Engineering Instrumentation and Control 4 Checkbook

H B Sutton
BTech, MTech, PhD, CEng, MIMechE, MInstMC

Butterworth Scientific
London Boston Sydney Wellington Durban Toronto

First published 1982

British Library Cataloguing in Publication Data

Sutton, H.B.
Engineering instrumentation and control 4 checkbook.
1. Mensuration 2. Automatic control
I. Title
620'.044 T50

ISBN 0-408-00680-3
ISBN 0-408-00617-X Pbk

Typeset by Scribe Design, Gillingham, Kent
Printed by Hartnoll Print Ltd., Bodmin, Cornwall

Contents

Preface

The importance of accurate measurement and control of industrial plant and process arameters has been recognized increasingly during the last two decades. During this period the rapid transition from the research stages to industrial implementation of many measurement and control techniques has been fuelled by the tremendous advances in the electronics industry. The application of electronics to instrumentation technology has produced an unparalleled diversity of measurement techniques and enabled measurements to be made with a speed and accuracy hitherto unknown. Increasingly, computer and microprocessor controllers are being applied to multi-input, continuous-operation plant and are making even greater demands for accurate, reliable and compatible measurement systems.

Consequently, the role of engineering technicians is also changing, so that it is essential for them to have a fundamental knowledge of instrumentation and measurement techniques and a sound understanding of the characteristics of control systems.

Although the same measurement techniques are used for data acquisition and monitoring outside the control situation, it is the control function which is currently the predominant focus of attention in industry. Thus many modern engineering syllabi combine the subjects 'Instrumentation' and 'Control'' Furthermore, the mathematical procedures associated with the analysis and the synthesis of the dynamical behaviour of instruments and control systems are identical, so that it is appropriate to combine them in a common text.

This book is intended to cover primarily the topics described in the standard unit Engineering Instrumentation and Control, level 4, of the TEC Programme Committee A5. However, the text is extended beyond this level so that it will be of value to those students who wish to study the subject at Level 5 and the early stages of engineering HND and degree courses. Additionally, the book covers many of the topics described in the Plant and Process Control level 3 unit, the Process Control level 4 unit and the Control Engineering level 4 unit of the TEC Programme Committeee A4.

H.B. Sutton
Highbury College of Technology
Portsmouth

Acknowledgements

This book is dedicated to my wife Agnes and to my daughter Susan who have given m tremendous support and encouragement.

Thanks are due to Agnes for her unstinting support during the preparation of this book and for diligently and painstakingly typing the manuscript. Thanks are also due to Susan for assisting me with some of the calculations.

Note to Reader

As textbooks become more expensive, authors are often asked to reduce the number of worked and unworked problems, examples and case studies. This may reduce costs, ut it can be at the expense of practical work which gives point to the theory.

Checkbooks if anything lean the other way. They let problem-solving establish and exemplify the theory contained in technician syllabuses. The Checkbook reader can gain *real* understanding through seeing problems solved and through solving problems himself.

Checkbooks do not supplant fuller textbooks, but rather supplement them with an alternative emphasis and an ample provision of worked and unworked problems. The brief outline of essential data—definitions, formulae, laws, regulations, codes of practice, standards, conventions, procedures, etc—will be a useful introduction to a course and a valuable aid to revision. Short-answer and multi-choice problems are a valuable feature of many Checkbooks, together with conventional problems and answers.

Checkbook authors are carefully selected. Most are experienced and successful technical writers; all are experts in their own subjects; but a more important qualification still is their ability to demonstrate and teach the solution of problems in their particular branch of technology, mathematics or science.

Authors, General Editors and Publishers are partners in this major low-priced series whose essence is captured by the Checkbook symbol of a question or problem 'checked' by a tick for correct solution.

Butterworths Technical and Scientific Checkbooks

General Editors for Science, Engineering and Mathematics titles:
J.O. Bird and A.J.C. May, Highbury College of Technology, Portsmcuth.

General Editor for Building, Civil Engineering, Surveying and Architectural titles:
Colin R. Bassett, lately of Guildford County College of Technology.

A comprehensive range of Checkbooks will be available to cover the major syllabus areas of the TEC, SCOTEC and similar examining authorities. A comprehensive list is given below and classified according to levels.

Level 1 (Red covers)
Mathematics
Physical Science
Physics
Construction Drawing
Construction Technology
Microelectronic Systems
Engineering Drawing
Workshop Processes & Materials

Level 2 (Blue covers)
Mathematics
Chemistry
Physics
Building Science and Materials
Construction Technology
Electrical & Electronic Applications
Electrical & Electronic Principles
Electronics
Microelectronic Systems
Engineering Drawing
Engineering Science
Manufacturing Technology
Digital Techniques
Motor Vehicle Science

Level 3 (Yellow covers)
Mathematics
Chemistry
Building Measurement
Construction Technology
Environmental Science
Electrical Principles
Electronics
Microelectronic Systems
Electrical Science
Mechanical Science
Engineering Mathematics & Science
Engineering Science
Engineering Design
Manufacturing Technology
Motor Vehicle Science
Light Current Applications

Level 4 (Green covers)
Mathematics
Building Law
Building Services & Equipment
Construction Technology
Construction Site Studies
Concrete Technology
Economics for the Construction Indus
Geotechnics
Engineering Instrumentation & Contro

Level 5
Building Services & Equipment
Construction Technology
Manufacturing Technology

1 Instrumentation systems

A. FUNDAMENTAL PRINCIPLES OF INSTRUMENTATION SYSTEMS

(a) SYSTEM CLASSIFICATION

Introduction

1 Instruments can be classified as indicating instruments, recording instruments and controlling instruments and they perform two basic functions, namely, the collection of data and the control of plant and processes. Frequently, the same instruments perform both of these functions simultaneously.

Instrumentation systems comprise one or more instruments interconnected for the purpose of collecting information about the state or change of state of variable quantities such as temperature, pressure, force, strain, velocity, acceleration, displacement and others. Information collected in this way (**output**) is known as a **measurement** and the variable quantity being measured (**input**) is known as the **measurand**. The complexity of instrumentation systems depends upon the type of measurement being made and the accuracy to which the measurement is required, so that they are categorised as primary, secondary or tertiary instrumentation systems.

Primary systems

2 Primary systems are those in which the required information can be obtained without the use of additional equipment, that is, by the use of the primary senses such as sight and touch. The following examples illustrate primary measurements:

(a) The estimation of temperature difference between the contents of two water containers by inserting fingers.

(b) The estimation of the difference in length between two rods by comparing one rod with the other rod.

Clearly, such comparisons provide subjective information only, since the observer can deduce only that the contents of one container are hotter than the contents of the other container or that one rod is longer than the other rod. However, information is usually required to a much greater degree of certainty. The observer usually wishes to know the precise difference in temperature between the contents of the two containers or the precise difference in length between the two rods. In order to obtain quantitative data of this nature additional aids are required.

Secondary systems

3 Secondary systems involve one **translation**, that is, the conversion of the **primary signal** (measurand) into some other signal form (**secondary signal**). Devices which

achieve such conversions are known as **transducers**. The following examples illustrate secondary systems:

(a) The conversion of pressure into displacement by means of bellows (*Fig 1*). In this illustration, the application of a pressure above that of the atmosphere to the open end of the bellows causes the bellows to expand accordingly. Therefore,

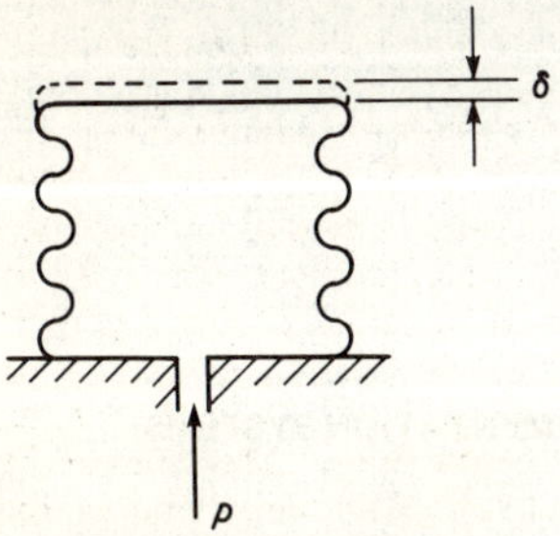

Fig 1 Bellows convert pressure into displacement

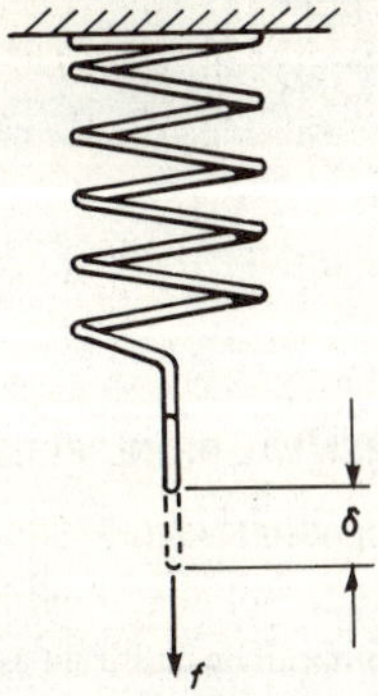

Fig 2 Springs convert force into displacement

the displacement of the bellows is a measure of the applied pressure. It can be shown mathematically that

$$\delta = Kp \qquad (1.1)$$

where

δ = bellows displacement (output)

p = variable pressure (input)

and

K = the constant of proportionality

so that the displacement varies **linearly** with the applied pressure, provided that the range of pressure variation is small. This simple device is used extensively in more complex pressure measurement and control systems.

(b) The conversion of force into displacement by means of a spring (*Fig 2*).

In this illustration, the application of a vertical force to the free end of the spring causes a corresponding spring deflection. Therefore, the spring deflection is a measure of the applied force. Spring stiffnes (S) is defined as that force which is necessary to cause unit spring deflection, so that

$$f = S\delta \qquad (1.2)$$

and

$$\delta = \frac{1}{S}f$$

or

$$\delta = Kf \qquad (1.3)$$

where

δ = spring deflection

f = applied force

and

K = the constant of proportionality

It is evident that in this case the displacement of the spring varies linearly with the applied force. This principle is exploited by the incorporation of various types of elastic members in many measuring devices.

Frequently, the secondary signals are very small as in the case of the bellows, so that it is necessary to amplify them in some way in order to improve the measurement accuracy. This means that a second translation is required in order to convert the secondary signal into a signal that can more easily be measured. The final or third signal is known as a **tertiary signal.**

Tertiary systems

4 A tertiary system involves two translations, that is, conversion of the primary signal into some other form (secondary signal) which in turn is converted into a third form (tertiary signal). The following examples illustrate tertiary systems:

(a) The measurement of **static** pressure using a Bourdon-tube pressure gauge (*Fig 3 and 4*).

In this illustration, the free end of the Bourdon-tube deflects in response to the primary pressure changes, giving rise to the secondary signal. The deflection of the tube is then amplified by the lever, quadrant and gear, and the pointer, so that the

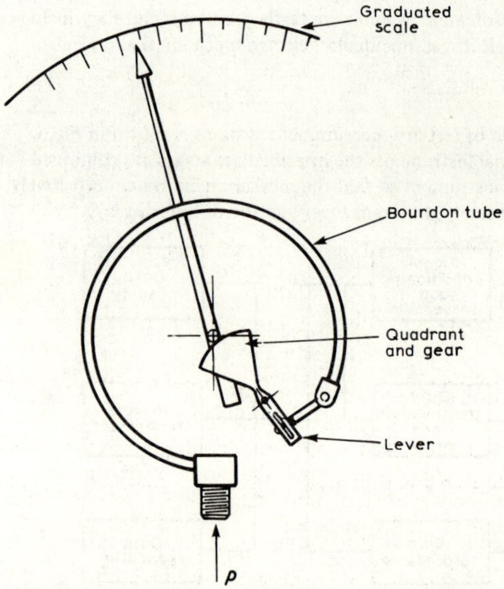

Fig 3 Bourdon-tube pressure gauge is a tertiary measurement system

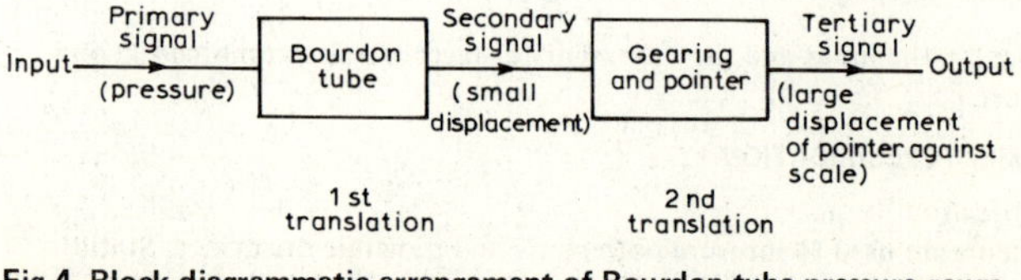

Fig 4 Block diagrammatic arrangement of Bourdon-tube pressure gauge

tertiary signal is the displacement of the pointer against the graduated scale. In this way large deflections of the pointer can be made to represent relatively small pressure changes.

(b) The measurement of angular velocity of a rotating shaft (*Fig 5*).

In this illustration, an *electro-mechanical transducer* can be used in order to sense the primary signal (angular velocity) and to convert it into the secondary

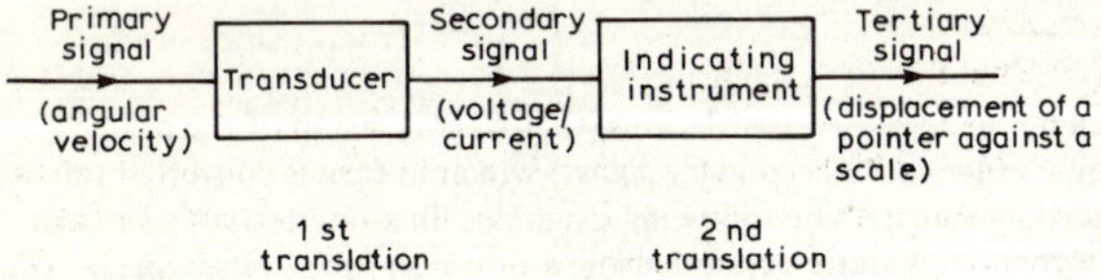

Fig 5 Block diagrammatic arrangement of a speed-measuring system

electrical signal (voltage). The secondary signal is then conditioned and converted into the movement of a pointer against a graduated scale by an indicating instrument.

Clearly, the majority of measurement systems are tertiary systems and they include a whole range of mechanical, electrical, pneumatic, electro-mechanical and electro-pneumatic instruments.

General configuration

5 The general configuration of tertiary measurement systems is shown in *Fig 6*.

Frequently, in industrial instruments the **intermediate stages** are combined with the **output stages** in one instrument so that the measurement system effectively reduces to two devices, namely, the transducer and the output display.

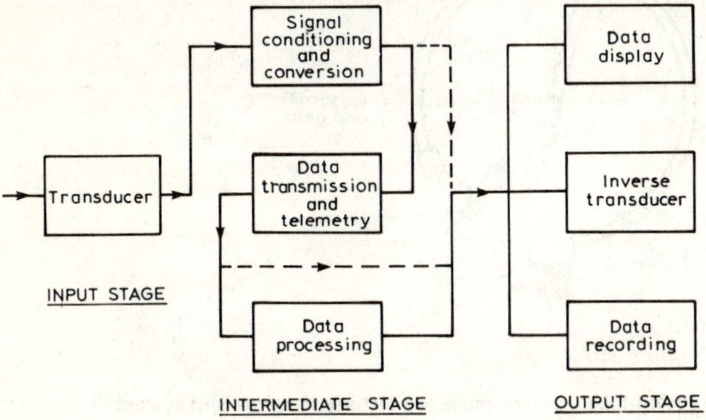

Fig 6 General configuration of measuring systems

Occasionally, the input and the intermediate stages are also combined in one transducer.

(b) INSTRUMENT SPECIFICATION

Signal classification

1 Instruments are used to measure both static and dynamic quantities. **Static** quantities do not change in value over a period of time whereas **dynamic** quantities

can change rapidly over a period of time. Frequently, in practical situations it is necessary to measure quantities which possess static and dynamic components simultaneously. The following examples illustrate static and dynamic components:

(a) The measurement of the static deflection of a cantilever beam (*Fig 7*).

In this illustration, the free end of the cantilever deflects as the mass is applied. If the applied mass is allowed to remain suspended over a period of time the corresponding cantilever deflection remains static.

(b) The measurement of the dynamic deflection of a cantilever beam (*Fig 8*).

In this illustration, the free end of the cantilever is deflected initially and then released which causes the cantilever to vibrate rapidly. The resulting varying deflection of the free end of the cantilever is a dynamic deflection.

(c) The measurement of the static and dynamic deflection of a cantilever beam (*Fig 9*).

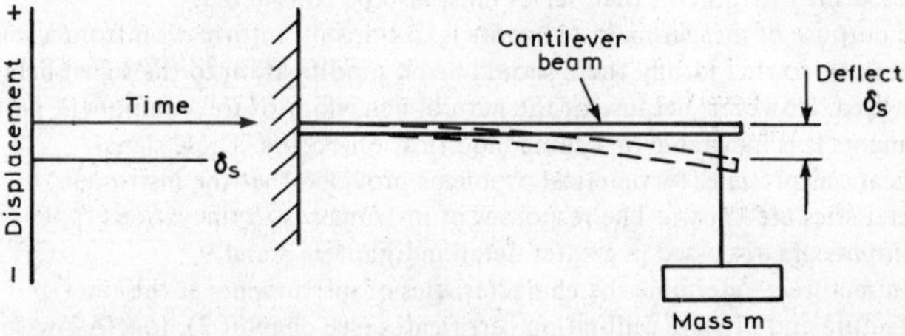

Fig 7 The application of mass *m* causes a static deflection of the free-end of the cantilever

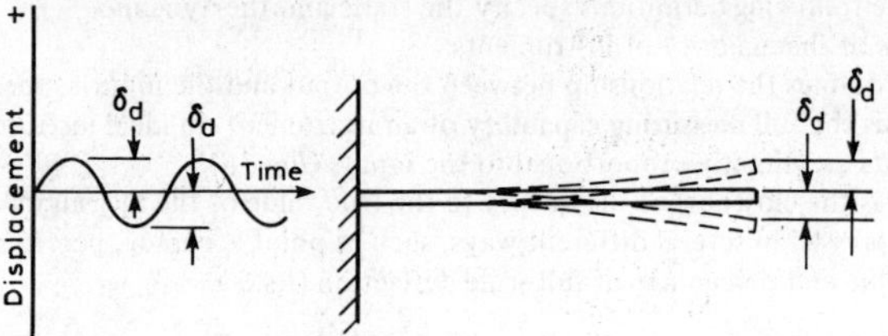

Fig 8 Vibration causes a dynamic deflection of the free end of the cantilever

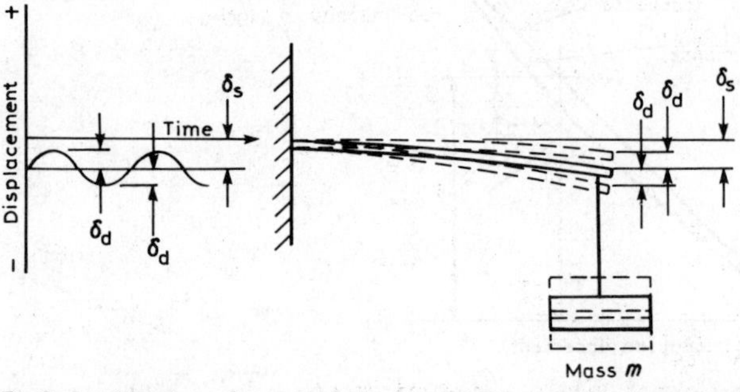

Fig 9 Combination of mass and vibration causes a combined static and dynamic free-end deflection

In this illustration, a mass is applied to the free end of the cantilever which gives rise to a static deflection of the free end. If the cantilever is then caused to vibrate, the resulting free-end total deflection is a combination of the static deflection and the dynamic deflection.

Instrument selection

2 The selection of instruments for particular applications is based upon a knowledge of the characteristics of the quantity being measured. It is desirable to know whether the measurand is static or dynamic or a combination of both of these states, the approximate magnitude of the measurand, the approximate frequency of the measurand if it has a dynamic component and the possible effects of interference such as might be experienced when working in hostile environments, i.e. in extreme heat or in extreme cold. In addition, the responses to the signals of the measuring instruments themselves must also be considered.

The purpose of measuring instruments is to transmit information from a **source** to a **receiver**, so that ideally there should be no modification to the signal being transmitted. However, because of the natural behaviour of the component parts of instruments it is inevitable that some modification occurs. These signal modifications present few practical problems provided that the instrument characteristics are known. The responses of instruments to the various types of signal inputs are discussed in greater detail in Chapters 3 and 9.

Manufacturers determine the characteristics of instruments at the time of manufacture and prepare calibration certificates (see chapter 3), together with specifications which enable the user to make objective assessments of the suitability of particular instruments in relation to the nature of the variables to be measured. The following definitions specify the static and the dynamic characteristics of the majority of instruments:

(a) **Linearity** defines the relationship between the output and the input as the input spans the full **measuring capability** of an instrument. In ideal instruments the outputs are directly proportional to the inputs (*Fig 10*).

(b) **Accuracy** is the closeness of the output to the true value of the measurand and can be expressed in several different ways, such as point accuracy, percentage of true value and percentage of full scale deflection (f.s.d.).

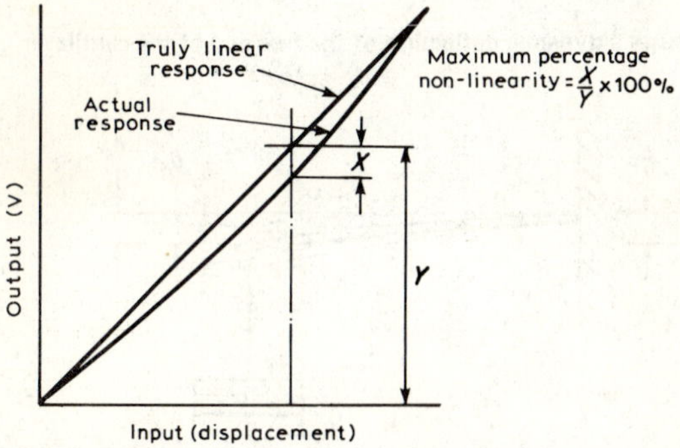

Fig 10 Relationship between output and input for a potentiometric displacement transducer

(c) **Tolerance** is the range of inaccuracy which can be tolerated in a measurement. For example, in the measurement of a pressure of 100 bar the inaccuracy which can be tolerated may be ± 1 bar, so that the tolerance is ± 1%.

(d) **Repeatability** is the ability of an instrument to reproduce the same reading for a group of measurements of the same measurand.

(e) **Range** is the maximum useable measuring capability of an instrument. For example, a pressure gauge might have a measuring range of 0–100 bar.

(f) **Sensitivity** is the ratio of the change in the output of an instrument to the corresponding change in the input and is usually required to be as high as possible.

(g) **Transverse-sensitivity** is the response of an instrument to an input which is not applied along the normal axis of measurement. This usually applies to transducers and is required to be as low as possible. For example, an accelerometer may have a transverse sensitivity of 5%, so that if an acceleration of lg is applied at 90° to the normal measurement axis this will produce an output which is equivalent to an acceleration level of 5% of lg applied along the normal measurement axis.

(h) **Resolution** is the smallest change in the measurand which can reasonably be measured by an instrument.

(i) **Lag** is a retardation or delay in the response of an instrument to changes in the measurand.

(j) **Fidelity** is the degree to which an instrument indicates changes in the measurand without dynamic error (this is occasionally referred to as 'finesse').

(k) **Dynamic error** is the difference between the true value of an input and the actual value indicated by an instrument when measuring a dynamic quantity.

(l) **Dead band** is the largest change in the measurand which produces no response from the instrument. This situation arises as a result of friction, backlash and hysteresis (see Chapter 3).

(m) **Zero stability** is the ability of an instrument to return to a zero reading as the measurand returns to zero.

(n) **Frequency response** is the maximum frequency of the measured variable that an instrument is capable of following without error. This applies particularly to the measurement of dynamic quantities and is the most important single factor to be considered when selecting instruments for this purpose. The usual requirement is that the frequency of the measurand should not exceed 60% of the natural frequency of the measuring instrument.

B. WORKED PROBLEMS ON INSTRUMENTATION SYSTEMS

Problem 1 A pencil-type U/V recorder galvanometer is to be selected for recording a gas pressure which pulsates at an estimated frequency of 100 Hz. The maximum recorder trace displacement must not exceed ±5 cm about a mean datum. The following galvanometers are available:

Type	*Natural frequency* (Hz)	*Terminal resistance* (Ω)	*Maximum safe current* (mA rms)	*Sensitivity* (mA/cm)	*Sensitivity* (mV/cm)
1	24	52	5	0.00058	0.030
2	40	45	10	0.0016	0.072
3	100	75	10	0.0025	0.187
4	200	70	10	0.010	0.70
5	400	120	15	0.030	3.60

(a) Explain the meaning of each term in this specification in relation to these galvanometers.
(b) Select the most appropriate galvanometer for the application described, giving reasons for your choice, and state the maximum input voltage and the maximum input current that is necessary in order to generate the maximum trace deflection.

(a) **Natural frequency** is the frequency at which each of the galvanometers will freely oscillate without any input.
Terminal resistance is the electrical resistance of the windings of each of the galvanometers as measured at the terminals. This factor has particular significance in the electrical matching of galvanometers to the outputs of signal conditioning instruments (see Chapter 5).
Maximum safe current is the maximum current that can be applied to each of the galvanometers without causing damage. Since the galvanometers can be used for measuring static and dynamic quantities, this input current is usually expressed as a root mean square (r.m.s.) value.
Sensitivity is the relationship between each of the galvanometer outputs (trace deflections) and the inputs expressed in terms of either current or voltage. For example, the sensitivity of the type 1 galvanometer is 0.00058 mA/cm, which means that an input **current** of 0.00058 mA will cause a trace displacement of 1 cm. Similarly, an input voltage of 0.030 mV will cause a trace displacement of 1 cm.

Naturally, the relationship between the input voltage and the input current is given by $V = I \times$ terminal resistance, so that the input voltage = $0.00058 \times 52 = 0.030$ mV.

(b) The maximum frequency that can safely be measured by any galvanometer is limited to 60% of its natural frequency. The frequency that is required to be measured in this case is 100 Hz, so that the most appropriate galvanometer is the type 4 galvanometer. Since 60% of 200 Hz is 120 Hz, this indicates that the type 4 galvanometer can safely measure frequencies up to 120 Hz. The type 5 galvanometer is not chosen because this galvanometer is less sensitive than the type 4 galvanometer and therefore requires a larger input current to generate the desired trace deflection.

The maximum trace deflection is required to be 5 cm, so that the corresponding input current must be 0.010 mA/cm × 5 cm, i.e. 0.05 mA. Similarly, the input voltage must be 0.7 × 5 = 3.5 mV.

Problem 2 The manufacturer's specification for a potentiometric linear displacement transducer is as follows:

Range	0–50 mm
Linearity	Better than 0.15% of full-scale output at 70% displacement with a minimum load of 100 kΩ
Accuracy	Better than 0.1% of full-scale output
Repeatability	Better than 0.01% of full-scale output
Maximum sensitivity	0.2 V/mm
Resolution	0.1% of full-scale displacement
Input voltage	10 V d.c.
Full-scale voltage	9.9 V
Output voltage at zero displacement	0.1 V

Define each of these terms in relation to this particular transducer.

Range In this case the instrument is capable of measuring linear displacements from zero to a maximum of 50 mm, that is, the displacement of the slider from the fully retracted position to the fully extended position (see Chapter 2).

Linearity The maximum deviation from linearity is stated to be not more than 0.15% of the full-scale voltage output, that is, 0.15% of 9.9 V. Thus, the maximum deviation from the truly linear response will not exceed 14.85 mV. This maximum deviation occurs as the slider is extended to 70% of 50 mm, which is a displacement of 35 mm. However, in order to achieve this degree of linearity the output voltage measuring instrument must have an input resistance of at least 100 kΩ. This is the electrical load on the transducer.

Accuracy Stated to be better than 0.1% of the full-scale output, so that any output voltage reading will be within 0.1% of 9.9 V, that is, 9.9 mV. Naturally, because the accuracy is stated as a percentage of the full-scale output, the **percentage accuracy** will **decrease** for all output voltages less than the maximum.

Repeatability Stated to be better than 0.01% of the full-scale output, so that the transducer will always produce repeated measurement readings to within 0.99 mV.

Sensitivity The relationship between the output voltage and the input displacement is stated to be 0.2 V output for every millimetre of displacement. In general, instruments are said to be more sensitive as the output per unit input is increased, so that the degree of amplification which may be required in the later stages of measurement systems is correspondingly smaller.

Resolution The smallest displacement that the instrument is capable of detecting is 0.1% of 50 mm, that is, 0.05 mm.

Input voltage The recommended voltage which should be applied to the instrument input terminals.

Full-scale output voltage/Output voltage at zero displacement The maximum output voltage corresponding to the maximum displacement of 50 mm is stated to be 9.9 V. Similarly, at the zero displacement position there is a corresponding output voltage of 0.1 V. The **ideal** maximum output voltage is 10 V, **equal** to the **input voltage** and the ideal output at **zero displacement** is also **zero** (see Chapter 2). However, it is not physically possible for the sliders of potentiometric transducers to traverse completely the full extent of the measuring resistor, so that losses are incurred at each of the two extremities.

Problem 3 The vibration level of the drive shaft of a steam turbine generator set is monitored by a piezoelectric accelerometer. The accelerometer has the following specification:

Charge sensitivity	20 pC/g
Mounted resonant frequency	40 kHz
Frequency response	10 Hz to 15 kHz
Transverse sensitivity	2% maximum
Acceleration range	0–500 pK *g*.

Define each of these terms in relation to this transducer.

The output from the transducer is conditioned and amplified by a charge amplifier before being displayed by a recorder. If the amplifier is set to a gain of 0.5 mV/pC and the sensitivity of the recorder is 10 cm/V, estimate the maximum recorder displacement. Determine also the transducer output corresponding to a transverse vibration level of 3 *g*.

The vibration levels are estimated to be:

Maximum vibration frequency	1 kHz
Maximum vibration acceleration	50 *g*
Vibration mode	Assumed to be sinusoidal

Charge sensitivity The output from piezoelectric transducers can be expressed in terms of the charge output or the voltage output. However, such transducers are essentially capacitive transducers so that electrical charge is probably the most appropriate way of expressing the output. In this case the charge sensitivity is 20 pC output for every 9.81 m/s^2 of acceleration (g).

Mounted resonant frequency The natural frequency of this transducer when it is mounted in the measuring position is 40 kHz. This is the frequency at which the transducer will resonate if it were caused to vibrate at the same frequency (see Chapter 9).

Frequency response Specified as 10 Hz to 15 000 Hz, is the range of input frequencies that the transducer can accurately and safely follow.

Transverse sensitivity The sensitivity of the accelerometer to an input which is not applied along the normal axis of measurement. In this case the maximum transverse sensitivity is 2%, so that if an acceleration level of 1 *g* is applied along an axis at 90° to the normal axis of measurement, then the transducer output will be 2% of 20 pC, that is 0.4 pC.

Acceleration range The range of acceleration levels that the accelerometer is capable of measuring is from zero up to a maximum of 500 *g*. Since the vibration mode is generally assumed to be sinusoidal, the maximum acceleration levels are the peak levels (pK), that is, acceleration amplitudes.

The maximum transducer output corresponding to the maximum acceleration level is

$20\ pC/g \times 50g \quad = \quad \mathbf{1000\ pC}$

The resulting maximum output from the charge amplifier is

$0.5\ mV/pC \times 1000\ pC \quad = \quad \mathbf{500\ mV}$

Since the recorder sensitivity is 10 cm/V, the corresponding recorder displacement is

$10\ cm/V \times 0.5\ V \quad = \quad \mathbf{5\ cm}$

The transducer output corresponding to a transverse acceleration level of 3 g is given by

$$\frac{2}{100} \times 3g \times 20\ pC/g \quad = \quad \mathbf{1.2\ pC}$$

C. FURTHER PROBLEMS IN INSTRUMENTATION SYSTEMS

(a) SHORT-ANSWER PROBLEMS

1 The three main instrument classifications are . . . . , ... and . . . .
2 The two basic functions of instruments are . . . . . . and . . . . . .
3 The input to a measuring system is known as the . . . . . . and the output is known as a . . . . . .
4 The degree of complexity of instrumentation systems depends upon the . . . . . . and the . . . . . .
5 Primary measuring systems involve the use of . . . . . . only.
6 The first signal translation in a measuring system is the conversion of the . . . . . . into the . . . . . . signal.
7 Systems which involve one translation only are known as . . . . . . systems.
8 Tertiary systems involve . . . . . translations in which the . . . . . . signal is converted into the . . . . . . signal, which in turn is converted into the . . . . . . signal.
9 Primary sensors are known as . . . . . .
10 Typical tertiary measuring systems comprise . . . . . , ... and . . . . . .

(b) MULTI-CHOICE PROBLEMS (answers on page 184)

1 The measurand is:
(a) the output, (b) the secondary signal; (c) the measured variable.
2 Secondary instruments are used in order to:
(a) sense the measured variable; (b) condition and transmit the secondary signal; (c) display the measured variable.
3 The output stage of a measuring system may comprise:
(a) a recorder; (b) a signal conditioner, (c) a transducer.
4 In industrial measuring systems, display instruments are frequently combined with:
(a) transducers; (b) signal processors; (c) the measurand.
5 Dynamic quantities:
(a) vary rapidly with time;
(b) remain constant over a period of time;
(c) are displaced from a zero position.

6. The linearity of instruments is:
   (a) the range of inaccuracy that can be tolerated;
   (b) the maximum useable capability;
   (c) the relationship between the output and the input.
7 The resolution of instruments is:
   (a) the retardation of the response,
   (b) the smallest change in the measurand that can be measured,
   (c) the difference between the true value of the input and the indicated value.
8 The largest change in the measured variable which produces no instrument response is known as the:
   (a) dynamic error; (b) lag; (c) dead band.
9 Instrument specifications enable:
   (a) instruments to be calibrated;
   (b) objective instrument selection;
   (c) the instrument range to be determined.
10 The purpose of instruments is to:
   (a) transmit information,
   (b) change signals;
   (c) allow measurements to be made.

(c) CONVENTIONAL PROBLEMS

1 Explain the difference between an instrument and a measurement.
2 Define the terms 'input' and 'output'.
3 Describe a practical tertiary measuring system and illustrate your description by drawing a block diagrammatic arrangement of the system.
4 Explain why it is frequently necessary to amplify secondary signals.
5 Explain the difference between recording instruments and indicating instruments.
6 Define the basic information that is necessary for the selection of instruments for specific applications.
7 Explain the significance of the frequency response of instruments in relation to the measurement of dynamic quantities.
8 Explain why it is necessary for manufacturers to prepare instrument specifications.
9 A pen recorder has the following specification:

Maximum sensitivity	2.5 mV/100 mm
Accuracy at f.s.d.	± 0.1%
Resolution	Infinite
Linearity	0.1% f.s.d.
Repeatability	0.1% f.s.d.
Dead band	± 0.2 mm

Explain the significance of each of these terms in relation to this particular instrument.

10 A piezoelectric transducer is to be used for the measurement of machine tool vibration acceleration levels, and a transducer having the following specification has been selected from the available range of transducers:

Voltage sensitivity	45 mV/g
Mounted resonant frequency	32 kHz
Frequency response	2 Hz to 6 kHz
Transverse sensitivity	5% maximum
Acceleration range	0–1000 pK g sinusoidal in any direction

Explain the significance of each of these terms in relation to this transducer.

As the machine tool is cutting, the vibration levels are estimated to be as follows:

Peak acceleration	100 × the acceleration due to gravity
Peak vibration frequency	500 Hz
Vibration mode	Approximately sinusoidal

Determine:

(a) the suitability of the transducer specified above for this application; (b) the estimated peak output voltage from the transducer, (c) the sensitivity of the transducer to a transverse vibration level of 2 *g*.

[(a) Transducer is suitable since the estimated peak acceleration level and the estimated maximum frequency are within the ranges specified for the transducer;
(b) 4.5 V,
(c) 4.5 mV]

2 Principles of electro-mechanical transducers

A. GENERAL PRINCIPLES OF ELECTRO-MECHANICAL TRANSDUCERS

(a) WHEATSTONE BRIDGE

Introduction

1 The operation of many primary sensors depends upon the variation of the electrical resistance of a conductor in response to variations in the measured variable. Generally, these devices can be categorised as those in which small changes in electrical resistance are generated and those in which large changes in electrical resistance are generated. The method of generating and of measuring these variations in resistance is different in each case. The large variations in resistance of the latter category can usually be measured directly, but it is necessary to use an intermediate method of measuring the small variations in resistance of the former category.

The Wheatstone Bridge technique is used in conjunction with **resistive transducers** whose electrical **resistance variations** are relatively **small**. Electrical resistance strain gauge sensors and thermo-resistive temperature sensors are typical of the various types of transducers which are in this category.

There are two ways of using the Wheatstone Bridge technique, the choice of which depends primarily upon the type of measurement being undertaken. In the first of these techniques the Wheatstone Bridge is used in the **balanced condition** (null condition), while in the second technique the Wheastone Bridge is used in the **unbalanced condition.**

Balanced Bridge

2 *Fig 1* shows the electrical circuit diagram for the typical Wheatstone Bridge arrangement.

In this arrangement, one limb of the bridge can be a resistive transducer whose **nominal** resistance is R_1, while a variable resistor whose **nominal** resistance is R_4 is connected in an **adjacent** limb. The fixed resistances R_2 and R_3 complete the bridge. In order for the bridge to be balanced, **no current** must flow through the measuring instrument that is indicated in the figure as a galvanometer. Thus, if the bridge initially is balanced and then the transducer changes its electrical resistance due to a change in the measured variable, electrical current flows through the galvanometer so that the bridge is unbalanced.

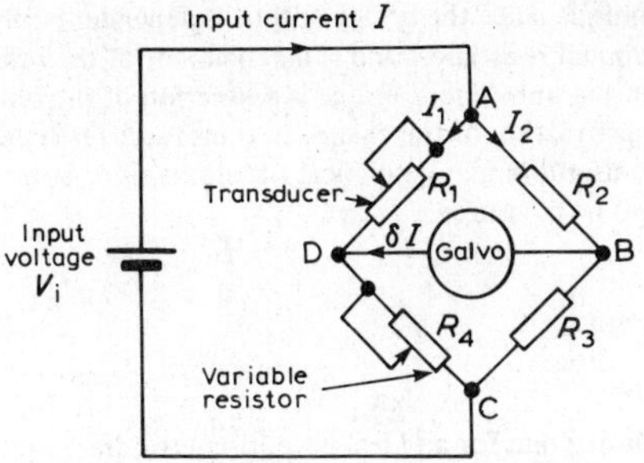

Fig 1 Wheatstone bridge arrangement

In order to rebalance the bridge, the variable resistor R_4 is adjusted until the galvanometer again indicates zero current. The **measured change** in the resistance of R_4 is a measure of the **unknown change in resistance** of the transducer.

In practical situations, a calibrated scale is attached to the variable resistor R_4 so that adjustments can be read directly as changes in resistance. However, frequently this scale is calibrated in units that are appropriate to the type of measurement being undertaken. For example, the scale can be calibrated in strain units or in temperature units or in force units etc., provided that the characteristics of the transducer with which the bridge is being used are known. That is, the relationship between the change in resistance with strain or the change in resistance with temperature etc.

This measurement technique is known as the **null technique** and is frequently used in applications where the measured variable is either **static** or changing very slowly with time (**quasi-static**). In applications such as the measurement of temperature, the resistors R_2, R_3 and R_4 are usually included in commercially manufactured instruments which also provide the measuring facility and the power supply, so that the only external connections are those required to connect the transducer to the instrument. However, in strain gauge applications, it is frequently necessary to construct the Wheatstone Bridge externally before connecting the **bridge** leads to an instrument that provides the measuring facility and the power supply.

Unbalanced Bridge

3 In this measurement technique the electrical configuration of the Wheatstone Bridge is the same as that shown in *Fig 1*, except that in this case R_4 can be a fixed resistor. As before, if the bridge is initially balanced and then the transducer changes its electrical resistance due to changes in the measured variable, electrical current flows through the galvanometer. However, in this case the Wheatstone Bridge is **not rebalanced** and the deflection of the galvanometer is taken to be a measure of the unknown change in resistance of the transducer.

Frequently, for static measurements, the measuring scale of the galvanometer is calibrated directly in units appropriate to the variable being measured, as in the previous case. However, the **main advantage** of the unbalanced bridge technique is that **dynamic** quantities can also be measured, so that the pointer and scale mechanism of the simple galvanometer is inadequate for many practical situations. Therefore in this case, it is more usual for the electrical output from the bridge to be **amplified** and **displayed** on either an oscilloscope or a recorder.

The **null technique** is a **more accurate** means of measuring resistance changes than the **unbalanced bridge technique** since the bridge output is **dependent** only upon the **ratios** of the bridge **nominal resistances** and is **independent** of the bridge **supply voltage**. The output from the unbalanced bridge is a function of the bridge supply voltage and is a non-linear function of the change in transducer resistance. However, this technique is more useful in many practical situations since both static and dynamic quantities can be measured.

(b) POTENTIOMETRIC TRANSDUCERS

Ideal potentiometers

1 *Fig 2* shows the electrical circuit diagram for an ideal potentiometric transducer.

In this device, the movement of the slider across the resistor results in a relatively large variation in the electrical resistance R_o and a corresponding variation in the voltage output. If the slider is connected to a component whose

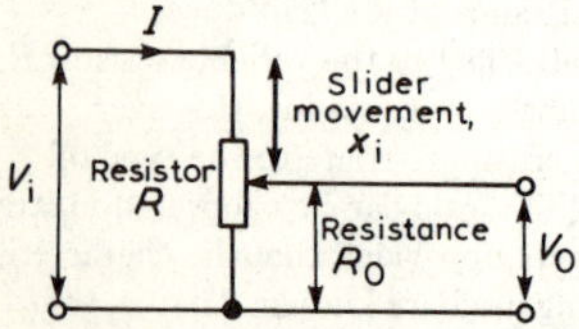

Fig 2 Ideal potentiometer

displacement is required to be measured, then the voltage output from the potentiometer is a measure of displacement. With the slider in the upper extreme position $R_o = R$, so that $V_o = V_i$. Similarly, with the slider in the lower extreme position $R_o = 0$, so that $V_o = 0$. Hence, as the slider traverses the full extent of the resistor the output voltage varies from zero to V_i.

It is evident from *Fig 2* that

$$V_i = IR \quad (2.1)$$

and that

$$V_o = IR_o \quad (2.2)$$

provided that no current is drawn from the output terminals. In order to achieve this, the voltmeter used to measure V_o must have an infinitely high input resistance. Thus

$$\frac{V_o}{V_i} = \frac{IR_o}{IR} = \frac{R_o}{R}$$

so that

$$V_o = \frac{V_i\, R_o}{R} \quad (2.3)$$

Since V_i and R are constants and R_o is a variable quantity that is dependent upon the displacement of the slider x_i, then

$$V_o = \text{const.}\ x_i \quad (2.4)$$

This is the law of an ideal instrument and implies that the instrument will faithfully reproduce any form of the input displacement. In this type of instrument there are no delays or distortions of the input signal, so that such devices are known generally as **zero-order** instruments.

Practical potentiometers

2 In practical situations, the voltage outputs from potentiometric transducers are measured by instruments such as voltmeters which may not have infinitely high

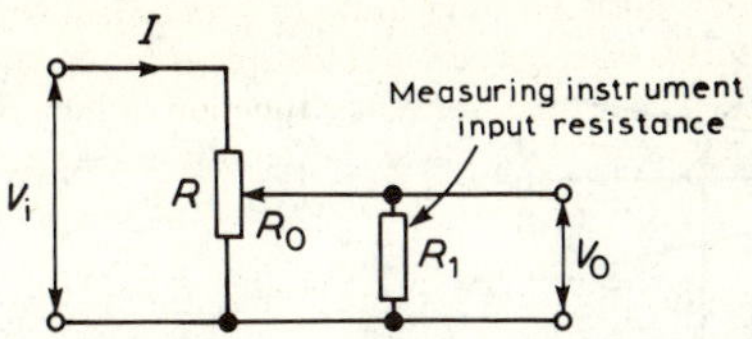

Fig 3 Practical potentiometer

input resistances. In such cases, the ideal circuit is modified by the output measuring instrument. This has the effect of electrically loading the primary sensor. *Fig 3* represents the electrical circuit diagram for an actual measuring system. It can be shown that in this case

$$\frac{V_o}{V_i} = \frac{1}{\frac{R}{R_o} + \frac{R}{R_1}\left(1 - \frac{R_o}{R}\right)} \tag{2.5}$$

(see *Worked Problem 6*).

Since R and R_1 are constants and R_o is a variable quantity that is dependent upon the displacement of the slider, it is evident that in this case the relationship between V_o and x_i is non-linear, except in the situation where $R_1 \rightarrow \infty$. In this situation, $R/R_1 \rightarrow 0$ and equation (2.5) reduces to equation (2.3). The acceptable ratio of $R_1:R$ is approximately 15:1. This means that the resistance of the measuring instrument must be **at least** 15 times **larger** than the potentiometer resistance in order to maintain an acceptable linearity.

(c) ELECTROMAGNETIC TRANSDUCERS

Introduction

1 There are many types of transducers that operate in accordance with the principles of electromagnetism. However, two common types of transducers depend upon the **displacement of a core** in order to vary the electromagnetic **self-inductance** of a coil or a series of coils, and the **relative movement of two coils** in order to vary the **mutual inductance** of those coils. Generally, these devices require the supply of electrical energy from an external source but in other cases this is not necessary since the laws of electromagnetism can be utilised in a manner that requires no external energy supply.

Self-inductive and mutual-inductive transducers are known as **passive** transducers since **energy is required** to be supplied from an external source, while the alternative forms of electromagnetic transducers are known as **active** transducers since the output signals can be generated **without the supply of energy** from an external source. In this way, **all transducers** can be categorised as passive or active transducers.

Passive electromagnetic transducers

2 If a current i A passes through a coil having N turns and an air core (*Fig 4*), then a magnetic flux of ϕ Wb is generated such that

$$\phi \propto Ni \tag{2.6}$$

or

$$Ni = S\phi \tag{2.7}$$

where S is known as the **reluctance** of the coil

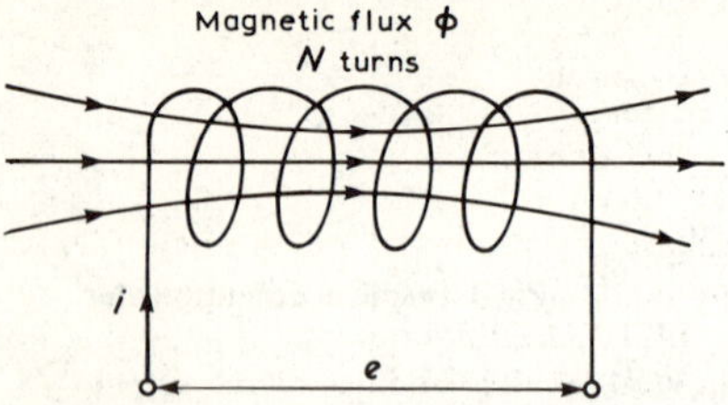

Fig 4 Flux linking

The **inductance** of the coil is a measure of the magnitude of the magnetic flux, and is defined as

$$L = \frac{N\phi}{i} \tag{2.8}$$

Combining equations (2.7) and (2.8) gives

$$L = \frac{N^2}{S} \tag{2.9}$$

It can also be shown that the reluctance is given by

$$S = \frac{l}{\mu_o \mu_r A} \tag{2.10}$$

so that

$$L = \frac{N^2 A \mu_o \mu_r}{l} \tag{2.11}$$

where A is the cross-sectional area of the coil, l is the length of the magnetic path, μ_o is the permeability of free space and has the value $4\pi \times 10^{-7}$ H/m and μ_r is the relative permeability of the core of the coil. The value of μ_r depends upon the core material, and for air $\mu_r = 1$.

Clearly, the self-inductance of the coil is dependent upon the number of turns of the coil, the geometrical configuration of the circuit (A and l) and the permeability of the core, so that variations in any of these quantities also vary the inductance. Similarly, where two coils are used then such variations can also cause variations in the mutual inductance between the coils.

Practical transducers based upon this principle usually measure linear and angular displacement or linear and angular velocity so that a movable member of the transducer causes the variation of one of the quantities described previously. These devices require external a.c. power supplies and are usually connected to form a.c. bridge networks. The supply signals for such transducers are usually known as **carrier signals** and the frequencies of the carrier signals are known as the **carrier frequencies**.

Active electromagnetic transducers

3 There are several types of active electromagnetic transducers and their operation depends upon two well-known principles. The first principle indicates that if a conductor is caused to move with a velocity v m/s through a magnetic field in a plane perpendicular to the magnetic field, then an e.m.f. is generated along the conductor (*Fig 5*).

The relationship between the e.m.f. generated and the velocity is given by

$$e = Blv \tag{2.12}$$

where e is the generated e.m.f., B is the flux density, l is the conductor length and v is the conductor velocity.

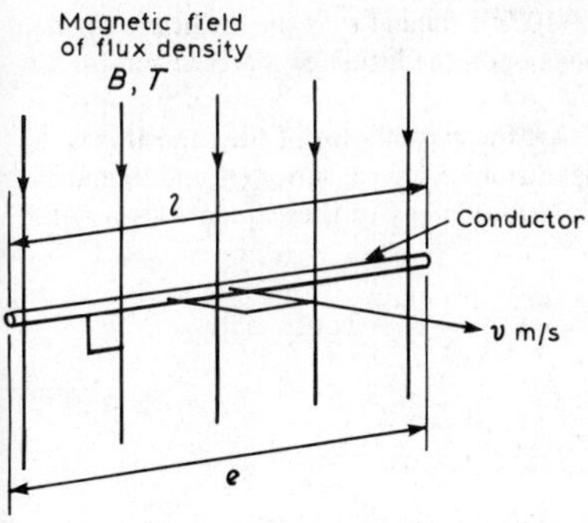

Fig 5 Flux cutting

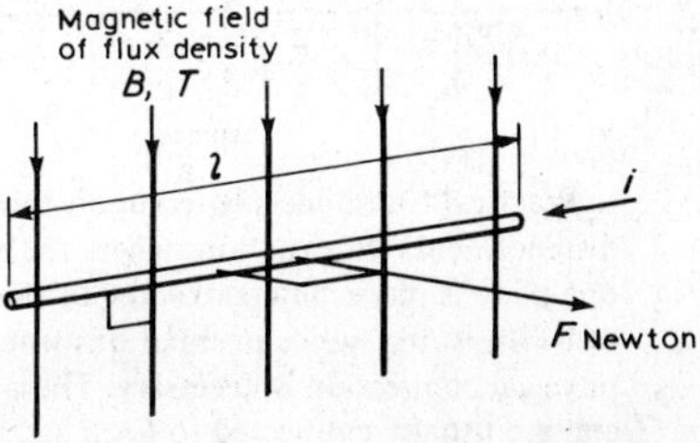

Fig 6

The second principle is the reverse of the first. This indicates that if a conductor is placed in a magnetic field such that its longitudinal axis forms a right angle to the lines of flux and a current is allowed to flow through the conductor, then a mechanical force is generated which acts on the conductor in a direction perpendicular to the lines of flux and to the conductor (*Fig 6*).
The relationship between the generated force and the current is given by

$$F = Bil \qquad (2.13)$$

where F is the generated force, B is the flux density, l is the conductor length and i is the conductor current.

It is evident from equation (2.12) that if B and l are maintained constant, then $e \propto v$. In this case, the e.m.f. generated along the conductor is a measure of the velocity of the conductor. Clearly, transducers based upon this principle can be used for measuring velocities and are frequently used in angular speed measurement, in vibration measurement and in fluid flow measurement.

Similarly, it is evident from equation (2.13) that if B and l are maintained constant, then $F \propto i$. In this case, the force generated is proportional to the current flowing through the conductor. This principle forms the basis of most moving-coil and moving-magnet measuring instruments.

(d) CAPACITIVE TRANSDUCERS

A *capacitor* comprises two or more metal plate conductors separated by an insulator. As a voltage is applied across the plates, equal and opposite electric charges are generated on the plates (*Fig 7*).

Capacitance is defined as the ratio of the charge to the applied voltage and for a parallel-plate capacitor is given by

$$C = \frac{\epsilon_o \, \epsilon_r A}{d} \text{ farads} \qquad (2.14)$$

where A is the plate overlap area, d is the plate separation, ϵ_o is the permittivity of free space and has the value 8.854×10^{-12} F/m and ϵ_r is the dielectric constant for the insulator. The value of ϵ_r depends upon the insulator material and for air $\epsilon_r = 1$.

From equation (2.14) it is evident that the capacitance of the capacitor is dependent upon the geometrical configuration of the capacitor (*A* and *d*) and the permittivity of the insulator, so that variations in any of these quantities vary the capacitance.

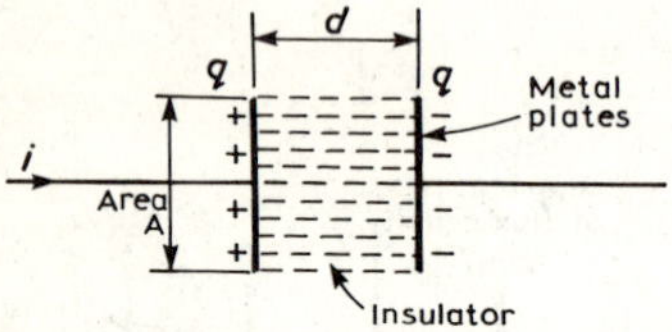

Fig 7 Capacitive effect

Practical transducers based upon this principle usually measure small displacements. In situations where the overlap area or the plate separation varies, one plate is physically connected to the component whose displacement is required to be measured, while in situations where the permittivity is caused to vary no physical connection is necessary. These devices require external a.c. power supplies and are usually connected to form a.c. bridge networks although other circuits can be used; for example, in frequency modulated systems.

(e) PIEZOELECTRIC TRANSDUCERS

Certain naturally occurring and artificial crystals generate electrical charges as they are mechanically deformed. This characteristic is known as the **piezoelectric effect**. The piezoelectric effect is reversible, for if a potential difference is applied across opposite faces of the material the crystal changes its physical dimensions. The most common natural materials that exhibit the piezoelectric characteristic are quartz and rochelle salt, while artificial crystals are frequently manufactured from lead zirconate titanate ceramics.

The piezoelectric effect can be produced by deforming the crystals in different ways. For example, by thickness expansion or compression, by transverse expansion or compression, by thickness shear or by face shear. Metal electrodes are attached to the selected faces of a crystal in order to detect the electrical charge generated (*Fig 8*).

The generated charge is given by

$$q = dF \text{ coulomb} \qquad (2.15)$$

where *d* is the crystal sensitivity in *C*/*N* and is a constant for particular crystals and

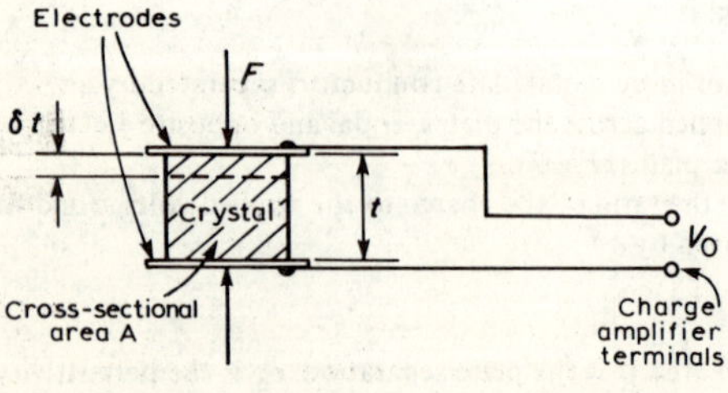

Fig 8 Piezoelectric effect

the manner in which they are cut. The relationship between the force F and the change in thickness δt is given by

$$F = \frac{EA \times \delta t}{t} \tag{2.16}$$

where the modulus of elasticity E is given by stress/strain, A is the crystal cross-sectional area, t is the crystal thickness and δt is the change in crystal thickness. The charge generated at the electrodes gives rise to a voltage, such that

$$V_o = \frac{q}{C_{cr}} \tag{2.17}$$

where C_{cr} is the capacitance between the electrodes. Furthermore, it is evident from equation (2.14) that

$$C = \frac{\epsilon_o \, \epsilon_r \, A}{t} \tag{2.18}$$

so that combining equations (2.15), (2.17) and (2.18) gives

$$V_o = gtP \tag{2.19}$$

where

$g = \dfrac{d}{\epsilon_o \, \epsilon_r}$ = crystal voltage sensitivity, Vm/N and P is the applied pressure, F/A.

Fig 9 indicates the equivalent circuit for a piezoelectric measuring system. In this measuring system the **impedance** of the transducer is **usually very high** so that the following amplifier must have a correspondingly **higher input impedance.** The connecting cable capacitance can be significant especially where long cables

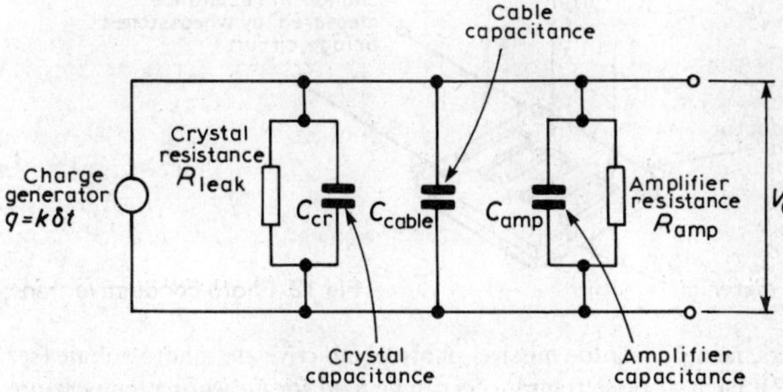

Fig 9 Piezoelectric equivalent circuit

are used and this frequently has to be taken into consideration when determining the transducer sensitivity.

If a static force is applied to the transducer, a charge is generated but the charge is slowly dissipated through the internal resistance of the crystal. This decay is slow if R_{leak} is high. However, because of this characteristic, piezoelectric transducers are used mainly for measuring dynamic quantities that are functions of force, for example, acceleration and pressure, although quasi-static quantities can be measured by using special amplifiers.

(f) PHOTOELECTRIC TRANSDUCERS

Photoelectric transducers are sensors that produce electrical signals in response to changes in the intensity of incident light. There are three types of photoelectric

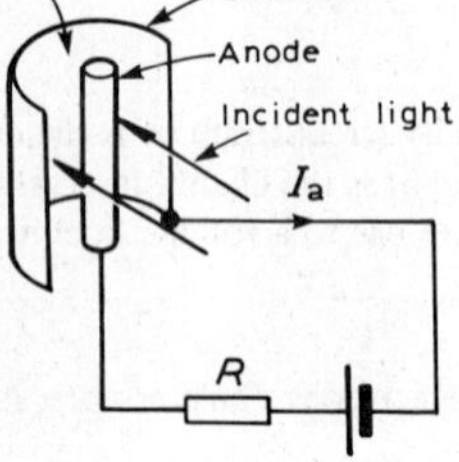

Fig 10 Photo-emissive transducer

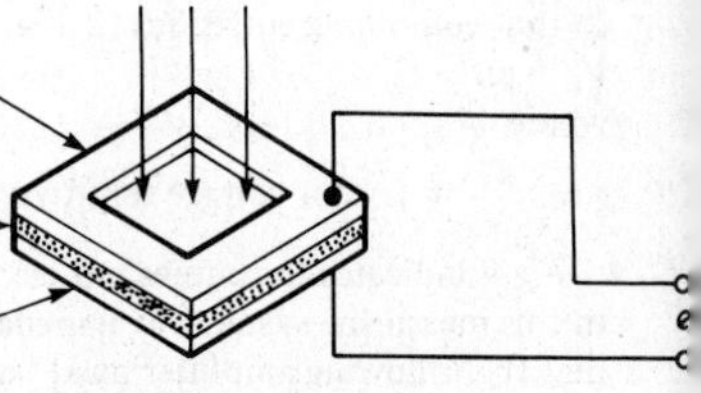

Fig 11 Photo-voltaic transducer

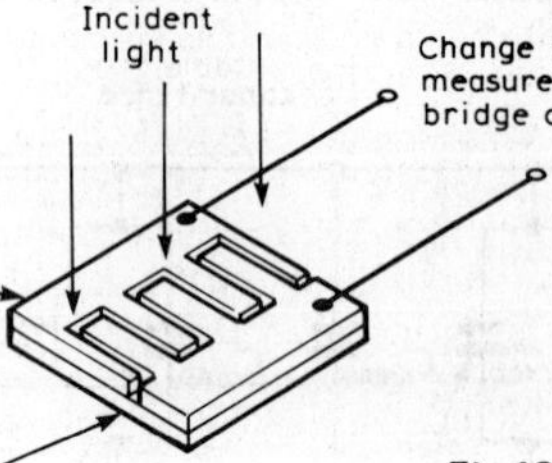

Fig 12 Photo-conductive transducer

transducers, namely, photo-emissive, photo-conductive and photo-voltaic (see *Figs 10, 11, 12*). Each of these transducers can be used for measuring temperature, light intensity and pulse counting. However, the photo-voltaic transducers are used mainly in light meters but are rarely used in precision instruments.

B. THERMO-ELECTRIC TRANSDUCERS

(a) THERMOCOUPLES

When two dissimilar metals are joined together at two points to form a closed loop and a temperature difference exists between the junctions, an electrical potential also exists between the junctions. Such an arrangement is known as a thermocouple and is frequently used for the measurement of temperature. A typical thermocouple measuring system is indicated in *Fig 13*.

In this arrangement, the two wires of dissimilar metals are insulated from each other but joined together at one point. In industrial thermocouples the wires are encapsulated within a metal sheath so that only the extremities of the two wires

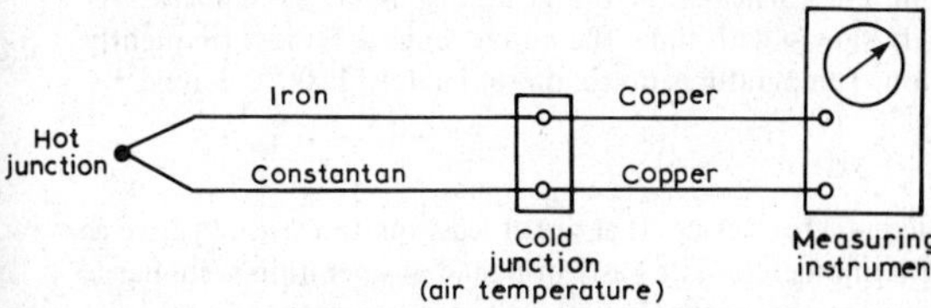

Fig 13 Thermocouple measuring system

protrude. The cold junction is formed by the junction of the thermocouple wires with the terminals of a measuring instrument such as a d.c. millivoltmeter. At this junction, both of the thermocouple wires are at the same room temperature so that the thermocouple responds as though the two wires were joined together at this point. If the room temperature remains essentially constant and heat is applied to the hot junction, an e.m.f. will be detected by the millivoltmeter. This e.m.f. is directly proportional to the temperature difference between the junctions so that if the room temperature is known, then the heat source temperature can be measured.

The most common metal combinations are iron-constantan, copper-constantan, chromium-aluminium and platinum-rhodium. Each of these combinations is suitable for measuring a specific range of temperatures but the maximum temperature that can be measured in this way is approximately 1500°C using the platinum-rhodium combination.

There are four basic laws that influence thermocouple performance and use:

a) The thermal e.m.f. of a thermocouple having junction temperatures of T_1 and T_2 is unaffected by temperature elsewhere in the circuit if the two metals are homogeneous.

b) If a third homogeneous metal is introduced into the circuit, the thermocouple e.m.f. is unaffected provided that the junctions of the thermocouple wires with the additional wire are at the same temperature. This law is frequently referred to as the 'law of intermediate metals'.

c) If the thermal e.m.f. of two metals A and C is V_{AC} and the thermal e.m.f. of two metals B and C is V_{BC}, then the thermal e.m.f. of metals A and B together is $V_{AC} + V_{BC}$.

d) If a thermocouple generates an e.m.f. of V_1 when its junctions are at temperatures T_1 and T_2, and an e.m.f. of V_2 when its junctions are at temperatures T_2 and T_3, then it will generate an e.m.f. of $V_1 + V_2$ when the junctions are at temperatures T_1 and T_3. This law is frequently referred to as the 'law of intermediate temperatures'.

b) THERMO-RESISTIVE TRANSDUCERS

Resistance thermometers

The operation of thermo-resistive transducers depends upon the property that the electrical resistance of most metals varies with variations in temperature. Naturally, these transducers are used in order to measure temperature.

Resistance thermometers usually are constructed so that a wire is wound to form a helix around a cylindrical former. The wire material is frequently platinum but it can also be nickel or copper. The assembly is coated with a layer of heat resisting cement which forms the insulation for the wire and makes the element rigid.

In order to measure the changes in the electrical resistance, the thermometer is connected as one limb of a Wheatstone Bridge arrangement. As temperature usually varies relatively slowly with time, the null technique is most frequently used in this application. Temperatures up to approximately 1100°C can be measured in this way.

Thermistors

2 Thermistors are semiconductor devices that are at least ten times as sensitive as platinum resistance thermometers. The basic principle of operation is similar to that of resistance thermometers in that variations in temperature generate corresponding variations in the resistance of the semiconductor. However, the resistance-temperature relationship is non-linear so that the range of operation of any particular thermistor is limited. The main advantages of thermistors are that they are physically very small and have very fast response times, so they are used frequently in temperature control systems. The measurement technique is the same as that used in the case of resistance thermometers.

The most common materials used in the manufacture of thermistors are manganese, nickel and cobalt oxides. These materials are milled and mixed with binders before being pressed and sintered.

Thermistors are commercially available in the form of beads, probes, discs and rods and are frequently coated with glass. The usable temperatures range from approximately −250°C to approximately 600°C.

C. WORKED PROBLEMS ON TRANSDUCERS

Problem 1 Assuming that the Wheatstone Bridge configuration of *Fig 1* is balanced, derive the relationship that exists between the resistors R_1, R_2, R_3 and R_4. Hence show that as the resistance R_1 is changed a corresponding change in R_4 will rebalance the Wheatstone Bridge.

If the Wheatstone Bridge is balanced, the electric current flowing through the galvanometer, δI, is zero. Hence, the potential difference across the resistor R_1 is $I_1 R_1$, and the potential difference across the resistor R_2 is $I_2 R_2$. Since $\delta I = 0$, then

$$I_1 R_1 = I_2 R_2 \qquad (2.20)$$

Similarly,

$$I_1 R_4 = I_2 R_3 \qquad (2.21)$$

since the current flowing between D and C is I_1, and the current flowing between B and C is I_2.

Dividing equation (2.20) by equation (2.21) gives

$$\frac{I_1 R_1}{I_1 R_4} = \frac{I_2 R_2}{I_2 R_3}$$

from which

$$\frac{R_1}{R_4} = \frac{R_2}{R_3} \qquad (2.22)$$

An alternative form of equation (2.22) is

$$\frac{R_1}{R_2} = \frac{R_4}{R_3} \qquad (2.23)$$

Equations (2.22) and (2.23) are alternative forms of the same relationship and indicate that the Wheatstone Bridge can be balanced only when the ratios of the resistances in adjacent limbs of the bridges are equal.

Let R_1 be changed by an amount δR_1, and in order to rebalance the bridge, let the corresponding change in R_4 be δR_4.

Equation (2.23) must be satisfied if the bridge is to be balanced, so that

$$\frac{R_1 + \delta R_1}{R_2} = \frac{R_4 + \delta R_4}{R_3} \qquad (2.24)$$

Dividing the left side of equation (2.24) by R_1 and the right side of equation (2.24) by R_4, yields

$$\frac{1 + \delta R_1/R_1}{R_2/R_1} = \frac{1 + \delta R_4/R_4}{R_3/R_4} \qquad (2.25)$$

However,

$$\frac{R_2}{R_1} = \frac{R_3}{R_4}$$

in view of equation (2.23), so that equation (2.25) reduces to

$$\frac{\delta R_1}{R_1} = \frac{\delta R_4}{R_4} \qquad (2.26)$$

Alternatively,

$$\delta R_1 = \frac{R_1}{R_4}.\delta R_4 \qquad (2.27)$$

Clearly, δR_4 is a measure of the unknown quantity δR_1, since the ratio R_1/R_4 is constant.

Problem 2 *Fig 14* indicates a measuring system in which four resistors of equal magnitude are connected to form a Wheatstone Bridge arrangement. If the measuring galvanometer has an internal resistance R_G, derive expressions for the output current and the output voltage if the resistance in limb (1) increases by an amount δR.

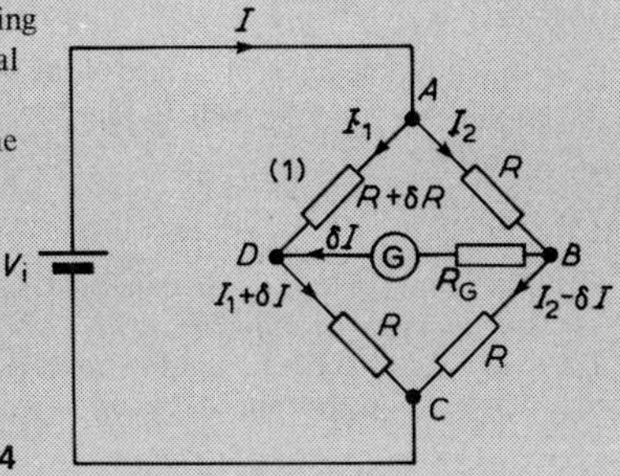

Fig 14

Applying Kirchhoff's laws to the analysis of the Wheatstone Bridge circuit (alternatively the Thèvenin analysis can be used), consider first the circuit ADC, so that

$$V_i = I_1(R + \delta R) + (I_1 + \delta I)R$$

from which

$$V_i = 2I_1R + I_1\delta R + \delta IR \qquad (2.28)$$

Consider next the network ABD, so that

$$I_2R + \delta IR_G = I_1(R + \delta R)$$

from which

$$I_2R - I_1R + \delta IR_G - I_1\delta R = 0 \qquad (2.29)$$

Finally, consider the network BCD, so that

$$(I_1 + \delta I)R + \delta IR_G = (I_1 - \delta I)R$$

from which

$$I_1R - I_2R + 2\delta IR + \delta IR_G = 0 \qquad (2.30)$$

The addition of equation (2.30) to equation (2.29) gives

$$2\delta I R_G + 2\delta I R - I_1 \delta R = 0$$

so that

$$I_1 = \frac{2\delta I(R + R_G)}{\delta R} \qquad (2.31)$$

Substituting for I_1 in equation (2.28) gives

$$V_i = \frac{4\delta I R(R + R_G)}{\delta R} + \frac{2\delta I \delta R(R + R_G) + \delta I R}{\delta R}$$

which reduces to

$$V_i = \frac{4\delta I R(R + R_G)}{\delta R} + 3\delta I R + 2\delta I R_G \qquad (2.32)$$

In practical situations, the first term of this equation is usually very large in relation to the remaining terms, so that for all practical purposes

$$V_i = \frac{4\delta I R(R + R_G)}{\delta R} \qquad (2.33)$$

so that the output current is

$$\delta I = \frac{V_i}{4(R + R_G)} \left(\frac{\delta R}{R}\right) \qquad (2.34)$$

and the output voltage (p.d. across DB) is

$$V_o = \frac{V_i R_G}{4(R + R_G)} \left(\frac{\delta R}{R}\right) \qquad (2.35)$$

Frequently, the input resistance of the output voltage measuring instrument can be considered to be very high. In this case, $R_G \to \infty$ and equation (2.35) becomes

$$V_o = \frac{V_i}{4}\left(\frac{\delta R}{R}\right) \qquad (2.36)$$

Problem 3 In a practical situation, the resistances of the Wheatstone Bridge circuit of *Fig 14* possess the following values: AB = 10 Ω, BC = 20 Ω, CD = 20 Ω and DA = 5 Ω. Calculate the output current from the bridge if the input voltage is 5 V and the measuring instrument has an internal resistance of 100 Ω.

Consider circuit ADC:

$$5I_1 + (I_1 + \delta I)20 = 5 \qquad (2.37)$$

and

$$5I_1 + 4\,\delta I = 1 \qquad (2.38)$$

Consider network ABD:

$$10I_2 + 100\,\delta I = 5I_1 \qquad (2.39)$$

and

$$2I_2 - I_1 + 20\,\delta I = 0 \qquad (2.40)$$

Consider network BCD:

$$(I_1 + \delta I)20 + 100\,\delta I = (I_2 - \delta I)20 \qquad (2.41)$$

and

$$I_1 - I_2 + 7\,\delta I = 0 \qquad (2.42)$$

In order to solve these three simultaneous equations, multiply equation (2.42) by 2 and add it to equation (2.40), so that

$$I_1 + 34\,\delta I = 0 \qquad (2.43)$$

and

$$I_1 = -34\,\delta I \qquad (2.44)$$

Substituting for I_1 in equation (2.38) gives

$170\ \delta I + 4\ \delta I = 1$ (2.45)

so that

$\delta I = -\dfrac{1}{166} =$ **6 mA**

flowing in a direction from D to B.

NOTE: (a) The negative sign indicates that the current is flowing in the opposite direction to the direction initially assumed.

(b) The solution of the three simultaneous equations (2.38), (2.40) and (2.42) can be performed by any appropriate method.

Problem 4 A thermo-resistive transducer is used in order to measure the temperature of a heat treatment furnace. The transducer is connected as one limb of a Wheatstone Bridge arrangement as indicated in *Fig 15*. If the transducer has a nominal resistance of 130 Ω and its sensitivity is 0.01 Ω/°C, calculate the voltage output from the bridge when the furnace temperature is 500°C. The bridge supply voltage is 5 V and the measuring instrument internal resistance is 50 Ω.

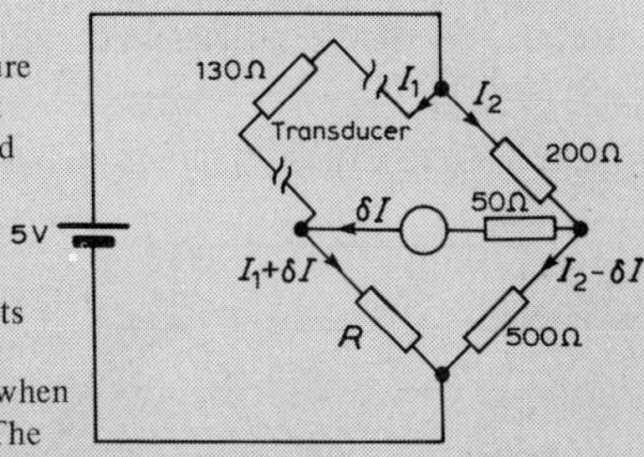

Fig 15

If the bridge is initially balanced,

$$\frac{130}{R} = \frac{200}{500}$$

so that

$R = 325\ \Omega$

The change in resistance of the transducer due to the increase in furnace temperature = 0.01 × 500 = 5 Ω

Consider circuit ADC:

$135 I_1 + 325(I_1 + \delta I) = 5$ (2.45)

or

$92 I_1 + 65\ \delta I = 1$ (2.46)

Consider network ABD:

$200 I_2 + 50\ \delta I = 135 I_1$ (2.47)

or

$4 I_2 + \delta I - 2.7 I_1 = 0$ (2.48)

Consider network BDC:

$325(I_1 + \delta I) + 50\ \delta I = 500(I_2 - \delta I)$

or

$6.5 I_1 + 17.5\ \delta I - 10 I_2 = 0$ (2.49)

Multiplying equation (2.48) by 2.5 and adding to equation (2.49) gives

$I_1 = 80\ \delta I$ (2.50)

Substituting for I_1 in equation (2.45) gives

$7360\ \delta I + 65\ \delta I = 1$ (2.51)

so that

$\delta I = 0.135\text{mA}$, flowing from B to D

The output voltage is given by

$V_o = \delta I R_G$ (2.52)

from which

$\mathbf{V_o = 6.74\ mV}$

Problem 5 A Wheatstone Bridge circuit used in a strain measurement system comprises four strain gauges of equal magnitude, one gauge connected into each limb of the bridge. The nominal resistance of each gauge is 100 Ω, the bridge supply voltage is 10 V and the output measuring instrument has an internal resistance of 20 Ω.

Determine the output voltage from first principles if one gauge increases its resistance by 1%. Compare this result with the voltage obtained by using equation (2.35).

Refer to *Fig 16*, and let R_1 increase its resistance by 1%.

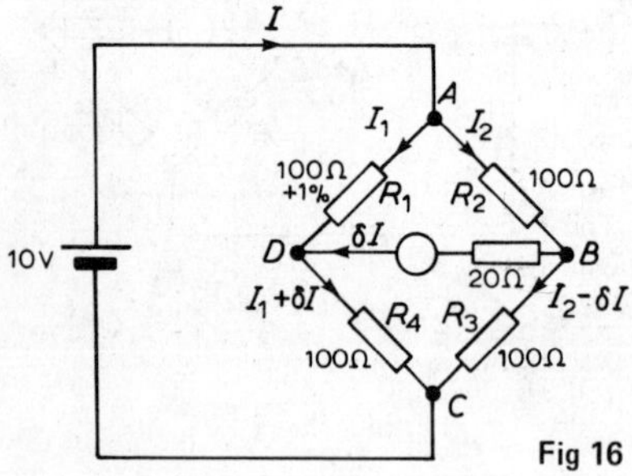

Fig 16

Consider circuit ADC:

$101I_1 + 100(I_1 + \delta I) = 10$ (2.53)

or

$20.1I_1 + 10\,\delta I = 1$ (2.54)

Consider network ABD:

$100I_2 + 20\,\delta I = 101I_1$ (2.55)

or

$5I_2 + \delta I - 5.05I_1 = 0$ (2.56)

Consider network BDC:

$100(I_1 + \delta I) + 20\,\delta I = 100(I_2 - \delta I)$

or

$5I_1 + 11\,\delta I - 5I_2 = 0$ (2.57)

Adding equation (2.57) to equation (2.56) gives

$I_1 = 240\,\delta I$ (2.58)

Substituting for I_1 in equation (2.54) gives

$\delta I = 2.068 \times 10^{-4}\ \text{A}$

and

$V_o = 2.068 \times 10^{-4} \times 20$

$= \mathbf{4.14\ mV}$

Substituting values in equation (2.35) gives

$$V_o = \frac{10 \times 20}{4(100 + 20)} \left(\frac{1}{100}\right) \text{V}$$

so that

V_o = **4.17 mV**

In this case, since all the resistances of the bridge are of **equal magnitude** initially, the percentage error resulting from the use of equation (2.35) is 0.72%. This degree of error is acceptable in practical situations.

Problem 6 Show that the ratio of the output voltage to the input voltage of a practical potentiometric transducer can be expressed as equation (2.5).

In a particular transducer, the transducer resistance is 2 kΩ, and the load resistance is 5 kΩ. Determine the loading error for this transducer in relation to an ideal potentiometer by plotting its response graph.

Circuits equivalent to *Fig 3* are shown in *Fig 17* and *Fig 18*.

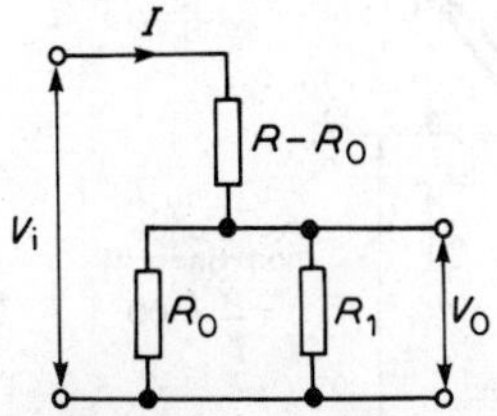

Fig 17

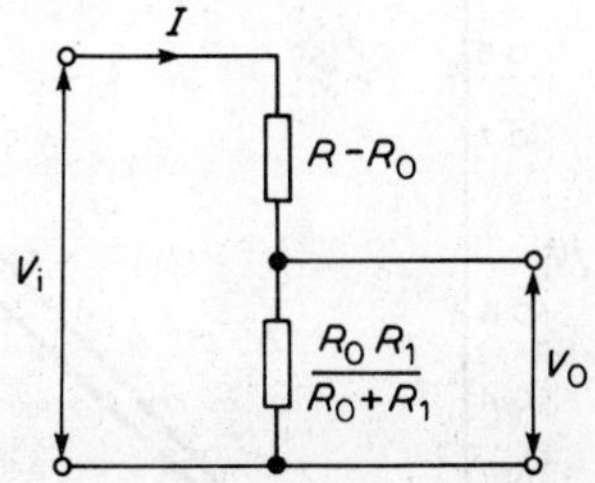

Fig 18

Resistors R_o and R_1 connected in parallel are equivalent to a single series resistor of magnitude

$$\frac{R_o R_1}{R_o + R_1} \qquad (2.59)$$

Thus, it is evident from *Fig 18* that

$$V_i = I\left[(R - R_o) + \frac{R_o R_1}{R_o + R_1}\right] \qquad (2.60)$$

and

$$V_o = \frac{I R_o R_1}{R_o + R_1} \qquad (2.61)$$

so that

$$\frac{V_o}{V_i} = \frac{R_o R_1}{(R_o + R_1)\left[(R - R_o) + \dfrac{R_o R_1}{R_o + R_1}\right]} \qquad (2.62)$$

Equation (2.62) reduces to

$$\frac{V_o}{V_i} = \frac{R_o R_1}{(R_o + R_1)(R - R_o) + R_o R_1} \qquad (2.63)$$

from which

$$\frac{V_o}{V_i} = \frac{R_o R_1}{R_o R + R_1 R - R_o^2} \qquad (2.64)$$

Dividing the numerator and the denominator of equation (2.64) by $R_o R_1$ gives

$$\frac{V_o}{V_i} = \frac{1}{\frac{R}{R_o} + \frac{R}{R_1}\left(1 - \frac{R_o}{R}\right)} \tag{2.65}$$

which is the same as equation (2.5).

The total displacement of the transducer, x_t, causes a change in resistance R, while any intermediate displacement, x_i, causes a change in resistance R_o, so that equation (2.65) can be written as

$$\frac{V_o}{V_i} = \frac{1}{\frac{x_t}{x_i} + \frac{R}{R_1}\left(1 - \frac{x_i}{x_t}\right)} \tag{2.66}$$

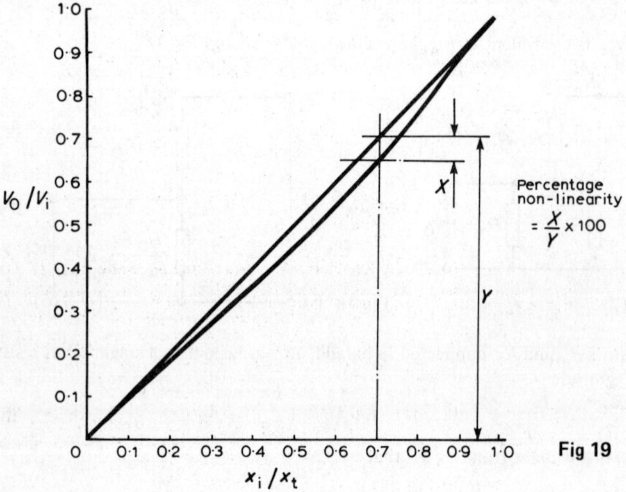

Fig 19

Substituting values in equation (2.66) and letting $x_i = x_t/4, x_t/2, 3x_t/4$ and x_t respectively, corresponding values for V_o/V_i can be calculated as follows:

(a) $x_i = x_t/4$, $\frac{V_o}{V_i} = 0.23$

(b) $x_i = x_t/2$, $\frac{V_o}{V_i} = 0.45$

(c) $x_i = 3x_t/4$, $\frac{V_o}{V_i} = 0.70$

(d) $x_i = x_t$ $\frac{V_o}{V_i} = 1.0$

The corresponding response graph is indicated in *Fig 19*, from which the maximum percentage non-linearity is 8.7% and occurs at approximately x_i/x_t = 0.7.

Problem 7 A recorder galvanometer contains a 200-turn coil that is 20 mm square and can rotate about a vertical axis. The movement of the coil is controlled by a spring that exerts a restoring torque of 2×10^{-6} N m per degree of rotation on the coil. If the galvanometer is inserted into a magnetic field of flux density 0.18T, calculate the galvanometer sensitivity in degrees per milliampere.

The force causing rotation of the coil is given by equation (2.13). The effective length of the coil is given by

$\ell = 200 \times 20 \times 10^{-3}$ (one side)

and the **torque** causing rotation is $2F \times 10 \times 10^{-3}$ N m.

For any particular current, this torque is balanced by the spring restoring torque, so that

$2F \times 10 \times 10^{-3} = 2 \times 10^{-6}$

and

$F = 10^{-4}$ N/degree

The current flowing through the coil that produces this force is

$$i = \frac{F}{B\ell} = \frac{10^{-4}}{0.18 \times 200 \times 20 \times 10^{-3}}$$

from which

$$i = \frac{1}{7.2} \text{ mA/degree}$$

and the sensitivity is **7.2 degrees/mA**

Problem 8 An active electromagnetic velocity transducer has a magnetic flux density of 1.0 T. The moving coil has 100 turns and is wound on a core 40 mm in diameter. If the electrical output from the transducer is observed to be a sinusoidal signal with an amplitude of 0.2 V r.m.s. and a frequency of 200 Hz, calculate the amplitude and the frequency of the armature displacement.

The transducer output is given by equation (2.12). The **maximum** output voltage is $0.2\sqrt{2}$, since the output voltage quoted is an r.m.s. voltage. The maximum velocity can be calculated by substituting values into equation (2.12), thus

$0.2\sqrt{2} = 1 \times \pi \times 40 \times 10^{-3} \times 100 \times v$

from which

$$v = \frac{0.2\sqrt{2}}{4\pi} \text{ m/s} \qquad (2.67)$$

Since the output is sinusoidal, the armature movement must be sinusoidal, so that the *maximum* velocity is also given by

$$v = \omega \times \text{amplitude} \qquad (2.68)$$

where ω is the circular frequency of the armature

Therefore, equating equations (2.67) and (2.68), gives

$$\frac{0.2\sqrt{2}}{4\pi} = 2\pi \times 200 \times \text{amplitude}$$

so that

$$\text{amplitude} = \frac{0.2\sqrt{2}}{4\pi \times 400\pi}$$

from which

Amplitude = 17.91 μm

It is evident that the maximum armature displacement is 17.91 μm and that the frequency is 200 Hz.

Problem 9 Describe the principles of operation of the three types of photo-electric transducer.

(i) *Photo-emissive transducers*
Fig 10 indicates a typical arrangement for a photo-emissive transducer. In this arrangement, a potential difference is applied across the photocell and a resistor is connected in a series circuit. The cathode of the photocell emits electrons in response to the intensity of light incident upon it and the electrons are collected on the anode. The anode current I_a is then proportional to the intensity of the incident light.

(ii) *Photo-voltaic transducers*
Fig 11 indicates a typical arrangement for a photo-voltaic transducer. In this arrangement, incident light causes an e.m.f. to be generated between the collecting ring and the base metal such that the e.m.f. generated is proportional to the intensity of the incident light.

(iii) *Photo-conductive transducers*
Fig 12 indicates a typical arrangement for a photo-conductive transducer. In this arrangement, incident light causes a change in the electrical resistance between the two semiconductor segments such that the change in resistance is proportional to the intensity of the incident light. It is necessary to use the Wheatstone Bridge circuit in order to measure the relatively small changes in resistance.

Problem 10 Describe how the four basic thermocouple laws influence industrial usage of thermocouples.

Law 1 indicates that only the junction temperatures are significant, so that variations in the environmental temperature will not affect the thermocouple output unless it affects one of the junction temperatures.
Law 2 indicates that the addition of connecting leads will not affect the thermocouple output provided that the connections are at the same temperature. This implies that a measuring instrument can be connected anywhere in the thermocouple circuit without influencing the temperature reading.
Law 3 indicates that all possible pairs of metals need not be calibrated, since individual metals can be calibrated against one standard metal which is usually platinum. The responses of any other metal combinations can then be calculated.
Law 4 indicates that the cold junction (sometimes known as the reference junction) can be at a temperature other than zero temperature, and a measurement made relative to zero temperature. For example, consider the situation where the cold junction temperature is 20°C and a voltmeter reads 1.8 mV. This temperature reading indicates the difference in junction temperatures relative to the cold junction temperature of 20°C. It is evident from standard tables, that if the mV output from two junctions, one at zero temperature and the other at 20°C is 0.71 mV, then the actual measured temperature relative to 0°C is 0.71 + 1.8 = 2.51 mV. This reading can then be converted to a temperature reading by using standard tables.

D. FURTHER PROBLEMS ON TRANSDUCERS

(a) SHORT-ANSWER PROBLEMS

1 The two methods of using Wheatstone Bridge circuits are known as the .... and the ....

2 In many applications the Wheatstone Bridge arrangement is included in .... while in strain gauge applications the bridge has to be ....

3 The unbalanced bridge technique can be used to measure .... and .... quantities but the balanced bridge technique can only be used to measure .... quantities.

4 The null technique is more accurate than the unbalanced bridge technique because the bridge output in this case is dependent only upon the .... and is independent of the ....

5 Ideal potentiometric transducers are known as .... instruments because the output is .... to the displacement of the slider.

6 The influence of measuring instruments upon transducers is known as the .... effect and produces a .... characteristic unless the ratio of the internal resistance of the measuring instrument is .... in relation to the transducer resistance.

7 Transducers can be classified as .... transducers or .... transducers depending upon whether .... is supplied to them.

8 The variation in the inductance of passive electromagnetic transducers can be accomplished by varying the .... of the coil or the .... of the circuit or the .... of the core.

9 Thermocouples are used in order to measure .... and comprise .... joined together at two points.

10 The relationship between temperature and the resistance of thermistors is ...., but their main advantages are that they are .... and have .... so that they are frequently used in ....

(b) MULTI-CHOICE PROBLEMS (answers on page 184)

1 Wheatstone Bridge circuits are used in conjunction with:
(a) potentiometric transducers; (c) active electromagnetic transducers;
(b) resistive transducers; (d) thermocouples.

2 The unbalanced bridge method of using Wheatstone Bridge circuits compared with the null method is:
(a) more accurate; (c) less accurate
(b) more linear; (d) less dependent upon the bridge supply voltage.

3 In potentiometric transducers, large variations in resistance are produced by:
(a) extending an electrical conductor;
(b) moving a conductor through a magnetic field;
(c) thermally expanding a conductor,
(d) displacing a slider across a resistor.

4 Passive electromagnetic transducers are frequently used in order to measure:
(a) displacement, (c) dynamic quantities only;
(b) temperature; (d) static quantities only.

5 Linear or angular velocity can be measured by active transducers that depend upon:
(a) the movement of a conductor through a magnetic field;

(b) the generation of a force by passing a current through a conductor;
(c) varying the mutual inductance of two coils;
(d) varying the capacitance of a capacitor.

6 In certain capacitive transducers, no physical connection between the transducer and the quantity being measured is necessary, so that the transducer variable is the:
(a) area of the capacitor plates; (c) plate separation;
(b) permittivity of the insulator; (d) resistance.

7 An electric charge is generated as certain naturally occurring and artificial crystals are deformed. This characteristic is known as:
(a) the capacitive effect; (c) the piezoelectric effect;
(b) the thermoelectric effect; (d) the electromagnetic effect.

8 If a static force is applied to a piezoelectric transducer the electric charge generated will:
(a) increase over a period of time; (c) remain static;
(b) decrease over a period of time; (d) oscillate.

9 In a temperature measurement, the e.m.f. generated by a thermocouple is observed to be 4.25 mV when the cold junction temperature is 21°C. From standard tables, the e.m.f. corresponding to a temperature difference of 21°C for this thermocouple is 0.75 mV, so that according to the law of intermediate temperatures, the source temperature relative to zero degrees will be equivalent to:
(a) 5 mv; (b) 3.5 mV; (c) 3.19 mV; (d) 5.67 mV.

10 In order to detect the electrical output from thermocouples it is necessary to use:
(a) Wheatstone Bridge circuits; (c) transducers,
(b) current measuring instruments; (d) voltage measuring instruments.

(c) CONVENTIONAL PROBLEMS

1 A thermo-resistive temperature sensor is used in order to measure the exhaust temperature of an internal combustion engine. The sensor is connected in one limb of a Wheatstone Bridge arrangement and the four resistances that make up the bridge are each 200 Ω, while the temperature sensitivity of the sensor is 0.01 Ω/°C. Calculate the output from the bridge in volts when the exhaust temperature is 800°C, if the bridge supply voltage is 5 V and the measuring instrument internal resistance is 50 Ω.

[10 mV]

2 A Wheatstone Bridge circuit used in a strain measuring system comprises four strain gauges of equal magnitude, one connected into each limb of the bridge. The nominal resistance of each gauge is 100 Ω, the output measuring instrument has an infinitely high internal resistance and the supply voltage is 10 V. Determine the voltage output from the bridge if one gauge increases its resistance by 1%.
If a gauge in an adjacent limb decreases its resistance by 1% simultaneously, calculate the new voltage output. Comment on the result.

[25 mV; 50 mV. If one gauge increases its resistance and an adjacent gauge decreases its resistance by the same amount simultaneoulsy, the bridge sensitivity is doubled.]

3 Explain the difference between the null measurement technique and the out-of-balance bridge measurement technique. Two 120 Ω strain gauges are connected to form adjacent arms of a Wheatstone Bridge. The bridge is completed by two resistors of 1.2 kΩ each. If the bridge supply voltage is 4 V and the internal resistance of the output measuring instrument is 50 Ω, calculate the bridge

sensitivity in μA per percentage resistance change when only one gauge changes its resistance. Comment on this result.

[12.27μA/percentage change in resistance; this output is very low so that the output needs to be amplified.]

4 A transducer is connected to an ammeter which consists of a coil 16 mm square having 160 turns. The coil can rotate about the vertical axis and the suspension stiffness is 2.0×10^{-3} Nm per degree of rotation. The vertical sides of the coil move in a magnetic field of flux density 0.14 T, the field being directed radially relative to the axis of rotation. Calculate the sensitivity of the ammeter in degrees/A.

[2.87 degrees/A]

5 Discuss, with the aid of suitable diagrams, the operating principles of two types of transducers whose outputs are electrical signals proportional to static and dynamic linear or angular displacement.

6 Explain why it is desirable for the internal resistance of voltage measuring instruments to be at least 15 times greater than the resistances of potentiometric transducers. Show that the response of a typical potentiometric transducer circuit can be given by equation (2.66) and plot the response of a particular system where the transducer resistance is 5 kΩ and the measuring instrument resistance is 20 kΩ. Estimate the percentage non-linearity of this system.

[4.3% (approx.)]

7 An electromagnetic velocity transducer is used in order to detect the motion of an oscillating hydraulic ram. The transducer coil is wound on a core 15 mm in diameter, has 100 turns and is surrounded by a magnetic field of flux density 1.0 T. If the waveform output from the transducer is measured by an oscilloscope and is observed to be sinusoidal, having a frequency of 10 Hz and a magnitude of 2.0 V peak-to-peak, calculate the maximum velocity and the corresponding peak-to-peak displacement of the transducer armature.

[0.212 m/s; 6.75 mm]

8 Explain the principles of operation of piezoelectric transducers and state two natural materials that exhibit this characteristic. State three variables that can be measured by such transducers and explain why it is desirable that these transducers should be used for the measurement of dynamic quantities only.

9 State the law of intermediate temperatures and the law of intermediate metals. Discuss the influence of these laws on the industrial usage of thermocouples.

10 Compare the operation and usage of industrial thermocouples and thermo-resistive sensing elements.

3 Measurement errors

A. ERROR SOURCES

(a) INTRODUCTION

All instruments contain error sources and all measurements contain errors. Generally, errors are generated from two sources, namely, deficiencies in instrument performance and observer or environmental interference. Errors emanating from the deficiencies in instrument performance are usually consistent and predictable so that they can be reduced by calibration. However, errors emanating from observer and environmental interference can be erratic and random but they can be reduced by using statistical techniques.

Instrument deficiencies arise from manufacturing tolerances, elastic deformation of components, transmission losses, translation errors and component responses. Interference errors can arise if either the measuring instrument or the environment alters the measured variable or influences the measuring system. Observation errors can arise as a result of mistakes in taking readings, parallax, improper instrument location and inadequate lighting.

(b) INSTRUMENT PERFORMANCE ERRORS

Construction errors

1 Tolerances exist on the dimensions and the quality of mechanical and electrical components which in turn affect the overall instrument performances. These tolerances are evident in gearing backlash, friction between moving parts, inaccurate scale graduations, inaccuracies in electrical components, etc. Manufacturing quality can also influence instrument performance but strict quality control procedures can reduce this source of error to a minimum. Generally, instrument price reflects instrument quality.

Translation errors

2 There are two principal causes of inaccurate signal translation, namely, instrument dynamic behaviour and hysteresis losses.

The dynamic behaviour of instruments varies and depends largely upon the degree of damping present in instrument mechanisms and the magnitudes of the instrument moving masses. Damping can be intentional or unintentional and instruments can exhibit over-damped or under-damped characteristics. Also, different types of instruments exhibit different characteristics. For example, first-order instruments, which are effectively zero-mass instruments, exhibit

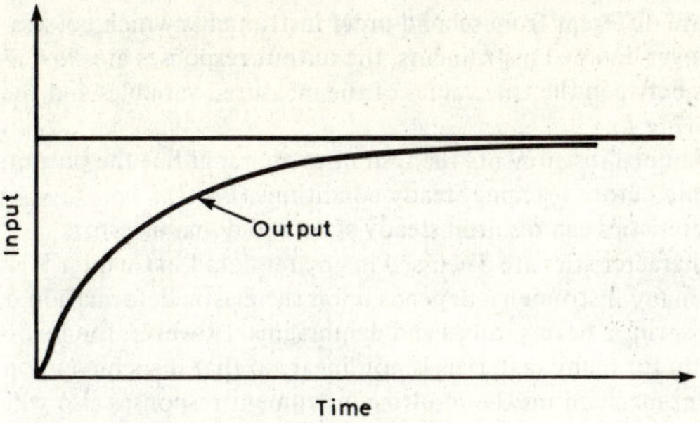

Fig 1 Overdamped response

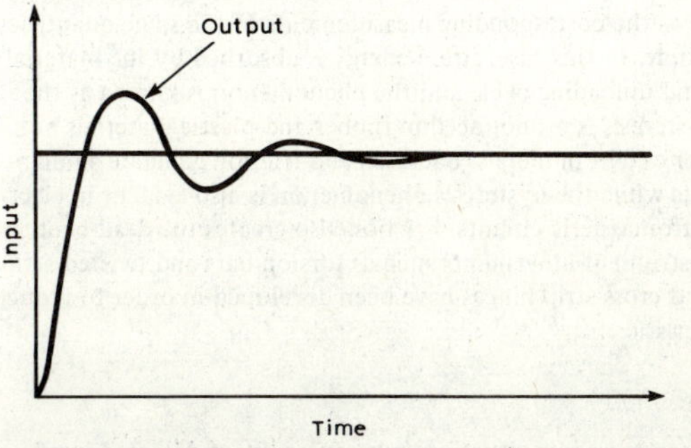

Fig 2 Underdamped response

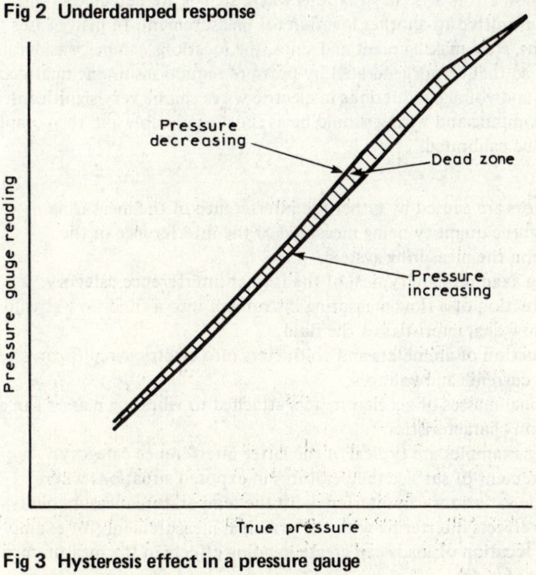

Fig 3 Hysteresis effect in a pressure gauge

characteristics that are different from second-order instruments which possess effective masses. In over-damped instruments, the output responses are slow and there are differences between the true values of the measured variables and the instrument readings (*Fig 1*).
However, in under-damped instruments the responses are rapid but the outputs overshoot and oscillate before reaching steady conditions (*Fig 2*).
Each of these characteristics can result in steady-state and dynamic errors. Dynamic response characteristics are discussed in greater detail in Chapter 9.

The operation of many instruments depends upon the elastic deformation of components such as springs, beams, tubes and diaphragms. However, the load-deflection relationship for many materials is not linear, so that if such components are used in instrument mechanisms the resulting instrument responses also will be non-linear. Furthermore, for many materials the unloading graph is not the same as the loading graph (*Fig 3*) so that measurements of increasing quantities are not necessarily the same as the corresponding measurements of the same quantities decreasing in magnitude. In this case, strain energy is absorbed by the material during the loading and unloading cycle and the phenomenon is known as the **hysteresis effect**. Hysteresis is pronounced in rubber and plastic materials but also occurs to a lesser extent in metals. Backlash and friction generate similar effects in instruments while the hysteresis phenomenon is also evident in electrical systems such as electromagnetic circuits. Friction also creates the dead-band characteristic and instrument movements such as torsion bars and twisted strips, roller movements and cross-strip hinges have been developed in order to reduce this undesirable characteristic.

Transmission errors

3 Signal transmission errors arise in situations where signals are detected in one location and transmitted to another location for measurement. In many cases such as power stations, steel making plant and ships, the locations can be considerable distances apart, so that errors generated by pressure reductions in pneumatic and hydraulic pipes and voltage reductions in electric wires can be very significant. In these situations, piping and wiring should be as short as possible and the complete systems should be calibrated.

Interference errors

4 Interference errors are caused by either the interference of the measuring instrument upon the quantity being measured or the interference of the environment upon the measuring system.

The following examples are typical of the former interference category:

(a) The introduction of a flow measuring instrument into a fluid flow stream can alter the flow characteristics of the fluid;

(b) the introduction of ammeters and voltmeters into electric circuits can alter the circuit currents and voltages;

(c) the additional masses of accelerometers attached to vibrating masses can alter the vibration characteristics.

The following examples are typical of the latter interference category:

(a) the measurement of surface temperatures in exposed situations where atmospheric variations can interfere with the temperature measurements;

(b) minor side effects interfering with the principal measurement, for example, inaccurate location of loads can create bending effects in the measurement of axial thrust (*Fig 4*);

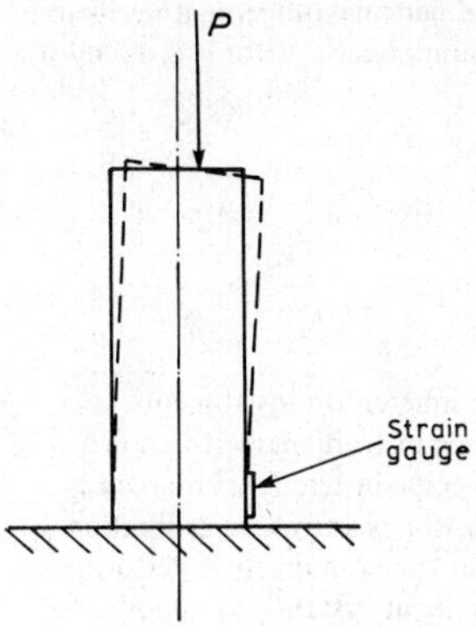

Fig 4 Inaccurate location of force *P* creates additional compressive bending strain

(c) locating measuring instruments where they can be subjected to intense heat, intense cold or vibration.

In each of these situations, the effects of the measuring instruments upon the measured variables mut be minimised. In addition, care must be exercised in order to ensure that only the desired measured variables are measured and not combinations of variables.

(c) RANDOM ERRORS

Random errors arise in all measurements and can be due to a multitude of minor, independent influences such as observation errors, vibration, draughts, electrostatic charges, variations in the mains voltage and frequency etc. In very accurate work, these errors must be minimised but they cannot be eliminated completely.

In these situations, it is usual to assume that if a large number of readings of a particular quantity is taken then the readings are distributed symmetrically about a mean reading. This distribution is known as the **Normal** or **Gaussian Distribution**. Generally, the mean value of a sample of readings is the best estimate of the mean value of the infinite population from which the sample is taken.

The spread of the readings about the sample mean value is determined by the **standard deviation**. The best estimate of the infinite population standard deviation is given by

$$\sigma_{est} = \sqrt{\left(\frac{n}{n-1}\right)} s \qquad (3.1)$$

where σ_{est} = the population standard deviation,
n = the number of readings in the sample,
s = the sample standard deviation.

Frequently, individual variables are measured and then substituted into formulae in order to calculate other quantities. In these cases, the individual measurement errors can become cumulative so that the error in the calculated quantity can be significantly greater than the individual measurement errors. The maximum possible error in the calculated quantity is given by the sum of the individual errors regardless of sign, so that the worst possible case is presented. However, in many cases this result can be too pessimistic and personal judgement needs to be exercised in individual applications. The maximum possible error is given by

$$\frac{\Delta X}{X} = \sum\left(\frac{\partial X}{\partial n} \times \frac{n}{X} \times \frac{\Delta n}{n}\right) \tag{3.2}$$

where X = any calculated quantity,
n = any measured quantity,
Δn = the measurement error

B. CALIBRATION

In order to assess the predictable errors that are inherent in instruments, it is necessary to compare the performance of working instruments with known standards or with the performance of reference grade instruments that are subjected to the same inputs. This act of comparison is known as **calibration.** Instruments must be calibrated regularly in order to maintain their performance and must be calibrated before use. Most measurement systems, as opposed to individual instruments, also need to be calibrated.

With the exception of dimensional measurements, there are few standard calibration procedures that can be applied to measurement systems. In many cases, calibration procedures are devised to suit the particular measurement problem and it is sometimes more difficult to calibrate measurement systems than to perform the measurement. Static calibration is usually the easiest and the most common form of calibration, but where extreme accuracies in dynamic measurements or in high or low temperature measurements are required it is necessary to simulate the actual working environment.

Usually in static calibration, the performance of one instrument is compared with the performance of another instrument that is maintained solely for calibration purposes. Alternatively, complete measurement systems or instruments can be calibrated by applying known standards such as standards of mass in force measuring systems, or standards of length in displacement measuring systems. As a general rule, the calibration standard must be at least ten times more accurate than the system or the instrument being calibrated.

Fundamental standards are maintained in the UK by the National Physical Laboratory and instruments can be referred to this institution for precise calibration. Additionally, there are centres in various parts of the UK that specialise in the calibration of particular types of instruments.

C. WORKED PROBLEMS ON MEASUREMENT ERRORS

Problem 1 The following data relates to the calibration of a Bourdon-tube pressure gauge. Plot the calibration graph, indicate the 'dead' zone and explain why this occurs. Using the calibration graph, plot the error and the correction curves for the gauge.

True pressure (bar)		10	20	30	40	50	60
Gauge reading (bar)	*Increasing*	9.0	15.5	26.0	33.5	45.5	56.0
	Decreasing	9.5	16.5	27.0	36.0	46.5	

The calibration graph for the pressure gauge is shown in *Fig 5*. The 'dead' zone occurs because of hysteresis in the Bourdon tube, backlash in the gear mechanism and friction between the moving parts. The combined effect of these factors is indicated by the differences in the gauge readings as the gauge is subjected to increasing and decreasing pressures.

The error graph for the pressure gauge is shown in *Fig 6* and the correction graph is shown in *Fig 7*.

The error graph is plotted by estimating the mean gauge error corresponding to each increment of true pressure. For example, when the true pressure is 10 bar, the estimated mean gauge reading is 9.25 bar, giving an error of –0.75 bar. Similarly,

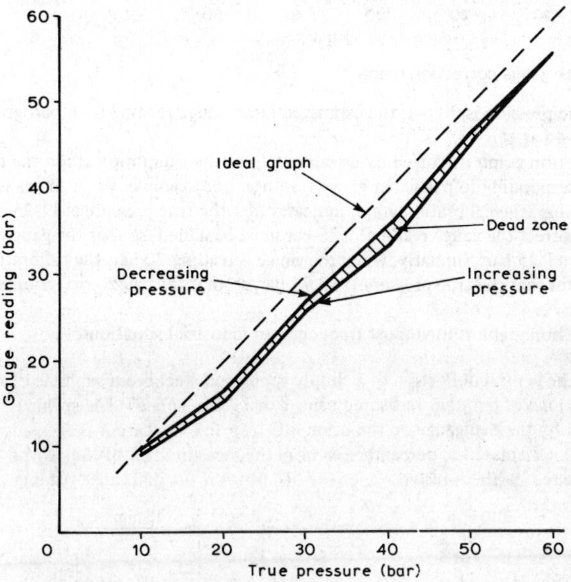

Fig 5 Pressure gauge calibration graph

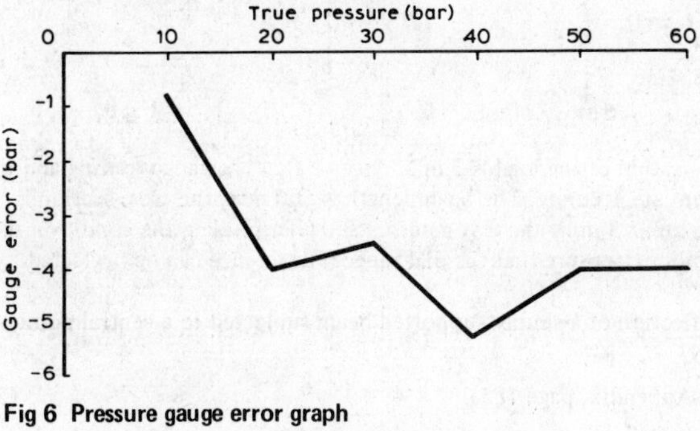

Fig 6 Pressure gauge error graph

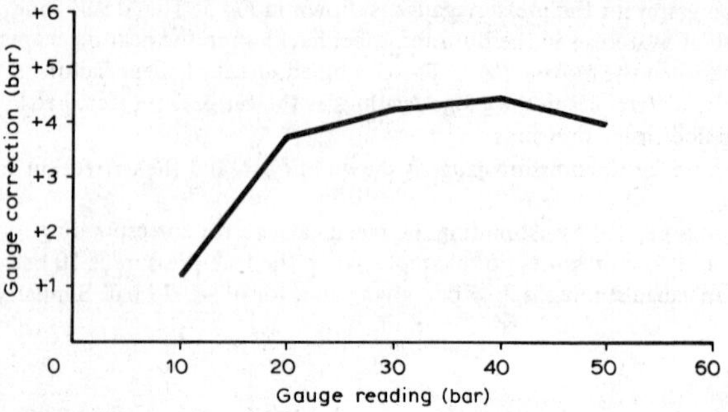

Fig 7 Pressure gauge correction graph

when the true pressure is 20 bar, the estimated mean gauge reading is 16 bar, giving an error of –4 bar.

The correction graph is plotted by estimating from the calibration graph the true pressure corresponding to particular gauge readings. For example, when the gauge is reading 10 bar, the calibration graph indicates that the true pressure is 11.25 bar. In order to correct the gauge reading, 1.25 bar must be added, so that the gauge correction is +1.25 bar. Similarly, when the gauge is reading 20 bar, the calibration graph indicates that the true pressure is 23.75 bar, so that the gauge correction is +3.75 bar.

The correction graph is used most frequently in industrial situations.

Problem 2 The central deflection of a simply supported steel beam subjected to a central point load of 0.5 kg is measured using a dial gauge (*Fig 8*). The spring force exerted by the dial gauge on the beam is $0.1R + 0.4N$, where R is the gauge reading (mm). Calculate the percentage error in the measurement of the central deflection caused by the interference of the dial gauge if the dial gauge reading

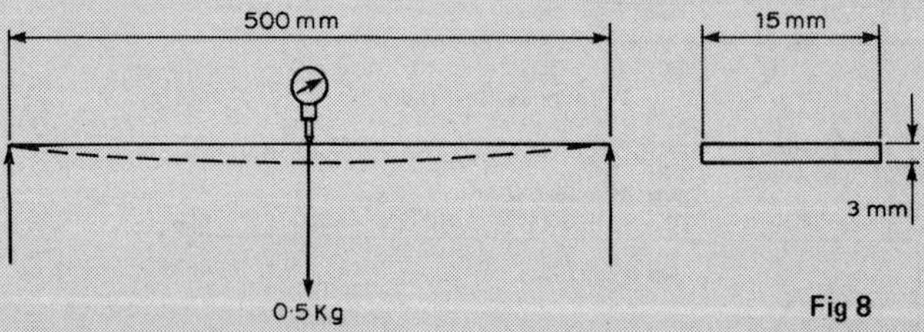

Fig 8

before the application of the load is 3 mm. Assume that the gauge reading and the beam dimensions are accurate. The beam length is 500 mm, the cross-section is rectangular, 15 mm × 3 mm, and E for steel is 200 GPa. Explain the condition that is required in order to ensure that the dial gauge interference can be neglected.

The central deflection of a simply supported beam subjected to a central point load is given by

$$\delta = \frac{FL^3}{48EI} \text{ (see Appendix, page 185)} \qquad (3.3)$$

where δ = the central deflection
F = the centrally applied load
L = the beam length
E = the modulus of elasticity of the beam material
and I = the second moment of area of the beam cross-section (see Appendix).

Thus,

$$\frac{L^3}{48EI} = \frac{500^3 \times 12}{48 \times 200 \times 10^3 \times 15 \times 3^3} \quad (3.4)$$

where all the dimensions are in millimetres,
so that

$$\frac{L^3}{48EI} = 0.3858 \text{ mm/N} \quad (3.5)$$

Neglecting the dial gauge force, the theoretical central deflection is given by $mg \times 0.3858$ so that the theoretical deflection

$$= 0.5 \times 9.807 \times 0.3858$$
$$= 1.8918 \text{ mm}$$

The force exerted by the dial gauge when the beam is deflected due to the applied mass is given by

$$F = [(0.1 \times 3) + 0.4] - 0.1\delta \quad (3.6)$$

where δ is the actual deflection
so that

$$F = 0.7 - 0.1\delta \quad (3.7)$$

The total force applied to the centre of the beam

$$= 0.5 \times 9.807 + (0.7 - 0.1\delta)$$
$$= 5.6035 - 0.1\delta$$

Therefore, the actual beam deflection is given by

$$\delta = (5.6035 - 0.1\delta)0.3858 \quad (3.8)$$

from which

$$\delta = 2.0815 \text{ mm}$$

Therefore,
the interference error $= 2.0815 - 1.8918$
$= 0.1897$ mm
and the percentage error = **10.03%**

In this case the beam deflection is large in relation to the load applied to it, so that the gauge force cannot be neglected. However, in order that the gauge force can be neglected, the beam must be less flexible so that its stiffness must be high.

Problem 3 A U/V recorder matching circuit is shown in *Fig 9*. Determine the interference error in the measurement of the potential difference across the 250Ω damping resistor using a voltmeter having an input resistance of 2 kΩ, and a voltmeter having an input resistance of 20 kΩ.

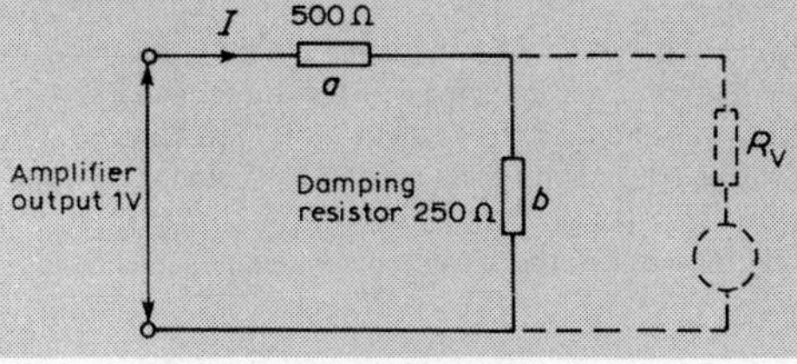

Fig 9

The theoretical potential difference across the damping resistor without the voltmeter connected in the circuit is given by

$$\text{p.d.} = I \times 250 \tag{3.9}$$

However, the current flowing in the circuit is given by

$$1 = 500I + 250I = 750I \tag{3.10}$$

so that

$$I = \frac{1}{750}\ \text{A} \tag{3.11}$$

and the p.d. across the damping resistor

$$= 250 \times \frac{1}{750} = 0.333\ \text{V}$$

With the 2 kΩ voltmeter connected, the potential difference across the damping resistor and the voltmeter connected in parallel is given by

$$\text{p.d.} = I \times \frac{R_b R_v}{R_b + R_v} \tag{3.12}$$

so that

$$\text{p.d.} = \frac{I \times 250 \times 2000}{250 + 2000} = 222.22I \tag{3.13}$$

Now

$$I = \frac{1}{(500 + 222.22)} = 1.385\ \text{mA}$$

so that the potential difference across the damping resistor is given by

$$\text{p.d.} = 1.385 \times 10^{-3} \times 222.22$$
$$= 0.3077\ \text{V}$$

and the percentage error is $\dfrac{(0.3077 - 0.3333)\,100}{0.3333} = \mathbf{-7.68\%}$

With the 20 kΩ voltmeter connected, the potential difference across the damping resistor is given by

$$\text{p.d.} = \frac{I \times 250 \times 20 \times 10^3}{250 + 20 \times 10^3} = 246.91I \tag{3.14}$$

and

$$I = \frac{1}{(500 + 246.91)} = 1.339\ \text{mA}$$

so that

$$\text{p.d.} = 1.339 \times 10^{-3} \times 246.91 = 0.3306\ \text{V}$$

In this case, the percentage error is

$$\frac{(0.3306 - 0.3333)100}{0.3333} = \mathbf{-0.81\%}$$

Clearly, the interference is reduced if the voltmeter input resistance is significantly greater than the source resistance.

Problem 4 The current flowing in the matching circuit shown in *Fig 9* is measured by a galvanometer connected alongside the damping resistor. Investigate the interference errors incurred if a galvanometer having a terminal resistance of 10Ω is used and a galvanometer having a terminal resistance of 1 Ω is used.

The current flowing in the circuit without the galvanometer connected is

$$I = \frac{1}{750}\ \text{A} = 1.3333\ \text{mA}$$

The current flowing with the 10 Ω galvanometer connected is

$$I = \frac{1}{760}\text{A} = 1.3158 \text{ mA}$$

so that the percentage error is

$$\frac{(1.3333 - 1.3158)100}{1.3333} = \mathbf{1.313\%}$$

The current flowing with the 1 Ω galvanometer connected is

$$I = \frac{1}{751}\text{ A} = 1.3316 \text{ mA}$$

so that the percentage error is

$$\frac{(1.3333 - 1.3316)100}{1.3333} = \mathbf{0.128\%}$$

Clearly, in current measuring systems the terminal resistance of the measuring instrument must be as low as possible.

Problem 5 The main journal diameter of an engine crankshaft was measured ten times and the following results were obtained:
54.010; 54.012, 54.014; 54.016; 54.018; 54.016; 54.016; 54.018; 54.016; 54.014 mm. Construct a frequency table and calculate the mean diameter of the journal and the sample standard deviation. Determine also the parameters of the infinite population from which these readings are assumed to be taken.

Reading	*frequency (f)*	*Deviation from assumed mean* of 54.016 (*x*)	*fx*	*fx*²
54.010	1	–0.006	–0.006	3.6×10^{-5}
54.012	1	–0.004	–0.004	1.6×10^{-5}
54.014	2	–0.002	–0.004	0.8×10^{-5}
54.016	4	0	0.000	0.000
54.018	2	+0.002	+0.004	0.8×10^{-5}
	$\Sigma f = 10$		$\Sigma fx = -0.010$	$\Sigma fx^2 = 6.8 \times 10^{-5}$

The deviation from the assumed mean $= \dfrac{\Sigma fx}{\Sigma f} = \dfrac{-0.010}{10} = -0.001$

Therefore the sample mean $= 54.016 - 0.001 = \mathbf{54.015\ mm}$

The sample standard deviation is given by

$$\sigma = \sqrt{\frac{1}{\Sigma f}\left[\Sigma fx^2 - \frac{(\Sigma fx)^2}{\Sigma f}\right]} \qquad (3.15)$$

so that in this case

$$\sigma = \sqrt{\frac{1}{10}\left[(6.8 \times 10^{-5}) - \frac{10^{-4}}{10}\right]}$$

from which

$$\sigma = \sqrt{\frac{1}{10} \times 5.8 \times 10^{-5}}$$

and

$\sigma = 2.408 \times 10^{-3}$ mm

Since the sample mean is the best estimate of the population mean, the population mean is 54.015 mm. The population standard deviation is estimated from equation (3.1), so that

$$\sigma_{est} = \sqrt{\frac{10}{10-1}} \times 2.408 \times 10^{-3}$$

and

$\sigma_{est} = 2.538 \times 10^{-3}$ mm

Problem 6 In an experiment to determine the coefficient of friction in a belt drive system, it is assumed that tensions T_1 and T_2 and the contact angle θ can be measured to an accuracy of 1%. Calculate the maximum possible error in the coefficient of friction when the ratio $T_1/T_2 = 1.5$ and 15. The expression relating the coefficient of friction to the belt tensions is

$$\frac{T_1}{T_2} = e^{\mu\theta} \qquad (3.16)$$

From equation (3.16), the coefficient of friction is given by

$$\mu = \frac{1}{\theta} \ln \frac{T_1}{T_2} \qquad (3.17)$$

Applying equation (3.2) to the errors associated with each of the variable quantities in turn gives

$$\frac{\Delta\mu}{\mu} = \frac{-1}{\theta^2} \ln \frac{T_1}{T_2} \times \frac{\theta}{\mu} \times \frac{\Delta\theta}{\theta} = \frac{-\mu}{\theta} \times \frac{\theta}{\mu} \times \frac{\Delta\theta}{\theta}$$

$$= -\frac{\Delta\theta}{\theta}$$

$$\frac{\Delta\mu}{\mu} = \frac{T_2}{\theta T_1 T_2} \times \frac{T_1}{\mu} \times \frac{\Delta T_1}{T_1} = \frac{1}{\theta} \times \frac{1}{\mu} \times \frac{\Delta T_1}{T_1}$$

$$= \frac{1}{\ln \frac{T_1}{T_2}} \times \frac{\Delta T_1}{T_1}$$

and

$$\frac{\Delta\mu}{\mu} = \frac{T_2 T_1}{\theta T_1 T_2^2} \times \frac{T_2}{\mu} \times \frac{\Delta T_2}{T_2} = \frac{1}{\theta} \times \frac{1}{\mu} \times \frac{\Delta T_2}{T_2}$$

$$= \frac{1}{\ln \frac{T_1}{T_2}} \times \frac{\Delta T_2}{T_2}$$

The maximum possible error in μ due to simultaneous errors in each variable is

$$\frac{\Delta\mu}{\mu} = \frac{\Delta\theta}{\theta} + \frac{1}{\ln \frac{T_1}{T_2}} \times \frac{\Delta T_1}{T_1} + \frac{1}{\ln \frac{T_1}{T_2}} \times \frac{\Delta T_2}{T_2} \qquad (3.18)$$

Substituting values in equation (3.18) for the case where $T_1/T_2 = 1.5$,

$$\frac{\Delta\mu}{\mu} = 1 + \frac{1}{0.4055} \times 1 + \frac{1}{0.4055} \times 1$$

so that in this case, the maximum possible error in μ is

$$\frac{\Delta\mu}{\mu} = 5.93\%$$

Substituting values in equation (3.18) for the case where $T_1/T_2 = 15$,

$$\frac{\Delta\mu}{\mu} = 1 + \frac{1}{2.7081} \times 1 + \frac{1}{2.7081} \times 1$$

so that in this case, the maximum possible error in μ is

$$\frac{\Delta\mu}{\mu} = 1.74\%$$

It is evident that in this experiment higher belt tension ratios produce greater accuracies in the calculation of the coefficient of friction, and that in each case the error in the calculated value is far greater than the individual measurement errors.

D. FURTHER PROBLEMS ON MEASUREMENT ERRORS

(a) SHORT ANSWER PROBLEMS

1 Errors are generated by the . . . . and by . . . .
2 Performance errors are usually . . . . while observer errors are usually . . . .
3 Instrument performance errors can be classified as . . . . errors, ... errors, ... errors and . . . . errors.
4 Random errors can be minimised by using . . . .
5 Translation errors are caused by the . . . . and . . . .
6 The hysteresis effect is evident in . . . . and is caused by . . . . being absorbed during . . . . and . . . .
7 Other causes of the hysteresis effect are . . . . , ... and . . . .
8 Errors that are caused by the influence of measuring instruments upon measured variables are known as . . . . errors.
9 The act of comparing the performance of instruments against precise standards is known as . . . .
10 Independent influences such as vibrations and draughts give rise to . . . . errors which can be minimised by taking . . . . of readings and calculating the . . . . mean.

(b) MULTI-CHOICE PROBLEMS (answers on page 184)

1 Instrument performance errors can be caused by:
(a) draughts; (b) parallax; (c) manufacturing tolerances; (d) observation errors.
2 Gearing backlash, friction between moving parts and scale inaccuracies are known generally as:
(a) construction errors; (c) interference errors;
(b) random errors; (d) calibration errors.
3 The dynamic behaviour of instruments is governed by:
(a) elastic deformation of components; (c) strain energy in materials;
(b) damping and inertia; (d) voltage reductions in wiring.
4 When subjected to suddenly applied inputs, the outputs of under-damped instruments:
(a) overshoot and oscillate before reaching steady conditions;
(b) reach steady readings very slowly;
(c) always read correctly;
(d) are independent of the masses of the moving parts.

5 Torsion bar mechanisms, roller movements and cross-strip hinges have been devised in order to:
(a) reduce the strain energy in elastic members;
(b) reduce damping;
(c) eliminate transmission errors;
(d) reduce dead-band and friction.

6 Errors that arise due to pressure and voltage reductions between locations are known as:
(a) interference errors,
(b) hysteresis errors;
(c) dynamic errors;
(d) transmission errors.

7 In order to reduce random errors, a sample of readings can be taken which are assumed to be distributed in accordance with the:
(a) Gaussian distribution;
(b) standard deviation;
(c) arithmetic mean,
(d) infinite population.

8 The best estimate of the infinite population mean value is the:
(a) standard deviation,
(b) sample mean value;
(c) normal distribution;
(d) number of readings in the sample.

9 Calibration is necessary in order to:
(a) reduce random errors;
(b) eliminate vibrations,
(c) reduce consistent errors;
(d) reduce damping.

10 Complete measurement systems can be calibrated by:
(a) comparing instruments with precision instruments;
(b) applying known standards to the input of the system and noting the corresponding outputs;
(c) referring to the National Physical Laboratory;
(d) applying statistical methods in order to analyse the systems.

(c) CONVENTIONAL PROBLEMS

1 Explain the causes of hysteresis and its influence upon measuring instruments.

2 Explain the causes of interference errors giving two examples of instrument interference and two examples of environment interference.

3 Describe a standard procedure that can be used in order to calibrate pressure gauges and pressure transducers, and explain the mode of operation of the equipment that is used in order to apply the known pressures.

4 Describe the Lissajous figure method of calibrating frequency-measuring instruments and state two time-interval calibration signal sources.

5 Explain two methods of calibrating temperature-measuring instruments, one method for temperatures below 500°C and the other method for temperatures in excess of 500°C.

6 Plot the calibration graph, the error graph and the correction graph for a Bourdon-tube pressure gauge having the following characteristics:

True pressure (bar)		20	30	40	50	60	70	80	90	100
Gauge reading	*Increasing*	19.5	28.0	38.5	47.5	58.0	67.5	76.0	86.0	95.5
	Decreasing	20.0	30.5	42.0	50.5	60.0	69.0	78.5	88.0	–

7 In order to calibrate a sensitive strain-gauge torque transducer, static torques are applied to one end of a solid torsion bar by means of a lever and dead weights. The

other end of the torsion bar is rigidly fixed. The angle of twist of the bar is obtained by measuring the end deflection of the lever using a dial gauge which exerts a force $F = 0.15\,R + 0.25$ newton when deflected, where R is the gauge deflection (mm). When the lever is in the initial horizontal position before the application of the load, the gauge deflection is 20 mm. Calculate the percentage error in the measurement of the angle of twist (degrees) due to the influence of the dial gauge, as a load of 2 kg is applied to the end of the lever.

The length and diameter of the torsion bar are 300 mm and 9 mm respectively, and the length of the lever is 400 mm. The bar dimensions and the lever length can

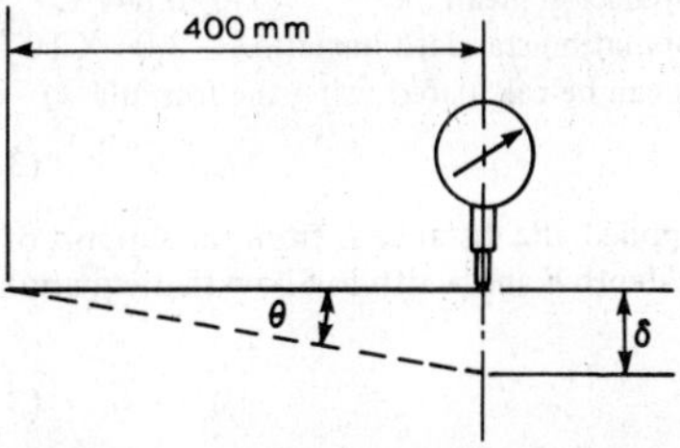

Fig 10

be assumed to be accurate and the modulus of rigidity for the torsion bar is 80 GPa.

Note: the angle of twist is given by the torsion formula

$\frac{T}{J} = \frac{G\theta}{L}$ (see Appendix), from which $\theta = \frac{L}{JG} \times T$.

Also, since the angle of twist is small, $\theta = \frac{\delta}{400}$ (*Fig 10*).

[theoretical angle of twist = 2.617°,
actual angle of twist = 2.677°;
percentage error = 2.28%.]

8 A U/V recorder matching circuit is shown in *Fig 11*. Calculate the interference errors incurred in the measurement of the current flowing through the circuit and

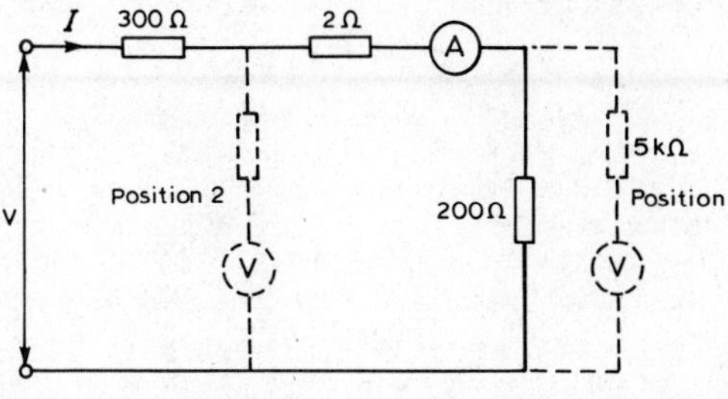

Fig 11

the potential difference across the 200 Ω damping resistor if an ammeter and a voltmeter are connected as shown in position 1. Determine the new interference errors if the voltmeter is connected between the 300 Ω resistor and the ammeter, position 2.

[percentage error in the voltage measurement = –2.74%; –1.76%;
percentage error in the current measurement = 1.15%; 1.2%.]

9 The time taken for a ball to fall through a known height was measured in an experiment to verify the acceleration due to gravity. Random errors in the form of

time lags and residual magnetism were known to be present in the measurement so that a number of readings were made. The following is a sample of 20 time readings: 0.641, 0.640, 0.639; 0.630, 0.644; 0.644; 0.641, 0.641; 0.640; 0.645; 0.643, 0.643, 0.641, 0.641; 0.640, 0.642; 0.642; 0.642, 0.639; 0.642 seconds. Construct a frequency distribution table and determine the mean and the standard deviation of the sample. Also, estimate the mean and the standard deviation of the population from which the sample is assumed to have been taken.

[sample mean = 0.641 s;
standard deviation = 2.98×10^{-3} s;
population mean = 0.641 s;
population standard deviation = 3.06×10^{-3} s.]

10 The surface stress in a cantilever beam can be calculated using the formula

$$\frac{\sigma}{y} = \frac{M}{I} \quad \text{(see Appendix)} \qquad (3.19)$$

In a particular case, an end load F is applied at a distance L from the support of a rectangular cantilever beam having a depth d and width b. Show that equation (3.19) can be reduced to

$$\sigma = \frac{6FL}{bd^2} \qquad (3.20)$$

and calculate the maximum possible error in the calculated value of σ if errors of 1% are incurred in the measurement of F, L, b and d. State the most critical measurement.

[5%; d]

4 Measuring instrument applications

A. MEASUREMENT CLASSIFICATION AND METHODS

(a) STRAIN MEASUREMENT

Mechanical strain gauges

1 Although mechanical strain gauges have been superseded by electrical-resistance strain gauges in many applications, extensometers are still used in applications where long gauge lengths and robust instruments are required. For example, in standard tensile testing and in structural steelwork. However, extensometers are capable of measuring static or quasi-static extensions only and require considerable working space.

As the extensions involved in strain measurements are usually very small, mechanical extensometers are lever operated. The purpose of the lever mechanism is to amplify the small extensions so that they can easily and accurately be displayed. The most common mechanical extensometers are Berry Extensometers, Mikrokator Extensometers, Lindly Extensometers and Huggenberger Extensometers. Each of these instruments is clamped in position on test specimens and extensions are detected by the relative movement between fixed knife edges and pivoted knife edges (see *Problem 1*).

The relative movement between fixed and movable knife edges can also be amplified optically, pneumatically, acoustically or electromagnetically.

Electrical-resistance strain gauges

2 Electrical-resistance strain gauges are not only used extensively in strain measurement but also in the measurement of many force-dependent variables when used in transducer form. There are three types of electrical-resistance strain gauges, namely, bonded, unbonded and semiconductor. Bonded strain gauges are the most versatile and the most common, since they can be purchased in matched packs so that 'home-made' measurement systems can be devised in order to solve specific measurement problems. The main advantages of resistance strain gauges are that they are simple to use, are very light so that there are no mass effects in dynamic applications, and they possess high frequency response characteristics. However, in situations where the gauges are attached to elastic members, their dynamic characteristics are governed by the characteristics of the elastic member as a whole.

The operation of electrical-resistance strain gauges depends upon the variation of the electrical resistance of metal wires as they are mechanically strained. A typical strain gauge configuration is shown in *Fig 1*.

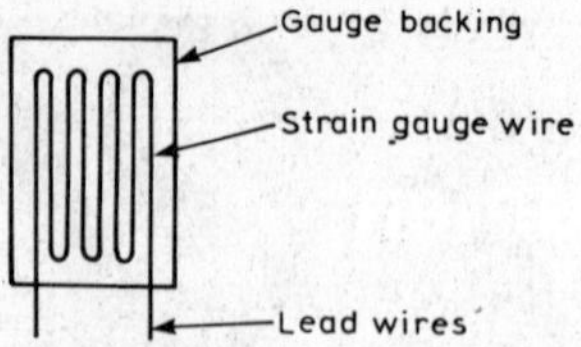

Fig 1 Typical bonded strain gauge

The relationship between the change in resistance and the strain is given by

$$\frac{\delta R}{R} = G\frac{\delta \ell}{\ell} \qquad (4.1)$$

where R is the wire resistance, δR is the wire change in resistance, $\delta \ell/\ell$ is the mechanical strain in the wire and G is the constant of proportionality which is known as the *Gauge Factor*. In the case of bonded strain gauges, the gauges are bonded to component surfaces so that the strain in the strain gauge wire is identical to the surface strain in the component. The gauge factor possesses particular values for particular gauges and depends upon the gauge material, the configuration of the gauge wire (or foil) and the mechanical loading. Generally, the gauge factor is approximately 2.0.

Particular care needs to be exercised in bonding the gauges to components in order to ensure perfect adhesion. Component surfaces must be accurately marked-out in order to locate the gauges accurately and must be smoothed and cleaned finally by wiping the surfaces with acetone. The adhesive must be carefully selected to suit the gauge backing material.

The usual method of measuring the small changes in resistance that occur in strain gauge usage is the Wheatstone Bridge method which is explained in Chapter 2.

Naturally, since electrical-resistance strain gauges are sensitive to very small displacements, they are also sensitive to temperature changes. In order to compensate for temperature effects in a particular application, the usual practice is to connect a **dummy strain gauge** in an adjacent limb to the **active strain gauge** in a Wheatstone Bridge circuit, as illustrated in *Fig 2.*

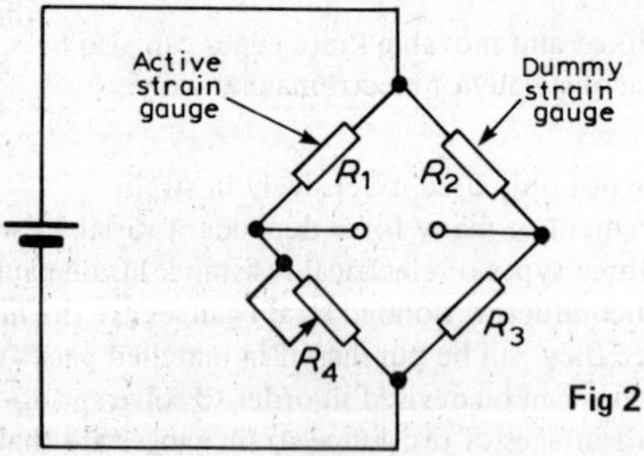

Fig 2

The dummy strain gauge is identical to the active strain gauge so that they form a **matched pair**, but the dummy gauge is bonded to a separate, unstrained component so that it suffers changes in resistance due to temperature only. In this way the bridge remains balanced, because both gauges suffer identical changes in resistance as they are subjected to the same temperature changes. Only the active gauge produces a bridge output, so that the bridge output is proportional to the strain in the strained component. This arrangement is known as a **quarter-bridge** configuration.

The electrical output from a quarter-bridge arrangement is usually very small so that it is desirable to increase the bridge output wherever possible. There are three fundamental measurement applications where the bridge sensitivity can be increased. These are:

(a) *Bending* Consider the cantilever beam illustrated in *Fig 3*.
In this case, one gauge is bonded to the upper surface of the beam and a second gauge is bonded to the lower surface of the beam and located precisely underneath

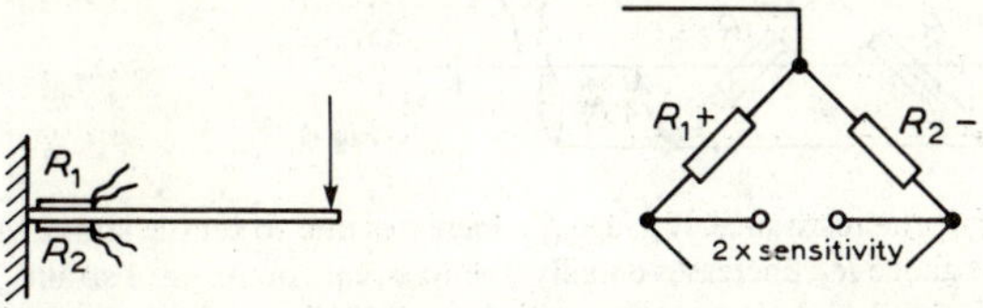

Fig 3

the first gauge. As the end load is applied to the beam, the resistance of gauge R_1 increases due to tensile strain whilst the resistance of gauge R_2 decreases due to equal compressive strain. The gauges are connected electrically to form adjacent limbs of a Wheatstone Bridge. This is known as a **half-bridge** configuration. In this case, not only is full temperature compensation achieved, but also the output from the bridge is doubled (see Conventional Problem 2 in Chapter 2). Furthermore, if two additional gauges are bonded alongside R_1 and R_2, the sensitivity can be increased by a factor of 4. In order to achieve this increase in sensitivity, the four gauges are connected electrically to form a **full-bridge** configuration as illustrated in *Fig 4*.

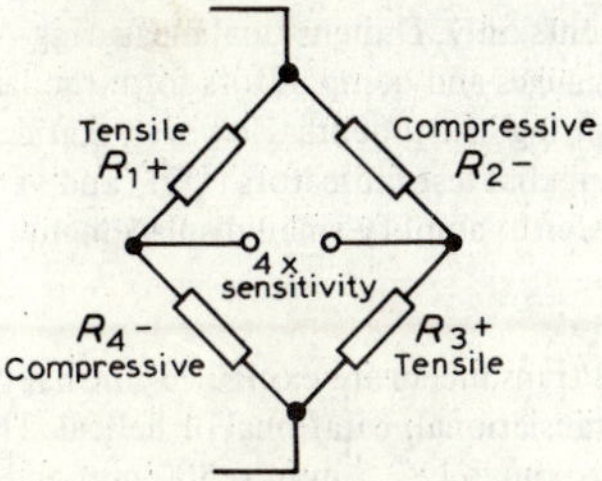

Fig 4

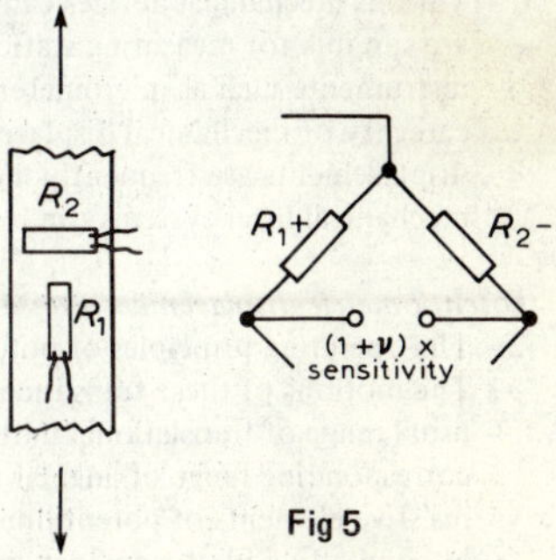

Fig 5

(b) *Direct tension or compression* Consider the tensile component illustrated in *Fig 5*.
In this case, one gauge is bonded longitudinally on the component and a second gauge is bonded transversely on the component. As the tensile load is applied to the component, the resistance of gauge R_1 increases due to tensile strain while the resistance of gauge R_2 decreases due to transverse compressive strain. As before, the gauges are connected electrically to form a **half-bridge** configuration. The sensitivity of this arrangement increases by a factor of $(1 + \nu)$, where ν is Poisson's ratio for the component material, and full temperature compensation is achieved. The sensitivity can be increased further by bonding two additional

gauges precisely in the same positions as R_1 and R_2 but on the opposite face of th component. These four gauges are connected electrically to form a **full-bridge** configuration similar to that indicated in *Fig 4*. In this case, the sensitivity is increased by a factor of $2(1 + \nu)$.

(c) *Torsion* Consider the torsion bar illustrated in *Fig 6*.
In the case of pure torsion, maximum tensile and compressive stresses occur at 45° to the axis of the torsion bar so that it is usual to locate strain gauges along these principal directions. As a **torque** is applied to the torsion bar, in the directio

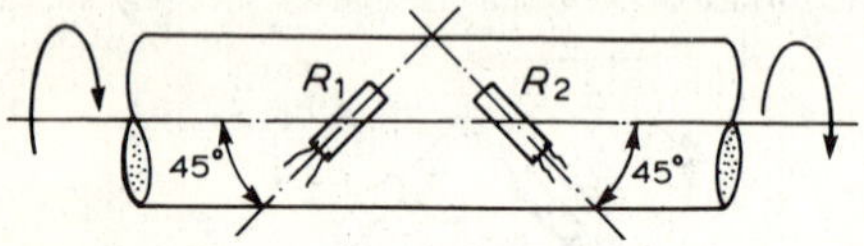

Fig 6

indicated in *Fig 6*, the resistance of gauge R_1 increases due to tensile strain while the resistance of gauge R_2 decreases **equally** due to equal compressive strain. The strain gauges are connected electrically to form a **half-bridge** configuration similar to that shown in *Fig 3*, so that the sensitivity of the Wheatstone Bridge is increase by a factor of 2 and full temperature compensation is achieved. The sensitivity of the bridge can be increased further by bonding two additional gauges diametricall opposite gauges R_1 and R_2. These four gauges are connected to form a **full-bridge** configuration similar to that shown in *Fig 4*. In this case, the sensitivity of the bridge is increased by a factor of 4.

(b) LINEAR AND ANGULAR DISPLACEMENT MEASUREMENT

Mechanical instruments

1 Various mechanical devices can be used in order to measure displacement but thes are suitable for measuring static displacements only. Dimensional measuring instruments such as micrometers, Vernier gauges and comparators form the larges category of mechanical displacement measuring instruments. However, static displacements are frequently measured using dial test indicators (DTI) and various mechanical lever systems can be used in order to amplify small displacements.

Potentiometric displacement transducers

2 The operating principles of potentiometric transducers are explained in Chapter 2 The motions of these transducers can be translational, rotational or helical. The usual range of translational motions is approximately 2.5 mm to 500 mm and the corresponding range of angular motions is approximately 10° to 60 full turns. The resistive elements of potentiometric transducers can be wire-wound, carbon film or conducting plastic and can be energised by a.c. or d.c. voltages.

Spurious output voltage fluctuations are sometimes evident during the operatio of these transducers. These fluctuations are known as **noise** signals and are caused by the motion of sliders across resistance elements.

Linear variable differential transformers

3 *Fig 7* illustrates a circuit diagram for an LVDT. The excitation voltages for these instruments are usually between 3 V and 15 V r.m.s. and the excitation frequencies are usually between 60 Hz and 20 kHz. In the transducer illustrated in *Fig 7*, sinusoidal voltages having the same frequency as the excitation voltage are electromagnetically induced in the two identical secondary coils, and the

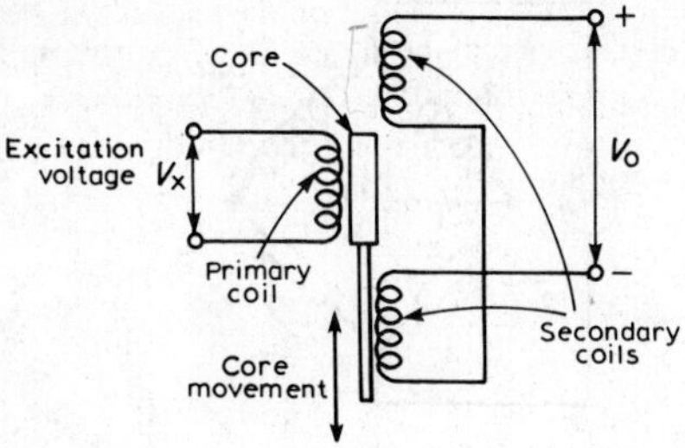

Fig 7

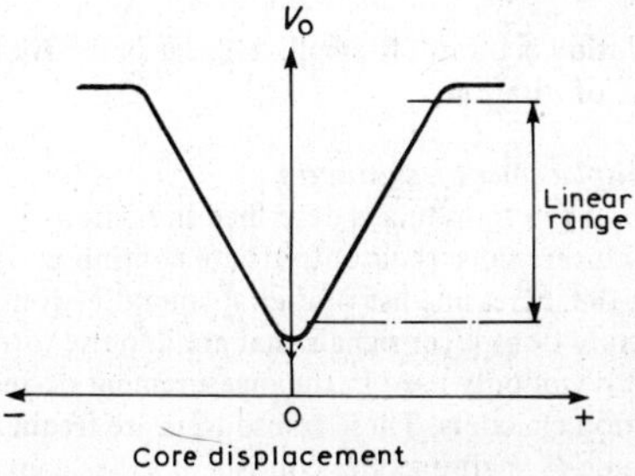

Fig 8 Typical LVDT response characteristics

amplitudes of these voltages vary with the movement of the core. With the secondary coils connected in series opposition, as shown in *Fig 7*, and the core centralised, the output voltage $V_0 = 0$. Motion of the core from this null position generates a larger mutual inductance in one coil and a smaller mutual inductance in the other coil so that V_0 is almost a linear function of the core displacement. A typical response graph is illustrated in *Fig 8*.

Static or quasi-static displacements can be measured by using directly-coupled voltmeters but for the measurement of high-frequency displacements, transducer outputs must be demodulated and filtered before being displayed on oscilloscopes or recorders (see Chapter 5).

The displacement range of these transducers is approximately 0.1 mm to 75 mm, and the non-linearity is usually about 0.5% of full scale, while the resolution is infinitely small. The dynamic responses of LVDT transducers are limited mainly by the excitation frequencies of the transducers so that the core displacement frequencies must not exceed approximately 1/10 of the excitation frequencies.

nductive displacement transducers

Inductive displacement transducers are similar in operation to LVDT transducers. In the transducer illustrated in *Fig 9*, the movement of a core varies the electromagnetic inductance of two coils which are connected to form a half-bridge configuration.

With the core in the central position, $V_0 = 0$ but as the core is displaced from this null position, the **reluctance** increases in one coil and decreases in the other coil so that a bridge output voltage proportional to displacement is induced.

The displacement range of these transducers is usually approximately 2.5 mm to 5 m, the non-linearity is usually between 0.02% and 1% of full scale, while the

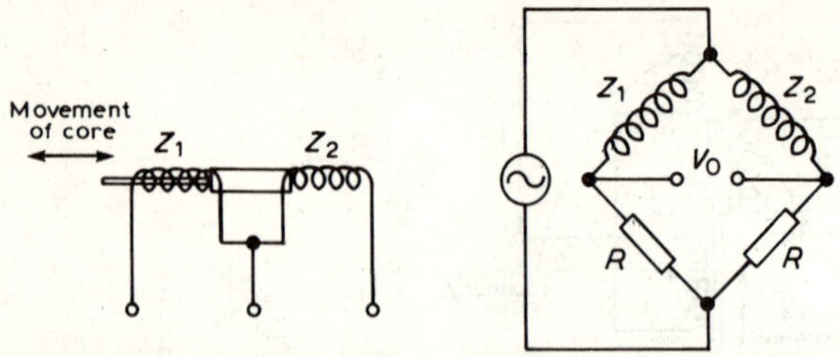

Fig 9 Electrical and physical configuration of an inductive displacement transducer

resolution is infinitely small. Angular inductive transducers can measure up to ± 45° of rotation.

Digital displacement transducers

5 Each of the transducers described in sections 1 to 4 are classified as analogue transducers since their outputs are continuous functions of their inputs. However, with the increasing use of digital computer controllers, it is frequently desirable to generate transducer signals that are in pulse form. The digital transducers that are most commonly used in the measurement of angular displacements are shaft-position encoders. These transducers are frequently used in machine-tool control systems. A shaft encoder consists of a disc containing a digitally coded scale which can be a series of translucent and opaque segments or a series of conducting and insulating surfaces. In the former type, the digitised signals are generated by photo-electric sensors whilst in the latter type, the signals are generated by contact brushes.

(c) FORCE MEASUREMENT

Mechanical instruments

1 Balances are the basic mechanical force measuring instruments and they measure force due to gravity or weight. There are two general types, namely, beam balances and spring balances. In the case of beam balances, unknown forces or masses are balanced by levers against known standard masses. In the case of spring balances, unknown forces or masses are balanced by spring restoring forces so that in this case, spring deflection is proportional to force (see Chapter 1).

Electro-mechanical instruments

2 The operation of most electro-mechanical transducers depends upon the deformation of elastic members in response to applied forces. Therefore, in principle, any form of elastic member whose deflection varies linearly with applied force can be used in order to measure force.

(a) *Strain gauge transducers* *Fig 10* illustrates a typical proving ring arrangement. This device consists of a ring of forged steel and forces applied across the ring cause axial deflections which can be measured by dial gauges, strain gauges, LVDT transducers or inductive transducers. This device can be calibrated by applying known static forces, using for example, a tensile testing machine.

Fig 11 illustrates a typical strain gauge tension/compression link. The arrangement of the strain gauges in this device gives automatic temperature

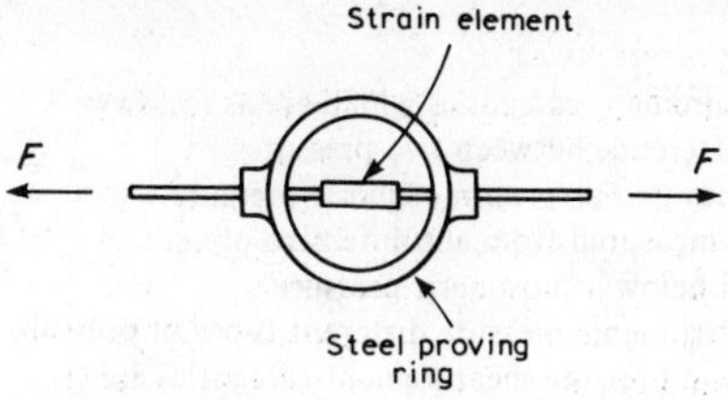

Fig 10

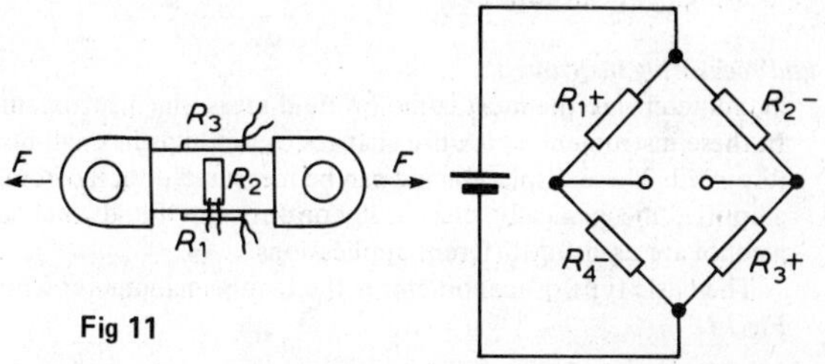

Fig 11

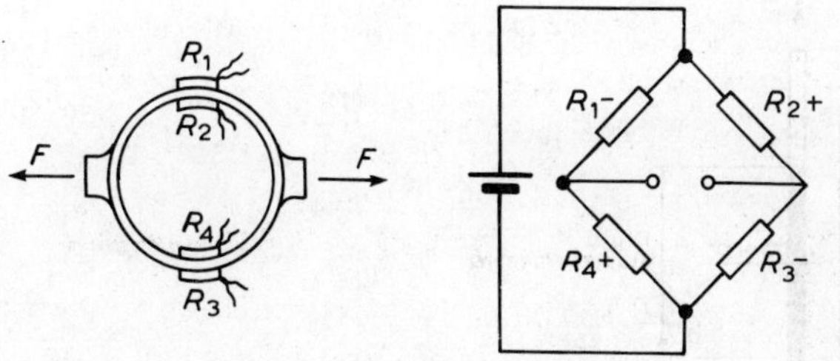

Fig 12

compensation, eliminates undesired bending and gives maximum sensitivity to direct thrust. The force range is governed only by the physical dimensions and the material of the link.

A more sensitive force link is illustrated in *Fig 12*. This arrangement can be used for measuring small forces.

Each of these devices can be calibrated statically by applying known forces and is suitable for measuring static and dynamic forces. However, the physical dimensions of these transducers tends to be large.

Strain gauges can be used in many ways for measuring force; purpose-made transducers need not be purchased as for many applications they can be 'home-made'.

(b) *Piezoelectric transducers* The principle of operation of piezoelectric transducers is described in Chapter 2. The construction of piezoelectric force transducers is similar to the construction of piezoelectric pressure transducers which are described later in this chapter. Piezoelectric force transducers are suitable mainly for measuring compressive dynamic forces and their physical dimensions are small.

(d) PRESSURE MEASUREMENT

There are four main pressure measurement categories which are as follows:

(i) **Differential pressure** is the difference between two pressures.

(ii) **Gauge pressure** is pressure measured above atmospheric pressure.

(iii) **Absolute pressure** is pressure measured from absolute zero pressure.

(iv) **Vacuum** is pressure measured below atmospheric pressure.

Generally, different types of instruments measure different types of pressure but in engineering the most common pressure measurement categories are (i) and (ii), so that this text is confined to instruments relating to these pressure measurement categories.

Fluid measuring instruments

1 Manometers are the most common fluid measuring instruments used in engineering. In these instruments, pressure changes cause fluids in small-bore tubes to be displaced. These displacements can be measured directly from scales or they can be amplified mechanically, electrically or optically. Fluids such as water, mercury and alcohol are used for different applications.

The basic type of manometer is the U-tube manometer which is illustrated in *Fig 13*.

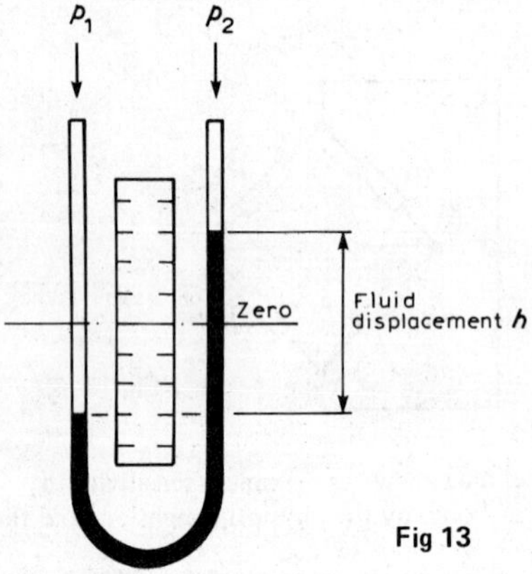

Fig 13

In this instrument, the fluid displacement is a measure of the differential pressure, $p_1 - p_2$, applied to the open ends of the tube. Equating forces in each limb of the tube gives

$$p_1 - p_2 = \rho g h \quad (4.2)$$

where ρ is the density of the manometer fluid, g is the acceleration due to gravity and h is the fluid displacement.

Simple manometer variations include cistern manometers and inclined-tube manometers. Manometers can be used to measure low differential pressures, low gauge pressures and vacuum pressures.

Mechanical measuring instruments

2 Mechanical pressure measuring instruments include Bourdon-Tube pressure gauges, bellows and diaphragms. The operation of Bourdon-Tube pressure gauges and bellows is described in Chapter 1.

A diaphragm is a thin, flat plate that is firmly fixed around its edges. As a pressure differential is applied across the diaphragm, the centre of the diaphragm deflects and provided that the deflection is small a linear relationship exists between the centre deflection and the differential pressure. Usually, the deflection is mechanically or electrically amplified.

Electro-mechanical transducers

3 There are numerous different types of electro-mechanical pressure transducers which operate using strain gauge, inductive, piezoelectric and capacitive principles. Three common types are described below.

(a) *Strain gauge transducers* There are numerous types of strain gauge pressure transducers, the operation of which depends upon the elastic deformation of materials in response to pressure changes. Static and dynamic pressures can be measured by this means but the physical dimensions of the transducers tend to be large. *Fig 14* illustrates a typical bellows and cantilever type of strain gauge pressure transducer.

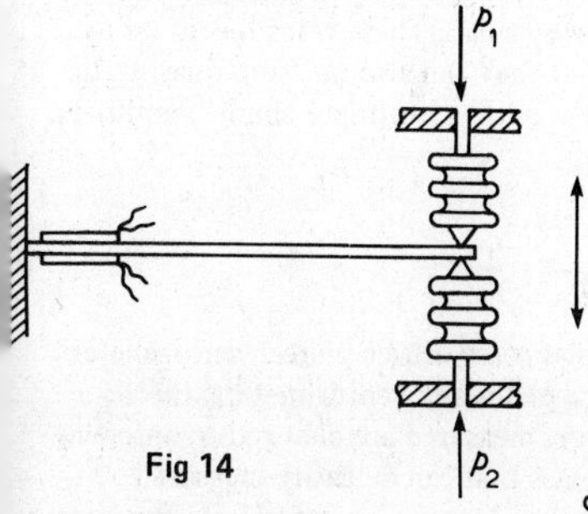

Fig 14

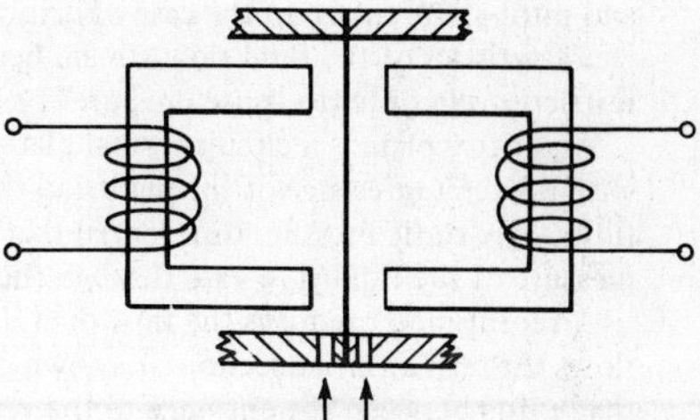

Fig 15

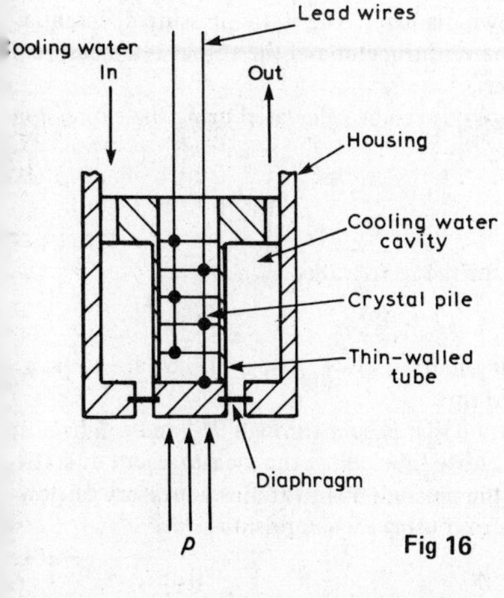

Fig 16

In this transducer, the pressure differential between p_1 and p_2 causes the cantileve to deflect. The deflection is sensed by the strain gauges which generate an electrica output proportional to the differential pressure.

(b) *Inductive transducers* A typical inductive transducer is illustrated in *Fig 15*. In this case, a differential pressure deflects a diaphragm which in turn increases the inductance of one coil and reduces the inductance in the other coil. The coils are usually connected to form an a.c. half-bridge circuit, so that the electrical output from the bridge is proportional to the differential pressure. These transducers can be used to measure static and dynamic pressures.

(c) *Piezoelectric transducers* A typical piezoelectric transducer is illustrated in *Fig 16*.

In this case, a pressure exerts a force on a crystal pile due to the deflection of a diaphragm. This force in turn generates an electrical charge proportional to the applied pressure.

Piezoelectric transducers have high natural frequencies which allow wide frequency ranges to be measured. They also have good linearities, high sensitivities and their physical dimensions are usually very small. These transducers are used mainly for measuring dynamic pressures but they can also measure quasi-static pressures when they are used in conjunction with appropriate charge amplifiers.

(e) FLUID FLOW MEASUREMENT

Restrictive instruments

1 The three most common restrictive flowmeters are orifice plates, venturimeters and pitot-static tubes. In the case of orifice plates and venturimeters, the characteristics of the fluid flow stream being measured are changed by inserting restrictions in order to cause pressure changes that can be easily measured.

An orifice plate is a circular metal plate that contains a central hole concentric with the circumference of the plate and through which the fluid being measured flows. The static pressure differential that exists across the orifice plate is a measure of the fluid **flow-rate** through the orifice plate.

A venturimeter reduces the flow duct diameter so that the fluid being measured flows through a throat section of known diameter. The static pressure differential that exists between the entrance to the venturimeter and the throat is a measure o the **flow-rate** through the venturimeter.

In each of the above cases, the flow-rates can be calculated using the expression

$$Q = C_d a_1 \sqrt{\frac{2g\,H}{m^2 - 1}} \qquad (4.3$$

where

Q is the flow-rate (m^3/s)
C_d is the coefficient of discharge for the restriction
a_1 is the approach area (m^2)
m is the ratio a_1/a_2
a_2 is the throat or orifice area (m^2), and
H is the differential pressure head (m)

A pitot-static tube is a small-bore tube that is bent through 90° and can be inserted into flow streams. Two concentric tubes allow the measurement of static pressure and kinetic pressure so that the pressure differential is a measure of flow **velocity**. Flow velocities can be calculated using the expression

$$v = C\sqrt{(2g\,H)} \qquad (4.$$

where

v is the flow velocity (m/s)

C is the tube constant, and

H is the differential pressure head (m)

These instruments measure flow velocities at points in flow streams so that it is necessary to obtain several readings across flow streams in order to obtain average velocities and consequently flow-rates. Velocity profiles of flow streams can be obtained by traversing pitot-static tubes horizontally and vertically across flow ducts.

The advantages of pitot-static tubes are that pressure losses caused by insertion are very small and costs are low compared with orifice meters and venturimeters. However, they are not as accurate and fluids must be moving with relatively high velocities in order to generate measurable differential pressures.

Variable area flowmeters

2 It is evident from equation (4.3), that **flow-rate** is a function of the differential pressure head, assuming that the orifice area remains constant. However, variable area flowmeters are designed so that the differential pressure head remains constant and the orifice area varies.

A variable area flowmeter contains a float that is located inside a tapered glass tube. The flowing fluid flows vertically upwards through the tube so that the float moves up the tube until the pressure differential across the float is zero. In this condition, the float maintains a stable position and the displacement of the float from a zero datum position is a measure of fluid **flow-rate**.

Electromagnetic flowmeters

3 The operation of electromagnetic flowmeters is described by equation (2.12). In this type of transducer, the flowing fluid being measured is the conducting medium. A localised magnetic field is generated across the duct carrying the fluid and electrodes are located on each side of the duct. As the fluid flows between the electrodes an e.m.f. is generated which is proportional to the **velocity** of the flowing fluid.

There are no moving parts in these transducers so that rapid and large flow fluctuations can be detected. The main limitation is that the measured fluids must be conductive; therefore these transducers cannot be used in the measurement of gas, steam or petroleum product flows. Equally, flow ducts must be non-conductive and non-magnetic.

(f) TIME, FREQUENCY AND SPEED MEASUREMENT

Time measurement

1 Industrial time measurement techniques include stop-watches, stop-clocks and electronic timers. Mechanical instruments such as stop-watches and stop-clocks possess inherent starting and stopping errors and are usually less accurate than electronic timers. However, mechanical instruments are frequently used in situations where convenience is more important than accuracy. Electronic timers can measure time accurately to 10^{-4} seconds, but obviously in order to obtain this degree of precision they need to be triggered automatically.

Frequency measurement

2 Electronic counters and frequency meters have largely superseded mechanical

counters. Mechanical counters are slow and can be used only in low-speed applications. Electronic counters are fast, accurate and easy to use and to read. Usually one instrument can measure frequency or speed and can be used for counting and timing. These instruments are activated by small voltage impulses generated by transducers, but in timing applications they can also be started and stopped manually.

Frequency is measured by counting the number of pulses received in a fixed time interval, and in electronic instruments the result is usually displayed in digital form giving readings in Hz. A similar process is used in speed measurement except that the timing periods are larger giving readings in revolutions per minute.

Speed measurement

3 Translational speeds can be measured by measuring the time taken for objects to travel fixed distances. However, special instruments are necessary in order to measure rotational speeds. These instruments can be mechanically or electrically operated.

(a) *Mechanical instruments* There are several types of mechanical tachometers which include the slipping clutch type and the centrifugal force type.

A centrifugal force tachometer comprises two masses attached to leaf springs which cause a loose collar to move along a shaft as the rotational speed varies. The collar actuates a pointer mechanism so that speed can be measured from a fixed scale. In operation, the conical end of the drive shaft of the tachometer is located manually in the end of the shaft of which the speed is required to be measured. The accuracy of these instruments is rarely better than ± 1%.

(b) *Electrical instruments* Stroboscopes are used extensively in rotational speed and frequency measurement since there is no physical contact between the measuring instrument and the rotating member. A stroboscope comprises a flashin light which illuminates the rotating member and the frequency of the flash is adjusted until the rotating member appears to be stationary. In this condition, the light is flashing at the same frequency as the rotating member so that the light frequency can be measured from a calibrated scale. However, it is also possible to obtain a stationary image if the light is flashing at a frequency that is a multiple of the speed of rotation. In this case, in order to establish the true speed, the flashing frequency is increased until two stationary images 180° apart are obtainec The flashing frequency is then halved in order to obtain a single image once more. This image represents the true speed.

Other forms of electrical tachometer include eddy current tachometers, a.c. tachogenerators, d.c. tachogenerators and capacitive tachometers.

Digital frequency meters can also be used in order to measure rotational speeds. In these cases, the small voltage impulses that are necessary in order to activate these instruments are generated by mounting toothed wheels or discs on the rotating members. A particular type of inductive transducer comprises a coil wour on a magnetic core that is located near to the edge of a toothed disc. As each toot passes through the magnetic field of the transducer, the lines of flux are broken sc that an e.m.f. pulse is induced in the coil. This pulse or series of pulses is transmit to the counter in order to obtain speed measurements.

Pulses can also be generated by using photoelectric transducers.

(g) VIBRATION MEASUREMENT

The measurement of vibration usually involves the measurement of one or more o the following variables: displacement, velocity, acceleration and frequency. The displacement and frequency measurement techniques described in sections (b) and (f) of this chapter can be used in vibration measurements. Additionally, inductive velocity transducers can be used and also strain gauge, inductive, potentiometric and piezoelectric accelerometers can be used. Frequently, in industrial practice, accelerometers are used in conjunction with integrating amplifiers so that displacement, velocity and acceleration can be measured by successive integration of the acceleration signals.

In accelerometers, the electrical signals are generated by seismic masses. A typical piezoelectric accelerometer is illustrated in *Fig 17*.

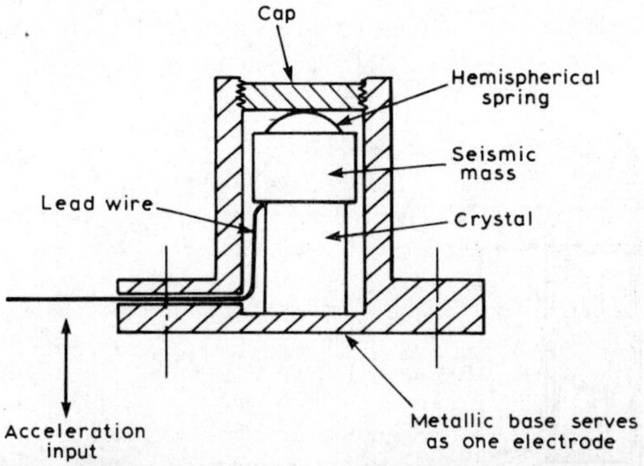

Fig 17

In this case, the accelerometer is bolted to a vibrating member so that the vibration is transmitted to a seismic mass. The acceleration forces acting on the mass cause deformations in the crystal which in turn generate proportional electrical charges.

Similar seismic arrangements are used in strain gauge, inductive and potentiometric accelerometers but in these cases the **displacements** of the seismic masses are detected by strain gauges, inductive or potentiometric displacement transducers.

h) TEMPERATURE MEASUREMENT

Common temperature measuring instruments are described in Chapter 2, page 00. However, these thermoelectric sensors are generally used for the measurement of relatively high temperatures. For the measurement of relatively low temperatures, a whole range of liquid-in-glass thermometers, bi-metallic thermometers and vapour thermometers is available. Liquid-in-glass thermometers find only limited use in industry whereas bi-metallic and vapour thermometers are used extensively. These instruments are robust and can remain in fixed positions for long periods of time.

Two types of measuring instruments can be used in order to measure the electrical outputs from thermocouples, these are millivoltmeters and potentiometers. Each of these types of measuring instruments is available commercially and is described in greater detail in Chapter 5.

B. WORKED PROBLEMS ON INSTRUMENT APPLICATIONS

Problem 1 Describe the operation of a Huggenberger extensometer and derive an expression relating the surface strain in a component to the pointer movement. Calculate the gain of a particular instrument having the dimensions: $m = 2$ mm, $L = 72$ mm, $n = 2$ mm and $R = 60$ mm.

Fig 18 illustrates the lever mechanism of a Huggenberger extensometer.
This extensometer is clamped firmly in position on a test specimen so that there can be no movement between the knife edges and the specimen, and the pointer reads zero on the strain scale. As the test specimen is strained, the movable

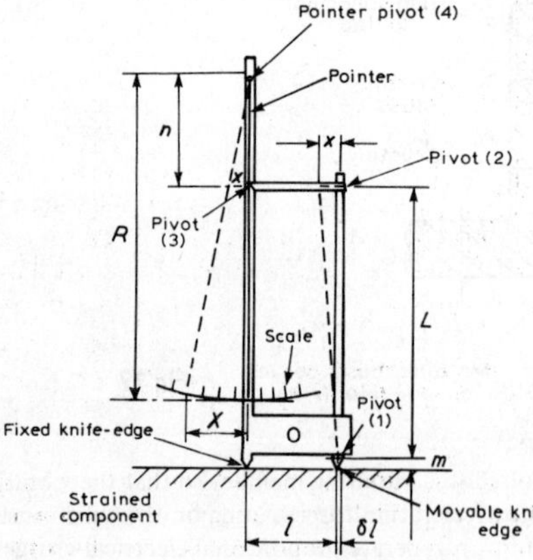

Fig 18

knife-edge pivots about the pivot point (1) causing a corresponding deflection at pivot point (2). This deflection is transmitted by a pivoted link to the pointer so that the pointer is caused to pivot about pivot point (4). The deflection of the free end of the pointer is the amplified movement of the movable knife-edge. The strain value is obtained by dividing the scale reading by a precisely known constant.

Consider the lever mechanism of the extensometer. As the movable knife edge deflects an amount $\delta\ell$, the corresponding lever movement at pivot point (2) is given by

$$\frac{\delta\ell}{m} = \frac{x}{L}$$

so that

$$x = \frac{L}{m} \times \delta\ell \qquad (4.5)$$

Also, at pivot point (3),

$$\frac{x}{n} = \frac{X}{R}$$

so that

$$x = \frac{n}{R} \times X \tag{4.6}$$

Equating equations (4.5) and (4.6) gives $\dfrac{nX}{R} = \dfrac{L}{m} \times \delta\ell$

so that

$$X = \frac{LR}{nm} \times \delta\ell \tag{4.7}$$

The magnification factor is known as the amplifer **gain** and is given by

$$\frac{LR}{nm}$$

The gain of the particular extensometer is given by

$$\frac{72 \times 60}{2 \times 2} = \mathbf{1080}$$

Problem 2 In a strain measuring system an active strain gauge and a dummy strain gauge are connected electrically to form a quarter-bridge configuration. The nominal resistance of the matched pair of strain gauges is 120 Ω and the gauge factor is 2.1. Calculate the strain in the component if the proportional change in resistance of a third limb of the bridge which restores balance is 1/1000.

In order to calibrate the bridge initially, a resistor R_p is connected in parallel with the active gauge. Determine an expression for the equivalent strain and calculate the equivalent strain if R_p = 50 kΩ.

It is evident from the way that the problem is worded, that the 'null' technique has been used. By referring to Chapter 2, *Problem 1*, equation (2.26) indicates that in this situation

$$\frac{\delta R_a}{R_a} = \frac{\delta R}{R}$$

where

R_a is the strain gauge nominal resistance
δR_a is the strain gauge change in resistance, and
$\delta R/R$ is the proportional change in resistance of the third limb of the bridge

Clearly, in this case

$$\frac{\delta R_a}{R_a} = \frac{1}{1000}$$

From equation (4.1)

$$\frac{\delta R_a}{R_a} = G \times \frac{\delta\ell}{\ell}$$

so that

$$\frac{1}{1000} = 2.1 \frac{\delta\ell}{\ell}$$

and

$$\frac{\delta\ell}{\ell} = \frac{1}{2.1 \times 1000}$$

Therefore, the strain in the component is $\dfrac{\delta\ell}{\ell} = \mathbf{4.76 \times 10^{-4}\ m/m}$

If a resistor R_p is connected in parallel with the active gauge R_a, then the resultant resistance in the active limb of the bridge is given by

$$\frac{1}{R} = \frac{1}{R_a} + \frac{1}{R_p} = \frac{R_p + R_a}{R_a R_p}$$

so that the resultant resistance is

$$R = \frac{R_a R_p}{R_p + R_a} \quad (4.8)$$

The **change** in resistance is given by

$$R_a - \frac{R_a R_p}{R_a + R_p} = \frac{R_a^{\ 2}}{R_a + R_p} \quad (4.9)$$

so that

$$\frac{\delta R_a}{R_a} = \frac{R_a}{R_a + R_p} \quad (4.10)$$

and the equivalent strain is given by

$$\frac{\delta \ell}{\ell} = \frac{1}{G}\left(\frac{R_a}{R_a + R_p}\right) \quad (4.11)$$

Substituting values into equation (4.11) gives

$$\frac{\delta \ell}{\ell} = \frac{1}{2.1}\left(\frac{120}{120 + 50 \times 10^3}\right)$$

so that

$$\frac{\delta \ell}{\ell} = \mathbf{1.14 \times 10^{-3}\ m/m}$$

Problem 3 A mild steel cantilever has a length of 0.5 m and a rectangular cross-section 50 mm wide and 15 mm deep. Four fully active strain gauges are bonded to the fixed end of the cantilever and are connected electrically to form a full-bridge configuration. The nominal resistance of the gauges is 120 Ω, the gauge factor is 2.1 and the bridge supply voltage is 12 V. If a calibration mass is applied at the free end of the cantilever, calculate the sensitivity of the system in mV/kg. The measuring instrument input resistance can be assumed to be infinitely high and the modulus of elasticity for mild steel is 200 GPa.

The arrangement of the gauges is similar to that described in section (a) 2(a) and *Fig 4*. Since the four gauges each have the same nominal resistance, equation (2.36) can be used. However, in this case the sensitivity is increased by a factor of 4, so that equation (2.36) becomes

$$V_o = 4\,\frac{V_i}{4}\left(\frac{\delta R}{R}\right) \quad (4.12)$$

Also,

$$\frac{\delta R}{R} = G\,\frac{\delta \ell}{\ell}$$

so that it is necessary to calculate the surface strain in the cantilever as the mass is applied to the free end.

Let a mass of 1 kg be applied to the free end of the cantilever. Since

$$\frac{\sigma}{y} = \frac{M}{I} \text{ (see Appendix A)}$$

$$\sigma = \frac{My}{I} = \frac{1 \times 9.81 \times 0.5 \times 0.0075 \times 12}{0.05 \times 0.015^3} \text{ Pa}$$

The surface strain is given by σ/E, so that

$$\frac{\delta \ell}{\ell} = \frac{9.81 \times 0.5 \times 0.0075 \times 12}{0.05 \times 0.015^3 \times 200 \times 10^9}$$

$$= \mathbf{1308 \times 10^{-5}\ m/m}$$

and

$$\frac{\delta R}{R} = 2.1 \times 1.308 \times 10^{-5}$$

$$= \mathbf{2.747 \times 10^{-5}}$$

The voltage output from the bridge corresponding to the applied mass of 1 kg is

$$V_o = 12 \times 2.747 \times 10^{-5}$$

$$= \mathbf{0.33\ mV}$$

so that the sensitivity of the system is **0.33 mV/kg**

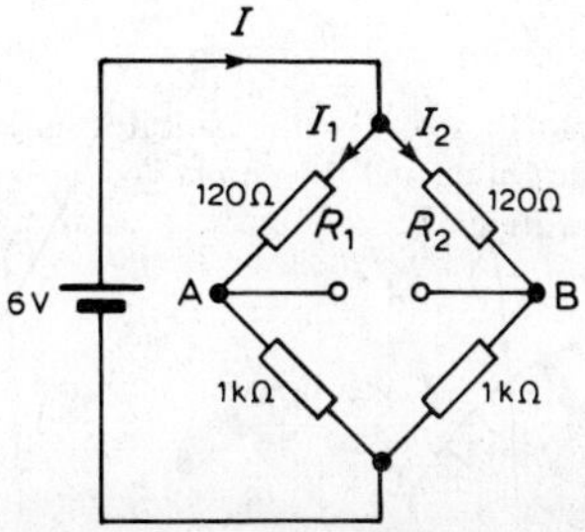

Fig 19

Problem 4 The torque transmitted by a propeller shaft is measured by two active strain gauges bonded at 45° to the axis of the shaft, such that one gauge detects tensile strains and the other gauge detects compressive strains. The nominal resistance of the gauges is 120 Ω and they are connected to form a half-bridge configuration. The bridge supply voltage is 6 V and it is estimated that the maximum strain will be 800×10^{-6} m/m. If the gauge factor is 2.09, calculate the bridge output, assuming an infinitely high input resistance to the measuring instrument and the bridge make-up resistors have a resistance of 1000 Ω each. (See *Fig 19*).

It is evident from equation (4.1) that

$$\frac{\delta R}{R} = 2.09 \times 800 \times 10^{-6}$$

so that

$$\delta R = 120 \times 2.09 \times 800 \times 10^{-6} = 0.2\ \Omega$$

It is also evident from *Fig 19* that the potential difference across R_1 is $120.2\, I_1$, and that the potential difference across R_2 is $119.8\, I_2$. Furthermore, the potential difference across the bridge is 6 V, so that

$$6 = 120.2\, I_1 + 1000\, I_1 \qquad (4.13)$$

since no current flows between A and B. In addition,

$$6 = 119.8\, I_2 + 1000\, I_2 \qquad (4.14)$$

From equation (4.13)

$$I_1 = \frac{6}{1120.2}\ \text{A}$$

and from equation (4.14)

$$I_2 = \frac{6}{1119.8}\ \text{A}$$

Therefore, the potential difference across R_1 is given by

$$\frac{120.2 \times 6}{1120.2} = 0.6438\ \text{V}$$

Also, the potential difference across R_2 is given by

$$\frac{119.8 \times 6}{1119.8} = 0.6419\ \text{V}$$

Therefore, the difference in potential between A and B is
0.6438 – 0.6419 = 1.9 mV
so that the bridge output is **1.9 mV**

Problem 5 Describe the operation of a dial test indicator. For the indicator shown diagrammatically in *Fig 20,* calculate the magnification and the number of revolutions of the pointer as the plunger moves 20 mm.

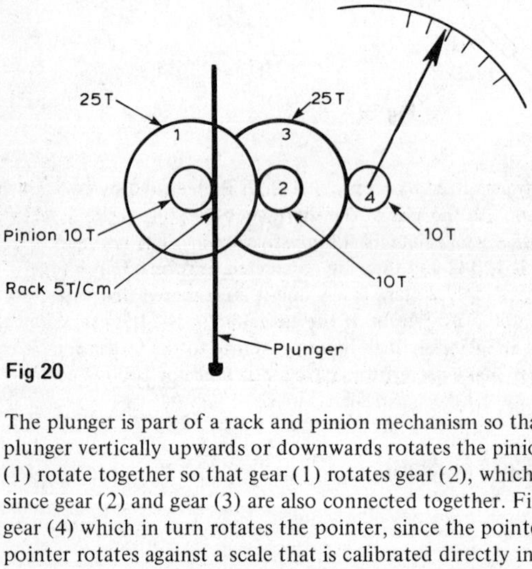

Fig 20

The plunger is part of a rack and pinion mechanism so that movement of the plunger vertically upwards or downwards rotates the pinion. The pinion and gear (1) rotate together so that gear (1) rotates gear (2), which in turn rotates gear (3), since gear (2) and gear (3) are also connected together. Finally, gear (3) rotates gear (4) which in turn rotates the pointer, since the pointer is attached to it. The pointer rotates against a scale that is calibrated directly in displacement units.

As the plunger moves 20 mm, the pinion rotates through one revolution since there are 5 teeth/cm on the rack and 10 teeth on the pinion. Gear (1) also rotates through one revolution causing 25/10 revolutions of gear (2). Similarly, gear (3) rotates through 25/10 revolutions. However, if gear (3) were to rotate only one revolution, gear (4) would rotate 25/10 revolutions, so that as gear (3) rotates 25/10 revolutions then gear (4) rotates

$$\frac{25}{10} \times \frac{25}{10} = 6.25\ \text{revolutions.}$$

Naturally, since the pointer is attached to gear (4), the pointer rotates **6.25 times** as the plunger moves 20 mm.

Problem 6 Compare the operation of spring balances and beam balances for measuring force. Calculate the position of the counterpoise of mass 0.25 kg if the beam balance illustrated in *Fig 21* measures a mass of 10 kg and $x = 100$ mm, $m = 50$ mm, $L = 25$ mm, $y = 200$ mm and $n = 100$ mm.

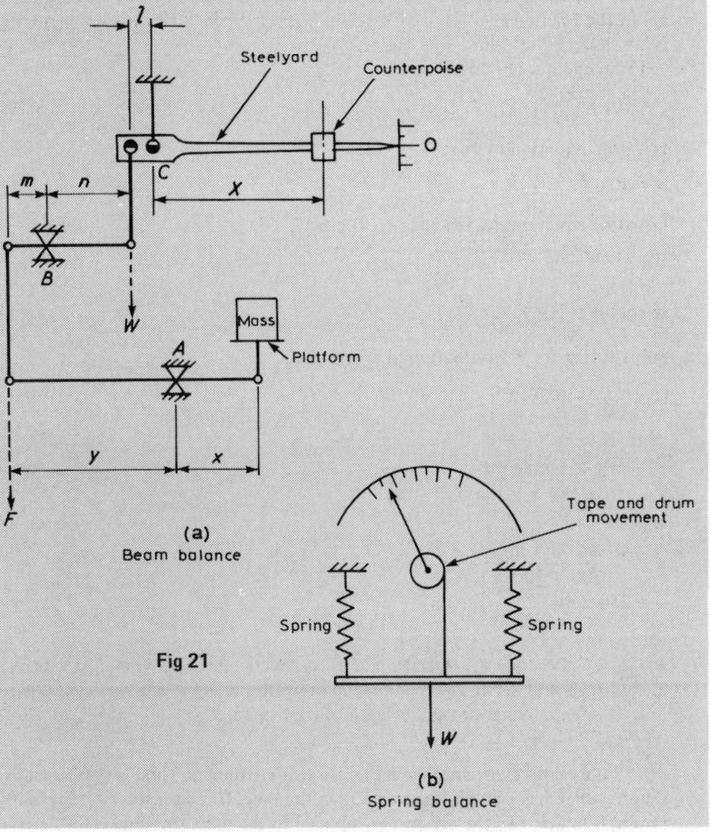

Fig 21

Fig 21 illustrates a beam balance and a spring balance.

In the case of the beam balance, as a mass is applied to the measuring platform the levers are displaced which in turn displace the steelyard. The displacement of the steelyard is detected as a movement against a scale. Balance is restored by adjusting the counterpoise until the steelyard position returns to zero. The weight of the mass is measured by reading the weight from a calibrated scale on the steelyard corresponding to the position of the counterpoise.

In the case of the spring balance, as a mass is applied to the weighing platform, the springs are deflected until the spring restoring forces balance the weight of the mass. The spring deflection is detected by a tape and drum movement and the weight is measured by the movement of a pointer against a calibrated scale.

Taking moments about the fulcrum A in *Fig 21*

$$10\,gx = Fy \qquad (4.15)$$

where F is a force necessary to maintain equilibrium. Similarly, taking moments about the fulcrum B

$$Fm = Wn \qquad (4.16)$$

where W is also a force necessary to maintain equilibrium. Finally, taking moments about the fulcrum C

$$WL = 0.25gX \qquad (4.17)$$

From equation (4.15)

$$F = 10g \times \frac{x}{y} \qquad (4.18)$$

but from equation (4.16)

$$F = W \times \frac{n}{m} \qquad (4.19)$$

Equating equations (4.18) and (4.19) gives

$$10g\,\frac{x}{y} = W\,\frac{n}{m}$$

so that $W = 10g \times \frac{x}{y} \times \frac{m}{n}$ (4.20)

Substituting for W in equation (4.17) gives

$$10g\,\frac{xmL}{yn} = 0.25gX$$

so that

$$X = \frac{10g \times x \times m \times L}{0.25\,g \times y \times n}$$

and

$$X = \frac{40 \times 100 \times 50 \times 25}{200 \times 100}$$

$= \mathbf{250\ mm}$

Problem 7 Describe the operation of cistern manometers and inclined tube manometers and derive the relationship between the input and the output in each case. Compare the advantages of each instrument.

Fig 22 illustrates a cistern manometer. In this instrument, fluid is contained in a cistern which has a much larger area than the tube. If the pressure p_1 applied to the cistern is larger than the pressure p_2 applied to the tube, the fluid is displaced up the tube. The height of the fluid in the tube can be measured by a scale fixed alongside the tube and is a measure of the differential pressure $p_1 - p_2$. Gauge pressure can be measured if p_2 is atmospheric pressure.

Let A_1 be the area of the cistern, A_2 be the area of the tube, d be the displacement of the fluid in the cistern and h be the displacement of the fluid in the tube

The volume of fluid displaced in the cistern is equal to the volume of fluid displaced in the tube, so that

$$A_1 d = A_2 h \qquad (4.21)$$

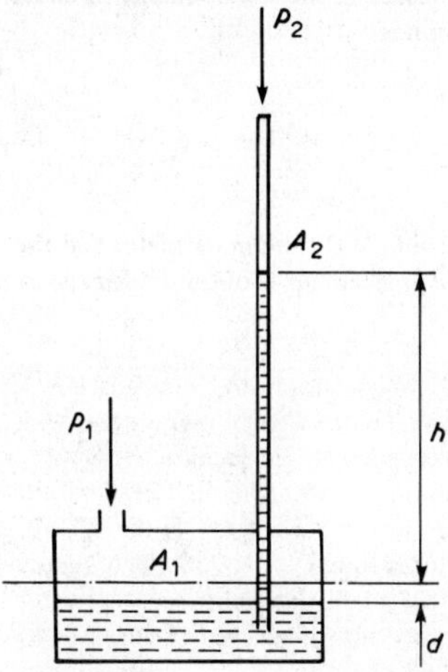

Fig 22

and

$$\frac{A_2}{A_1} = \frac{d}{h} \qquad (4.22)$$

Equating forces acting upon the fluid surfaces in the cistern and the tube respectively gives

$$p_1 = p_2 + \rho g\,(h + d) \qquad (4.23)$$

taking the lower fluid level as the datum level, and ρ is the fluid density.

Equation (4.23) can be written as

$$p_1 - p_2 = \rho g h\,(1 + d/h) \qquad (4.24)$$

and substituting equation (4.22) into equation (4.24) gives

$$p_1 - p_2 = \rho g h\,(1 + A_2/A_1) \qquad (4.25)$$

The ratio A_2/A_1 can be arranged to be negligible.

The advantage of this manometer is that a very narrow tube can be used and a reasonably long single scale, so that the measuring accuracy is better than the simple U-tube manometer.

Fig 23 illustrates an inclined tube manometer. The operation of this instrument is similar to the operation of the cistern manometer.

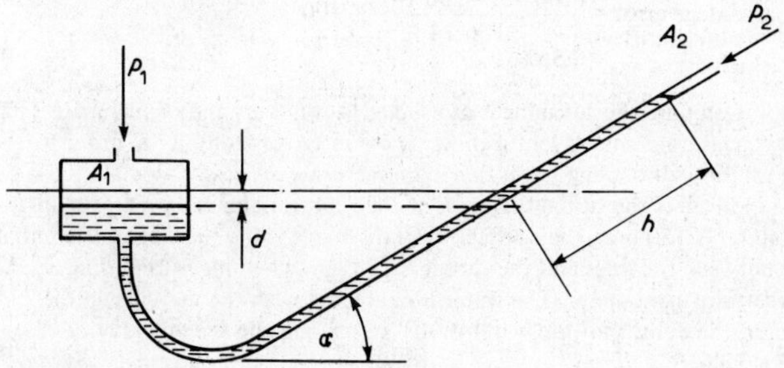

Fig 23

The volumetric displacement equation is derived in the same manner as equation (4.22). However, in this case the force equation is

$$p_1 = p_2 + \rho g\,(h \sin\alpha + d) \tag{4.26}$$

so that

$$p_1 - p_2 = \rho g h\,(\sin\alpha + d/h) \tag{4.27}$$

and

$$p_1 - p_2 = \rho g h\,(\sin\alpha + A_2/A_1) \tag{4.28}$$

The advantage of this manometer over the simple U-tube manometer and the cistern manometer is that an increased fluid displacement is obtained for the same differential pressure.

Problem 8 Steam is used in order to pre-heat the air supply to a combustion process. The steam pressure is monitored by a mercury U-tube manometer which shows a positive displacement of 42 mm above atmospheric pressure. However, it is observed that steam has condensed in the manometer resulting in a head of condensate of 60 mm in contact with the mercury in the U-tube. If the atmospheric pressure measured by a barometer is found to be 758 mm of mercury, calculate the absolute pressure of the steam. Calculate also the percentage error that would be incurred if the head of condensate were neglected. (Density of water $= 10^3$ kg/m^3, specific gravity of mercury = 13.6)

Refer to *Fig 13*. Since there is condensate in contact with the mercury in the left limb, it is necessary to analyse the forces acting in each limb, so that

$$p_1 + \rho_w g \times 0.06 = p_2 + \rho_m g \times 0.042 \tag{4.29}$$

where ρ_m is the density of the mercury and ρ_w is the density of the condensate. Re-arranging equation (4.29) gives

$$p_1 = p_2 + \rho_m g \times 0.042 - \rho_w g \times 0.06 \tag{4.30}$$

However, since the right limb is open to the atmosphere, p_2 is the atmospheric pressure, so that

$$p_2 = \rho_m g \times 0.758 \tag{4.31}$$

Substituting equation (4.31) into equation (4.30) gives

$$p_1 = \rho_m g \times 0.758 + \rho_m g \times 0.042 - \rho_w g \times 0.06 \tag{4.32}$$

so that

$$p_1 = 9.81 \times 10^3\,(13.6 \times 0.758 + 13.6 \times 0.042 - 0.06),$$

and

$$p_1 = \mathbf{106.14\ kPa}$$

Neglecting the condensate, i.e. neglecting the last term in equation (4.32) gives

$$p_1 = 106.73 \text{ kPa}$$

so that percentage error $= \dfrac{(106.73 - 106.14)}{106.14} \times 100$

$= \mathbf{0.56\%}$

Problem 9 Compare the advantages of using venturimeters and orifice meters in fluid flow measurements. A venturimeter is mounted horizontally in order to measure the flow of cooling water in a manufacturing process. Calculate the water flow-rate in m^3/h if the throat diameter of the venturimeter is 75 mm, the inlet duct diameter is 150 mm, the coefficient of discharge is 0.97 and the differential pressure between the inlet and the throat is 178 mm when measured using a mercury U-tube manometer. The water is in contact with the mercury in the manometer, the density of the water is 10^3 kg/m^3 and the specific gravity of mercury is 13.6.

The venturimeter is more accurate but is costly and not so easy to install, whereas the orifice meter is cheap, relatively easy to install but less accurate.

Referring to *Fig 13*, and analysing the differential pressure reading, it is evident that

$$p_1 - p_2 = h(\rho_m g - \rho_w g) \qquad (4.33)$$

since the water is in contact with the mercury. However, the equivalent differential pressure **head** H, referred to the fluid flowing through the venturimeter, is given by

$$h(\rho_m g - \rho_w g) = \rho_w g H \qquad (4.34)$$

so that

$$H = \frac{h(\rho_m g - \rho_w g)}{\rho_w g}$$

$$= h\left(\frac{\rho_m}{\rho_w} - 1\right) \qquad (4.35)$$

The flow through the venturimeter is calculated from equation (4.3), where

$$a_1 = \frac{\pi \times 0.15^2}{4} = 0.0177 \text{ m}^2$$

$$H = 0.178\left(\frac{13.6}{1} - 1\right) = 2.2428 \text{ m}$$

and

$$m = \frac{\pi d_1{}^2 4}{4\pi d_2{}^2} = \frac{0.15^2}{0.075^2} = 4.0$$

In this case

$$Q = 0.97 \times 0.0177\sqrt{\frac{2 \times 9.81 \times 2.2428}{15}}$$

so that

$$\mathbf{Q = 0.0294\ m^3/s = 105.86\ m^3/h}$$

Problem 10 A pitot-static tube is calibrated against a venturimeter which has a throat diameter of 60 mm and a coefficient of discharge of 0.98. Air flows through the 100 mm diameter horizontal duct in which the venturimeter is located and a differential pressure reading of 55 mm is obtained using a water U-tube manometer. The pitot-static tube is located downstream of the venturimeter and in this case an average differential pressure reading of 7.8 mm is obtained using a water U-tube manometer. Calculate the velocity of flow in the duct and the tube constant for the pitot-static tube. (Density of air = 1.225 kg/m³, density of water = 10³ kg/m³)

The flow of air is calculated from equation (4.3), where

$$a_1 = \frac{\pi \times 0.1^2}{4} = 7.854 \times 10^{-3} \text{ m}^2$$

$$H = 0.055\left(\frac{10^3}{1.225} - 1\right) = 44.843 \text{ m}$$

and

$$m = \frac{0.1^2}{0.06^2} = 2.778$$

In this case

$$Q = 0.98 \times 7.854 \times 10^{-3}\sqrt{\frac{2 \times 9.81 \times 44.843}{2.778^2 - 1}}$$

so that

$Q = 0.088 \text{ m}^3/\text{s}$

The mean velocity of flow through the duct is given by

$$Q = \text{duct area} \times \text{velocity}$$

so that

$$v = \frac{0.088}{7.854 \times 10^{-3}} = \mathbf{11.2 \text{ m/s}}$$

However, the velocity of flow measured by the pitot-static tube is given by equation (4.4), but in this case

$$H = 0.0078\left(\frac{10^3}{1.225} - 1\right) = 6.36 \text{ m}$$

so that

$v = C\sqrt{(2 \times 9.81 \times 6.36)}$

from which

$C = \mathbf{1.0}$

C. FURTHER PROBLEMS ON INSTRUMENT APPLICATIONS

(a) SHORT ANSWER PROBLEMS

1 The purpose of levers and gears in mechanical instruments is to . . . . small primary signals.

2 Electrical resistance strain gauges can be used in order to measure . . . . , ... , ... , ... and . . . .

3 The constant that relates the proportional change in resistance to mechanical strain in electrical resistance strain gauges is known as the . . . . and its value is dependent upon the . . . . , ... and . . . .

4 In order to compensate for changes in electrical resistance of strain gauges due to temperature changes, ... are connected in Wheatstone Bridge limbs . . . . . . to the . . . .

5 In order to increase the bridge sensitivity by a factor of four, as well as providing full temperature compensation . . . . strain gauges must be used in such a way that two gauges suffer . . . . strains and two gauges suffer . . . . strains.

6 In the situation described in question 5, the gauges must be connected to form a . . . . bridge configuration and the directions of the resistance changes must . . . . round the bridge.

7 Linear variable differential transformers are used in order to measure . . . . and the movement of a core causes variations in the . . . . of output voltages which have the same . . . . as the input voltage.

8 The principal types of force measuring instruments are . . . . and . . . . , ... transducers and . . . . transducers.

9 The difference between two pressures is known as a . . . . pressure whilst gauge pressure is . . . . and pressure measured below atmospheric pressure is known as an . . . . measurement.

10 Manometers can be used in order to measure . . . . , ... and . . . .

11 The advantages of piezoelectric transducers are that they have high . . . . which allow . . . . to be measured and they have good . . . . , high . . . . and are physically . . . .

12 Restrictive instruments such as . . . . , ... and . . . . are commonly used in order to measure . . . .

13 Mechanical frequency counters are . . . . and can be used only in . . . . applications, whereas electronic counters are . . . . , ... and . . . .

14 Transducers used in vibration measurements usually include . . . . masses which transmit the vibration . . . . or . . . . to the . . . .

(b) MULTI-CHOICE PROBLEMS (answers on page 184)

1 Mechanical strain gauges can measure:
(a) dynamic strains only; (c) static strains only;
(b) static and dynamic strains; (d) static and quasi-static strains.

2 Dummy strain gauges are:
(a) substandard strain gauges;
(b) the same as active strain gauges except that they are bonded to unstrained components;
(c) arranged so that they suffer temperature changes as well as mechanical strain;
(d) always connected in opposite Wheatstone Bridge limbs to active gauges.

3 The sensitivity of half-bridge arrangements in which two strain gauges suffer equal and opposite strains is:
(a) doubled, (b) quadrupled; (c) unity; (d) increased by $(1 + \nu)$.

4 In the case of pure torsion, strain gauges are bonded to the strain component:
(a) at 45° to the axis; (c) transversely;
(b) longitudinally, (d) in the direction of the applied torque.

5 In high-frequency displacement measurements, the outputs from linear variable differential transformers must initially be:
(a) amplified, (c) demodulated and filtered;
(b) directly coupled to voltmeters, (d) displayed on recorders.

6 Inductive displacement transducers are similar in operation to linear variable differential transformers except that in this case the movement of a core varies the coil:
(a) capacitance, (b) reluctance, (c) resistance, (d) displacement.

7 Manometers are:
(a) force measuring instruments, (c) frequency measuring instruments,
(b) flow measuring instruments; (d) pressure measuring instruments.

8 Strain gauge transducers and piezoelectric transducers can be used in order to measure any variable that is a function of:
(a) pressure, (b) velocity, (c) force; (d) strain.

9 Restrictive flowmeters are used in order to measure fluid flow-rates and involve the measurement of:
(a) differential pressure across a restriction,
(b) gauge pressure,
(c) differential pressure in a straight duct;
(d) vacuum pressure.

10 Pitot-static tubes are frequently used in order to measure:
(a) differential pressures in flow streams, (c) fluid flow-rates directly;
(b) fluid density, (d) flow velocity profiles.

11 The main limitation of electromagnetic flowmeters is that:
(a) there are no moving parts;
(b) the fluid must be electrically conductive;

(c) a localised magnetic field must be provided;
(d) the e.m.f. generated is proportional to the flow velocity.

12 Tachometers are used in order to measure:
(a) vibration; (b) time; (c) angular velocity, (d) displacement.

13 The main advantage of stroboscopes is that:
(a) no physical contact is necessary between the measuring instrument and the variable being measured,
(b) they use flashing lights;
(c) they measure multiples of angular speed;
(d) the stationary image can be easily observed.

14 Electronic digital frequency meters are activated by voltage pulses generated by:
(a) capacitive transducers;
(b) piezoelectric transducers,
(c) inductive transducers;
(d) accelerometers.

(c) CONVENTIONAL PROBLEMS

1 A Huggenberger extensometer has the following dimensions: m = 1.7 mm, L = 80 mm, n = 2.8 mm, R = 55 mm. Calculate the gain of the lever amplification mechanism and determine the strain indicated by the extensometer if the gauge length is 25 mm. Explain how the gain can be increased.

[Gain = 924.37; strain = extensometer reading/23109.24]

2 Electrical resistance strain gauges are used frequently for measuring static and dynamic tensile and compressive forces. Describe a strain gauge transducer that would be suitable for this application indicating the positions of the strain gauges, the electrical connections and how temperature compensation is achieved.

In an automatic weighing device, four strain gauges are used in order to measure the strain in a cylindrical compression member that is 25 mm in diameter. The gauges are arranged so that the sensitivity of the transducer is 2.6 and the gauge factor is 2.1. If the bridge supply voltage is 10 V, calculate the reading that would be indicated by a digital voltmeter having an infinitely high input resistance when the transducer is subjected to a load of 545 kg. The modulus of elasticity of the material of the compression member is 200 GPa. [V_o = 0.74 mV]

3 Explain the difference between the null method and the out-of-balance bridge method as applied to strain gauge usage. In an automatic sand feed system, the sand has to be supplied in batches by weight. The sand is weighed by a strain gauge load cell, the output of which is read from a digital voltmeter. Four strain gauges are used having a gauge factor of 2.0, and connected to form a Wheatstone Bridge. When the weight of sand is correct, the digital voltmeter reads 20 mV. If the bridge supply voltage is 5 V, calculate the stress in the load cell compression member. The modulus of elasticity for the load cell material is 208 GPa [Stress = 416 MPa]

4 Two strain gauges having nominal resistances of 120 Ω and a gauge factor of 2.1, are located so that one gauge is bonded to the upper surface and one gauge is bonded to the lower surface of the fixed end of a cantilever beam. The effective length of the cantilever is 0.5 m and its cross-section is rectangular, 30 mm wide and 10 mm deep. The strain gauges are connected to form two limbs of a Wheatstone Bridge, and the bridge is completed by two other resistances of 800 Ω each. If a mass of 2 kg is applied to the free end of the cantilever, calculate the change in resistance that is required to be applied to one of the 800 Ω resistances in order to restore balance. The modulus of elasticity for the cantilever material is 200 GPa.

[δR_4 = 0.165 Ω]

5 A 120 Ω strain gauge is used in conjunction with an identical dummy strain gauge in order to measure the surface strain in a component. The gauges are connected in adjacent limbs of a Wheatstone Bridge so that a half-bridge configuration is formed, and the bridge is completed by two 1.2 kΩ resistors. The output from the bridge is recorded by a pencil galvanometer that is inserted in a U/V recorder. If the bridge supply voltage is 4 V and the galvanometer input resistance is 50 Ω, calculate the bridge sensitivity in μA/percentage resistance change.

[Sensitivity = 12.27 μA/percentage change in resistance]

6 Compare the advantages and the disadvantages of the null method and the out-of-balance bridge method of strain gauge usage.

A Wheatstone Bridge circuit comprises two matched electrical resistance strain gauges each having a nominal resistance of 120 Ω and two matched resistances each having a nominal resistance of 500 Ω. The strain gauges are connected in adjacent limbs of the bridge and mounted on the elastic member of a force transducer so that one gauge senses positive strains as the other gauge senses equal negative strains. The voltage output from the bridge is measured by an amplifier that is set to a gain of 1000 and is connected to an oscilloscope that is set to a gain of 0.5 V/cm. The input resistance of the amplifier can be considered to be infinitely high. As a particular force is applied to the transducer, the oscilloscope deflection is observed to be 5.2 cm.

Calculate the change in resistance of the gauges and the magnitude of the applied force if the elastic member is subjected to pure bending, is rectangular in section, 15 mm wide by 5 mm deep, and the gauges are positioned 20 mm from the axis of the force. The bridge supply voltage is 10 V and the gauge factor is 2.1. Second-order of smallness terms can be neglected. E steel = 200 GPa.

[Change in resistance = 0.1 Ω, applied force = 248 N]

7 Compare the advantages and the disadvantages of mechanical force measuring instruments and electro-mechanical force measuring instruments. Calculate the position of the counterpoise if the beam balance described in worked problem 6 is used in order to weigh a mass of 8.2 kg. [Counterpoise position = 205 mm]

8 A simple U-tube manometer is used in order to measure the absolute pressure of water in a pipe. The water pressure is below atmospheric pressure and one limb of the manometer is open to the atmosphere. The height of a column of water that is in contact with the mercury in the manometer is 120 mm and the difference in mercury levels is 249 mm. Calculate the absolute pressure of the water given that the water density = 10^3 kg/m^3, mercury density = 13.6×10^3 kg/m^3 and atmospheric pressure = 100 kPa.

Explain how the sensitivity of this instrument can be increased and sketch a more sensitive instrument that operates on the same principle.

[Absolute pressure = 66.8 kPa]

9 A venturimeter tapers from 260 mm in diameter at the entrance to 100 mm in diameter at the throat, and the coefficient of discharge is 0.98. A differential mercury U-tube manometer is connected between the pressure tappings at the entrance and the throat. If the venturimeter is used in order to measure water flow-rate, calculate the flow-rate in m^3/s when the difference in mercury level is 60 mm and the water is in contact with the mercury. (Density of water = 10^3 kg/m^3, density of mercury = 13.6×10^3 kg/m^3)

[Flow-rate = 0.03 m^3/s]

10 Show that the relationship between differential pressure and manometer displacement for an inclined-tube manometer is given by the expression $p_1 - p_2 = \rho g h (\sin \alpha + A_2/A_1)$. The inclination of an inclined-tube mercury manometer is

30°, the diameter of the cistern is 50 mm and the diameter of the tube is 3 mm. If the scale reading of the manometer is 45 mm of vacuum and the barometric pressure is 764 mm of mercury, calculate the gauge pressure reading and the absolute pressure. (Density of mercury = 13.6×10^3 kg/m^3)

[Gauge pressure = –3.023 kPa, absolute pressure = 98.91 kPa]

11 As an initial method of ascertaining the amount of air blast supplying a cupola, a pitot-static tube is used in order to traverse the circular duct which is 0.2 m in diameter. With the pitot-static tube connected to a water U-tube manometer, the difference in water level was observed to be 40 mm. Assuming the tube coefficient for the pitot-static tube to be unity, determine the air velocity at this position and the corresponding flow-rate. (Density of air = 1.225 kg/m^3, density of water = 10^3 kg/m^3)

[Air velocity = 25.3 m/s; flow-rate = 0.795 m^3/s]

12 Describe the operation of two different types of transducers that can be used in order to measure vibration acceleration levels. Explain how the frequency of vibration can be measured.

5 Signal processing and display

A. SIGNAL PROCESSING

(a) INTRODUCTION

Signal processing or conditioning instruments provide energy for passive primary sensors and also amplify signals generated by passive and active primary sensors. The conditioned and amplified signals are then in forms that can be conveniently displayed, recorded or digitised.

Transducers such as strain gauges, thermo-resistive thermometers, potentiometers, capacitive and certain types of inductive transducers require power supplies as they are passive transducers, whereas thermocouples, tachogenerators, piezoelectric and certain other types of inductive transducers are active transducers and they do not require power supplies. Passive transducers can be energised by a.c. or d.c. power supplies, but the choice of power supply depends upon the type of transducer being energised. For example, inductive transducers require a.c. power supplies, whereas strain gauge transducers are usually d.c. supplied.

It is frequently necessary to process transducer signals further after amplifying them. For example, they may need smoothing, linearising, filtering or converting into digital form. The latter process is necessary in order to use transducers in conjunction with digital computers, digital controllers or multi-channel data loggers.

(b) AMPLIFIER SYSTEMS

Carrier amplifier systems

1 In a carrier system the transducer is energised by a high-frequency carrier signal which is used also as a reference signal in a demodulation process. The carrier signal is an a.c. voltage or current. If the transducer is an inductive or a resistive transducer, the normal carrier frequency is between 50 Hz and 20 kHz. However, if the transducer is a capacitive transducer then the carrier frequency is usually about 1 MHz.

Fig 1 is a block diagrammatic arrangement of a carrier system, in which the amplitude of the measured variable modulates the carrier signal which is then amplified, demodulated and filtered. The demodulation process is phase-sensitive so that the polarity of the d.c. output signal corresponds with the polarity of the measured variable. In this way, the direction of the output signal gives precise

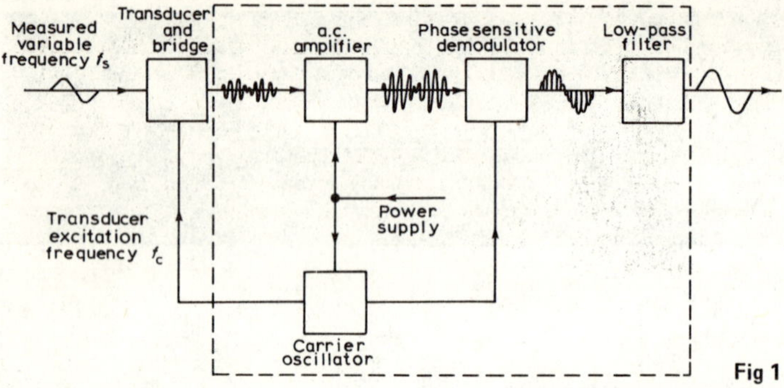

Fig 1

information about the direction of the measured variable. The carrier oscillator, amplifier, demodulator and filter are usually provided in one instrument so that the only external connections are to the transducer which provides the input and to a display or recording instrument which measures the output.

The advantages of carrier systems are that amplifier drift and spurious noise signals are not significant unless they modulate the carrier signals, and the mains frequency pick-up rejection is very high.

D.C. amplifier systems

2 *Fig 2* is a block diagrammatic arrangement of a d.c. system, in which the transducer generates a time-varying d.c. signal in response to the measured variable. This d.c. signal is amplified by the d.c. amplifier. The low-pass filter removes any high-frequency spurious noise signals that are occasionally present in the amplified signal, so that the time-varying d.c. output signal is an enlarged replica of the measured variable. The bridge balancing network, d.c. power supply, d.c. amplifier and low-pass filter are usually provided in one instrument so that the only external connections are to the transducer and to a display or recording instrument.

The advantages of d.c. systems are that they are easy to calibrate at low frequencies, they have the ability to recover rapidly from overload conditions, and with balanced differential inputs d.c. amplifiers have very good thermal and long-term stabilities. However, amplifier drift and low-frequency noise signals can be superimposed upon the output signals so that low-drift amplifiers need to be used.

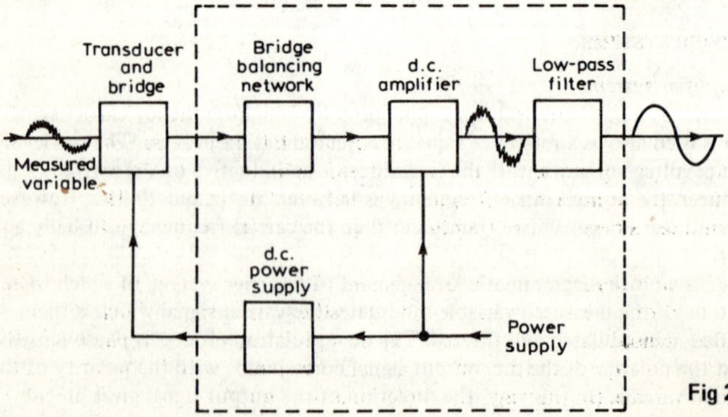

Fig 2

Charge amplifier systems

3 Charge amplifiers are used in order to amplify the output signals of piezoelectric and capacitive transducers. Naturally, in the case of piezoelectric transducers no power supply is required.

Fig 3 is a diagrammatic arrangement of a charge amplifier, which comprises an electronic operational amplifier with a feedback capacitor C_f connected across it. The gain of the amplifier is negative, so the output signal is opposite in sign to the input signal. The transducer is connected to the input terminals of the charge

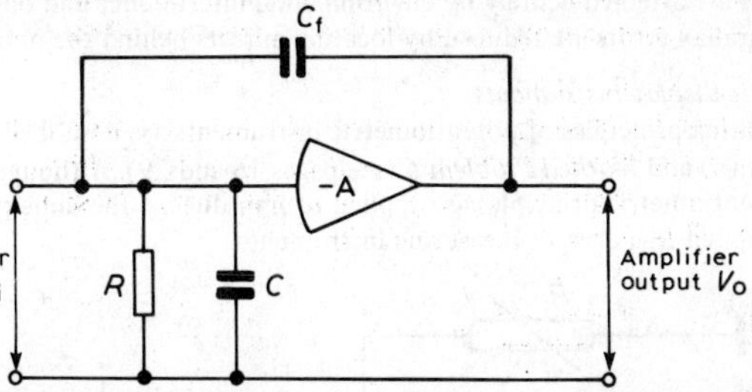

Fig 3

amplifier by a screened low-noise cable. The cable capacitance is important as it affects the charge generated by the transducer; the combined effect of the cable capacitance and the amplifier input impedance is to create a parallel *RC* circuit at the amplifier input.

The input terminal of a charge amplifier is effectively grounded so that loading effects due to lead capacitance and charge leakage in the transducer are reduced.

(c) DISPLAY INSTRUMENTS

Pointer and scale display instruments

1 Several examples of pointer-and-scale instruments are described in Chapter 1 and Chapter 4. Bourdon-tube pressure gauges, mechanical extensometers, tachometers and mechanical balances provide examples of this type of display instrument. Also, pointer-and-scale indicators are frequently used in moving-coil instruments such as millivoltmeters. The operating principles of moving-coil instruments are described in Chapter 2, section A.(c)3 and worked problem number 7.

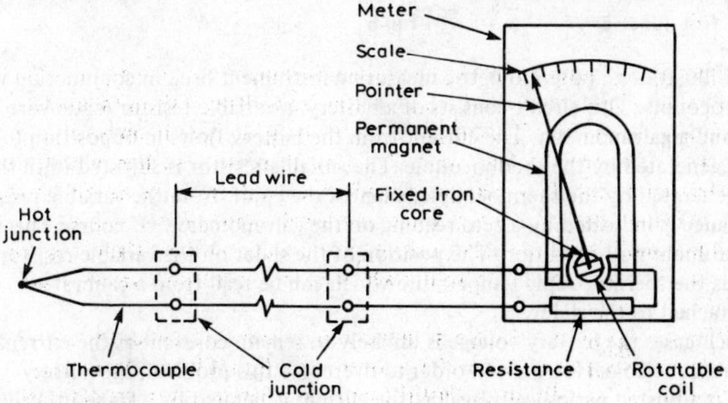

Fig 4

Fig 4 illustrates a typical millivoltmeter used in conjunction with a thermocouple. In this example, the e.m.f. generated between the junctions of the thermocouple causes an electric current to flow through the rotatable coil. Since the coil is located in a magnetic field, the force corresponding to the flowing current causes the pointer to rotate against the fixed scale. The scale can be calibrated directly in temperature units.

The frequency responses of pointer and scale indicators are very low so that they are suitable only for static or quasi-static measurements. Furthermore, reading accuracies are affected acutely by environmental interference and observation errors. Parallax errors are reduced by locating mirrors behind the pointers.

Potentiometric display instruments

2 The operating principles of potentiometric instruments are described in Chapter 2, section A.(b) and *Worked Problem 6* (see pages 16 and 29). Although in these cases potentiometric principles are applied to transducers, the same principles can be applied to a class of measuring instruments.

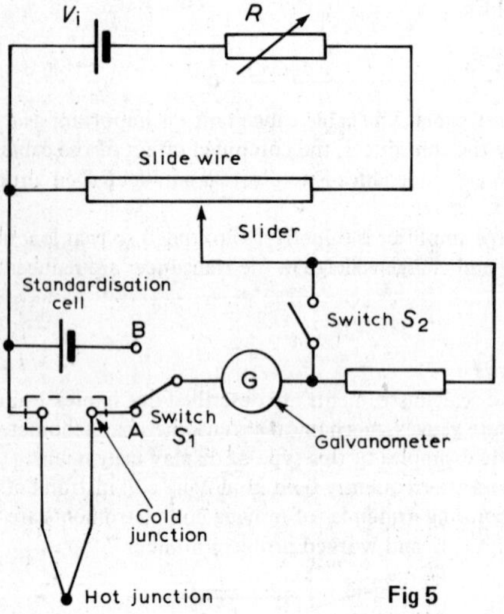

Fig 5

Fig 5 illustrates a potentiometric measuring instrument used in conjunction with a thermocouple. This circuit consists of a battery, a variable resistor (slide wire and slider) and a galvanometer. The current from the battery flows in opposition to the current generated by the thermocouple. The variable resistor is adjusted until the e.m.f. generated by the thermocouple balances the e.m.f. from the variable resistor, this balance is indicated by a zero reading on the galvanometer. Of course, this is the instrument **null** condition. The position of the slider on the variable resistor indicates the thermocouple temperature which can be read from a calibrated scale attached to the slider.

In such cases the battery voltage is unlikely to remain constant as the current drain is appreciable. However, in order to overcome this problem, the battery current is adjusted periodically against the current generated by a standard cell. This procedure is known as 'standardisation'.

Alphanumeric display instruments

3 Alphanumeric devices generate the letters of the alphabet, digits 0 to 9, punctuation marks and other symbols in common use. The characters can be generated by numerical indicator tubes (NIT), light emitting diodes (LED), liquid-crystal displays (LCD) or hot-filament indicators.

A numerical indicator tube comprises a metallic anode and 10 stacked cathodes enclosed in a gas-filled glass tube, the cathodes forming the alphanumeric display. As a sufficiently high voltage is applied between the anode and a cathode, light is emitted around the cathode so that a particular number is displayed. Naturally, a system of sequencing determines which number or letter is displayed in a particular case. A complete instrument display is formed by grouping together several such indicator tubes.

Light emitting diodes are semiconductor diodes that are manufactured from gallium phosphide or gallium arsenide phosphide crystals. Impurities are added to these crystals in controlled quantities and the display colours are determined by the diode material and the type of impurity added. These diodes are very small and produce small spots of light as electric current is passed through them. Individual numbers and letters are formed by the diode lighting sequence. The main advantage of LED displays is that they can be switched on and off relatively quickly.

A liquid crystal display comprises a film of liquid crystal that is sandwiched between two transparent electrodes. The electrodes form the display characters. As an electrical potential is applied to the electrodes, the liquid crystal forming the character becomes opaque. Light is not generated by the crystal but the apparent illumination is generated by light that is directed on to the crystal passing through or being reflected by the crystal. LCD indicators possess small power requirements so that they are suitable for battery operated instruments.

Hot-filament indicators comprise small bars of light-emitting tubes. The bars make up the characters of the display and are illuminated as electric currents flow through them. These displays possess slow response times compared with the other alphanumeric displays.

Graphic display instruments

4 *(i) Oscilloscopes* A cathode ray oscilloscope (CRO) is a voltage measuring instrument and has a high input impedance which reduces the loading on the input amplifier. This display instrument is used mainly to measure dynamic and transient signals.

Fig 6 is a diagrammatic arrangement of an oscilloscope. Electrons are released from the hot cathode and accelerated towards the screen by the positively charged anode. The position of the spot on the screen is controlled by applying voltages across the horizontal and the vertical deflection plates. The screen is coated with a phosphorescent material that emits light as the electron beam strikes it. Several hundred volts are usually required in order to deflect the beam across the full diameter of the screen so that low-level input signals require additional amplification.

The sweep generator produces a saw-tooth wave which provides a timebase for dynamic and transient input voltages. In this way, waveforms that represent changes in the measured variables with time can be displayed, so that not only can magnitudes of measured variables be measured but also the behaviour of measured variables can be observed.

Certain types of oscilloscopes can display two or more signals simultaneously

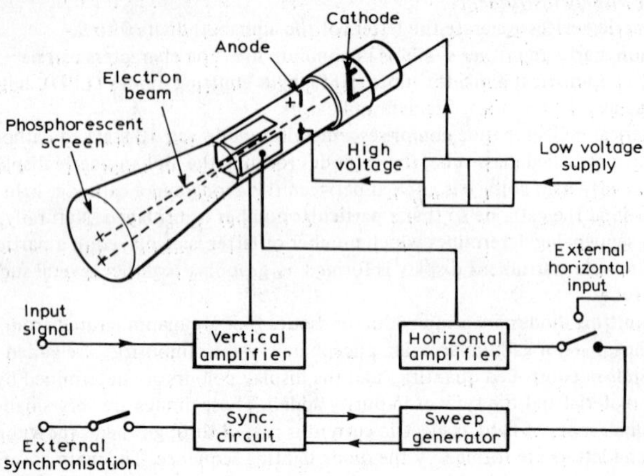

Fig 6

while more advanced oscilloscopes can store signals that can be recalled for analysis at a later time.

The measuring accuracies of oscilloscopes are usually no better than ± 3%, although there are virtually no frequency response limitations. Oscilloscopes do not provide permanent records of displayed signals but where permanent records are required the displayed signals can be photographed. However, the photographic processes can impose frequency response limitations.

(ii) Visual display units (VDU) A visual display unit is basically a cathode ray tube and is similar in appearance to a television set. Alphanumeric, graphic and pictorial data can be displayed in this way. The characters that are displayed by VDU instruments are formed by 9 X 7 dot matrices and 1024 X 780 individual points can be energised for graphic displays, so that straight lines, curves and complex slopes can be formed point-by-point.

Frequently, VDU instruments are used in conjunction with digital computers and this combination can replace numerous conventional pointer and scale instruments. In this technique, the operator selects only the information that is required and in fault diagnosis or emergency situations the computer can automatically display appropriate data.

(d) RECORDING INSTRUMENTS

Oscillographs

1 An oscillograph is a moving-coil current recording instrument that uses the D'Arsonval principle described in Chapter 2, section A.(c)3 (page 18) and section (c)1 of this chapter. There are basically two types of oscillograph recorders, namely, direct writing or stylus recorders and light-beam recorders. The same operating principles are used in both of these types of recorders.

(i) Direct writing recorders Fig 7 illustrates the D'Arsonval principle. In this type of instrument, electric current from an amplifier flows through the rotatable coil and as the coil is located in a magnetic field generated by a permanent magnet, the coil

rotates against the suspension spring as the current flows through the coil. The coil suspension is also the electrical conductor. If the current remains steady, the deflection of the coil and consequently the pointer is a measure of the magnitude of the flowing current. However, if the current fluctuates, the pointer also

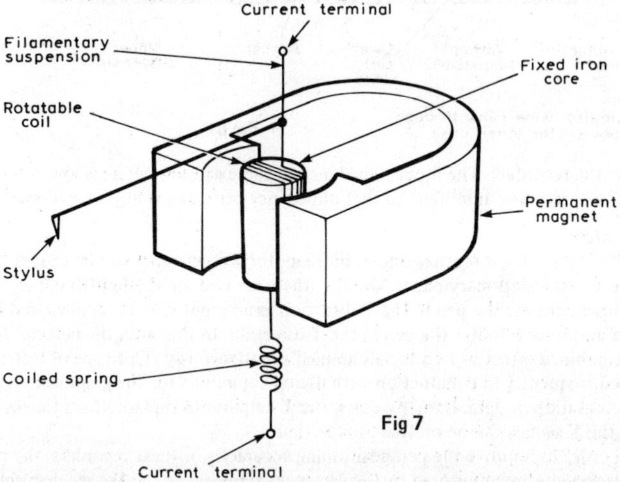

Fig 7

fluctuates, so that as a paper is passed underneath the pointer a graphic display is obtained. The display timebase depends upon the paper speed, so that different timebases can be obtained by varying the paper speed.

There are three types of writing styli, namely, ink writing, pressure writing and heat writing. Ink writing styli are simply ink pens that write directly on normal paper. However, pressure writing and heat writing styli write on pressure-sensitive and heat-sensitive paper respectively.

The frequency response characteristics of these recorders are limited by pen inertia and are usually low. The maximum measured variable frequency can rarely be more than approximately 100 Hz.

(ii) Light-beam recorders (U/V recorders) The operation of a light-beam recorder is identical to the operation of a direct writing recorder except that a mirror is attached to the rotating coil instead of a pointer. In this case the mirror reflects a beam of ultra-violet light that is generated within the recorder, on to photo-sensitive paper. This paper develops as it is subjected to daylight and produces a permanent trace if it is stored in subdued light.

The frequency response characteristics of these recorders are much higher than those of direct writing recorders but they depend upon the galvanometer characteristics. Since a galvanometer movement depends upon a mass, a spring and some form of damping, the resulting response to a dynamic input signal is that of a second-order instrument (see Chapters 1 and 9). The limiting input frequency is assumed to be 60% of the natural frequency of the galvanometer.

A typical U/V recorder galvanometer is illustrated in *Fig 8.* These galvanometers are frequently known as pencil galvanometers and are located in magnet blocks

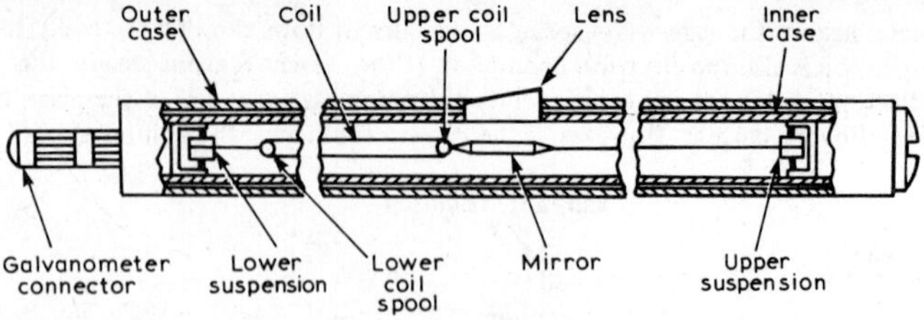

Fig 8

inside the recorders. The input impedance of these galvanometers is low compared with the preceding amplifiers so that impedance matching is usually necessary.

X-Y recorders

2 An $X-Y$ recorder comprises one or more motorised pens that can be caused to move across a stationary paper. Usually, there are two input amplifiers; one amplifier actuates the pen in the Y direction as an input signal is applied and the other amplifier actuates the pen in the X direction. In this way, the pen can trace the combined effect of two signals applied simultaneously. This type of instrumen is used frequently in conjunction with digital computers for the graphical representation of data. In many cases, the X amplifier is replaced by a timebase so that the Y signals can be plotted against time.

In order to improve the pen positioning accuracies of these recorders, the pen displacements are monitored by displacement transducers and the mechanisms are arranged to form closed-loop positional control systems (see Chapter 7). Very high positioning accuracies are achieved with these recorders but because of the considerable pen inertias the frequency responses are limited to very low frequencies. The pen slewing speeds are important in assessing the response characteristics, the slewing speed being the maximum constant velocity that a pen is capable of achieving.

Magnetic tape recorders

3 Magnetic tape recorders are used in order to record transducer signals over very wide frequency ranges. A magnetic tape comprises a coating of fine magnetic iron oxide particles laid upon a plastic ribbon. A recording is achieved by electromagnetically altering the magnetic structure of the iron oxide particles.

The advantages of magnetic tape recorders are that signals ranging from d.c. to MHz frequencies can be recorded, tapes can be replayed an infinite number of times, replay speeds can be different from recording speeds and tapes can be erased and re-used. However, the main disadvantage of magnetic tape recorders is that the recorded signals are not visually displayed.

B. WORKED PROBLEMS ON SIGNAL PROCESSING AND DISPLAY

Problem 1 Explain amplitude modulation and demodulation.

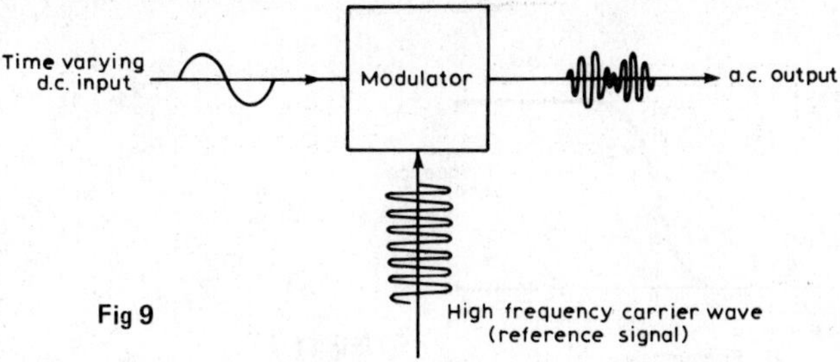

Fig 9

The conversion of direct current into alternating current is a form of amplitude modulation, whereas the conversion of alternating current into direct current is a form of demodulation. *Fig 9* illustrates the modulation process.

In this example, a modulator is energised by a high-frequency carrier signal. If a time-varying d.c. input signal is applied to the modulator, the **amplitude** of the carrier signal is modulated according to the waveform of the input signal. Consequently, the output from the modulator is a signal that has the d.c. input signal superimposed upon the base carrier signal.

Transducers are the modulators in measuring systems and the generation of amplitude modulated a.c. signals enable a.c. amplifiers to be used. In these cases, the frequency spectrums of d.c. input signals must not exceed 10% of the carrier frequencies.

In most a.c. measuring systems, phase-sensitive demodulation is used in order to recover the algebraic sign of the original d.c. information. This necessitates the use of the carrier signals as reference signals in demodulators in order to ensure precise synchronisation. Demodulator outputs are distorted representations of the input signals so that low-pass filters are usually required in order to remove high-frequency components.

Problem 2 Describe the effects of low-pass, high-pass and band-pass filters.

Filters are used in measuring systems in order to reject unwanted frequencies and distortions and to pass only the desired frequencies. Generally, there are three filter categories, namely, low-pass, high-pass and band-pass filters.

(a) Low-pass filters transmit all frequencies below certain cut-off frequencies. Ideally, there is no attenuation (reduction in amplitude) of the transmitted frequencies. *Fig 10* illustrates the effects of low-pass filters.

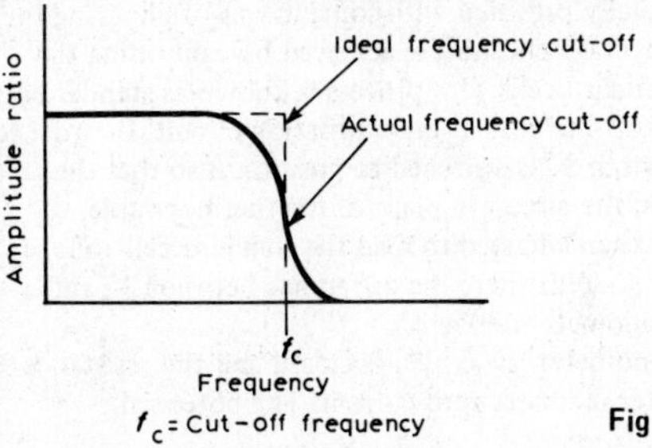

Fig 10

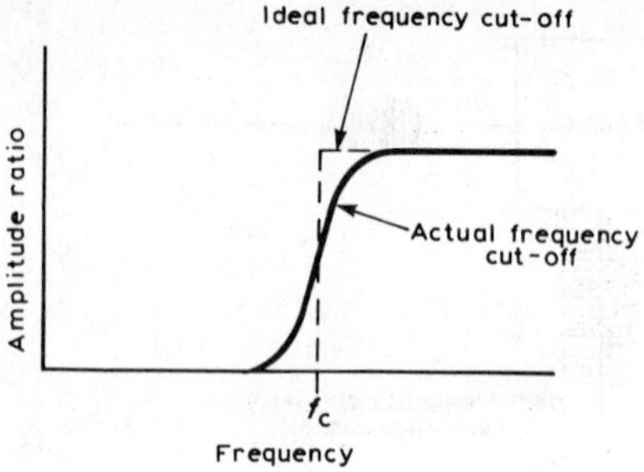

Fig 11

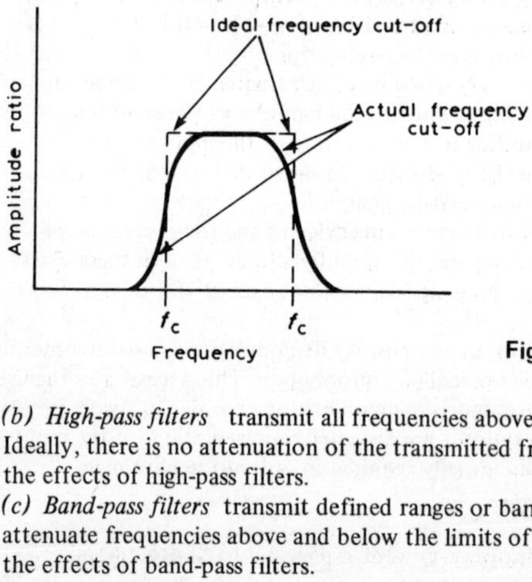

Fig 12

(b) High-pass filters transmit all frequencies above certain cut-off frequencies. Ideally, there is no attenuation of the transmitted frequencies. *Fig 11* illustrates the effects of high-pass filters.

(c) Band-pass filters transmit defined ranges or bands of frequencies and attenuate frequencies above and below the limits of these ranges. *Fig 12* illustrates the effects of band-pass filters.

Problem 3 Explain the term 'standardisation' and describe the voltage dividing method of using potentiometric display instruments.

Many applications require measured variables to be monitored over lengthy periods of time and consequently difficulties can be experienced in maintaining constant supply voltages in battery-operated instruments. In order to overcome this problem, these instruments are usually provided with some means of checking the supply voltages. Frequently, this voltage checking is achieved by calibrating the battery supply voltages against standard cells. This process is known as **standardisatio**

The potentiometer circuit of *Fig 5* includes a standardisation circuit. In order to standardise this potentiometer, switch S_1 is switched to position B so that the standardisation cell is connected in the circuit in place of the thermocouple. The slider of the potentiometer is then adjusted to read the standard cell voltage (usually 1.0186 V) on the voltage scale. If there is a difference between V_i and the standard cell voltage, the galvanometer deflects.

In order to re-balance the galvanometer, switch S_2 is closed and the resistance R is adjusted until the galvanometer indicates zero current. The potential difference across the potentiometer slider is then precisely equal to the standard cell voltage and the potentiometer scale is calibrated to read volts directly.

After standardisation, the thermocouple can be re-connected by switching S_1 to position A and opening switch S_2. The slider is again adjusted until the galvanometer indicates zero current. The slider voltage scale then indicates the e.m.f. generated by the temperature difference between the thermocouple junctions.

This type of instrument must be standardised before being used and must be standardised periodically in long-term measurement situations. Potentiometers can also be used in order to calibrate other instruments such as direct reading temperature indicators.

Problem 4 Discuss the electrical matching requirements of U/V recorders.

In order to optimise the performance of galvanometer type measuring instruments, it is necessary to consider their electrical requirements and their damping requirements. The electrical requirements of galvanometers are related usually to the output resistances of the driving amplifiers (e.g. a.c. amplifiers or d.c. amplifiers, etc.). The driving currents that are necessary to generate desired galvanometer deflections must be determined together with the optimum input resistances that are necessary to prevent electrical loading of the driving amplifiers. Low-frequency galvanometers, i.e. below about 500 Hz, are usually damped electro-magnetically, so that it is necessary to choose resistors of appropriate magnitude in order to generate optimum galvanometer damping characteristics.

Usually, galvanometer manufacturers publish data that relate to their ranges of galvanometers together with graphical information that facilitates the selection of appropriate parallel and series resistors. As the magnitudes of these resistors are chosen, electrical matching networks can be connected between driving amplifiers and recorders. However, many manufacturers now produce U/V recorders that possess built-in amplifiers and matching networks, so that in these cases external matching networks are not required.

C. FURTHER PROBLEMS ON SIGNAL PROCESSING AND DISPLAY

(a) SHORT ANSWER PROBLEMS

1 Signal conditioning instruments usually provide energy for . . . . transducers and also . . . . their signals.

2 The advantages of a.c. systems are that . . . . and . . . . Also, ... pick-up is rejected.

3 The disadvantages of d.c. systems are that . . . . and . . . . signals can be superimposed upon the output signals.

4 The reading accuracies of pointer and scale instruments are affected by . . . . and . . . . errors.

5 Alphanumeric instruments are . . . . instruments that generate . . . . , ... and . . . . in common use.

6 Oscilloscopes are used mainly in order to measure . . . . and . . . . signals.

7 A direct writing recorder is an . . . . recorder in which a . . . . is attached to a . . . . coil so that a . . . . can be scribed on a paper.
8 A band-pass filter transmits . . . . between an upper and a lower limit and . . . . frequencies outside of this range.
9 The frequency responses of U/V recorder galvanometers are much . . . . than direct writing recorders and are governed by the . . . . , the . . . . and the . . . . of the galvanometers.
10 The advantages of magnetic tape recorders are that signals ranging from . . . . can be recorded, replay speeds can be . . . . and tapes can be . . . . , but the disadvantage is that they have no . . . .

MULTI-CHOICE PROBLEMS (answers on page 184)

1 A tachogenerator is a:
(a) thermoelectric transducer; (c) active transducer;
(b) passive transducer; (d) piezoelectric transducer.
2 Charge amplifiers are used in order to amply the output signals of:
(a) inductive transducers; (c) d.c. amplifiers;
(b) thermocouples; (d) piezoelectric and capacitive transducers.
3 The frequency responses of pointer-and-scale instruments are:
(a) very low; (b) very high; (c) linear; (d) stable.
4 A display instrument produces:
(a) recorded waveforms; (c) visual displays;
(b) data print-outs; (d) magnetic tape recordings.
5 Oscilloscope timebases are generated by:
(a) X amplifiers; (c) storage oscilloscopes;
(b) Y amplifiers; (d) sweep generators.
6 Visual display units are:
(a) cathode ray tubes, (c) recorders,
(b) television sets; (d) oscillographs.
7 An oscillograph recorder timebase is generated by:
(a) an amplifier, (c) the paper speed;
(b) the writing mechanism; (d) the type of stylus.
8 The basic operating principle of oscillograph galvanometers is:
(a) the piezoelectric principle; (c) the transducer principle;
(b) the D'Arsonval principle; (d) the photoelectric principle.
9 Filters that transmit all frequencies below a defined cut-off frequency are known as:
(a) low-pass filters; (c) band-pass filters,
(b) high-pass filters; (d) variable filters.
10 The slewing speed of an X–Y recorder is the:
(a) frequency response;
(b) relationship between the X channel and the Y channel;
(c) timebase;
(d) maximum constant velocity that the pen can achieve.

(c) CONVENTIONAL PROBLEMS

1 Explain the purpose of signal conditioning instruments.
2 State three types of passive transducers and three types of active transducers. Explain the types of power supply and the types of amplifiers required in each case.

3 Explain the processes that may be necessary in a measurement system after the amplification stage and give reasons for including such processes in measurement systems.
4 Describe a carrier-amplifier system and explain the difference between carrier amplifiers and d.c. amplifiers.
5 Describe a measurement situation where an a.c. amplifier can be used and a measurement situation where a d.c. amplifier can be used. Explain the reasons for using these amplifiers in each case.
6 Explain the significance of transducer connecting cable length in piezoelectric transducer applications.
7 Describe three different types of indicating instruments.
8 State two types of recording instruments and describe the operation of U/V recorders.
9 Compare the advantages and the disadvantages of oscilloscopes and U/V recorders.
10 Describe three different methods of producing a permanent data record.
11 Compare the frequency response limitations of oscilloscopes, U/V recorders and $X-Y$ recorders.
12 A thermocouple is used in conjunction with a null-balance instrument. Draw a suitable instrument circuit and explain the battery standardisation procedure.
13 The peak pressure of a gas in a small reservoir is required to be measured. It is estimated that the gas is pulsating at a frequency of 60 Hz. An inductive transducer is available together with a carrier amplifier system whose carrier frequency is 3 kHz. Explain whether this system is satisfactory for the measurement of the pulsating gas pressure and give reasons for your decision. Select an appropriate display instrument that can generate a permanent record of the pressure variation and discuss the limitations on the measurement frequency that this instrument imposes. If an oscilloscope were selected, explain how a permanent record could be obtained and discuss the limitations of this device.

6 Measuring system applications

A. WORKED PROBLEMS ON MEASURING SYSTEM APPLICATIONS AND MEASURING SYSTEM ASSIGNMENTS

Problem 1 In order to establish the axial force transmitted by a vehicle brake rod, a section of the brake rod is machined and an electrical resistance strain gauge is bonded longitudinally along the machined section. It is intended to connect a dummy strain gauge in a limb that is adjacent to the active gauge in the necessary Wheatstone Bridge circuit. However, it is anticipated that the force may not be transmitted precisely along the axis of the rod so that bending could occur. Examine the effects of bending on the measurement of the direct axial force and discuss possible alternative strain gauge arrangements that are sensitive to axial forces only.

Determine the sensitivity of the alternative gauge arrangement that is selected.

If bending occurs due to eccentric loading of the brake rod, the active strain gauge senses the bending strain in addition to the axial strain. Of course, the bending strain can be positive or negative relative to the strain gauge so that the output from the bridge is proportional to the axial strain plus or minus the bending strain. In this case, the measurement of the axial force can be grossly inaccurate.

In order to overcome this error, two alternative gauge configurations can be used. One alternative is the technique that is outlined in Chapter 4, section A.(a)2(b) (see page 53). However, because of the small diameter of the brake rod it is unlikely that there is sufficient width to physically locate transverse gauges on the rod unless the gauges are extremely small.

A second alternative method is to bond axially to the rod two matched gauges that are located precisely opposite to each other. Then, instead of connecting the gauges into adjacent limbs of a Wheatstone Bridge, they are connected into **opposite** limbs of a bridge. As the axial force is applied to the brake rod, both of the gauges sense identical axial strains. However, if bending is present, one gauge senses tensile strains as the other gauge senses equal compressive strains. Referring to Chapter 4 and *Fig 4*, reveals that Wheatstone Bridges remain **sensitive** to measured variables if **opposite** gauges deflect with the **same algebraic sign**, while bridges are **insensitive** to measured variables if **opposite** gauges deflect with **different algebraic signs**. Clearly, in this case the bridge illustrated in *Fig 1* is sensitive to axial strains and insensitive to bending strains.

Temperature compensation is not achieved without the addition of two dummy

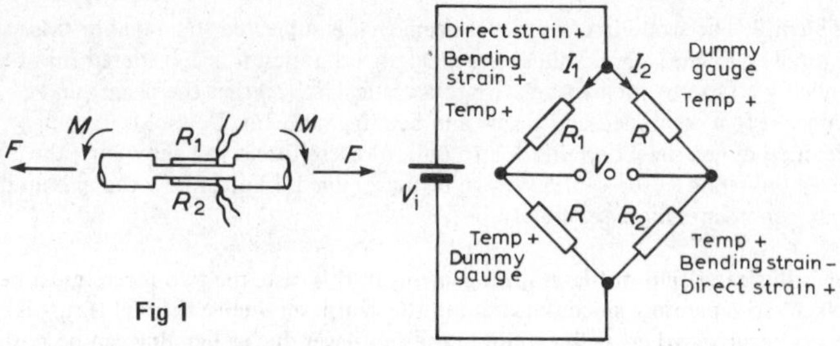

Fig 1

strain gauges in each of the other two limbs of the bridge since both of the active gauges respond identically to temperature changes. If two dummy gauges are included in the bridge then each of the four strain gauges respond identically to the same temperature changes so that the ratios of the limbs of the bridge remain unchanged and consequently the bridge remains insensitive to temperature changes.

Since the gauges are matched, let the nominal resistance of each gauge be R. Let R_1 change its resistance to $R + \delta R$ and R_2 change its resistance to $R + \delta R$ due to axial strain.

Applying Kirchhoff's laws to each branch of the bridge gives

$$V_i = I_1(R + \delta R) + I_1 R \tag{6.1}$$

and

$$V_i = I_2 R + I_2(R + \delta R) \tag{6.2}$$

assuming that the output measuring instrument has an infinitely high input resistance. Clearly, in this case

$$I_1 = I_2 = \frac{V_i}{(2R + \delta R)} \tag{6.3}$$

The potential difference across R_1

$$= \frac{V_i(R + \delta R)}{(2R + \delta R)} \tag{6.4}$$

and the potential difference across the adjacent dummy gauge

$$= \frac{V_i R}{(2R + \delta R)} \tag{6.5}$$

Therefore, the corresponding output voltage is given by

$$V_o = \frac{V_i(R + \delta R)}{(2R + \delta R)} - \frac{V_i R}{(2R + \delta R)}$$

$$= \frac{V_i\, \delta R}{(2R + \delta R)} \tag{6.6}$$

However, for practical purposes δR is small relative to $2R$, so that equation (6.6) reduces to

$$V_o = \frac{V_i}{2}\left(\frac{\delta R}{R}\right) \tag{6.7}$$

Equation (2.36) provides the expression for the output voltage in the case of the single-active-gauge system, so that clearly the sensitivity of the two-active-gauge system is double that of the single-active-gauge system.

Problem 2 The strain in a cantilever beam that is subjected to an end load is required to be measured. Due to practical uncertainties, it is considered that the applied load can be inclined relative to a vertical axis so that the beam can be subjected to a combined end thrust and bending moment. Devise strain gauge circuits that can detect strains due to both of these forces and show how the maximum strain in the cantilever can be determined. Explain how the maximum strain can be measured separately.

Fig 2 illustrates the cantilever arrangement. In this case, the two forces must be considered separately since the strain in the cantilever due to the end thrust is always negative, whereas the strain in the cantilever due to bending can be positive

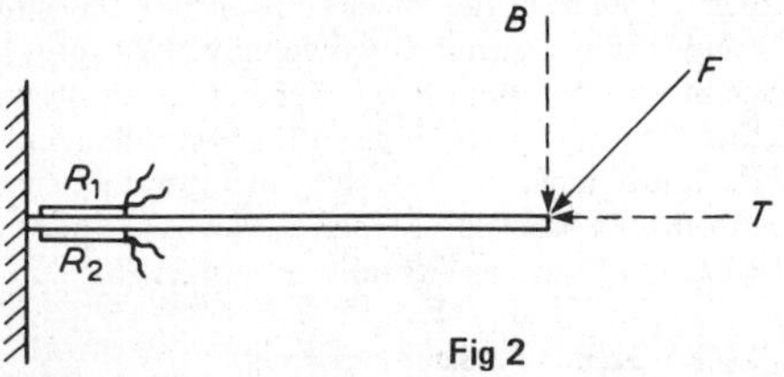

Fig 2

or negative. There are several ways in which gauges can be located on the cantilever and connected to form Wheatstone Bridges. However, the following is suggested.

(i) Bending strain measurement Two matched strain gauges are bonded on the upper and the lower surfaces at the root of the cantilever as illustrated in *Fig 2*. The gauges R_1 and R_2 are connected so that they form a half-bridge configuration and two similarly matched dummy gauges are connected so that they complete the bridge. This bridge arrangement is illustrated in *Fig 3*. Since the upper gauge R_1

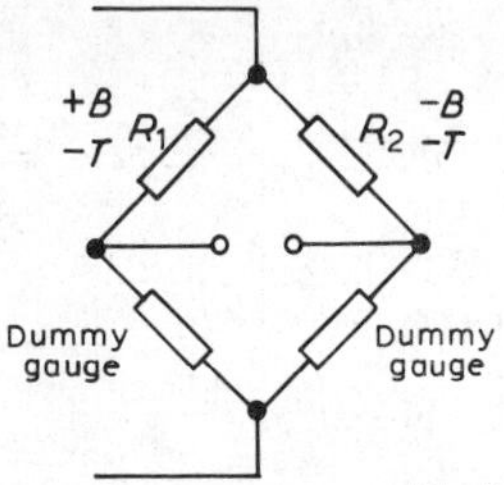

Fig 3

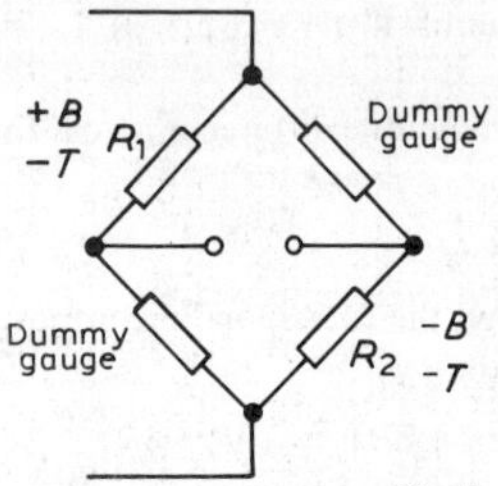

Fig 4

senses positive bending strains and the lower gauge R_2 senses negative bending strains, the bridge sensitivity to bending strains is double the sensitivity of a single-active-gauge system. Each of the gauges responds identically to the end thrust so that this bridge configuration is insensitive to axial strains.

(ii) Axial strain measurement *Fig 4* illustrates an alternative bridge arrangement using the same two strain gauges as in case (i) along with the same two dummy gauges. This arrangement is the same as the arrangement that is described in problem 1. In this case, the bridge is insensitive to bending strains and doubly sensitive to axial strains.

(iii) Maximum strain measurement The maximum strain in the cantilever is expected to occur in the lower surface at the root of the cantilever since both bending strains and axial strains combine negatively at this point. Therefore, the maximum surface strain can be determined by adding the strains measured by methods (i) and (ii).

Alternatively, gauge R_2 can be connected in a limb adjacent to a dummy gauge in order to form a quarter-bridge arrangement. In this case, the bridge output is proportional to the total strain in the cantilever.

Temperature compensation is achieved in each case since each gauge responds identically to temperature changes and the gauges are arranged so that each bridge configuration is insensitive to temperature changes.

Problem 3 The gauge factor of a batch of electrical resistance strain gauges is to be determined by testing a small sample of gauges from the batch. The usual four-point loading method is to be used.

Describe the four-point loading method and show that the gauge factor can be determined by measuring the central deflection of a beam.

Fig 5 illustrates the arrangement of the test equipment for the four-point loading test. In this arrangement a beam is simply supported at two points such that there is an equal overhang at each end of the beam. A dial gauge is located centrally so that as equal loads are applied to the ends of the beam the dial gauge measures the corresponding central deflection. In this condition, the bending moment is constant between the supports and is given by $F\ell$. Naturally, because the bending moment is

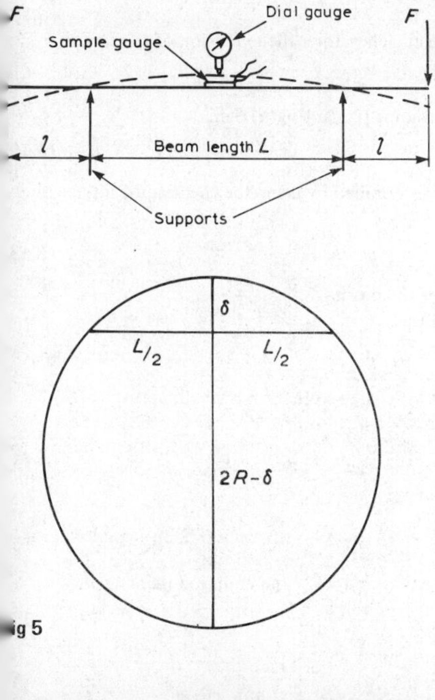

ig 5

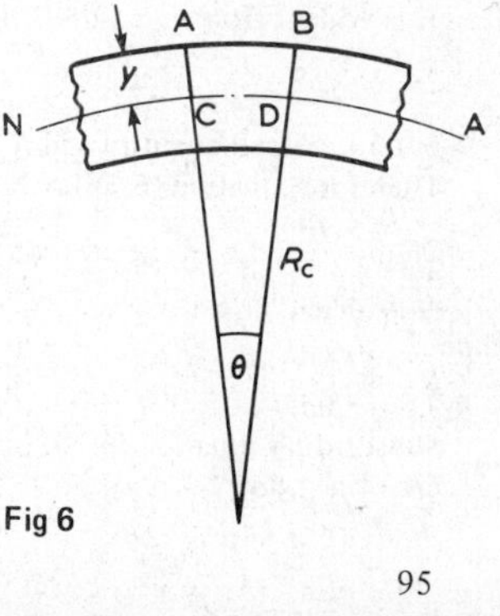

Fig 6

constant, the strain is constant between the supports and the beam deflects to form an arc of a circle since the radius of curvature is also constant. This latter condition can be observed from the bending formula

$$\frac{M}{I} = \frac{E}{R_c} \quad \text{(see Appendix)} \tag{6.8}$$

Since the bending moment M is constant between the supports and I for the beam section is constant, also E for the beam material is constant, then R_c must also be constant in order to satisfy equation (6.8).

A strain gauge from the sample is located between the supports and bonded longitudinally to the beam. The gauge is then connected in a Wheatstone Bridge configuration in the usual way. As the beam is deflected by applying equal loads to the ends of the beam, the corresponding central deflection and the strain gauge output is measured. The gauge factor can be calculated from these measurements.

Consider *Figs 5 and 6*. The fundamental relationship between the change in resistance of the strain gauge and mechanical strain is given by equation (4.1). Clearly, the ratio $\delta R/R$ is determined from the measured output from the Wheatstone Bridge, so that it is desired to obtain an expression for the surface strain in the beam in relation to the central deflection of the beam.

It is evident from *Fig 6*, that the extension of the upper surface of the beam is given by the distance AB less the distance CD, since CD lies along the neutral axis of the beam and remains unstrained. Let R_c be the radius of curvature of the beam and y be the distance from the neutral axis to the upper surface of the beam. Clearly, in this situation

$$\text{CD} = R_c\theta \tag{6.9}$$

and

$$\text{AB} = (R_c + y)\theta \tag{6.10}$$

assuming the angle θ to be very small. Therefore, the extension of the upper surface of the beam is given by

$$(R_c + y)\theta - R_c\theta = y\,\theta \tag{6.11}$$

and since strain is defined as extension/original length, then

$$\text{Strain} = \frac{y\theta}{R_c\theta} = \frac{y}{R_c} \tag{6.12}$$

The radius of curvature can be determined by using the theorem of intersecting chords, that is, from *Fig 5*,

$$\delta(2R_c - \delta) = \frac{L^2}{4} \tag{6.13}$$

where δ is the central deflection of the beam.
It is evident from equation (6.13) that

$$2R_c\delta - \delta^2 = \frac{L^2}{4} \tag{6.14}$$

but δ is a small quantity and R_c is very large so that δ^2 is small relative to $2R_c\delta$. Therefore equation (6.14) reduces to

$$2R_c\delta = \frac{L^2}{4} \tag{6.15}$$

from which

$$R_c = \frac{L^2}{8\delta} \tag{6.16}$$

Substituting equation (6.16) into equation (6.12) and equation (4.1),

$$\frac{\delta R}{R} = G \times \frac{8\delta y}{L^2} \tag{6.17}$$

so that

$$G = \frac{L^2}{8\delta y}\left(\frac{\delta R}{R}\right) \qquad (6.18)$$

It is evident from equation (6.18) that the gauge factor of the strain gauge can be determined by measuring only the bridge output and the central deflection of the beam. Naturally, the beam length between the supports, L and the thickness of the beam (y = half the beam thickness) are also required to be measured.

Problem 4 The inlet flow of air to a gas turbine operating at a steady speed is measured by a pitot-static tube that is connected to a U-tube water manometer. A small fast-response thermocouple is attached to the tip of the pitot-static tube which gives a steady temperature reading of 286 K. The upstream static pressure is measured from a separate static pressure tapping and is observed to be 7.2 kPa, gauge pressure. The local barometer reads 758 mm of mercury. If the tube constant for the pitot-static tube is 0.98 and a differential pressure head of 85 mm of water is recorded from the U-tube manometer, calculate the velocity of flow of the inlet air.

It can be assumed that the gas constant R for air is 287 J/kgK, the relative density of mercury is 13.6 and the density of water is 10^3 kg/m^3

Obviously, this is a compressible gas flow situation and the density of the inlet air varies with temperature so that it is necessary to determine the air density corresponding to the inlet conditions.

The equation of state for a perfect compressible gas is

$$\frac{P}{\rho} = RT \qquad (6.19)$$

where ρ is the gas density, P is the gas pressure, T is the absolute temperature of the gas and R is the gas constant. In this case,

$$\rho_a = \frac{P}{RT} \qquad (6.20)$$

The absolute pressure of the inlet air is the barometric pressure plus the gauge pressure, so that

$$P = 13.6 \times 10^3 \times 9.81 \times 0.758 + 7.2 \times 10^3,$$

and

$$\rho_a = \frac{13.6 \times 10^3 \times 9.81 \times 0.758 + 7.2 \times 10^3}{287 \times 286} = 1.32 \text{ kg/m}^3$$

The velocity of flow is given by equation (4.4). Furthermore, it is evident from equation (4.35) that $H = 0.085\left(\frac{10^3}{1.32} - 1\right)$

$$= 64.31 \text{ m}$$

so that

$$v = 0.98\sqrt{(2 \times 9.81 \times 64.31)}$$
$$= \mathbf{34.81\ m/s}$$

Problem 5 Discuss the relevance of the following factors to the selection and matching of U/V recorder galvanometers that are used for acquiring data on dynamic variables:
(a) frequency distortion, (b) phase distortion; (c) transient distortion.

True fidelity is the perfect reproduction of all input signals, so that signal distortion is the lack of fidelity.

(a) *Frequency distortion* is the unequal response of a measuring instrument to all input frequencies. In the case of recorder galvanometers, these must be selected so that they possess uniform responses to all the desired data frequencies. The frequency range of uniform response for a galvanometer is known as the **flat frequency response** and is usually considered to be between zero and 60% of the natural frequency of the galvanometer. Galvanometer selection is easily achieved if the highest frequency that is to be recorded is known. However, there are frequently other limitations such as higher unwanted frequencies that can be superimposed upon the data frequency or limitations imposed by other parts of measuring systems such as amplifiers or transducers. Each of these additional factors must be considered as part of the selection process.

In many cases, it is possible that the highest data frequencies can extend beyond the natural frequencies of galvanometers having the widest flat responses. However, such harmonic frequencies usually diminish in amplitude so that frequency distortion by inadequate flat response can be acceptable in such cases.

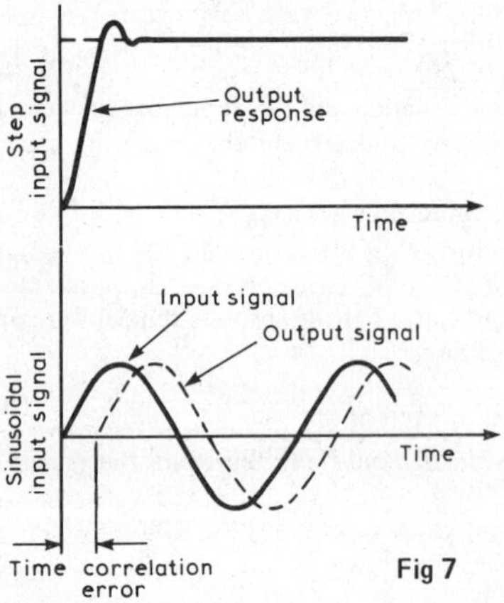

Fig 7

(b) *Phase distortion* is the phase difference between the output response of an instrument and the input signal. Phase distortion can contribute to non-fidelity in two ways, namely inaccurate time correlations between separate channels of information and non-linear relationships between phase angle and the ratio data frequency/galvanometer natural frequency. However, with optimum galvanometer damping the latter relationship is virtually linear for simple sinusoidal inputs.

Fig 7 illustrates examples of phase distortion in recorded signals. In general, phase distortion can be reduced by selecting a galvanometer that has a higher natural frequency than is necessary from a frequency consideration.

(c) *Transient distortion* is the undesirable spurious response of a galvanometer to transient inputs. The major transient response is overshoot which is governed largely by galvanometer damping. If a galvanometer is underdamped it overshoots and oscillates wildly as a step input is applied to it but if the galvanometer is overdamped its ability to follow rapidly changing signals is impaired.

B. MEASURING SYSTEM ASSIGNMENTS

Assignments can be classified as minor projects and involve experimental or theoretical investigations of real or hypothetical problems. In order to generate maximum learning and experience situations, assignments need to be related to real practical problems but this is sometimes difficult to achieve in college environments. However, assignments can be carefully selected so that academic learning can be enhanced by applying theoretical knowledge to the solution of typical industrial problems.

Engineering problems invariably involve constructing physical hardware that frequently serves little purpose in satisfying the overall learning objectives of assignments. However, such constructions are inevitable but care needs to be exercised in order to minimise the time devoted to this aspect of assignments. Where hardware construcion is necessary, this must involve greater use of college technician skills but a better arrangement is to combine college activities with the daily work of the student in industry. This arrangement leads to the ideal interface between college and industry.

The assignments that are suggested in this chapter have been selected in order to minimise hardware construction, to maximise instrumentation knowledge and experience and to present students with real engineering situations. All of the assignments involve decision making, planning, analysing requirements, selecting equipment, conducting experiments and analysing results.

Assignment 1 Consider the situation posed by *Worked Problem 2*. The hypothesese that are postulated for the solution of this problem can be verified relatively easily and inexpensively. A small amount of hardware is required but the design of an experimental rig and arranging for its construction forms a component of the learning process.

The cantilever can be simulated by a length of rectangular section mild steel bar having the approximate dimensions 25 mm × 6 mm × 400 mm, although any reasonable dimensions will suffice. The inclined load can be generated by attaching a wire or strong twine to one end of the cantilever and passing the wire over a pulley that is set back relative to the free-end of the cantilever. The fixed end of the cantilever can be clamped conveniently to a bench. Naturally, a convenient method of clamping the pulley in order to ensure that the angle of the applied force remains constant is required to be designed. *Fig 8* illustrates such an

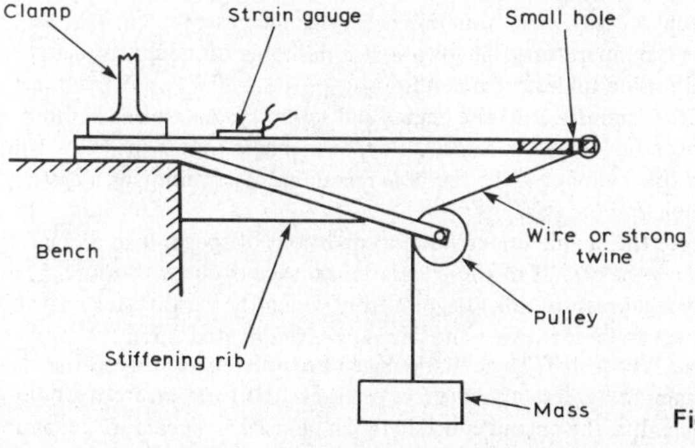

Fig 8

arrangement. The application of a mass to the wire applies an inclined load to the free-end of the cantilever such that if the angle of inclination is known then the bending force and the end thrust can be calculated. The corresponding strains in the cantilever can also be calculated.

The strain gauge procedures that are described in *Problem 2* can be carried out sequentially in order to verify the hypotheses within reasonable experimental tolerances. The experimental work involves bonding active strain gauges to the cantilever and dummy strain gauges to separate scraps of mild steel, connecting the gauges electrically in order to form the various circuit configurations, selecting suitable strain gauge energising and measuring equipment, conducting an error analysis, analysing the results and forming conclusions.

Assignment 2 Consider the measurement of cylinder pressures in a multi-cylinder or a single-cylinder diesel or petrol engine. Usually, single-cylinder diesel engines provide the best results. No equipment construction is necessary in this assignment but an engine test bed is required along with a considerable amount of expensive instrumentation. However, such equipment is available in most colleges and care must be exercised in handling and setting-up the equipment.

The first stage in the assignment is to define the problem and to estimate the magnitude and the highest frequency of the cylinder pressure. It is to be noted that harmonic frequencies are superimposed upon the fundamental frequency so that the highest signal frequency is considerably in excess of the frequency due to combustion. However, usually these harmonic frequencies possess low amplitudes. Naturally, this factor can affect the choice of recording instruments.

Secondly, select an appropriate pressure transducer and a corresponding measuring system that is suitable for measuring pulsating pressures at high temperatures and the characteristics of the particular engine being examined. Such transducers are usually inductive or piezoelectric transducers and the corresponding signal processing instruments are respectively a.c. power supplies and amplifiers or charge amplifiers. In addition, select an instrument that is suitable for recording or displaying the pressure signals. This can be either a U/V recorder or an oscilloscope. If a U/V recorder is selected, a galvanometer must be chosen that is capable of responding to the high-frequency harmonics. If an oscilloscope is selected and a permanent record of the pressure signals is required then an oscilloscope camera must be attached to the oscilloscope.

Thirdly, calibrate the measuring system using a pressure gauge dead-weight tester. Of course, this is a static calibration that is performed at low temperatures whereas the actual measurement situation is a dynamic measurement that is performed at high temperatures. Therefore, it is desirable to judge the relative value of the calibration under these conditions.

Next, attach the transducer to the engine and set-up the measuring equipment. The transducer can be located in a spark plug, or in a hole that is specially drilled and tapped into one cylinder, or in the hole remaining after removing a diesel engine heater plug.

Finally, operate the engine under various conditions of speed, load and ignition timing and observe the effects of these variations on the cylinder pressure. The resulting display is a pressure-time diagram from which the various stages of the combustion cycle can be identified and should be commented upon.

In certain cases, crankshaft angle markers can be superimposed upon the pressure-time diagram by detecting degrees of crankshaft rotation from a notched disc that is attached to the engine crankshaft. These marker signals are generated by an electromagnetic pick-up and smoothed and amplified before being displayed. The notched disc is initially adjusted until a particular mark on the disc coincides with the top-dead-centre of the piston in the particular cylinder under examination. The disc is usually notched at 15° intervals. In this case, it is possible to relate the cylinder pressure variations to the rotation of the crankshaft which in turn can be related to the volume swept by the piston if the engine stroke is known. Clearly, a pressure-volume diagram can be plotted from such data so that additional information can be obtained.

This assignment can be used as a paper assignment since the measurement problem can be investigated without conducting actual experiments. Obviously, it is more beneficial if the practical work is undertaken, nevertheless considerable useful knowledge can be gained without the practical experience.

Assignment 3 Consider the measurement of vibration levels in a milling machine slide. The objective of this assignment is to measure the vibration levels along three axes of a milling machine slide as the machine performs a cutting operation. The assignment requires minimal equipment construction, one accelerometer and its associated signal processing and recording instruments, and an accelerometer calibration set.

The first stage of the assignment is to define the measurement problem and to estimate the magnitude and the highest frequency of the vibration acceleration levels. Clearly, this is related to the cutter type, the cutter speed, the depth of cut, the feed rate and the material being machined. Therefore, each of these parameters needs to be defined initially and to be maintained at constant levels thereafter.

Secondly, select an appropriate accelerometer and a corresponding measuring system that is suitable for measuring the acceleration and the frequency levels that are estimated initially. Such accelerometers can be potentiometric, inductive or piezoelectric transducers and the corresponding signal processing instruments are respectively d.c. or a.c. power supplies and corresponding amplifiers, a.c. power supplies and amplifiers or charge amplifiers. In addition, select an instrument that is suitable for recording or displaying the vibration acceleration signals. This can be either a U/V recorder, an oscilloscope or a tape recorder. If a U/V recorder is selected, a galvanometer must be chosen that is capable of responding to the estimated frequency levels. If an oscilloscope is selected and a permanent record of the vibration signals is required then an oscilloscope camera must be attached to the oscilloscope. Probably, the most suitable measuring instrument in this application is the U/V recorder.

Thirdly, calibrate the measuring system. The calibration of accelerometers is rather difficult since known acceleration levels need to be generated. However, certain manufacturers produce calibration weight sets that enable accelerometers to be calibrated statically while certain other manufacturers produce calibration vibrators that generate a precise acceleration level at a frequency of 50 Hz. A third calibration alternative, not so precise as the previous methods, is to accept the accelerometer specification and the measuring instrument specification and to calculate the display instrument deflection that corresponds to a particular acceleration input to the accelerometer. For example, if the accelerometer sensitivity is 20 mV/g, the amplifier gain is 10 V/V, and the oscilloscope amplifier gain is 10 cm/V, then an acceleration level of 1 g generates an oscilloscope deflection of $20 \times 10^{-3} \times 10 \times 10 = 2$ cm. Assuming that the response of each instrument is linear, then an acceleration level of 2 g generates an oscilloscope deflection of 4 cm, etc.

Next, construct a simple adaptor that enables the accelerometer to be bolted conveniently to the milling machine slide. This can be in the form of a small length of flat mild steel bar having a central tapped hole in order to support the transducer. Two clearance holes can be drilled at each end of the bar and spaced so that they match the slots in the milling machine slide. In this way, the accelerometer can be attached to the upper surface of the slide, the end of the slide and the front surface of the slide. The vibration levels can be measured at each location with the machine operating at a constant cutting speed, a constant cutting depth and a constant feed rate.

Finally, compare the vibration levels at each location and relate these levels to the cutting conditions, considering also the transverse-sensitivity of the transducer. Examine the possible effects of vibration on the finish of the machined surface.

This assignment can also be used as a paper assignment since the measurement problem can be investigated without conducting actual experiments.

C. FURTHER PROBLEMS ON MEASURING SYSTEM APPLICATIONS

1 In work involving electrical resistance strain gauges, temperature compensation is necessary. Explain why it is necessary and how it can be achieved in practice. A long column carries an eccentric load as illustrated in *Fig 9*. Explain with the aid of diagrams where electrical resistance strain gauges can be located on the column and how they can be connected electrically in order to obtain maximum sensitivity to bending and to eliminate end thrust. Explain how the end thrust and temperature responses are eliminated and state the sensitivity of the system.

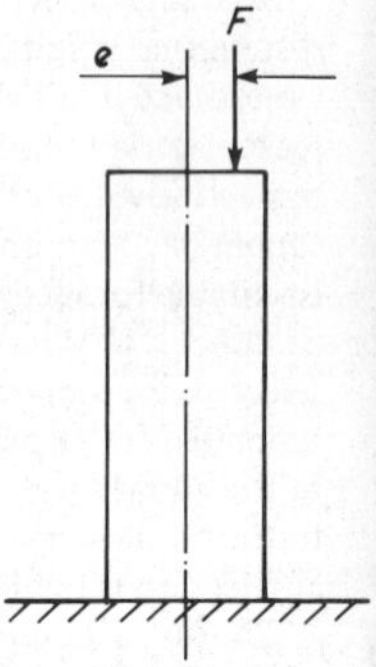

Fig 9

2 A cantilever beam is subjected to a load at its free end. The load is inclined relative to the vertical axis. Indicate the number of strain gauges required and their location on the beam in order to ensure maximum sensitivity to the vertical component of the load. Sketch the electrical circuit that is necessary and show that this circuit is insensitive to the horizontal component of the load and to changes in ambient temperature. Describe a strain gauge transducer that uses the above arrangement in order to measure differential pressure.

3 At a stage in the development of a ship's propulsion system, it is required to measure the torque transmitted to the propeller. This is achieved by applying strain gauges to the propeller shaft. Indicate the positions in which the gauges should be applied and explain how they should be connected electrically in order to produce maximum output. Discuss the practical difficulties that may be encountered in connecting the rotating gauges to stationary measuring equipment.

4 Two electrical resistance strain gauges are to be used for the measurement of torsional strain in a motor vehicle drive shaft as it is rotating. Indicate:

(a) the desirable positions of the gauges on the shaft;
(b) how the gauges should be connected electrically;
(c) how temperature compensation can be achieved;
(d) whether the gauges are influenced by axial loading;
(e) the degree of sensitivity that can be achieved.

5 Describe a type of transducer that can be used in conjunction with a counter-timer. State the four main components of a counter-timer and explain their function. Describe how such an instrument can be used to measure time and frequency, and for counting.

6 Select two electro-mechanical transducers that can be used for the measurement of dynamic pressures. Describe their mode of operation and indicate their limitations. Discuss the type of instrumentation system that is necessary in each case.

7 Describe a simple method of converting the angular position of a rotating shaft into a binary signal. State the main purpose of such devices.

8 One of the basic laws of electromagnetism relates the e.m.f. induced in a conductor to the velocity of the conductor as it is moving through a magnetic field. Illustrate how this law can be utilised in practice in order to measure fluid flow. State two advantages and two limitations of such devices in industrial environments.
If the associated voltage measuring instrument were not calibrated in flow units, explain how this system could be calibrated.

9 A transducer is to be used for the measurement of a dynamic variable and is supplied with an a.c. carrier signal. Describe how modulation of the carrier signal occurs and explain the significance of phase-sensitive demodulation. State the limitation that is imposed upon the measured variable frequency by the carrier signal.

10 Describe the signal processing systems that are required for the following types of electro-mechanical transducer:
(a) resistive, (b) inductive; (c) piezoelectric.
Define zero drift and noise in relation to the transducer amplifiers and describe the effects of three different types of filter.

11 Explain the terms fidelity, phase distortion, transient distortion and amplitude modulation as applied to the measurement of dynamic quantities.

12 In many measuring systems the output from a transducer is fed to an amplifier which in turn drives a U/V recorder. Explain why it is necessary to match the output impedance of the amplifier to the impedance of the recorder galvanometer. State the factors that influence the responses of these systems.

13 Explain the principle of operation, the different recording techniques available, the response limitations and the matching requirements of direct recording oscillographs.

FURTHER MEASURING SYSTEM ASSIGNMENTS

Determine Poisson's ratio for steel. Bond two electrical resistance strain gauges to a rectangular bar of mild steel. Bond one gauge longitudinally and the other gauge transversely. Connect each gauge to form one limb of a Wheatstone Bridge circuit along with a dummy strain gauge. Apply a tensile load to the bar using a tensile testing machine and measure the longitudinal strain and the transverse strain. The ratio of the two strains yields Poisson's ratio. Bond two additional gauges on the opposite side of the bar in order to verify that an increase in bridge sensitivity can be obtained.

Determine the modulus of elasticity for a metal. Bond a strain gauge to a length of rectangular section metal bar. Connect the gauge to form a Wheatstone Bridge along with a dummy gauge. Clamp the bar firmly to a bench at one end and apply known vertical loads at the free end. Measure the strain in the bar corresponding to increments of load and calculate the modulus of elasticity. Increase the number of active gauges and repeat the loading procedure in order to verify the appropriate increases in the bridge sensitivity.

3 Design a torque transducer that can be used in order to calibrate torque wrenches. Calculate a suitable circular bar size for an appropriate torque range. One end of the bar can be drilled and tapped axially so that an appropriate set screw can be screwed into the end. This enables a standard socket torque wrench to be applied. Machine two flats on the other end of the bar so that the bar can be clamped to a bench. Bond an appropriate number of gauges to the bar and connect them to form a Wheatstone Bridge. Calibrate the torque transducer by applying known torques to the free end of the bar. This assignment can also be conducted without constructing hardware.

4 Measure dynamic deflections due to impact forces on a cantilever. Construct a cantilever arrangement as described in assignment 2. Drill a small hole in the free end of the cantilever and insert a vertical rod so that it is suspended by the cantilever. Attach a mass to the rod so that it is free to slide along the rod. Locate an end stop to the rod so that the mass is captive. Using the maximum number of active strain gauges for maximum sensitivity, the instantaneous strain (or deflection by appropriate static calibration) caused by allowing the mass to fall on to the end stop can be recorded.

5 Assess the problem of transmitting transducer signals from rotating machinery to stationary measuring instruments. This is a common problem and certain types of equipment are available for this purpose. Obtain information from appropriate equipment manufacturers and survey the transmitting equipment that is available, quoting the advantages and the limitations of each device and typical applications. This assignment does not require hardware construction.

6 Determine the sensitivity of a pressure transducer. Use a pressure gauge dead-weight tester in order to calibrate statically a pressure transducer and its associated signal processing and measuring instruments. Compare the calibrated sensitivity with the manufacturer's specification.

7 Compare the responses of thermocouples. Obtain several thermocouples having either the same metal combination and different diameters or the same diameter and different metal combinations. Connect each thermocouple in turn to a recording instrument and plunge each thermocuple in turn into a small furnace that is maintained at a constant temperature. Compare and comment upon the different responses that are obtained. This assignment does not require hardware construction.

8 Measure the displacement levels in a vibrating beam. Vibrating beam experiments are usually conducted in many colleges so that the basic vibration equipment can be readily available. Calibrate a small displacement transducer and its associated measuring equipment by applying known displacements. Locate the transducer at several positions in succession along the length of the beam and measure the displacement of the beam as it vibrates at a constant frequency. Plot the displacement curve for the beam. This assignment may need a minimum amount of hardware construction.

9 Design a liquid level measuring system. Define a liquid level problem and devise a system for measuring and continuously monitoring the liquid level. Such a system can be simulated by constructing a perspex tank and a float system. Attach a displacement transducer to the float. Calibrate the float displacement measuring system by applying known displacements.

10 Solve an industrial measurement problem. Define and analyse an industrial problem. Survey the measuring equipment that is available and propose a suitable measuring system. Describe an experimental procedure and explain methods of analysing results.

Note. In each of these suggested assignments it is assumed that students analyse the measurement problems, select appropriate measuring instruments, calibrate the measuring systems, devise experimental procedures, analyse the errors and analyse the experimental results.

7 Control systems

A. INTRODUCTION TO CONTROL SYSTEMS

(a) GENERAL INTRODUCTION

A control system is a group of separate components or sub-systems that are connected together in order to regulate a variable quantity or several variable quantities simultaneously. Such systems require input signals and they generate corresponding output signals. The input signals are frequently known as **command** signals since the desired values of the controlled variables are determined by these commands and the output signals regulate the variables. A control system that regulates a variable in response to a **fixed** command signal is known as a **regulator** system, whereas a control system that accurately follows **changes** in the command signal is known as a **follow-up** system. However, control systems are frequently classified according to the actions of their controllers, and there are discrete-time proportional controllers, continuous-time proportional controllers, derivative controllers, integral controllers, adaptive controllers, optimal controllers, etc.

In view of the historical development of control system technology, there are two system categories, namely, positional control systems (sometimes known as servomechanisms) and process control systems. Identical mathematical procedures are used in the analysis of the dynamical behaviour of both of these control system categories. Complex process control systems frequently incorporate servo-mechanisms as sub-systems. The following examples illustrate positional control systems:

Machine tool cutter and slide positioning;
Automatic pilots in aircraft steering and stabilising;
Automatic ship steering and stabilising;
Gun-turret positioning;
Motor vehicle assisted steering and anti-skid devices.

The following examples illustrate process control systems:

Liquid and bulk level control systems;
Flow control systems;
Boiler plant control systems;
Room temperature control systems;
Automatic liquid and bulk-weighing systems.

(b) OPEN-LOOP AND CLOSED-LOOP SYSTEMS

Control systems can be classified as open-loop systems or closed-loop systems. In an open-loop system there is no connection between the output from the system and the input to the system. *Fig 1* is a block diagrammatic arrangement of an open-loop hydraulic control system. In this system, as the control valve is opened manually, possibly by a lever, high-pressure oil flows into a hydraulic actuator (possibly a piston and cylinder arrangement). However, since oil continues to flow as long as the valve remains open the actuator simply moves to its full-stroke

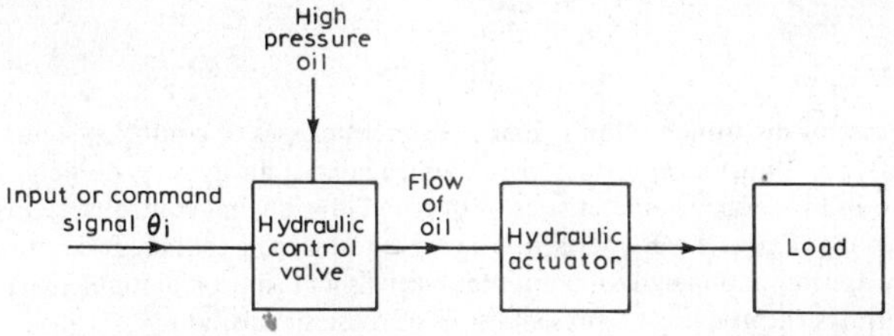

Fig 1

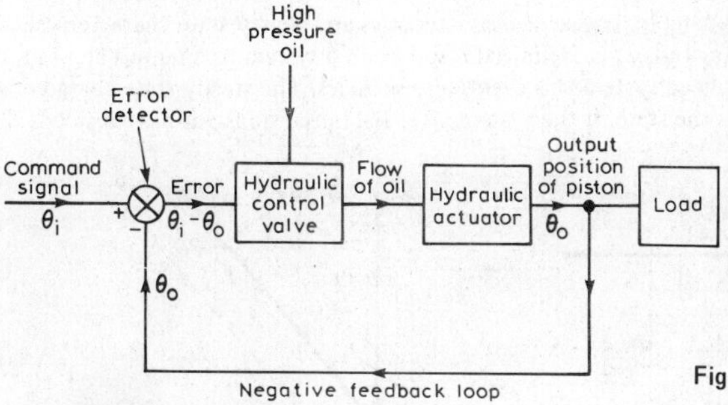

Fig 2

position. In this case intermediate positions of the actuator can only be obtained by manually manipulating the control valve and accurate positioning of the actuator is extremely difficult. Such imprecise systems are used frequently in hydraulically actuated earthmoving plant.

Fig 2 is a block diagrammatic arrangement of a closed-loop hydraulic control system. In this case, the movement of the actuator is monitored by a displacement transducer that feeds a signal back to the input. This output signal is compared with the command signal in an error detector (or comparator) which in turn generates an error signal. Clearly, this is an error-actuated system that moves the actuator only if there is a difference between the desired position of the actuator (command signal) and the actual position of the actuator (the output signal). As the actual actuator position approaches the desired actuator position, the error signal approaches a zero value and gradually closes the valve accordingly so that eventually no oil flows to the actuator. In this way, the actuator moves precisely to any position, within the limits of its stroke, that is determined by the command signal.

Complete closed-loop control systems comprise error detectors, controllers, output elements and feedback measuring instruments. The feedback measuring instruments and their associated signal processing instruments can be used also to monitor the movement of the output element or the controlled variable separately. Naturally, an appropriate power source is also required in order to energise the components of a control system. For example, the hydraulic system described previously requires a hydraulic pump driven by an electric motor, a reservoir, pressure regulator valves and filters. Typical individual control system components are considered in section (d) of this chapter. Additional feedback loops can also be used in complex systems and such multi-loop control systems are considered in Chapters 8 and 9.

(c) TEST SIGNALS

As in the case of instrumentation systems, different classes of control systems possess different dynamical characteristics which are not always easy to determine. In order to examine the characteristics of instrumentation and control systems various test input signals were devised. The three test signals that are used most frequently are step input signals, ramp input signals and sinusoidal input signals. *Fig 3* illustrates the graphical representations of these signals.

The dynamical characteristics of most systems can be reduced to two components, namely, transient characteristics and steady-state characteristics. The transient characteristic is the initial response of a system to an input and in a correctly designed system this eventually subsides. The steady-state characteristic of a system is the state of the system after the initial transient has subsided. The

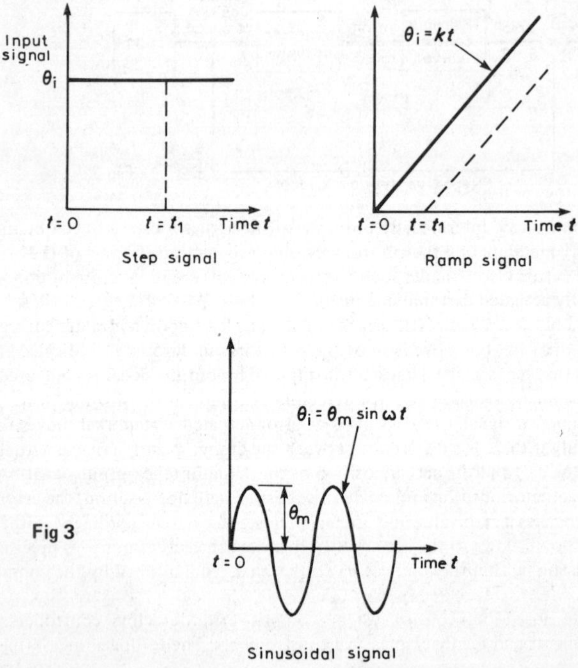

Fig 3

complete response of a system to an input is the sum of the two states. However, there are certain conditions under which the most carefully designed system will not settle to a steady state and in some cases systems can oscillate violently and destructively. This is considered to be an unstable condition. Transient, steady-state and instability conditions are considered in greater detail in Chapters 9 and 10.

The three main test signals are defined as follows:

ʻtep signals

Step input signals are used in order to examine the initial transient characteristics of instrumentation and control systems. A step signal is a suddenly applied signal such as can be experienced by the rapid operation of a valve.

ʻamp signals

Ramp input signals are used in order to examine the ability of instrumentation and control systems to accurately follow uniformly varying inputs. The ramp is a signal that varies uniformly with time such as can be experienced in machining a uniform taper in a copying machine.

ʻinusoidal signals

Sinusoidal input signals are used in order to examine the steady-state characteristics of instrumentation and control systems and are frequently used in order to assess the stability of control systems. The application of sinusoidal signals in this way is known as frequency response testing and is considered in greater detail in Chapter 10.

d) CONTROL SYSTEM COMPONENTS

ʻrror detectors

The purpose of error detectors is to compare the actual outputs of control systems with the desired outputs and to generate corresponding error signals. Of course, the desired outputs are represented by the command signals, so that the generated error signals are proportional to the sum of the feedback signals and the command signals. Only in exceptional situations is positive feedback used, so that in the majority case of negative feedback systems, the error signals are proportional to the difference between the command signals and the feedback signals.

There are many different types of error detectors used in the control of many different variables. Frequently, mechanical, pneumatic and hydraulic control systems are interfaced with electrical error detectors so that they form electro-mechanical, electro-pneumatic and electro-hydraulic control systems. However, error detectors can also be wholely mechanical or wholely pneumatic; but electro-mechanical transducers are usually the most convenient instruments for generating feedback signals, so that electrical error detectors are probably used most frequently.

(i) Mechanical error detectors

Mechanical differentials can be used in order to detect positional errors in rotating systems where the outputs are not remote from the inputs. *Fig 4* illustrates a mechanical differential.

Consider the situation where the output shaft of the differential is locked in position but the input shaft rotates. In this case, the rotation of the input bevel gear causes the intermediate bevel gears to rotate about their own axes and also about the axis of the output shaft providing that the casing is also allowed to rotate. Because of the rotation of the intermediate bevel gears about the output

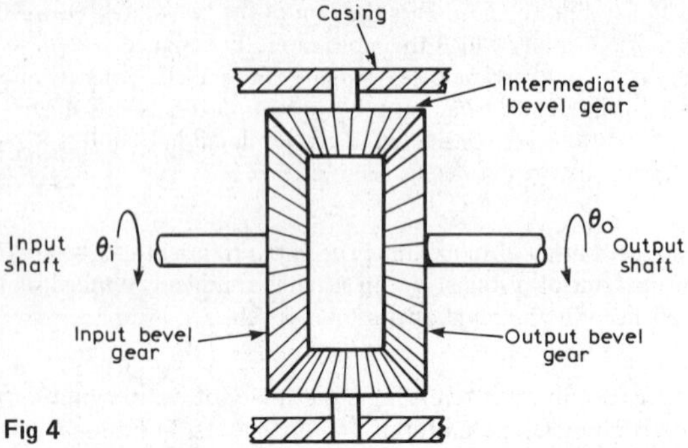

Fig 4

shaft axis and simultaneously about the input shaft axis, the casing rotates by an angle that is equal to half of the input shaft angular rotation. A similar angular rotation of the casing is obtained as the output shaft rotates relative to the input shaft. Therefore, if both of the shafts rotate simultaneously with the output shaft rotating in an opposite direction to the input shaft, then the angle of rotation of the casing is given by

$$\frac{\theta_i - \theta_o}{2}$$

It is evident that in this case the rotation of the differential casing is proportional to the difference between the angular displacement of the input shaft and the output shaft.

There are two fundamental disadvantages of mechanical devices of this type. The first disadvantage is that the two shafts cannot be located remotely and the second disadvantage is that backlash in the gears results in the non-linear characteristic of dead-band.

2 **Positional gyroscopes** are used in situations where no fixed reference points are available. Aircraft and ship steering and stabilisation systems are typical applications for these error detectors. In these applications, transducers such as potentiometers can measure only relative displacements between the hulls of ships or aircraft and the controlled variables, since these vehicles are themselves

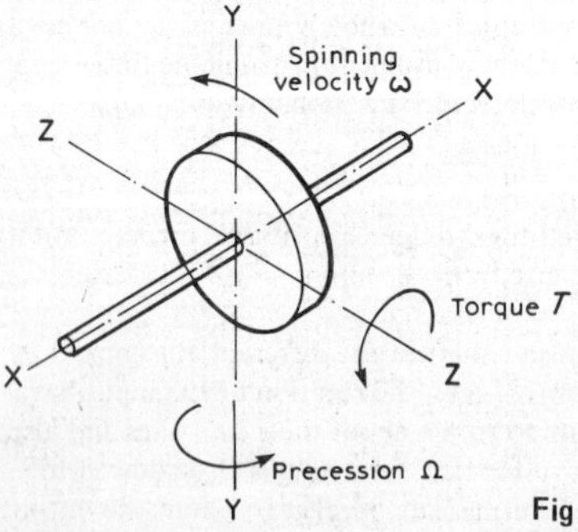

Fig 5

moving relative to the horizon. Positional gyroscopes sense deviations from set-points without the need for fixed reference points.

Fig 5 illustrates a positional gyroscope. In this device, a circular mass that is known as a spinner is rotated at high speed about its own axis by an electric motor. The gyroscope can be aligned initially so that this stable condition corresponds to a reference plane such as the horizon. If a torque is applied to the axis of the gyroscope in the manner indicated in *Fig 5*, then the gyroscope rotates about the vertical axis YY. This rotation is known as a precession. In a control system situation, the gyroscope is freely suspended by a double gimbal and tends to maintain its preset axial alignment. However, bearing friction and unbalance of the gimbals can cause changes in the initial axial alignment which needs resetting periodically. The torque can be caused by the roll of an aircraft or a ship and the precession can be detected by an angular displacement transducer that energises a controller which in turn applies a corrective signal to the aircraft or ship stabilising surfaces.

The relationship between torque, spin velocity and the precession velocity is given by

$$\Omega = \frac{T}{J\omega} \tag{7.1}$$

where Ω is the precession velocity (rad/s), T is the applied torque (Nm), ω is the spin velocity (rad/s) and J is the polar moment of inertia of the spinning mass (kgm^2) (See Appendix).

Rate gyroscopes are used in order to detect changes in angular velocities in situations where no fixed reference points are available. For example, the rate of roll, pitch or yaw of aircraft, missiles or ships.

A rate gyroscope is similar in operation to a positional gyroscope except that the spinner is suspended in an inner frame which in turn is suspended in an outer frame. The inner frame is attached to the outer frame by a torsion bar spring so that as the outer frame rotates due to the movement of the host vehicle a torque is applied to the inner frame. This torque is restrained by the torsion bar spring so that the **displacement** of the **inner frame** is proportional to the **angular velocity** of the **outer frame**.

(ii) Electrical error detectors

Potentiometers can be used in order to detect positional errors in angular or translational position control systems. In this case, the outputs can be remote from the inputs. A common arrangement for an angular position error detector is

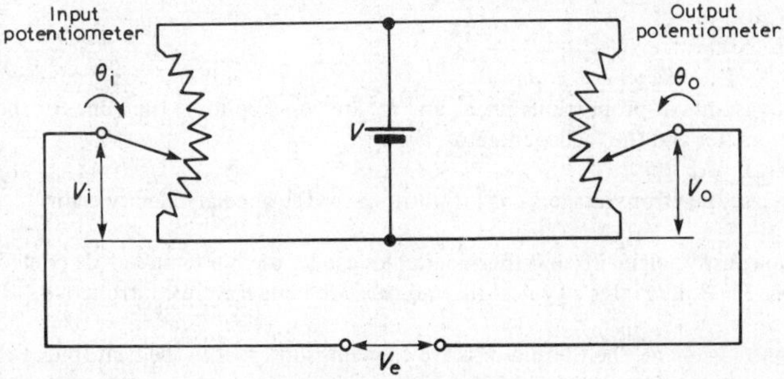

Fig 6

illustrated in *Fig 6*, where the movement of the input potentiometer sets the desired angular displacement of an output shaft (set point) so that $V_i \propto \theta_i$. The output potentiometer is connected to the output shaft of a control system so that as the output shaft rotates in accordance with the command signal V_i, the output potentiometer generates a signal $V_o \propto \theta_o$.

It is evident that

$V_i = K_i\theta_i$

and that

$V_o = K_o\theta_o$

If the constant of proportionality, K is designed to be the same in each potentiometer,

then

$$V_i - V_o = K(\theta_i - \theta_o) \quad (7.2)$$

Thus the error voltage V_e is proportional to the displacement error.

2 **Potentiometers and tachogenerators** can be combined in speed control systems. *Fig 7* illustrates a typical speed control error detector, in which the movement of the input potentiometer sets the desired angular velocity of an output shaft so that $V_i \propto \omega_i$, where ω_i is the desired angular velocity. The tachogenerator senses the actual angular velocity of the output shaft and generates a voltage $V_o \propto \omega_o$, where ω_o is the actual angular velocity. If the potentiometer and the tachogenerator are

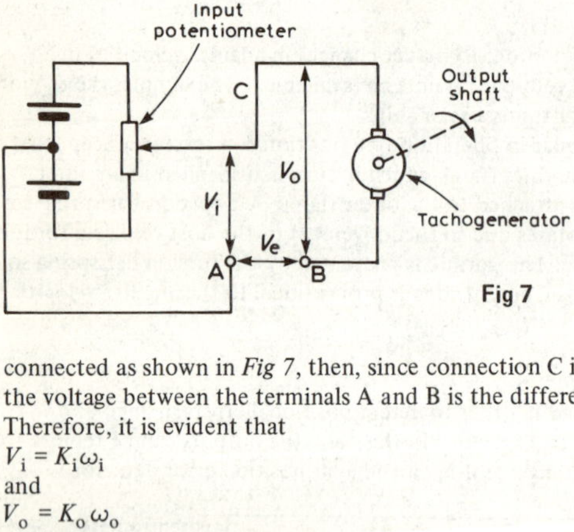

Fig 7

connected as shown in *Fig 7*, then, since connection C is a common connection, the voltage between the terminals A and B is the difference between V_i and V_o. Therefore, it is evident that

$V_i = K_i\omega_i$

and

$V_o = K_o\omega_o$

so that

$V_e = V_i - V_o = K_i\,\omega_i - K_o\,\omega_o$

If the constants of proportionality K_i and K_o are designed to be the same for the potentiometer and the tachogenerator, then

$$V_e = K(\omega_i - \omega_o) \quad (7.3$$

In this case the error voltage V_e is proportional to the angular velocity error.

3 **Thermo-resistive elements and thermocouples** can be used in temperature control systems. *Fig 8* illustrates a typical thermo-resistive temperature control error detector.

In this arrangement, the thermo-resistive element is inserted in the heat source that is to be controlled so that variations in the source temperature cause corresponding variations in the resistance of the thermo-resistive element. The heat source temperature is regulated by the output from the Wheatstone Bridge and the bridge is balanced initially. If the variable resistance is adjusted initially in order to provide the **desired** heat source temperature and the initial source temperature is zero, then the instantaneous output from the bridge is V_e. However, as the source

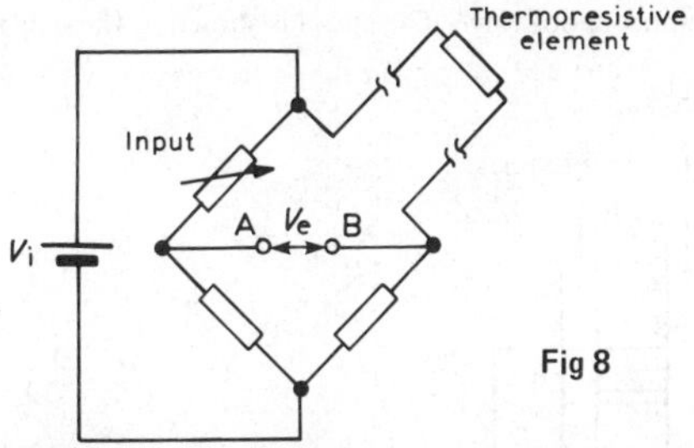

Fig 8

temperature increases in response to V_e the ratios of the bridge resistors in each branch of the bridge become more closely related (see Chapter 2) and V_e diminishes. As the heat source temperature approaches the desired temperature, $V_e \rightarrow 0$, so that V_e is proportional to the difference between the set-point temperature and actual temperature, i.e. the temperature error. Variations in the source temperature from the set-point temperature result in corrective voltages from the bridge.

Controllers

The purpose of controllers is to accept the low-power signals from error detectors and to present high-power signals to actuators. The high-power signals must be in a physical form that is compatible with the requirements of the actuators. For example, in the case of a hydraulic control system, the output from the controller must be high-pressure oil flow. Generally, a controller does not generate power but regulates power that is generated from an external source. The case of the hydraulic system that is described in section A.(b) is a typical example of this. Controllers can be classified as mechanical, electrical, hydraulic and pneumatic.

1 *Mechanical controllers* There are few controllers that operate upon purely mechanical principles. However, one such controller is a mechanical governor. This controller can be used in an engine speed control system where the engine speed is monitored by a rotating shaft which in turn rotates the governor fly weights. The movement of the fly weights due to centrifugal force actuates a fuel control valve which in turn regulates the engine fuel flow and consequently the engine speed. Of course, the main disadvantage of mechanical error detectors and controllers is that the input and the output of a system must be physically close together.

2 *Electrical controllers* Electrical controllers are frequently in the form of amplifiers. These can be electronic amplifiers, magnetic amplifiers or rotary amplifiers. Electronic amplifiers are generally low-power controllers whereas magnetic amplifiers and rotary amplifiers are high-power controllers. The theory of these amplifiers is beyond the scope of this text.

3 *Hydraulic controllers* Hydraulic control systems can be classified as pump-controlled systems or valve-controlled systems. In a pump-controlled system a variable-stroke pump delivers high-pressure oil to a fixed-stroke motor. The moto speed is controlled by regulating the flow of oil from the pump. In this case, the controller is the variable-stroke pump.

In a valve-controlled system, the motor speed can be controlled by a fast-operating valve that is frequently known as a servo-valve. *Fig 9* illustrates a simple servo-valve, in this case a five-port spool valve. The spool is shown in the central o

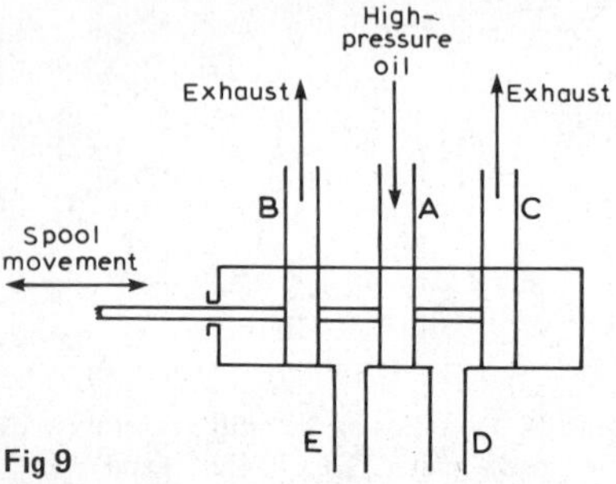

Fig 9

null position so that port A is effectively sealed and no oil can flow through the valve. However, as the spool is moved to the right the centre spool opens port A and the right-hand spool opens port C, but port B remains closed due to the position of the left-hand spool. In this case, high-pressure oil flows through the valve to the outlet port E while returning oil flows from port D to the exhaust port C.

As the spool is moved to the left from the null position, ports A and B are opened while port C remains closed. Thus high-pressure oil flows from port A to port D while low-pressure oil flows from port E to the exhaust port B. Clearly, th control valve controls the flow of oil in each direction so that reciprocating motions can be controlled. Generally, in this type of valve the flow-rate through the valve is assumed to be proportional to the spool displacement.

There are many practical variations on the simple spool valve. For example, th spool can be operated manually, mechanically, electrically, hydraulically or pneumatically.

4 *Pneumatic controllers* Air is normally the energy medium in pneumatic control systems. Low-pressure pneumatic systems are frequently used in process control applications and higher-pressure systems are frequently used in mechanisation systems such as in mechanical handling and manufacturing. In both of these applications, air is compressed by a compressor, stored in a reservoir and regulate by valves before being exhausted to the atmosphere after doing useful work.

Pneumatic valves and actuators are similar in construction to hydraulic valves and actuators; however, air is compressible whereas oil is frequently assumed to b incompressible so that pneumatic valves need to be pressure-locked in position. The essential difference between pneumatic systems and hydraulic systems is tha hydraulic control valves control **oil flow** whereas pneumatic control valves contrc **air pressure**.

Fig 10 illustrates a typical nozzle-flapper type of control valve that is used

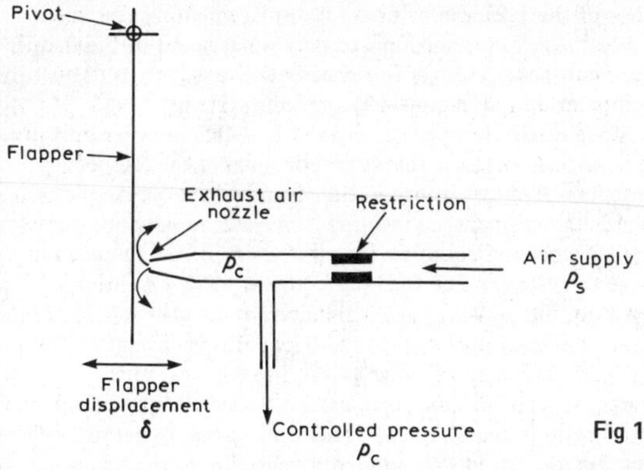

Fig 10

extensively in low-pressure process control systems. Air is supplied to the control valve at a constant pressure p_s and the restriction generates a pressure reduction. As the flapper is in its null position, air exhausts through the gap between the flapper and the nozzle so that the pressure p_c remains at a steady value. However, as the flapper is moved towards the nozzle, the gap between the flapper and the nozzle is reduced and the pressure p_c increases. The maximum value of p_c is reached as the nozzle tends to be fully closed and $p_c \rightarrow p_s$. As the flapper is moved away from the nozzle, the gap between the flapper and the nozzle is increased and the pressure p_c is reduced to a minimum value.

Clearly, the movement of the flapper regulates the controlled pressure p_c so that this pressure can be used in order to operate an output actuator. However, this simple controller is very non-linear except over a limited range of flapper displacements and is extremely sensitive so that in practical situations the valve is de-sensitised.

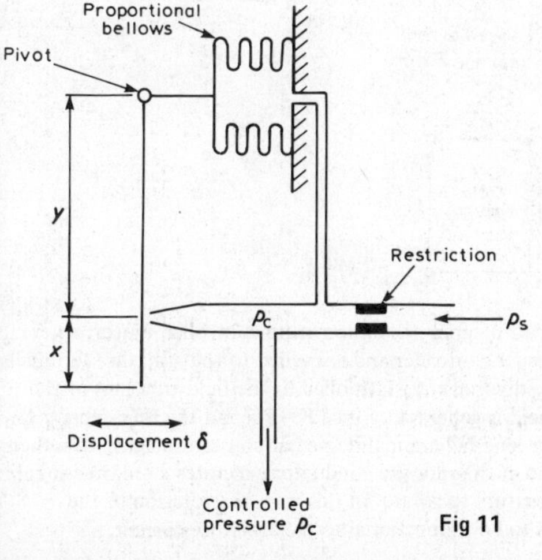

Fig 11

Nozzle-flapper valves of this type can be used for displacement measurement since the controlled pressure p_c is proportional to the displacement of the flapper over a limited displacement range. This type of pneumatic transducer is frequently used in pneumatic comparators and in multi-head gauging systems.

Fig 11 illustrates a de-sensitised nozzle flapper valve in which negative pressure feedback generates a controlled pressure that is proportional to the flapper displacement. This principle is known as **proportional control action**. As the flapper is moved towards the nozzle, the pressure p_c increases rapidly and causes the bellows to expand. The bellows act upon the pivoted end of the flapper and increase the gap between the flapper and the nozzle until a stable condition is obtained. In this condition, the pressure p_c is maintained at a higher value than the null pressure and its increase is proportional to the flapper displacement δ. The sensitivity of this arrangement can be adjusted by varying the ratio x:y.

More complex arrangements of this proportional controller are used in order to generate various control actions, see Chapter 9. The higher-pressure control valves that are used in mechanisation systems are similar in operation to the hydraulic spool valve that is described in the previous section (3).

Output elements

Output elements generate high-power outputs in response to controller signals. These outputs are usually in the form of physical quantities such as position, speed, temperature, flow, etc. so that the output elements can also take many different forms. For example, speed control can be obtained by controlling an electric motor or by controlling an internal combustion engine. Obviously the torque and power that is generated in each of these cases is different and the output element that is chosen in a particular situation is determined by such factors.

Three typical classes of control system output elements are described here:

1 *D.C. motor* D.C. electric motors can be used in positional or speed control systems where the power requirements are relatively low. These output elements are frequently known as servomotors. Servomotors can be armature-controlled or field-controlled.

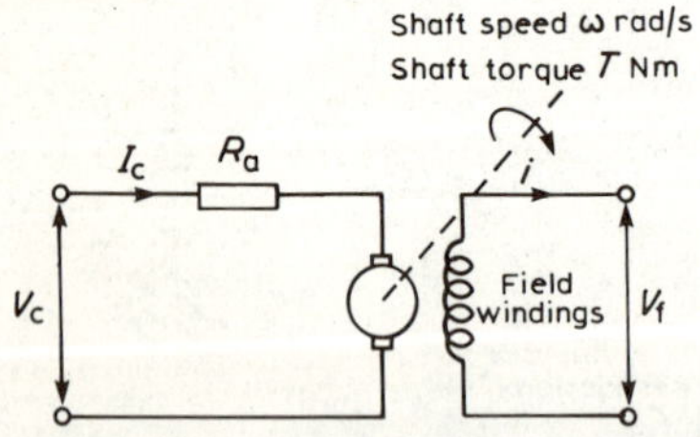

Fig 12

Fig 12 illustrates the circuit diagram for an armature-controlled motor, where V_c is the output voltage from a controller and is applied to the armature terminals of the motor. A separate field voltage, V_f is applied to the field windings of the motor so that a magnetic field is generated. Since $F = Bi\ell$ and the flux density B and the armature conductor length ℓ are maintained at constant magnitudes, then the force that is generated in each armature conductor generates a unidirectional torque which causes the armature to rotate. In this way, the rotation of the armature can be considered to be proportional to the armature current.

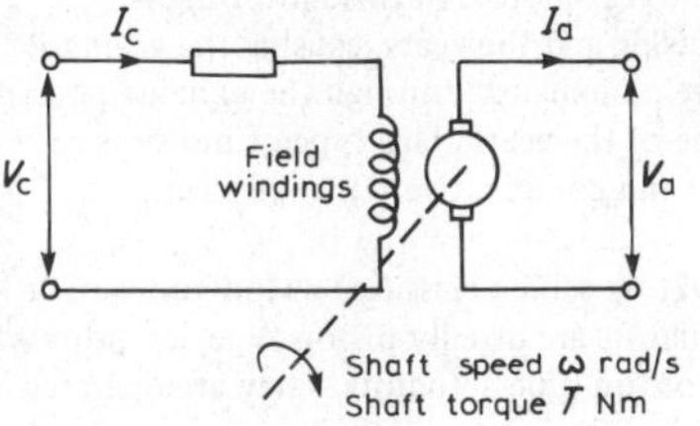

Fig 13

Fig 13 illustrates the alternative field control form, in which the armature current I_a is maintained at a constant level while the controller output voltage V_c is applied to the field windings of the motor. Here the motor torque can be considered to be proportional to the field voltage but the motor speed is independent of the voltage and the torque. Because of this situation, velocity feedback is necessary in order to avoid the generation of uncontrolled speeds. However, the main advantage of field control is that small input currents can be used which enable these motors to be energised directly from electronic controllers.

Hydraulic actuators These actuators can be in the form of hydraulic motors or hydraulic piston devices, and are available in a wide range of power capacities, torque capacities and speeds.

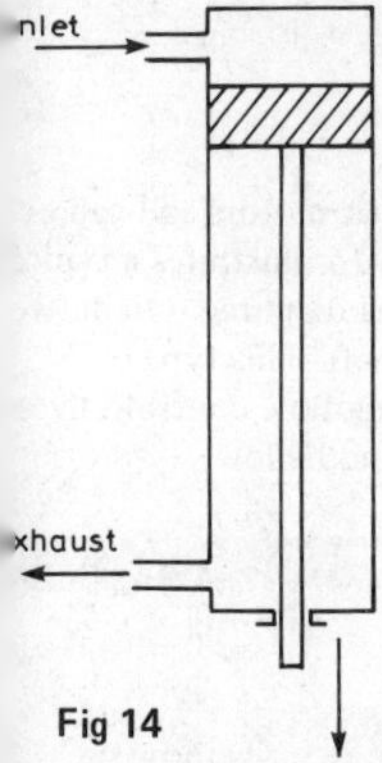

Fig 14

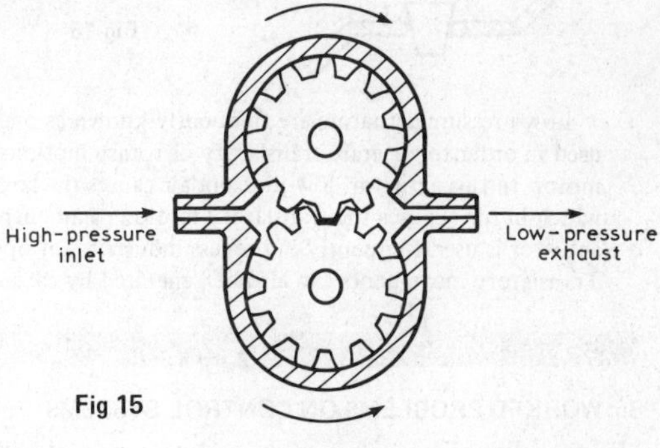

Fig 15

Fig 14 illustrates a typical double-acting piston and cylinder actuator. Coulomb friction affects the performance of these actuators and pressure differentials as high as 30% of the supply pressure can be necessary in order to overcome this resistance to motion. The mathematical equations that govern the motions of these actuators under steady conditions are:

$$Q = L_p p + A_p v \tag{7.4}$$

and

$$F = A_p p \tag{7.5}$$

where Q is the flow of oil into the cylinder, L_p is the leakage flow coefficient for the piston, A_p is the piston area, v is the piston velocity, F is the force that is generated by the piston and p is the pressure differential across the piston.

Fig 15 illustrates a typical hydraulic gear motor. In this motor high-pressure oil is forced between the housing and the gears, causing the gears to rotate in opposition. The low-pressure oil exhausts through the exhaust port. An output drive shaft is connected to one of the gears. This type of motor is easy to manufacture, is efficient in operation and comparatively inexpensive.

3 *Pneumatic actuators* Pneumatic actuators can be classified as low-pressure or hig pressure actuators. High-pressure actuators are usually piston-type actuators whic are similar in operation to hydraulic piston-type actuators. They are operated usually by spool-type control valves.

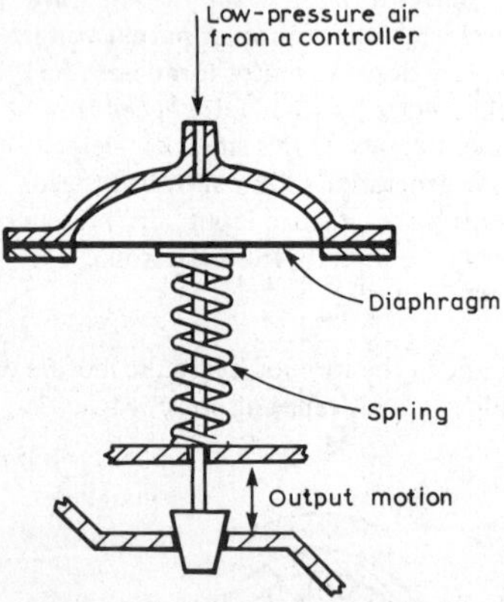

Fig 16

Low-pressure actuators are frequently known as pneumatic motors and can be used in order to generate translatory or rotary motions. *Fig 16* illustrates a typica motor. In this actuator, low-pressure air causes the large-area diaphragm to deflec which in turn causes the translatory motion of an output shaft. This type of actuator is used frequently in process industries for operating flow control valves Translatory movements can also be generated by capsules and bellows.

B. WORKED PROBLEMS ON CONTROL SYSTEMS

Problem 1 Define the main features of synchro-systems and describe how such systems can be used as error detectors.

Synchro-systems can be used in order to perform two main functions. Firstly, a synchro pair, which comprises a synchro transmitter and a synchro receiver, can be used in order to indicate remotely the angular position of an output shaft. Th transmitter converts an input shaft rotation into an electrical signal which in turr causes the receiver output shaft to rotate through an angle that is similar to the rotation of the input shaft.

Secondly, a synchro pair can be used also to generate error signals in positiona control systems. In this case, a synchro transmitter is used in conjunction with a synchro control transformer. *Fig 17* illustrates a typical synchro error detector

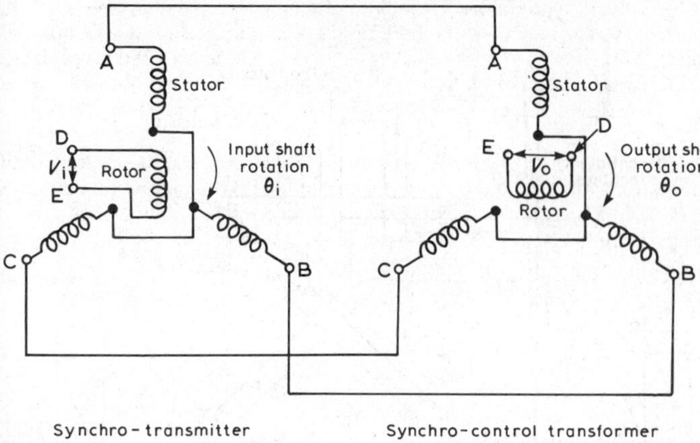

Fig 17

arrangement in which the transmitter rotor is connected to an a.c. power supply so that an e.m.f. is induced in each of the three stator coils of the control transformer. The control transformer rotor is connected to the output shaft of the device being controlled and is positioned initially so that $V_o = 0$. However, as the transmitter rotor is rotated to a new position, the new magnetic field surrounding the transformer stator induces an e.m.f. in the rotor coils so that $V_o \neq 0$. This output voltage drives the controlled device to a new position which in turn rotates the transformer rotor until $V_o \to 0$ once more. It can be shown that over a limited range of operation, $V_o = K(\theta_i - \theta_o)$, where K is a constant of proportionality. Clearly, the output voltage is essentially proportional to the difference in the angular displacement between the input shaft and the output shaft over a range of approximately 70°.

Problem 2 Explain how a differential lever can be used in order to provide feedback in a hydraulically operated steering mechanism for a mobile crane.

Fig 18 illustrates a possible arrangement for a hydraulically operated steering system. The hydraulic spool valve and the actuator are arranged to be in the null positions as the steering lever is in the vertical position so that a movement of the steering lever to the left or to the right operates the valve. As the steering lever is moved to the right by an amount x_i, the differential lever pivots initially about point A and causes the spool valve to open an amount x_v. This movement causes high-pressure oil to flow into the actuator port D while low-pressure oil is exhausted from the actuator port E. A pressure differential now exists across the actuator piston so that the piston moves to the left and turns the road wheels accordingly.

However, as the piston moves, the differential lever pivots about point C′ and gradually closes the spool valve. In this way, the resulting road wheel position is proportional to the initial steering lever movement. Naturally, the piston moves as soon as the valve is opened so that the actual valve opening at any instant in time is a function of the difference between x_i and x_o (see Chapter 8).

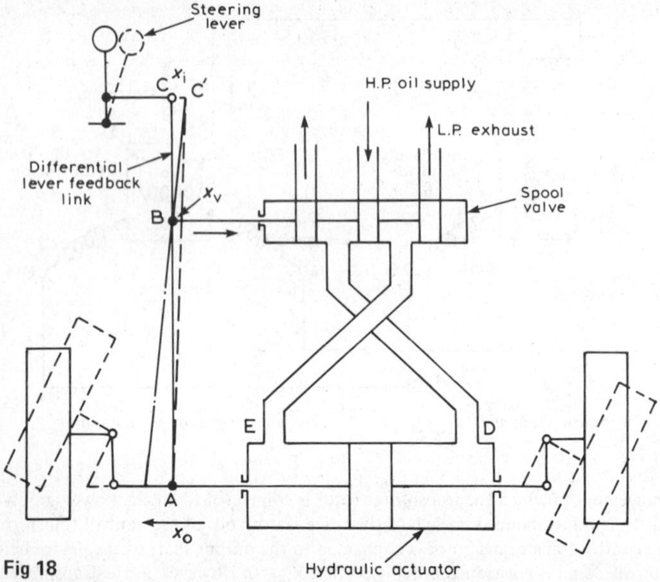

Fig 18

Problem 3 Fig 19 illustrates a liquid level control system. Explain how the system operates and draw a block diagrammatic arrangement of the system. Explain the function of each sub-system.

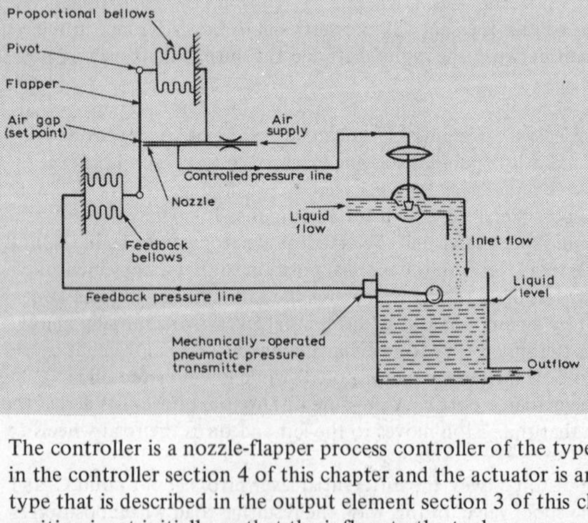

Fig 19

The controller is a nozzle-flapper process controller of the type that is described in the controller section 4 of this chapter and the actuator is an air motor of the type that is described in the output element section 3 of this chapter. The flapper position is set initially so that the inflow to the tank corresponds to the mean outflow from the tank and the liquid remains at a desired level (set-point). However, if the flow demand from the tank increases in relation to the set point, the liquid level tends to fall. The ball cock then senses the reduction in the liquid level and actuates the pressure transmitter, which reduces the air pressure in the feedback pressure line, causing the feedback bellows to contract. The contraction of the bellows opens the nozzle air gap which reduces the controlled pressure. The reduction in the controlled pressure causes the air motor to open the flow control valve which in turn increases the inflow in order to maintain the liquid at a constant level.

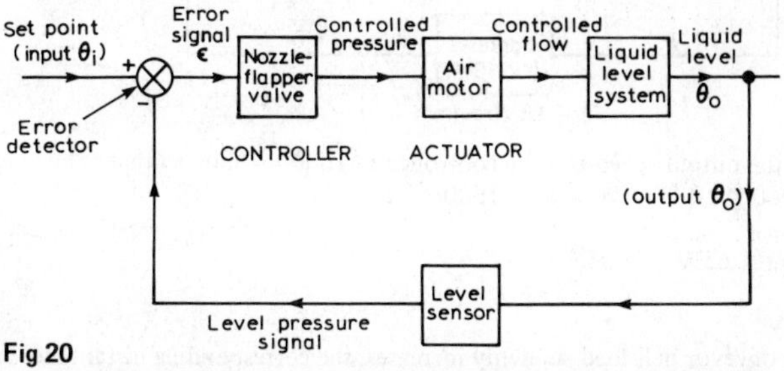

Fig 20

The block diagrammatic arrangement of the system is illustated in *Fig 20*. Here the differential lever of the nozzle-flapper valve is the error detector since it detects changes from the set-point. The nozzle-flapper valve is the controller and the air motor is the control actuator. The ball cock and the pressure transmitter provide the feedback link to the differential lever. In practical situations, the feedback bellows and the nozzle-flapper valve are contained within the same casing along with the means to adjust the set-point and to monitor deviations from the set-point.

Problem 4 The speed of a conveyor belt on which castings are transported from one location to another is regulated by the closed-loop control of the speed of an electric motor. An error-actuated current amplifier drives a high-power relay which in turn drives the electric motor. The motor speed is sensed by a tachogenerator which feeds a voltage signal to an error detector. Draw a block diagram of the arrangement. The gains of the current amplifier, the relay and the electric motor are respectively 60 mA/V, 190 V/A and 85 rev/min/V while the sensitivity of the tachogenerator is 3 mV/rev/min. Calculate the input voltage that is required in order to maintain a motor speed of 1600 rev/min with a particular load on the conveyor belt.

If the load on the conveyor belt is increased suddenly so that the speed falls instantaneously to 1350 rev/min, calculate the instantaneous change in the error voltage.

Fig 21 illustrates the block diagrammatic arrangement of the system. The voltage output from the tachogenerator corresponding to the motor speed of 1600 rev/min is given by

$V_o = 3 \times 10^{-3} \times 1600$ volts $= 4.8$ volts (7.6)

and the corresponding error voltage is

$\epsilon = V_i - 4.8$ (7.7)

The output from the amplifier is $(V_i - 4.8)60 \times 10^{-3}$ A, and the output from the relay is $(V_i - 4.8)60 \times 10^{-3} \times 190$ V, so that the output speed from the motor is

$(V_i - 4.8)60 \times 10^{-3} \times 190 \times 85$ rev/min (7.8)

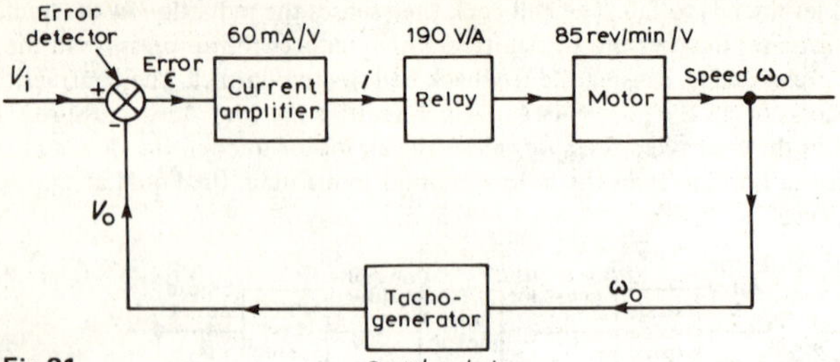

Fig 21

However, the output speed is to be controlled at 1600 rev/min, so that

$(V_i - 4.8)60 \times 10^{-3} \times 190 \times 85 = 1600$

from which

$(V_i - 4.8) = 1.65$ V (7.9)

Therefore

V_i = **6.45 V**

As the conveyor belt load suddenly increases, the corresponding instantaneous error voltage is given by

$6.45 - (3 \times 10^{-3} \times 1350) = 2.4$ V (7.10)

Since the initial error voltage is 1.65 V, from equation (7.9), the instantaneous change in the error voltage is

$2.4 - 1.65 =$ **+ 0.75 V**

Clearly, as the conveyor belt speed falls the error voltage increases. Conversely, as the conveyor belt speed increases due to the removal of castings the error voltage decreases. This situation illustrates the effect of negative feedback.

Problem 5 A closed-loop error-actuated electro-hydraulic servomechanism is used in order to accurately position a die in a die-casting operation. The servomechanism comprises an amplifier which operates a servo-valve and a linear actuator. Negative positional feedback is provided by a displacement transducer which generates a voltage that is proportional to the actuator displacement. Draw a block diagrammatic arrangement of this system.

Estimate the displacement of the die 0.4 s after the sudden application of a command voltage of 12 mV, if the amplifier gain is 1825 mA/V, the servo-valve gain is 0.36×10^{-3} m^3/s.mA, the actuator bore diameter is 85 mm and the transducer sensitivity is 86 mV/m. It may be assumed that the velocity of the actuator is approximately uniform over the specified time period and that the actuator starts from rest. Also, calculate the error signal in mV after this time interval.

Fig 22 illustrates the block diagrammatic arrangement of this system. The instantaneous error signal resulting from the application of the command voltage is

$\epsilon = (12 \times 10^{-3} - 86 \times 10^{-3}\theta_o)$ V (7.11)

so that the amplifier output is

$i = 1825 \times 10^{-3}(12 - 86\theta_o)$ mA (7.12)

The corresponding flow of oil from the servo-valve to the actuator is

$q = 1.825 \times 0.36 \times 10^{-3}(12 - 86\theta_o)$ m^3/s (7.13)

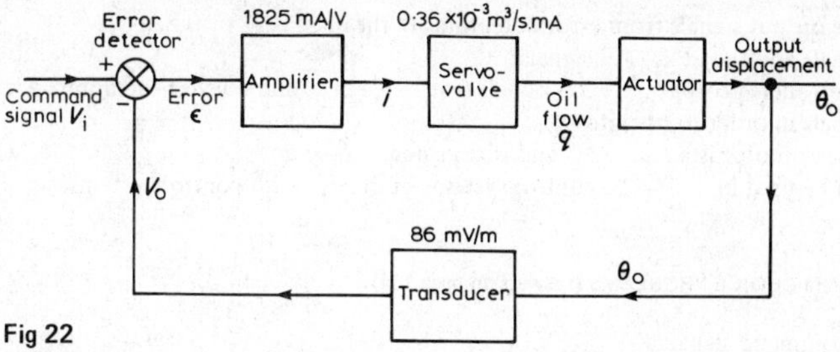

Fig 22

However, neglecting leakage, the rate of oil flow to the actuator is given by equation (7.4), and in this case

$$A_p = \frac{\pi \times 0.086^2}{4}$$

and since the piston velocity is assumed to be uniform

$$v = \frac{\theta_o}{t}$$

Equating equations (7.13) and (7.4) gives

$$1.825 \times 0.36 \times 10^{-3}(12 - 86\theta_o) = \frac{\pi \times 0.086^2}{4} \times \frac{\theta_o}{0.4} \qquad (7.14)$$

from which θ_o = **111 mm**

The corresponding error signal after this time interval is

$\epsilon = 10^{-3}(12 - 86 \times 0.111)$

so that

ϵ = **2.45 mV**

. FURTHER PROBLEMS ON CONTROL SYSTEMS

) SHORT ANSWER PROBLEMS

A control system that regulates a variable in response to a fixed command signal is known as a . . . . system and a control system that follows changes in command signals is known as a . . . . system.

. . . . and . . . . are two types of controllers.

A control system that has no connection between the output and the input is known as an . . . . control system, whereas an error-actuated control system is a . . . . control system.

Error-actuated control systems comprise . . . . , ... and . . . .

The transient characteristic of an instrumentation system or a control system is the . . . . to an input, whereas the steady-state characteristic is the . . . . and the complete response is the . . . .

A system which does not settle to a . . . . after a disturbance is known as an . . . . system.

Control systems usually require . . . . power sources and hydraulic systems require . . . ., ... and . . . . valves.

8 The output signals from error detectors are the . . . . of the . . . . signals and the . . . . signals.
9 Controllers accept . . . . signals from . . . . and convert them into . . . . . . signals in order to operate . . . .
10 A servomotor is a . . . . and is considered to be an . . . . , ... whic can be used in . . . . control systems or in . . . . control systems.

(b) MULTI-CHOICE PROBLEMS (answers on page 184)

1 A command signal is:
(a) the output from a control system;
(b) the input to a control system;
(c) a step signal;
(d) a ramp signal.
2 A servomechanism is generally considered to be:
(a) a process control system;
(b) a temperature control system;
(c) a complex control system;
(d) a positional control system.
3 A control sub-system is:
(a) a control system component;
(b) a controller;
(c) a feedback loop;
(d) a minor system within a control system.
4 Control systems that are used in boiler plant systems are:
(a) process control systems;
(b) positional control systems;
(c) automatic systems,
(d) open-loop control systems.
5 Step input test signals are used in order to examine:
(a) the follow-up characteristics of instrumentation and control systems;
(b) the frequency response characteristics of instrumentation and control systems;
(c) the transient response characteristics of instrumentation and control system
(d) the complete responses of instrumentation and control systems.
6 A step input signal:
(a) starts from zero and rises to a value in zero time;
(b) starts from zero and rises uniformly with time;
(c) changes rapidly with time;
(d) starts from zero, rises to a value and returns to zero in zero time.
7 A control system error detector:
(a) compares the actual output with the desired output;
(b) generates a high-power output signal;
(c) regulates a variable quantity;
(d) amplifies the error signal.
8 A multi-loop control system possesses:
(a) one feedback loop only;
(b) more than one feedback or feedforward loop;
(c) one feedforward loop;
(d) more than one controller.

9 Positional gyroscopes are used in:
   (a) angular velocity control systems where there are no fixed reference points;
   (b) servomechanisms;
   (c) positional control systems where there are no fixed reference points;
   (d) process control systems.

10 Potentiometers and tachogenerators can be combined in order to generate error signals in:
   (a) temperature control systems;
   (b) speed control systems;
   (c) positional control systems;
   (d) electro-hydraulic control systems.

(c) CONVENTIONAL PROBLEMS

1 Distinguish between open-loop control and closed-loop control and give examples of one type of control system in each case. Explain the disadvantages of open-loop control systems.

2 Define three common test signals and explain their principal functions.

3 Describe the operation of a mechanical error detector and an electrical error detector and explain the principal uses of each type.

4 Describe the operation of a hydraulic controller and a pneumatic controller and explain the principal uses of each type. Explain the essential difference between hydraulic control systems and pneumatic control systems.

5 Explain how the control system components described in section (d), (ii), 2 can be used in order to control the speed of an electric motor.

6 Explain the difference between regulator control systems and follow-up control systems. Describe the operating principles of hydraulic, valve-operated, closed-loop positional servo-systems, indicating two ways of generating the feedback signals. State the basic requirements for providing a safe, high-pressure, closed-circuit oil supply for such systems.

7 Explain the following terms:
(a) command signal; (b) error detector; (c) output element. Give examples of the types of equipment that can perform each of these functions.

Linear potentiometers are frequently used in control systems. Describe the operating principles and the main uses of these instruments, clearly illustrating their limitations. Explain how they would normally be used as error detectors in control systems and derive a simple expression for the output signal.

9 The closed-loop control of the speed of a d.c. electric motor can be accomplished by using the following additional sub-systems:
(a) an operational amplifier, (b) a power amplifier; (c) a tachometer generator. Draw a block diagram of a suitable control system arrangement and state the purpose of each sub-system.

In a continuous plant temperature control system, the temperature of a fluid is required to be maintained at 200°C. This is achieved by a process controller that feeds a signal to an electro-pneumatic converter which then feeds a signal to a pneumatic control valve. The control valve regulates the flow of a heating fluid through a heat exchanger. The controlled temperature is measured by a thermocouple which feeds a signal negatively to an error detector. The electro-pneumatic converter has a gain of 6 kPa/mA, the control valve has a gain of 5×10^{-3} m^3/s/kPa, and the relationship between the heating fluid flow and the controlled fluid temperature is 1000°C/m³/s. The sensitivity of the process controller is 2 mA/mA of error.

Draw a block diagram of the arrangement and calculate the feedback sensitivity that is necessary if the input current is 20 mA. Calculate the input signal that is required in order to maintain the same temperature if the feedback sensitivity is increased by 30%.

[Thermocouple sensitivity = 0.0833 mA/°C; input current = 25 mA

10 In a closed-loop electro-hydraulic servomechanism, the error signal is fed to an electronic amplifier that has a gain of 1500 mA/V of error. The signal from the amplifier drives an electro-hydraulic servo-valve which delivers oil to a hydraulic ram. A linear displacement transducer measures the displacement of the ram and feeds a signal to an error detector which compares the feedback signal with the command signal in order to generate the error voltage. Draw a block diagram of th arrangement.

If the valve gain is 0.09×10^{-3} m³/s.mA, the ram bore diameter is 40 mm and the transducer sensitivity is 90 mV/m, calculate the displacement of the ram after a time interval of 1.5 s when the command voltage is 8 mV. Determine the error voltage after this time interval. It may be assumed that the velocity of the ram is uniform over the specified time period.

[Ram displacement = 83.15 mm; error signal = 0.517 mV

11 A closed-loop speed control system is used in order to regulate the speed of a conveyor belt. In this system, an error-actuated current amplifier drives a high-power relay which in turn drives an electric motor. The motor speed is monitored by a tachogenerator which feeds a voltage signal negatively to an error detector. If the gains of the current amplifier, the relay and the electric motor are respectively 50 mA/V, 150 V/A, 75 rev/min/V and the sensitivity of the tachogenerator is 1.5 mV/rev/min, calculate the command voltage that is necessary in order to maintain a speed of 1400 rev/min. If the load on the conveyor belt suddenly increases so that instantaneously the speed falls to 1200 rev/min, calculate the ne error voltage.

[Command voltage = 4.59 V; error voltage = 2.79 V

12 Describe a typical closed-loop control system that can be used in order to control one of the following processes:

(a) control of thickness in a continuous strip mill; (b) control of liquid flow.

Draw a block diagram of the arrangement and indicate the role of any instrumentation that is used. Discuss the merits of using feedback in this application.

13 Devise and describe an automatic control system that can be used in order to deliver sand at a uniform rate to a continuous moulding plant.

8 Transfer functions

A. TRANSFER FUNCTIONS AND TRANSFER OPERATORS

In the control systems that are considered mathematically in Chapter 7, it is assumed that the dynamical behaviour of their sub-systems is linear, that is their outputs are directly proportional to their inputs. However, many control sub-system possess non-linear outputs although their behaviour is assumed to be governed by linear equations of motion. Linear equations of motion can be established for control systems and for control sub-systems. If these equations are expressed in terms of the ratio output/input, they are known as transfer functions or transfer operators. This ratio can be expressed in terms of the Laplace variable s in which case the ratio is known as a transfer function, alternatively the ratio can be expressed in terms of the operator D in which case it is known as a transfer operator. The Laplace variable s is a complex variable and can be written in the form $\alpha + j\omega$. This is a complex number and complex numbers comprise real parts and imaginary parts. In this case, the real part is α and the imaginary part is $j\omega$, where j is defined as $\sqrt{(-1)}$. Complex numbers are considered in greater detail in Chapters 9 and 10.

The Laplace method and the operator D method are both methods of solving linear differential equations, that is, differential equations that can be solved in two parts. However, for the purposes of this text, the variable s and the operator D are considered to be interchangeable. Furthermore, the operator D method of solving differential equations is considered to be more appropriate for solving the relatively simple linear equations that are considered in this text.

WORKED PROBLEMS

THE DERIVATION OF TRANSFER OPERATORS

Problem 1 Derive the transfer operator for the simple damped-spring system that is illustrated in *Fig 1*. Assume that the motion of the spring is viscously damped, that is, damped by an oil-filled dashpot.

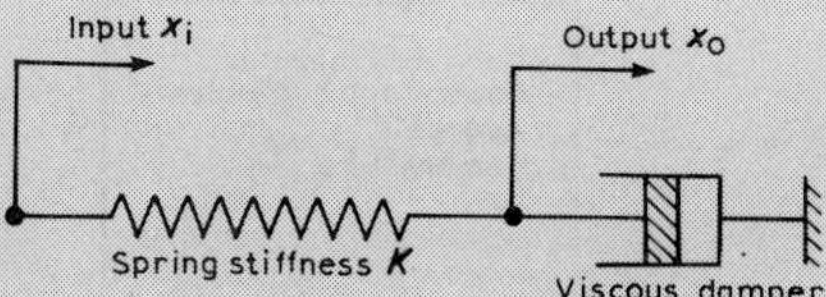

Fig 1

Let the free-end of the spring be displaced by an amount x_i, then the resulting displacement of the attached end of the spring is x_o. The restoring force that is developed by the spring due to the instantaneous spring compression is

$$K(x_i - x_o) \quad (8.1)$$

where K is the spring stiffness (N/m).

The viscous damper generates a force that resists the motion of the attached end of the spring. It is generally assumed that such dampers generate damping forces that are proportional to the dashpot velocities so that in this case the damping force is

$$C\frac{dx_o}{dt} \quad (8.2)$$

where C is the constant of proportionality and is frequently known as the damping coefficient. In order for this system to be in dynamic equilibrium,

$$C\frac{dx_o}{dt} = K(x_i - x_o) \quad (8.3)$$

Rearranging equation (8.3) and expressing the differential dx_o/dt in terms of the operator D as Dx_o gives

$$(CD + K)x_o = Kx_i \quad (8.4)$$

so that

$$\frac{x_o}{x_i} = \frac{K}{CD + K} \quad (8.5)$$

Equation (8.5) can be simplified by dividing the numerator and the denominator of the right side of the equation by K, so that

$$\frac{x_o}{x_i} = \frac{1}{\tau D + 1} \quad (8.6)$$

where τ is the ratio C/K. Since this ratio is the ratio of two constants and possesses units of time, it is known as the **time constant** for the system.

Equation (8.6) is the transfer operator for the damped-spring system and since the differential term is a first-order term this system is known as a first-order system. Frequently, such systems are known as **simple lag** or **simple delay** systems. The solution of first-order differential equations is considered in Chapter 9.

Problem 2 Components requiring heat treatment are heated to a particular steady-state temperature in a gas-fired furnace. As the components are placed in the furnace the temperature of the furnace falls to a minimum temperature. Show that as the furnace temperature rises gradually to its previous steady-state temperature, the time relationship between the furnace temperature and the temperature that is generated by the gas burners is a simple lag relationship.

Fig 2 illustrates the furnace system. Let the thermal capacitance of the furnace be C joule/degree, the gas burner temperature be T_i and the furnace temperature be

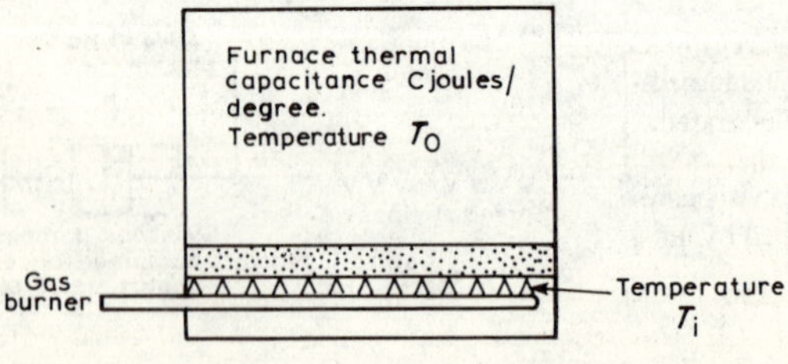

Fig 2

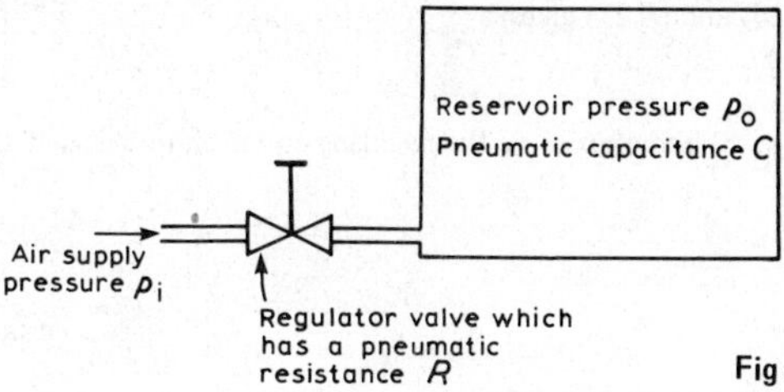

Fig 4

Therefore, if q is the rate of flow of air through the valve at an instant in time, then

$$R = \frac{p_i - p_o}{q} \qquad (8.20)$$

and

$$q = \frac{p_i - p_o}{R} \qquad (8.21)$$

Assuming that there are no air leaks, this flow of air increases the pressure in the reservoir, so that

$$q = C\frac{dp_o}{dt} \qquad (8.22)$$

Equating equations (8.21) and (8.22) gives

$$C\frac{dp_o}{dt} = \frac{p_i - p_o}{R} \qquad (8.23)$$

Rearranging equation (8.23) and expressing the resulting equation in terms of the operator D, gives

$$(RCD + 1)p_o = p_i \qquad (8.24)$$

so that

$$\frac{p_o}{p_i} = \frac{1}{\tau D + 1} \qquad (8.25)$$

where $\tau = RC$ and is the system time-constant.

Problem 5 Derive the transfer operator that governs the dynamical performance of the electrical system that is illustrated in *Fig 5*. Assume that no current is drawn from the output terminals.

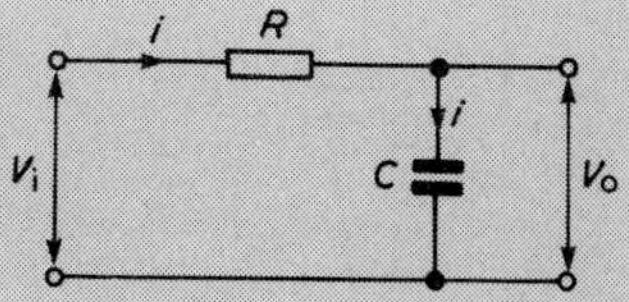

Fig 5

This electrical circuit contains an electrical resistance and an electrical capacitance, so that the system is analogous to the thermal, the liquid level and the pneumatic systems that are considered in *Problems 2, 3 and 4*. In this case, the current flow is equivalent ot the heat flow, the liquid flow or the air flow in the previous cases, so that

$$i = \frac{V_i - V_o}{R} \qquad (8.26)$$

and

$$i = C\frac{dV_o}{dt} \qquad (8.27)$$

Equating equations (8.26) and (8.27) gives

$$C\frac{dV_o}{dt} = \frac{V_i - V_o}{R} \quad (8.28)$$

Rearranging equation (8.28) and expressing the resulting equation in terms of the operator D, gives

$$(RCD + 1)V_o = V_i \quad (8.29)$$

so that

$$\frac{V_o}{V_i} = \frac{1}{\tau D + 1} \quad (8.30)$$

where $\tau = RC$ and is the system time constant.

Problem 6 Derive the transfer operator for the hydraulic steering system that is illustrated in Chapter 7, *Fig 18* (see page 120).

The differential lever movement is illustrated in two parts in *Fig 6*. Referring to *Fig 6(a)*, the initial instantaneous movement of the lever x_i causes an instantaneous valve movement v_i. The relationship between x_i and v_i is given by

$$\frac{x_i}{a+b} = \frac{v_i}{b} \quad (8.31)$$

However, as the actuator movement commences this tends to close the valve by an amount v_o. *Fig 6(b)* illustrates this situation. The relationship between x_o and v_o is given by

$$\frac{x_o}{a+b} = \frac{v_o}{a} \quad (8.32)$$

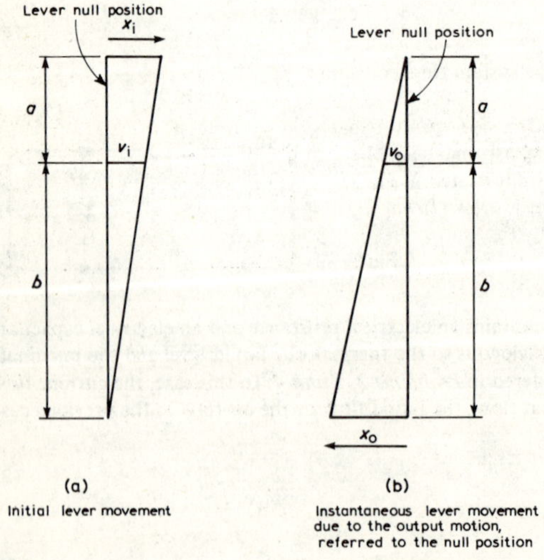

Fig 6

Therefore, the instantaneous valve opening is given by

$$\nu_i - \nu_o = \nu \quad (8.33)$$

From equation (8.31),

$$\nu_i = \frac{bx_i}{a+b} \quad (8.34)$$

while from equation (8.32),

$$\nu_o = \frac{ax_o}{a+b} \quad (8.35)$$

so that

$$\nu = \frac{bx_i}{a+b} - \frac{ax_o}{a+b} \quad (8.36)$$

The rate of flow of oil through the valve to the actuator is assumed to be proportional to the valve opening ν, and if leakage is neglected the piston velocity is proportional to the flow of oil to the actuator.

Therefore, $$\frac{dx_o}{dt} = C\nu \quad (8.37)$$

where dx_o/dt is the piston velocity and C is the constant of proportionality.

Substituting equation (8.36) into equation (8.37) gives

$$\frac{dx_o}{dt} = \frac{C}{a+b}(bx_i - ax_o) \quad (8.38)$$

so that

$$\frac{a+b}{C} \times \frac{dx_o}{dt} + ax_o = bx_i \quad (8.39)$$

Rearranging equation (8.39) and expressing the resulting equation in terms of the operator D, gives

$$\frac{x_o}{x_i} = \frac{b/a}{\tau D + 1} \quad (8.40)$$

where $\tau = (a+b)/aC$ and is the system time constant. The ratio b/a is the final magnification of the movement and is known as the system **gain**. Clearly, this system is a simple lag system.

Problem 7 Show that the transfer operator for the mechanical system illustrated in *Fig 7* can be expressed in the form

$$\frac{x_o}{x_i} = \frac{1}{\tau_1 D^2 + \tau_2 D + 1}$$ where τ_1 and τ_2 are time constants.

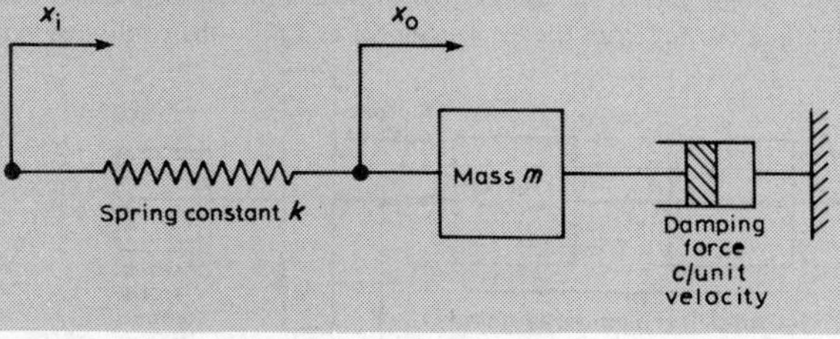

Fig 7

Let the free end of the spring be displaced by an amount x_i, then the resulting displacement of the attached end of the spring is x_o. The restoring force that is developed by the spring due to the instantaneous spring compression is

$$K(x_i - x_o) \quad (8.41)$$

where K is the spring stiffness (N/m). The viscous damper generates a force that resists the motion of the attached end of the spring and, referring to problem 1, it is evident that the damping force is

$$C\frac{dx_o}{dt} \tag{8.42}$$

There is an additional mass in this system so that an additional force is necessary in order to overcome the inertia of the mass. This force is given by Newton's second law of motion, force = mass × acceleration, so that the inertia force is

$$m\frac{d^2x_o}{dt^2} \tag{8.43}$$

In this case, the total resistance to motion is

$$m\frac{d^2x_o}{dt^2} + C\frac{dx_o}{dt} \tag{8.44}$$

while the applied force is the spring force. Therefore, in order for this system to be in dynamic equilibrium,

$$m\frac{d^2x_o}{dt^2} + C\frac{dx_o}{dt} = K(x_i - x_o) \tag{8.45}$$

Rearranging equation (8.45) and expressing the resulting equation in terms of the operator D, gives

$$(mD^2 + CD + K)x_o = Kx_i \tag{8.46}$$

from which

$$\frac{x_o}{x_i} = \frac{K}{mD^2 + CD + K} \tag{8.47}$$

Dividing the numerator and the denominator of equation (8.47) by K gives

$$\frac{x_o}{x_i} = \frac{1}{\tau_1 D^2 + \tau_2 D + 1} \tag{8.48}$$

where $\tau_1 = m/K$ and $\tau_2 = C/K$ are time constants. Clearly, there is an acceleration term in this transfer operator so that this system is a second-order system. Such systems are sometimes known as complex lag systems.

Problem 8 A positional control system comprises an error detector, an amplifier and an electric motor. The motor rotates a flywheel mass that has an inertia I against a viscous damping torque and unity positional feedback is provided. Draw a diagram of the system and derive the transfer operator for the system.

Fig 8 illustrates the block diagram of the system. Assume that the sub-systems are ideal, that is, the amplifier and the electric motor do not introduce transfer delays. Let T be the torque output from the electric motor and K be the combined gain of

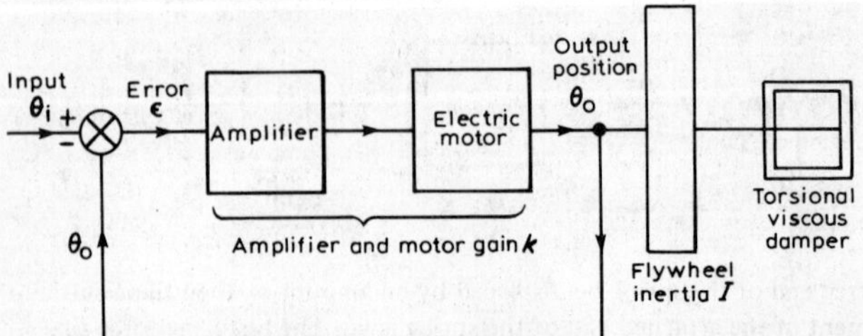

Fig 8

the amplifier and the electric motor. Since this is an error-actuated system, then the torque output from the motor is proportional to the error, so that

$$T = K(\theta_i - \theta_o) \qquad (8.49)$$

However, this output torque has to overcome the viscous damping torque and provide sufficient torque in order to accelerate the flywheel mass. Reference to problems 1 and 7 indicates that in this case the damping **torque** is

$$C\frac{d\theta_o}{dt} \qquad (8.50)$$

and the torque that is necessary in order to accelerate the flywheel mass is

$$I\frac{d^2\theta_o}{dt^2} \qquad (8.51)$$

where I is the flywheel moment of inertia (which is equivalent to mass in translatory systems), $d^2\theta_o/dt^2$ is the angular acceleration of the flywheel, C is the damping torque/unit angular velocity and $d\theta_o/dt$ is the angular velocity of the viscous damper.

It is evident that the total resisting torque is

$$I\frac{d^2\theta_o}{dt^2} + C\frac{d\theta_o}{dt} \qquad (8.52)$$

so that

$$I\frac{d^2\theta_o}{dt^2} + C\frac{d\theta_o}{dt} = K(\theta_i - \theta_o) \qquad (8.53)$$

Rearranging equation (8.53) and expressing the resulting equation in terms of the operator D, gives

$$(ID^2 + CD + K)\theta_o = K\theta_i \qquad (8.54)$$

from which

$$\frac{\theta_o}{\theta_i} = \frac{K}{ID^2 + CD + K} \qquad (8.55)$$

Dividing the numerator and the denominator of equation (8.55) by K gives

$$\frac{\theta_o}{\theta_i} = \frac{1}{\tau_1 D^2 + \tau_2 D + 1} \qquad (8.56)$$

where $\tau_1 = I/K$ and $\tau_2 = C/K$ are time constants.

Clearly, this torque proportional to error system is a second-order system since there is an acceleration term and equation (8.54) is the equation of motion for the system, while equation (8.56) is the transfer operator for the system.

Problem 9 In order to improve the performance of the torque proportional to error positional control system that is described in *Problem 8*, an additional negative velocity feedback loop is added. Draw a diagram of this multi-loop system and explain the influence of the additional feedback loop on the performance of the system.

Fig 9 illustrates the block diagram of the system. A tachogenerator is added to the system so that an additional feedback signal that is proportional to the angular velocity of the output shaft is combined with the error signal. Therefore, the signal that operates the amplifier and the electric motor is now

$$\epsilon - k_t\frac{d\theta_o}{dt} \qquad (8.57)$$

where ϵ is the error signal, k_t is the constant of proportionality for the tachogenerator (tachogenerator gain) and $d\theta_o/dt$ is the angular velocity of the output

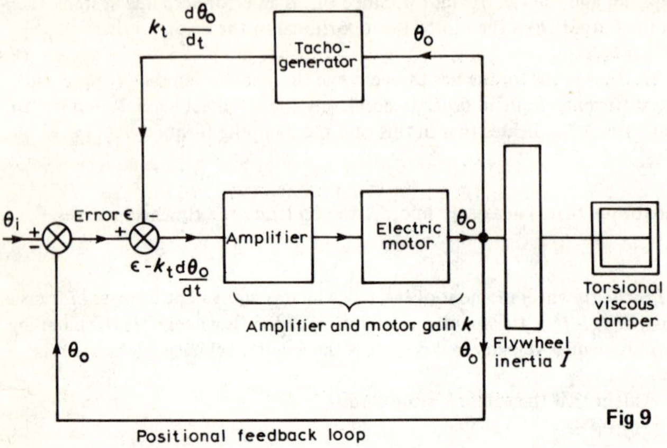

Fig 9

shaft. The torque output from the motor is proportional to this combined signal so that

$$T = K\left[\epsilon - k_t \frac{d\theta_o}{dt}\right] \tag{8.58}$$

or

$$T = K\left[\vartheta_i - \theta_o - k_t \frac{d\theta_o}{dt}\right] \tag{8.59}$$

Equating torques as in problem 8, gives

$$I\frac{d^2\theta_o}{dt^2} + C\frac{d\theta_o}{dt} = K\left[\vartheta_i - \theta_o - k_t \frac{d\theta_o}{dt}\right] \tag{8.60}$$

Rearranging equation (8.60) and expressing the resulting equation in terms of the operator D, gives

$$[ID^2 + (C + Kk_t)\,D + K]\;\theta_o = K\theta_i \tag{8.61}$$

It is evident, by comparing equation (8.61) with equation (8.54), that an additional damping term Kk_t has been generated in the multi-loop system.

The effect of this term is to increase the degree of damping that is present in the system in a way that can be regulated. Since C represents the natural damping that is present in all systems, this cannot be regulated but the tachogenerator circuit can be designed so that different values can be assigned to k_t, for example, by including a potentiometer in this feedback loop. In this way, it is possible to design systems that possess precisely regulated damping characteristics. The technique of creating particular characteristics artificially is known as **synthesis**.

There are many different kinds of feedback and feedforward loops that can be used in order to modify the dynamical behaviour of systems. Some of these feedback and feedforward loops are considered in Chapter 9.

(b) THE ANALYSIS OF MULTI-LOOP SYSTEMS

Problem 10 Determine the open-loop transfer function for a system that comprises three elements that are connected in cascade.

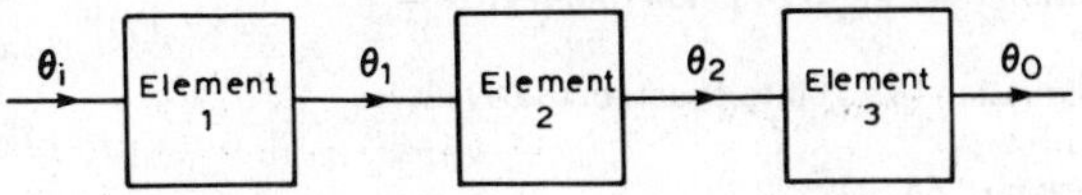

Fig 10

Fig 10 illustrates three control elements connected in cascade. Let the transfer functions of elements 1, 2 and 3 respectively be G_1, G_2 and G_3. Since there are no feedback loops, this is an open-loop system so that the overall open-loop transfer function is θ_o/θ_i. However,

$$\frac{\theta_o}{\theta_i} = \frac{\theta_1}{\theta_i} \times \frac{\theta_2}{\theta_1} \times \frac{\theta_o}{\theta_2} \qquad (8.62)$$

so that

$$\frac{\theta_o}{\theta_i} = G_1 G_2 G_3 \qquad (8.63)$$

Thus the overall open-loop transfer function is given by the product of the transfer functions of the individual elements. This relationship applies to all elements that are connected in cascade.

Problem 11 Derive the closed-loop transfer function for a single-loop closed-loop system that has non-unity feedback, and define open-loop, closed-loop and forward-path transfer functions in this context.

Fig 11 illustrates a block diagrammatic arrangement of the closed-loop system. Let G be the transfer function of all the forward path elements, that is, all the elements whose signals pass from left to right in *Fig 11*. In this case, G is the forward-path

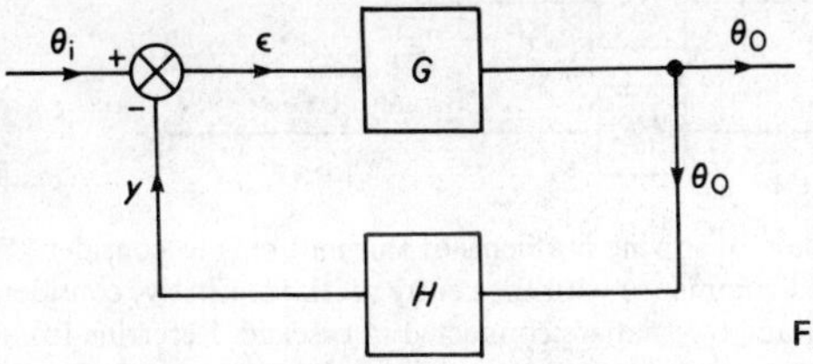

Fig 11

transfer function. Let H be the transfer function of the feedback elements, θ_i be the input signal, θ_o be the output signal and ϵ be the error signal. The forward-path transfer function is

$$\frac{\theta_o}{\epsilon} = G$$

so that

$$\theta_o = G\epsilon \qquad (8.64)$$

Similarly, the feedback transfer function is

$$\frac{y}{\theta_o} = H$$

so that

$$y = H\theta_o \qquad (8.65)$$

Finally, the error signal

$$\epsilon = \theta_i - y \qquad (8.66)$$

Substituting equation (8.66) into equation (8.64) gives

$$\theta_o = G(\theta_i - y) \tag{8.67}$$

and substituting equation (8.65) into equation (8.67) gives

$$\theta_o = G(\theta_i - H\theta_o) \tag{8.68}$$

Rearranging equation (8.68) gives

$$\frac{\theta_o}{\theta_i} = \frac{G}{1 + GH} \tag{8.69}$$

Equation (8.69) is the closed-loop transfer function for the closed-loop system, G is the forward-path transfer function for the closed-loop system and the product GH is the open-loop transfer function for the closed-loop system. In the case of unity feedback, $H = 1$, and in the case of positive feedback the denominator becomes $1 - GH$.

Problem 12 Reduce the multi-loop control system that is illustrated in *Fig 12* to a single-block diagram and determine the overall transfer function for the system.

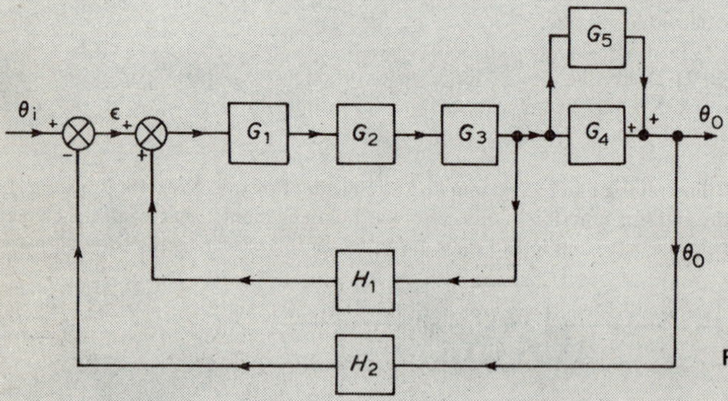

Fig 12

The most convenient method of solving problems of this nature is to consider sections of the systems and commence with the centre sections. Firstly, consider the three elements G_1, G_2 and G_3 that are connected in cascade. Referring to problem 10, it is evident that these three elements can be reduced to a single block whose transfer function is $G_1 G_2 G_3$. Secondly, consider the inner closed-loop H_1. The closed-loop transfer function of this inner loop is given by

$$\frac{G_1 G_2 G_3}{1 - G_1 G_2 G_3 H_1} \tag{8.70}$$

so that this part of the system can be represented by a single block whose transfer function is given by equation (8.70). Thirdly, consider the two elements G_4 and G_5 that are connected in parallel. This part of the system contains a forward path element and a feedforward element. These elements have a common input signal which is processed differently in each case and then recombined at a later stage. Following the procedure that is described in *Problem 11*, it can be shown easily that the overall transfer function for parallel elements is given by the sum of the individual transfer functions. Therefore, in this case the parallel elements G_4 and G_5 can be represented by a single block whose transfer function is $G_4 + G_5$. *Fig 13* illustrates the modified block diagram at this stage.

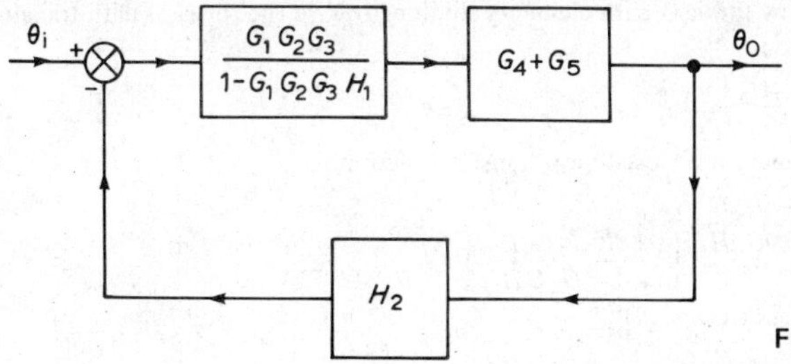

Fig 13

Fourthly, combine the two forward path cascade elements, so that the final forward path transfer function is

$$\frac{G_1G_2G_3(G_4+G_5)}{1-G_1G_2G_3H_1} \tag{8.71}$$

Finally, the overall closed-loop transfer function is

$$\frac{\theta_o}{\theta_i} = \frac{G_1G_2G_3(G_4+G_5)}{(1-G_1G_2G_3H_1)\left[1+\dfrac{G_1G_2G_3(G_4+G_5)H_2}{1-G_1G_2G_3H_1}\right]} \tag{8.72}$$

which reduces to

$$\frac{\theta_o}{\theta_i} = \frac{G_1G_2G_3(G_4+G_5)}{1-G_1G_2G_3H_1+G_1G_2G_3(G_4+G_5)H_2} \tag{8.73}$$

In this way, the multi-loop control system can be represented by a single block whose transfer function is given by equation (8.73).

Problem 13 *Fig 14* is a block diagrammatic arrangement of a multi-loop control system. Reduce the system to a single-block arrangement and determine the closed-loop transfer function for the system.

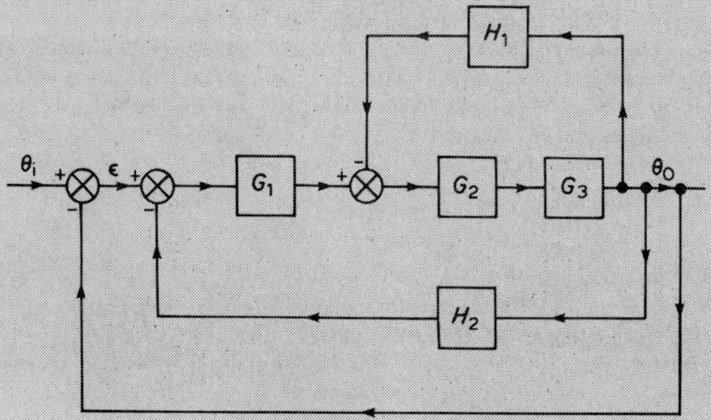

Fig 14

(i) The cascade elements G_2 and G_3 combine to give G_2G_3.

(ii) The transfer function of the feedback loop H_1 is

$$\frac{G_2G_3}{1+G_2G_3H_1} \tag{8.74}$$

(iii) The new forward path elements combine to give the forward path transfer function

$$\frac{G_1 G_2 G_3}{1 + G_2 G_3 H_1} \qquad (8.75)$$

(iv) The inner loop closed-loop transfer function is

$$\frac{G_1 G_2 G_3}{(1 + G_2 G_3 H_1)\left[1 + \dfrac{G_1 G_2 G_3 H_2}{1 + G_2 G_3 H_1}\right]}$$

which reduces to

$$\frac{G_1 G_2 G_3}{1 + G_2 G_3 H_1 + G_1 G_2 G_3 H_2} \qquad (8.76)$$

(v) The overall closed-loop transfer function is

$$\frac{\theta_o}{\theta_i} = \frac{G_1 G_2 G_3}{(1 + G_2 G_3 H_1 + G_1 G_2 G_3 H_2)\left[1 + \dfrac{G_1 G_2 G_3}{1 + G_2 G_3 H_1 + G_1 G_2 G_3 H_2}\right]} \qquad (8.77)$$

since the overall feedback loop gain is unity. Equation (8.77) reduces to

$$\frac{\theta_o}{\theta_i} = \frac{G_1 G_2 G_3}{1 + G_2 G_3 H_1 + G_1 G_2 G_3 H_2 + G_1 G_2 G_3} \qquad (8.78)$$

Equation (8.78) is the overall closed-loop transfer function.

Problem 14 An electro-hydraulic servo controls the position of a machine tool slide in accordance with a command signal from punched tape. A tape reader converts this signal into an electrical command voltage θ_i while a linear displacement transducer feeds back negatively the output position of the slide θ_o which is then compared with θ_i. In addition to the positional feedback, an accelerometer delivers an electrical signal to an operational amplifier which integrates the accelerometer signal and produces a negative voltage that is proportional to velocity. The sum of the error signal and the velocity signal is then fed to an electronic amplifier which has a gain of 20 mA/V input. This amplifier in turn drives an electro-hydraulic control valve. The flow of oil q from the valve operates the hydraulic cylinder which positions the slide.

If the transfer operators for the various sub-systems are:

(i) Valve/cylinder/slide combination, $\dfrac{10}{D(1 + 0.4D)}$;

(ii) positional feedback loop, 50;

(iii) velocity feedback loop, 0.5D,

draw a block diagram for the arrangement and derive the forward path and the closed-loop transfer operators for the complete system.

The block diagrammatic arrangement of the system is illustrated in *Fig 15*.

(i) Combining the cascade elements, namely, the amplifier and the valve/cylinder/slide combination, gives

$$\frac{200}{D(1 + 0.4D)} \qquad (8.79)$$

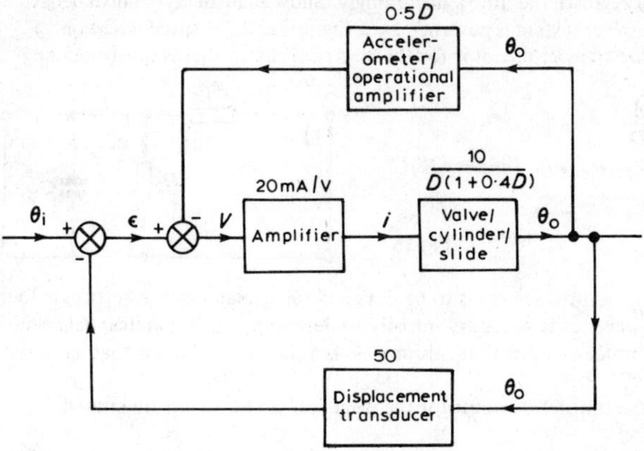

Fig 15

(ii) The closed-loop transfer operator for the inner loop is

$$\frac{200}{D(1+0.4D)\left[1+\dfrac{200\times 0.5D}{D(1+0.4D)}\right]}$$

which reduces to

$$\frac{200}{D(1+0.4D)+100D} \qquad (8.80)$$

Equation (8.80) is the forward path transfer operator for the closed-loop system.

(iii) Finally, the overall closed-loop transfer operator is given by

$$\frac{200}{\left[D(1+0.4D)+100D\right]\left[1+\dfrac{200\times 50}{D(1+0.4D)+100D}\right]} \qquad (8.81)$$

which reduces to

$$\frac{200}{D(1+0.4D)+100D+10000} \qquad (8.82)$$

so that

$$\frac{\theta_o}{\theta_i}=\frac{200}{0.4D^2+101D+10^4} \qquad (8.83)$$

C. FURTHER PROBLEMS ON TRANSFER FUNCTIONS AND TRANSFER OPERATORS

1 Explain the difference between a transfer operator and a transfer function.
2 Derive the transfer operator for a typical first-order pneumatic process.
3 Explain the term 'time constant'. A process control system is required in order to regulate the level of a liquid in a container. In order to design a suitable control system, it is first necessary to establish the dynamical characteristics of the liquid level system. The demand for liquid from the container can vary so that the control

system must regulate the inflow accordingly. Show that the dynamical behaviour of the liquid level system is governed by a first-order differential equation.

4 Show that the transfer operator for the electrical circuit that is illustrated in *Fig 16* is

$$\frac{\theta_o}{\theta_i} = \frac{A}{(A\tau D + 1)}$$

where $A = R_2/(R_2 + R_1)$ and $\tau = R_1 C$.

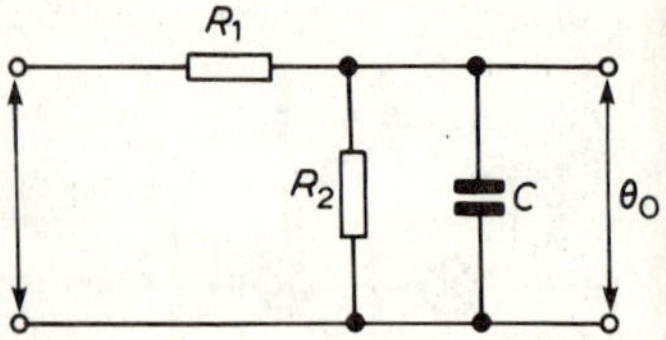

Fig 16

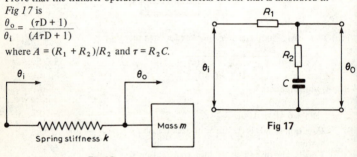

5 A closed-loop control system is to be designed for a small-batch electrical induction furnace. However, it is necessary initially to determine the dynamical behaviour of the thermal process. Show that this process is a simple lag process that has a time constant τ.

6 Prove that the transfer operator for the electrical circuit that is illustrated in *Fig 17* is

$$\frac{\theta_o}{\theta_i} = \frac{(\tau D + 1)}{(A\tau D + 1)}$$

where $A = (R_1 + R_2)/R_2$ and $\tau = R_2 C$.

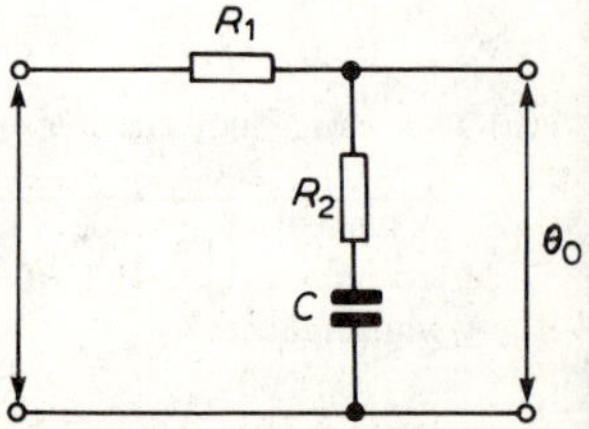

Fig 17

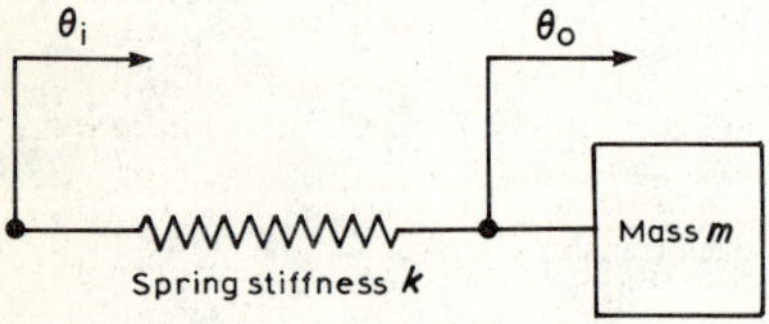

Fig 18

7 Show that the transfer operator for the mechanical system that is illustrated in *Fig 18* is

$$\frac{\theta_o}{\theta_i} = \frac{1}{\tau D^2 + 1}$$

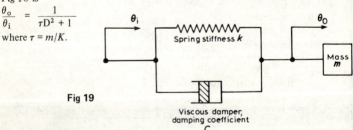

where $\tau = m/K$.

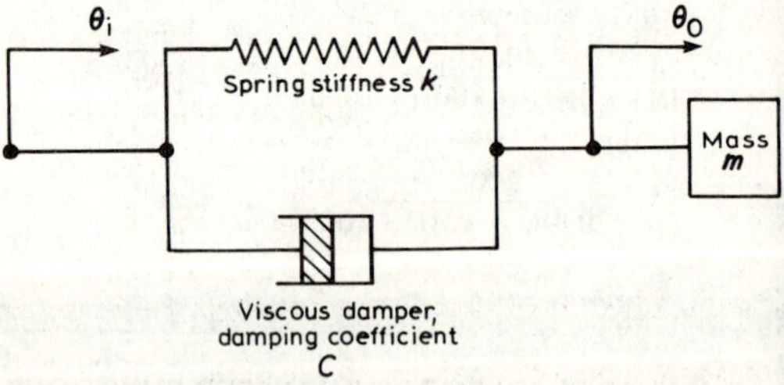

Fig 19

8 Show that the transfer operator for the mechanical system that is illustrated in *Fig 19* is

$$\frac{\theta_o}{\theta_i} = \frac{(\tau_1 D + 1)}{(\tau_2 D^2 + \tau_1 D + 1)}$$

where $\tau_1 = C/K$ and $\tau_2 = m/K$.

9 Prove that the electrical circuit that is illustrated in *Fig 20* is dynamically equivalent to the mechanical system that is illustrated in *Fig 19*.

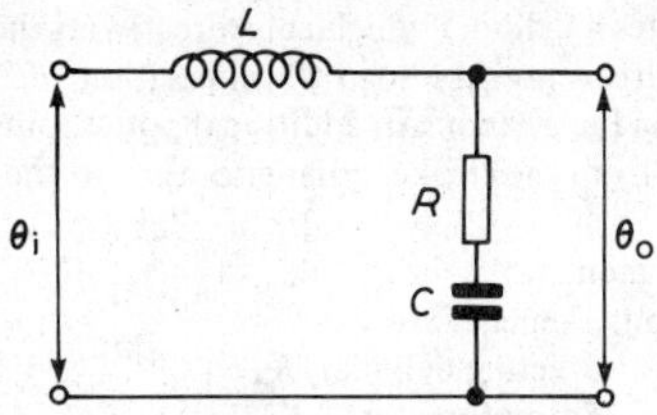

Fig 20

0 The performance of the positional control system that is illustrated in *Fig 8* is to be synthesised by adding a positive acceleration feedback loop. In this case, the signal that actuates the controller is

$$\epsilon + k_a \frac{d^2\theta_o}{dt^2}$$

Show that the equation of motion for the system is

$$[(I - Kk_a)D^2 + CD + K]\theta_o = K\theta_i,$$

and explain the effect of this additional feedback loop upon the system performance.

[The effect of the additional feedback loop is to reduce the effective inertia of the system. This means that the system behaves as though it were driving a smaller mass. This technique is particularly useful in large-mass systems.]

1 In order to regulate the damping of the control system that is illustrated in *Fig 8*, a proportional-plus-derivative controller is connected between the error detector and the amplifier. This type of controller generates a signal that is proportional to the error and also to the first derivative of the error. If the signal that actuates the amplifier is $k_a\epsilon + k_b D\epsilon$, where ϵ is the error signal, show that the transfer operator for the modified system is

$$\frac{\theta_o}{\theta_i} = \frac{Kk_b D + Kk_a}{ID^2 + (C + Kk_b)D + Kk_a}$$

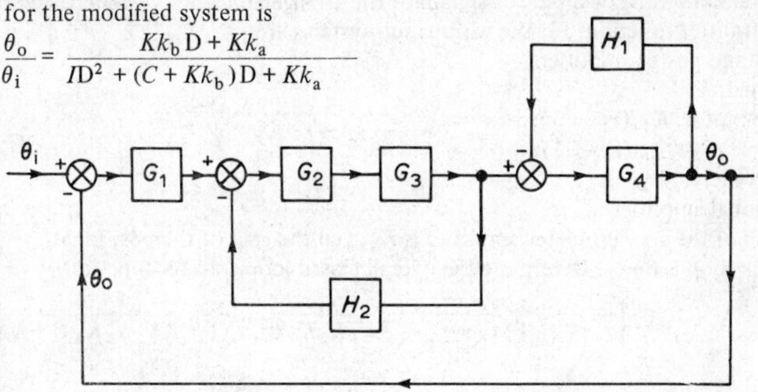

Fig 21

2 *Fig 21* illustrates the block diagrammatic arrangement of a multi-loop control system. By reducing this diagram to a single block, establish the overall transfer operator for the system.

$$\left[\frac{G_1 G_2 G_3 G_4}{1 + G_2 G_3 H_2 + G_4 H_1 + G_2 G_3 G_4 H_1 H_2 + G_1 G_2 G_3 G_4}\right]$$

3 An electro-hydraulic control system is used in order to steer a mechanical digger. The steering-wheel position is sensed by a potentiometric displacement transducer which provides an input θ_i to an amplifier. The amplifier output drives the electro-hydraulic valve which controls the stroke of a variable displacement pump via a

stroke cylinder. Oil from the pump operates a cylinder which acts directly on the steering mechanism. A second potentiometer senses the road wheel position and provides the primary negative feedback for the system. An additional potentiomete provides a second negative feedback loop from the stroke cylinder output to the amplifier input.

(i) Draw a block diagram of this arrangement.

(ii) If the transfer functions for the various elements are:

Amplifier and valve, $K_1/(\tau s + 1)$;	Steering cylinder, K_4/s;
Stroke cylinder, K_2/s;	Potentiometer 2, K_5;
Pump, K_3,	Potentiometer 3, K_6.

Determine, by block diagram reduction, the closed-loop transfer function.

$$\left[\frac{K_1K_2K_3K_4}{s[s(\tau s + 1) + K_1K_2K_5] + K_1K_2K_3K_4K_6}\right]$$

14 The position of a rotatable mass is controlled by an electric motor. The actual position of the mass is sensed by a potentiometer which feeds a negative electrical voltage to an error detector where the feedback signal is compared with a positive electrical command signal. The error signal from the error detector feeds a current amplifier which in turn feeds a power amplifier. The output from the power amplifier drives the electric motor.

In order to improve the performance of this system, negative velocity and positive acceleration feedback is added. This is achieved by mounting an angular accelerometer to the output shaft. In order to complete the acceleration loop, the output from the accelerometer is connected to an amplifier which in turn is connected positively to the input of the current amplifier. The velocity loop is completed by connecting the accelerometer output to an operational amplifier which integrates the acceleration signal and provides a negative voltage that is proportional to the output velocity. This voltage is also fed to the input of the current amplifier. Draw a block diagram of the arrangement.

The transfer functions for the various sub-systems are:

Current and power amplifiers

Combined, K;

Electric motor, $K_1/(\tau_1 s + 1)$;

Rotatable mass, $1/s(\tau_2 s + 1)$,

Accelerometer, $K_2 s^2$,

Operational amplifier, K_3/s.

The gain of the accelerometer amplifier is K_4, and the gain of the positional feedback loop is unity. Determine the overall closed-loop transfer function.

$$\left[\frac{KK_1}{\tau_1\tau_2 s^3 + (\tau_1 + \tau_2 - KK_1K_2K_4)s^2 + (1 + KK_1K_2K_3)s + KK_1}\right]$$

9 Dynamic characteristics of instrumentation and control systems

A. INSTRUMENT AND CONTROL SYSTEM CHARACTERISTICS

Mathematical introduction – the generalised equation of motion

The differential equations that govern the dynamical behaviour of instruments and control systems are usually assumed to be linear and can be expressed in the general form

$$a_n \frac{d^n \theta}{dt^n} + a_{n-1} \frac{d^{n-1} \theta}{dt^{n-1}} + \ldots\ldots\ldots a_1 \frac{d\theta}{dt} + a_o \theta = f(t) \tag{9.1}$$

The function of time indicated on the right side of equation (9.1) is the input or driving function and can be a step input, a ramp input, a sinusoidal input or any other input function. The left side of equation (9.1) contains the mathematical terms that determine the fundamental behaviour of the system or sub-system that is represented by this equation. The value of the power n determines the system order. For example, if $n = 1$ the system that is represented by this equation is known as a first-order system; if $n = 2$ the system is known as a second-order system. Most instruments and systems can be classified in this way.

Consider the equation of motion for an ideal potentiometer,

$$\theta_o = K\theta_i \tag{9.2}$$

where θ_o is the output, θ_i is the input and K is the constant of proportionality. This is a zero-order equation since $n = 0$, and is the equation of an ideal instrument since equation (9.2) indicates that the output is a faithful reproduction of the input.

Similarly, temperature measuring instruments are first-order instruments since their equations of motion have the form

$$\tau \frac{dT_o}{dt} + T_o = T_i \tag{9.3}$$

where T_o is the indicated temperature, T_i is the input temperature and τ is a time constant.

Furthermore, accelerometers usually contain seismic masses so that there is an acceleration term that generates a second-order equation of the form

$$m \frac{d^2 \theta_o}{dt^2} + C \frac{d\theta_o}{dt} + K\theta_o = K\theta_i \tag{9.4}$$

where m is the seismic mass, C is the viscous damping force, K is the spring stiffness, θ_o is the output reading and θ_i is the input. Naturally, accelerometers of this type are second-order instruments.

Control systems can also be classified in this way (see *Worked Problems 2, 3, 4, 5, 6 and 8* in Chapter 8).

Linear differential equations that possess constant coefficients and are characterised by equation (9.1) can be solved by the method of superposition. Th is, such equations can be solved in two stages and the complete solution is determined by adding the two separate solutions. These two solutions are known the **transient solution** and the **steady-state** solution, so that the complete response of a system to an input is the sum of the transient state and the steady state.

(a) FIRST-ORDER SYSTEMS

Consider a first-order system that has a transfer operator of the type

$$\frac{\theta_o}{\theta_i} = \frac{1}{\tau D + 1} \quad (9.$$

The equation of motion for this system is

$$(\tau D + 1)\theta_o = \theta_i \quad (9.$$

This equation can be solved in a variety of ways, but there is a relatively simple systematic way of determining the transient solutions for first-order and second-order systems. However, there are no systematic ways of determining steady-state solutions. Since only first-order and second-order systems are considered in this text, only the systematic method of determining transient solutions is considered. Also, only the particular operational methods relating to step, ramp and sinusoidal inputs are considered for steady-state solutions.

The solution of equation (9.6) can be determined as follows:

(i) Construct and solve the auxiliary equation. This equation is formed by replacir the differential operator by an algebraic variable m and equating θ_i to zero. This equation determines the free response of the system, that is, the response of the system when there is no forcing function. The auxiliary equation that arises from equation (9.6) is

$$\tau m + 1 = 0 \quad (9.$$

from which $m = -1/\tau$ (9.

(ii) Determine the transient solution from the form of the solution of the auxiliar equation. It is evident from equation (9.8), that the solution of the auxiliary equation is a single real root, which is always the case for first-order systems. It can be shown that in this case, the transient solution has the accepted form

$$\theta_{ot} = A \exp(mt) \quad (9.$$

where $m = -1/\tau$ and A is a constant.

(iii) Determine the steady-state solution. The method of determining the steady-state solution depends upon the nature of the driving function. Consider the case of a step input. A step input is effectively a constant-valued input, and the first derivative of a constant is zero. This is the basis for the operational method of determining the steady-state solution. In this case, the procedure is simply to set the operator D equal to zero in the left side of the equation of motion so that the value of θ remaining is the steady-state value. Applying this method to equation (9.6) gives

$$\theta_{oss} = \theta_i \quad (9.1$$

Equation (9.10) clearly indicates that in this case the steady-state output is exactl equal to the input.

(iv) Determine the complete response. The complete response is the sum of the transient response and the steady-state response so that in this case the output from a first-order system that is subjected to a step input is

$$\theta_o = A \exp(-\frac{1}{\tau} t) + \theta_i \quad (9.11)$$

(v) Determine the value of the constant A. Clearly, A is an unknown constant which can be evaluated only if the output at a particular instant in time is known. In the case of a step input, it is usual to assume that $\theta_o = 0$ at the instant $t = 0$. This assumption implies that the system is stationary at the instant that the input is applied. Applying this initial condition to equation (9.11) gives

$$0 = A \exp(0) + \theta_i \quad (9.12)$$

and since exp(0) = 1, then

$$A = -\theta_i \quad (9.13)$$

(vi) Determine the particular response. The response of the system relating to particular conditions is determined by substituting the particular value of the constant into the equation that represents the complete response. Therefore, substituting equation (9.13) into equation (9.11) gives

$$\theta_o = -\theta_i[\exp(-t/\tau)] + \theta_i \quad (9.14)$$

or

$$\theta_o = \theta_i[1 - \exp(-t/\tau)] \quad (9.15)$$

The graphical representation of equation (9.15) is shown in *Fig 1*.

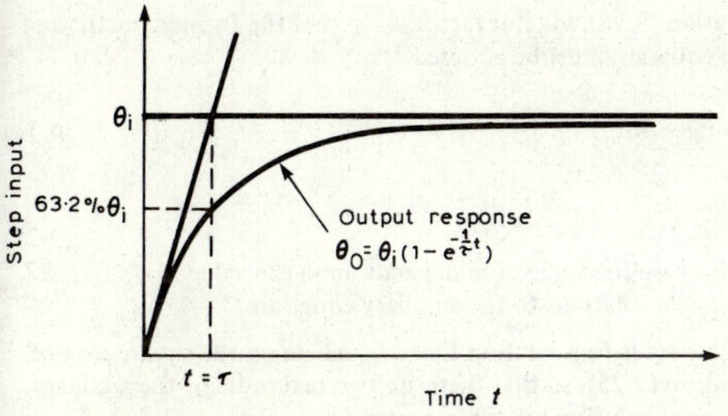

Fig 1

It is evident from *Fig 1* that if the initial rate of change of the output remained at a constant value, then the tangent to the response curve at $t = 0$ cuts the line that represents the input after a time $t = \tau$. Furthermore, if $t = \tau$,

$$\theta_o = \theta_i[1 - \exp(-t/t)] \quad (9.16)$$

so that

$$\theta_o = \theta_i[1 - \exp(-1)] \quad (9.17)$$

and

$$\theta_o = 0.632\, \theta_i \quad (9.18)$$

Equation (9.18) implies that after a time interval of τ, the output reaches 63.2% of its steady-state value. Additionally, when $t = 5\tau$, the output reaches 99.3% of its steady-state value, so that $t = 5\tau$ is a reasonable estimate of the time taken for a first-order system to reach its steady-state.

The frequency response of first-order systems is considered in Chapter 10.

(b) SECOND-ORDER SYSTEMS

The mathematical procedures that were adopted in order to determine the response characteristics of first-order systems can also be applied to second-order systems. Consider the equation of motion for the positional control system that is depicted in Chapter 8, *Problem 8*, namely, equation (8.54) which is repeated here as

$$(ID^2 + CD + K)\theta_o = K\theta_i \tag{9.19}$$

This equation can be expressed in a slightly more convenient form by dividing both sides of the equation by I and letting

$$\frac{C}{I} = 2\zeta\omega_n \tag{9.20}$$

and

$$\frac{K}{I} = \omega_n^2 \tag{9.21}$$

where ζ is a constant that is known as the damping ratio and ω_n is the **undamped natural frequency** of the system. This frequency is the frequency at which the system freely oscillates as it is disturbed if there is no damping present. Substituting equations (9.20) and (9.21) into equation (9.19) gives the alternative form of equation (9.19)

$$(D^2 + 2\zeta\omega_n D + \omega_n^2)\theta_o = \omega_n^2\theta_i \tag{9.22}$$

Equation (9.22) can be solved by following the procedures that are described in section (a), so that the auxiliary equation that is associated with equation (9.22) is

$$m^2 + 2\zeta\omega_n m + \omega_n^2 = 0 \tag{9.23}$$

It is evident that equation (9.23) will not factorise, so that the formula method of solving this quadratic equation must be adopted.

Therefore

$$m = \frac{-2\zeta\omega_n \pm\sqrt{(4\zeta^2\omega_n^2 - 4\omega_n^2)}}{2} \tag{9.24}$$

which reduces to

$$m = -\zeta\omega_n \pm \omega_n\sqrt{(\zeta^2 - 1)} \tag{9.25}$$

It is evident that in this case the value of m depends upon the value of ζ, so that there can be three possible solutions to the auxiliary equation.

Case 1, ($\zeta > 1$) This case leads to a solution that depends upon the square root of a real number in equation (9.25), so that there are two real roots of the auxiliary equation and the transient solution has the accepted form

$$\theta_{ot} = A\exp(m_1 t) + B\exp(m_2 t) \tag{9.26}$$

Of course, this solution is compatible with the transient solution of the first-order system that is considered previously. Equation (9.26) is the sum of two exponential terms so that the transient response graph for this system is similar to the transient response graph of the first-order system. In the case of the second-order system, ζ is large so that the exponential response characteristic is the characteristic of a heavily damped system. Such systems respond slowly and are usually unsuitable for many control applications.

Case 2, ($\zeta = 1$) This is the critical damping case which leads to two equal-valued real roots of the auxiliary equation. The responses of critically damped systems are exponential in form but the degree of damping is just sufficient to prevent any oscillation. Critically damped systems respond more rapidly than overdamped systems but because of their relatively sluggish initial responses they are usually unsuitable for most control applications.

Case 3, ($\zeta<1$) This case leads to a solution that depends upon a pair of complex roots of the auxiliary equation. The majority of instrumentation and control systems are in this category since rapid initial responses are obtained although they can take longer to reach steady states.

Consider equation (9.25). If $\zeta<1$, then $\sqrt{(\zeta^2 - 1)}$ leads to the square root of a negative number which cannot physically be obtained. However, equation (9.25) can be rewritten so that

$$m = -\zeta\omega_n \pm j\omega_n\sqrt{(1 - \zeta^2)} \qquad (9.27)$$

remembering from Chapter 8, section A, that $j = \sqrt{(-1)}$. It is usual to let $\omega = \omega_n\sqrt{(1 - \zeta^2)}$, where ω is the **damped natural frequency** of the system, so that equation (9.27) becomes

$$m = -\zeta\omega_n \pm j\omega \qquad (9.28)$$

The damped natural frequency is the frequency at which the system freely oscillates as it is disturbed when damping is present. It is evident from equation (9.28) that in this case the two roots of the auxiliary equation are $m_1 = -\zeta\omega_n + j\omega$ and $m_2 = -\zeta\omega_n - j\omega$, which are both complex numbers. The only different between these numbers is the sign of the complex parts so that they are known as a **complex conjugate pair**. In such cases, the accepted form of the transient solution is

$$\theta_{ot} = \exp(-\zeta\omega_n t) \times (A \sin \omega t + B \cos \omega t) \qquad (9.29)$$

so that there are two unknown constants A and B and the transient response is oscillatory.

The procedure that is described in section (a) can be followed in order to obtain the steady-state solution for second-order systems. In the case of step inputs, set the operator $D = 0$ in the left side of equation (9.22) so that

$$\omega_n^2\,\theta_o = \omega_n^2\,\theta_i$$

and

$$\theta_{oss} = \theta_i \qquad (9.30)$$

Equation (9.30) indicates that in this case the steady-state output is exactly equal to the magnitude of the step input.

The complete response of second-order systems to step inputs is given by

$$\theta_o = \theta_i + \exp(-\zeta\omega_n t) \times (A \sin \omega t + B \cos \omega t) \qquad (9.31)$$

The constants A and B can be determined by inserting the usually assumed initial conditions relating to step inputs, namely, $\theta_o = 0$ and $D\theta_o = 0$ when $t = 0$.

Fig 2 illustrates the response of a second-order control system to a step input as the system is overdamped, critically damped and underdamped.

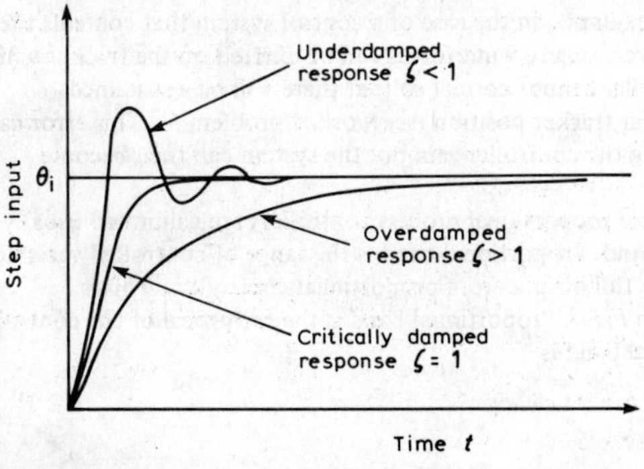

Fig 2

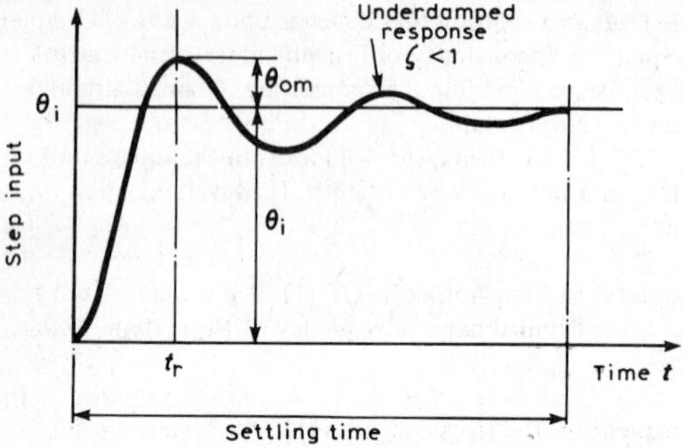

Fig 3

Fig 3 illustrates the underdamped response graph in greater detail. It is evident from *Fig 3* that t_r is defined as the rise-time and that $100\,\theta_{om}/\theta_i$ is defined as the percentage overshoot. The settling time is the time taken for the system to reach a steady state. It can be shown that

$$t_r = \frac{\pi}{\omega} \tag{9.32}$$

and that

$$\text{percentage overshoot} = 100 \exp(-\zeta\omega_n\,\pi/\omega) \tag{9.33}$$

Alternatively,

$$\text{percentage overshoot} = 100 \exp[-\zeta\pi/\sqrt{(1-\zeta^2)}] \tag{9.34}$$

CONTROL ACTIONS

Proportional control action

1 Proportional controllers generate corrective signals that are directly proportional to error signals. In this case, the output from a proportional control system is defined as

$$\delta V = K\epsilon \tag{9.35}$$

where δV is the change in the output variable that is required in order to achieve a correction, K is the constant of proportionality or the gain of the proportional controller and ϵ is the error. The main disadvantage of proportional controllers is that in cases where there is a sustained disturbance on the output side of a control system, the controller takes no corrective action so that there is an accompanying steady-state error. For example, in the case of a control system that controls the position of a radar tracker, steady wind forces can be exerted on the tracker which the proportional controller cannot correct so that there will be a sustained misalignment in the radar tracker position (see worked problem 5). This error can be reduced by increasing the controller gain but the system can then become unstable.

Commercially available proportional process controllers are calibrated usually in terms of **proportional band**. Proportional band is the range of controlled variable deviations that generate full output from proportional controllers. This is illustrated graphically in *Fig 4*. Proportional band is the reciprocal of the controller gain so that proportional band is

$$\text{P.B.} = \frac{100}{K} \tag{9.36}$$

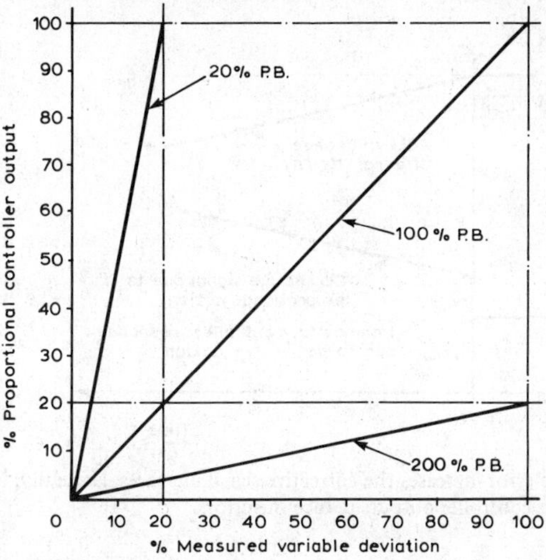

Fig 4

Derivative control action

Derivative controllers generate corrective signals that are proportional to time derivatives of error signals. In this case, the output from a derivative control system is defined as

$$\delta V = K_{\mathrm{d}} \frac{\mathrm{d}\epsilon}{\mathrm{d}t} \tag{9.37}$$

where K_{d} is the gain of the derivative controller. Derivative controllers respond to the **rates of change** of error signals so that these controllers generate outputs as soon as the error signals begin to change. In this way, rapid initial responses are generated in anticipation of eventual errors. However, derivative controllers do not respond to steady-state errors, that is, constant errors, so that they must be combined with proportional controllers.

The output from a proportional plus derivative control system is defined as

$$\delta V = K\epsilon + K_{\mathrm{d}} \frac{\mathrm{d}\epsilon}{\mathrm{d}t} \tag{9.38}$$

which can also be written as

$$\delta V = K(\epsilon + \frac{K_{\mathrm{d}}\,\mathrm{d}\epsilon}{K\mathrm{d}t}) \tag{9.39}$$

Commercially available proportional plus derivative controllers are usually calibrated in terms of proportional band and derivative action time. Derivative action time is defined as the ratio K_{d}/K. Although these controllers generate fast initial responses, sustained deviations still exist in the case of constant errors.

The response of a typical proportional-plus-derivative controller to a uniformly varying error is illustrated in *Fig 5*. In this case, as the error signal begins to change at a uniform rate $\mathrm{d}\epsilon/\mathrm{d}t$ at the instant $t = t_1$, the derivative controller generates an immediate signal that is proportional to $\mathrm{d}\epsilon/\mathrm{d}t$ and that is a constant signal since $\mathrm{d}\epsilon/\mathrm{d}t$ is constant. An additional corrective signal is generated due to proportional

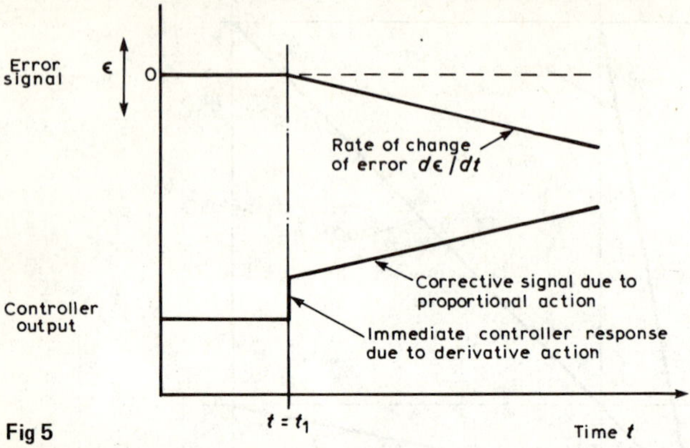

Fig 5

action such that as the error increases the corrective signal increases. Naturally, in practical situations the controller outputs reduce the errors.

Integral control action

3 Integral controllers generate corrective signals that are proportional to time integrals of error signals. In this case, the output from an integral control system is defined as

$$\delta V = K_t \int \epsilon(\mathrm{d}t) \qquad (9.40$$

where K_t is the gain of the integral controller. By differentiating both sides, equation (9.40) can be expressed as

$$\frac{\mathrm{d}\delta V}{\mathrm{d}t} = K_t \epsilon \qquad 9.41$$

Equation (9.41) indicates that the corrective action occurs at a **rate** that is proportional to the error so that an integral controller generates corrective signals until the error is reduced to zero. Therefore, these controllers eliminate steady-state offset but unfortunately they tend to generate oscillatory motions and can become unstable. The stability of these controllers can be improved by combining them with proportional controllers.

The output from a proportional plus integral control system is defined as

$$\delta V = K\epsilon + K_t \int \epsilon(\mathrm{d}t) \qquad (9.42$$

which can also be written as

$$\delta V = K\left[\epsilon + \frac{K_t}{K} \int \epsilon(\mathrm{d}t)\right] \qquad (9.43$$

Commercially available proportional-plus-integral controllers are usually calibrated in terms of proportional band and integral action time. Integral action time is defined as the ratio K/K_t. The response of a typical proportional-plus-integral controller to a step change in error is illustrated in *Fig 6*.

The error signal is considered to remain at a constant value after the instant $t = t_1$. The proportional controller generates an immediate signal that is proportional to the constant error. An additional corrective signal is generated due to integral control action which increases at a rate that is proportional to the error until the error is eliminated.

Proportional, derivative and integral control actions are usually combined in commercial controllers. Such controllers are known as **three-term controllers.**

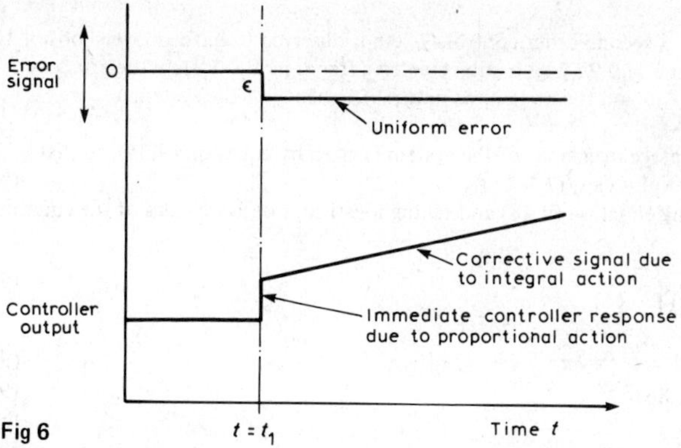

Fig 6

Two-step control action

The previously described controlling devices generate control actions that are continuous within specified ranges of operation. However, two-step controllers possess only two states, namely, 'on' and 'off'. Such controllers regulate variables within specified upper and lower limits so that these controlled variables oscillate continually between these limits. The range through which a controlled variable moves between the upper and the lower limit is known as the **controller differential**. This type of controller is used frequently in relatively inexpensive systems that do not require precise control of variables, such as home heating systems and liquid level systems.

. WORKED PROBLEMS ON THE DYNAMIC CHARACTERISTICS OF INSTRUMENT AND CONTROL SYSTEMS

Problem 1 A thermocouple is plunged into a furnace whose temperature remains steady at 900°C. It is observed that after a time interval of 3 s, the thermocouple indicates a temperature of 750°C. Calculate the thermocouple time-constant, assuming that the temperatures are measured relative to absolute zero temperature.

Consider equation (9.15) since the thermocouple is a first-order instrument and is effectively subjected to a step input as it is plunged into the furnace. Substituting appropriate values into equation (9.15) gives

$$750 = 900[1 - \exp(-3/\tau)] \qquad (9.44)$$

so that

$$-150 = -900 \exp(-3/\tau) \qquad (9.45)$$

and

$$\exp(-3/\tau) = 1/6 \qquad (9.46)$$

Taking logarithms on both sides of equation (9.46) gives

$$-3/\tau = \ln 1/6 \qquad (9.47)$$

from which

$\boldsymbol{\tau = 1.674}$ **s**

Problem 2 A second-order control system is observed to have an overshoot of 10% in a rise-time of 0.2 s as it is subjected to a step input. Calculate the effective damping ratio and the undamped natural frequency of the system.

The percentage overshoot of the system is given by equation (9.34), so that

$$10 = 100 \exp[-\zeta\pi/\sqrt{(1-\zeta^2)}] \quad (9.48)$$

Rearranging equation (9.48) and taking logarithms on both sides of the equation gives

$$\ln 0.1 = \frac{-\zeta\pi}{\sqrt{(1-\zeta^2)}} \quad (9.49)$$

so that

$$2.3026\sqrt{(1-\zeta^2)} = \zeta\pi \quad (9.50)$$

$$1-\zeta^2 = 1.8615\zeta^2 \quad (9.51)$$

and

$\boldsymbol{\zeta = 0.591}$

Following equation (9.27), the damped natural frequency, ω is given by

$$\omega = \omega_n\sqrt{(1-\zeta^2)} \quad (9.52)$$

and from equation (9.32), the rise-time, t_r is given by

$$t_r = \frac{\pi}{\omega} \quad (9.53)$$

However, in this case $t_r = 0.2$ s, so that $\omega = \dfrac{\pi}{0.2}$ (9.54)

Substituting for ω in equation (9.52) gives

$$\frac{\pi}{0.2} = \omega_n\sqrt{(1-\zeta^2)} \quad (9.55)$$

so that the undamped natural frequency, ω_n is given by

$$\omega_n = \frac{\pi}{0.2\sqrt{(1-0.591^2)}} \quad (9.56)$$

from which

$\omega_n = 19.47$ rad/s

or

$f_n = \dfrac{\omega_n}{2\pi} = \mathbf{3.1\ Hz}$

Problem 3 The motion of a moving-coil galvanometer type of instrument can be represented by a second-order differential equation. It is observed that as the instrument pointer is displaced and suddenly released it oscillates at a frequency o[f] 12 Hz. Also, as the instrument is subjected to a step input signal it is observed tha[t] the pointer overshoots by 12%. Calculate:

(a) the effective damping ratio;
(b) the damping force per unit velocity;
(c) the restoring spring stiffness if the effective inertia is estimated to be 0.05 kg m^2.

From equation (9.34),

$$12 = 100 \exp[-\zeta\pi/\sqrt{(1-\zeta^2)}] \quad (9.5$$

Following the procedure described in *Worked Problem 2*,

$\boldsymbol{\zeta = 0.559}$

Also, ω_n can be calculated by following the procedure that is described in worke[d] problem 2, since in this case the damped natural frequency, ω is $12 \times 2\pi = 24\pi$ rad/s, so that $\omega_n = 90.93$ rad/s.

The damping torque per unit angular velocity can be calculated by using equation (9.20), so that

$$C = 2\zeta\omega_n I \tag{9.58}$$

and

$C = 2 \times 0.559 \times 90.93 \times 0.05$

from which

$\mathbf{C = 5.08}$ **Nm/rad/s**

Similarly, the restoring spring stiffness can be calculated by using equation (9.21), so that

$$K = \omega_n^2 I \tag{9.59}$$

and

$K = 90.93^2 \times 0.05$

from which

$\mathbf{K = 413.41}$ **Nm/rad**

Problem 4 The angular position of a rotatable mass which is driven by an electric motor is controlled by an input potentiometer using a closed-loop control system. Draw a block diagram of the system and set up the differential equation assuming that viscous friction is present.

Sketch waveforms showing the output responses that are to be expected from a sudden change in the input as the system is (a) overdamped, (b) critically damped, (c) underdamped.

If the moment of inertia of the moving parts is 900 kg m², the viscous friction force is 1900 Nm/rad/s and the overall forward path gain is 4 kN/rad of misalignment, show that the transient motion is oscillatory. Calculate the percentage overshoot which results from a step input signal.

A block diagrammatic arrangement of the system is illustrated in *Fig 8* of Chapter 8 (see page 000) and the differential equation is derived in *Problem 8* in Chapter 8 (page 000). Equation (8.46) is the equation of motion for the system.

The response waveforms corresponding to the various degrees of damping are illustrated in *Fig 2*.

Substituting values in equations (9.20) and (9.21) gives

$$2\zeta\omega_n = \frac{1900}{900} = \frac{19}{9} \tag{9.60}$$

and

$$\omega_n^2 = \frac{4 \times 10^3}{900} = \frac{40}{9} \tag{9.61}$$

Substituting for ω_n in equation (9.60) gives

$$2\zeta\sqrt{\frac{40}{9}} = \frac{19}{9}$$

from which

$\boldsymbol{\zeta = 0.5}$

Clearly, since $\zeta < 1$ the transient motion of the system is oscillatory.

The percentage overshoot is given by equation (9.34), so that

percentage overshoot = $100 \exp[-0.5\pi/\sqrt{(1 - 0.5^2)}]$

and

percentage overshoot = 16.3%

Problem 5 A closed-loop control system is used to control the position of a radar tracker. The system can be considered to be a second-order system with unity feedback of position and viscous damping. If the tracker is subjected to a steady wind force that exerts a torque T Nm on the control system, show that in the absence of a command signal the steady-state offset is

$$\theta_{oss} = \frac{T}{K}$$

The inertia of the tracker can be considered to be 10^3 kg m^2 and its response as the control system is subjected to a step input is such as to generate an overshoot of 20% in a time of 0.1 s. Calculate the steady-state error as the system is subjected to a ramp input of 20 rev/min with a wind torque of 800 Nm.

Sketch the type of response that is expected.

Fig 8 in Chapter 8 (page 134) illustrates the arrangement of this system, and equation (8.54) is the equation of motion neglecting the wind torque. However, th wind torque effectively provides an additional input and since equation (8.54) is a torque equation, then this equation is modified by the additional torque so that

$$(ID^2 + CD + K)\theta_o = K\theta_i + T \tag{9.62}$$

If the input is zero, then equation (9.62) becomes

$$(ID^2 + CD + K)\theta_o = T \tag{9.63}$$

Clearly, in this case the driving torque is constant, so that the steady-state displacement is obtained by setting D = 0 in the left side of equation (9.63). Therefore,

$$\theta_{oss} = \frac{T}{K} \tag{9.64}$$

The steady-state error that is present in the system as the ramp input is applied can be obtained by modifying equation (9.62). Let

$$\epsilon = \theta_i - \theta_o \tag{9.65}$$

so that

$$\theta_o = \theta_i - \epsilon \tag{9.66}$$

Substituting equation (9.66) into equation (9.62) and neglecting the wind torque gives

$$(ID^2 + CD + K)(\theta_i - \epsilon) = K\theta_i \tag{9.67}$$

from which

$$(ID^2 + CD + K)\epsilon = (ID^2 + CD)\theta_i \tag{9.68}$$

Since in this case the input is a ramp, then $D\theta_i$ is a constant (i.e. constant velocity). Let $D\theta_i = \omega_i$, then $D^2\theta_i = D\omega_i = 0$ since ω_i is a constant. Clearly, equation (9.68) becomes

$$(ID^2 + CD + K)\epsilon = C\omega_i \tag{9.69}$$

The steady-state error is obtained by setting D = 0 in the left side of equation (9.69) since the right side of the equation is constant.

Thus,

$$K\epsilon_{ss} = C\omega_i \tag{9.70}$$

so that

$$\epsilon_{ss} = \frac{C\omega_i}{K} \tag{9.71}$$

Equation (9.71) represents the form of the steady-state error for all second-order systems. Clearly, if K is large then the steady-state error is reduced. However, practical high-gain systems tend to become unstable.

In the case of the radar tracker, the total steady-state error is

$$\frac{C\omega_i}{K} + \frac{T}{K} \tag{9.72}$$

Since ω_i is given, and T is given, then C is required to be calculated before K can be calculated.

The percentage overshoot is given by equation (9.34), so that

$$0.2 = \exp[-\zeta\pi/\sqrt{(1-\zeta^2)}]$$

and

$$\ln 0.2 = -\frac{\zeta\pi}{\sqrt{(1-\zeta^2)}}$$

so that

$$\zeta = 0.456$$

Also, combining equations (9.52) and (9.53) gives

$$\frac{\pi}{t_r} = \omega_n\sqrt{(1-\zeta^2)} \tag{9.73}$$

so that

$$\frac{\pi}{0.1} = \omega_n\sqrt{(1-0.456^2)}$$

and

$$\omega_n = 35.3 \text{ rad/s}$$

The damping torque per unit angular velocity can be calculated by using equation (9.58), so that

$$C = 2 \times 0.456 \times 35.3 \times 10^3$$

and

$$C = 32.19 \times 10^3 \text{ Nm/rad/s} \tag{9.74}$$

Also, from equation (9.59)

$$K = 35.3^2 \times 1000$$

so that

$$K = 1246.09 \text{ kNm/rad} \tag{9.75}$$

Substituting equations (9.74) and (9.75) into equation (9.72) gives

$$\epsilon_{ss} = \frac{39.19 \times 10^3 \times 2\pi \times 20}{1246.09 \times 10^3 \times 60} + \frac{800}{1246.09 \times 10^3} \text{ rad}$$

so that

$$\epsilon_{ss} = 3.14°$$

The response of this system to a ramp input is illustrated in *Fig 7*.

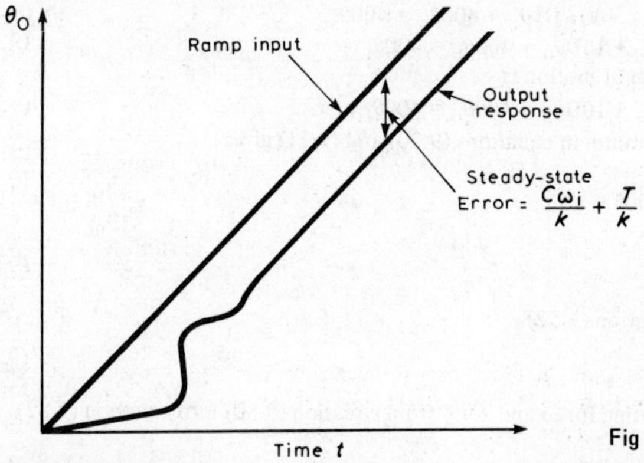

Fig 7

Problem 6 A closed-loop servomechanism is designed in order to control the angular position of a rotatable mass and is stabilised by means of additional acceleration feedback. The moment of inertia of the system is 1.0 kg m², the viscous damping torque per radian per second is 10.0 Nm and the motor torque is given by

$$T = 400\left[\epsilon + \frac{k\,d^2\theta_o}{dt^2}\right] \text{ Nm}$$

where $\epsilon = (\theta_i - \theta_o)$ is the angular position error in radians between the input and the output shafts, and $k\,d^2\theta_o/dt^2$ is the additional feedback signal. Show that the equation of motion for the system is

$$[(1 - 400k)D^2 + 10D + 400]\theta_o = 400\theta_i$$

Determine the value that is to be assigned to k in order that the damped natural frequency of the transient response, ω shall be 40 rad/s, and calculate the corresponding damping ratio.

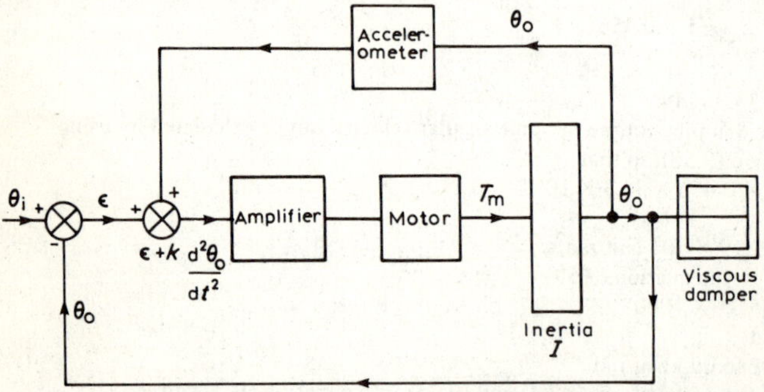

Fig 8

The system is illustrated in *Fig 8*. Refer also to conventional *Problem 10* in Chapter 8. Equating the inertia torque and the damping torque to the driving torque gives

$$I\frac{d^2\theta_o}{dt^2} + C\frac{d\theta_o}{dt} = 400\left[\epsilon + \frac{kd^2\theta_o}{dt^2}\right] \tag{9.76}$$

so that

$$D^2\theta_o + 10D\theta_o - 400\,kD^2\theta_o + 400\theta_o = 400\theta_i \tag{9.77}$$

$$(1 - 400k)D^2\theta_o + 10D\theta_o + 400\theta_o = 400\theta_i \tag{9.78}$$

and the equation of motion is

$$\mathbf{(1 - 400k)D^2\theta_o + 10D\theta_o + 400\theta_o = 400\theta_i} \tag{9.79}$$

Substituting values in equations (9.20) and (9.21) gives

$$2\zeta\omega_n = \frac{10}{1 - 400k} \tag{9.80}$$

and

$$\omega_n^2 = \frac{400}{1 - 400k} \tag{9.81}$$

Also, from equation (9.52)

$$\frac{\omega^2}{\omega_n^2} = 1 - \zeta^2 \tag{9.82}$$

so that substituting for ω and for ζ from equation (9.80) into equation (9.82)

$$\frac{1600}{\omega_n^2} = 1 - \frac{5^2}{\omega_n^2\,(1 - 400k)^2}$$

from which

$$1600(1 - 400k)^2 = \omega_n^2(1 - 400k)^2 - 5^2 \qquad (9.83)$$

Substituting equation (9.81) into equation (9.83) gives

$$1600(1 - 400k)^2 = \frac{400}{1 - 400k}(1 - 400k)^2 - 5^2$$

so that

$$64(1 - 400k)^2 = 16(1 - 400k) - 1 \qquad (9.84)$$

Rearranging equation (9.84) gives

$$10.24 \times 10^6 k^2 - 4.48 \times 10^4 k + 49 = 0$$

and

$$k = \frac{4.48 \times 10^4 \pm \sqrt{(2.007 \times 10^9 - 2.007 \times 10^9)}}{20.48 \times 10^6}$$

so that

$\mathbf{k = 2.19 \times 10^{-3} s^2}$

Using equation (9.81),

$$\omega_n^2 = \frac{400}{1 - (400 \times 2.19 \times 10^{-3})}$$

so that

$\omega_n = 56.8$ rad/s

Substituting for ω_n in equation (9.80) gives

$$\zeta = \frac{5}{56.8[1 - (400 \times 2.19 \times 10^{-3})]}$$

from which

$\boldsymbol{\zeta = 0.71}$

Problem 7 A control system is required to be designed in order to control the position of a winding drum which rotates in frictionless bearings. A proportional controller is to be used which develops a torque of 12 Nm/radian of error. The specification for the system is as follows:

Drum inertia	1.8 kg m^2
Maximum overshoot due to a step input	9% of step magnitude
Rise-time	Not greater than 0.9 s
Overall feedback	Negative, unity

In order to meet this specification, negative velocity and positive acceleration feedback loops are added. Calculate the gains which must be allocated to each of these loops.

The basic system is similar to that illustrated in *Fig 8*, except that here there is no viscous damping and there is an additional negative velocity feedback loop.

In this case, the torque output from the controller is

$$K\left[\epsilon + k_a\frac{d^2\theta_o}{dt^2} - k_v\frac{d\theta_o}{dt}\right]$$

where K is the overall forward gain, k_a is acceleration loop gain and k_v is the velocity loop gain. This torque drives the winding drum so that

$$ID^2\theta_o = K[(\theta_i - \theta_o) + k_a D^2\theta_o - k_v D\theta_o] \qquad (9.85)$$

and

$$[(I - Kk_a)D^2 + Kk_v D + K]\theta_o = K\theta_i \qquad (9.86)$$

Equation (9.86) is the equation of motion for the control system.

From equation (9.34),

$0.09 = \exp[-\zeta\pi/\sqrt{(1-\zeta^2)}]$

so that

$\zeta = 0.608$

It is evident from equation (9.86) that

$$2\zeta\omega_n = \frac{Kk_v}{(I - Kk_a)} \qquad (9.87)$$

and that

$$\omega_n^2 = \frac{K}{(I - Kk_a)} \qquad (9.88)$$

Also, using equation (9.52) and substituting for ω from equation (9.53)

$$\frac{\pi}{0.9} = \omega_n\sqrt{(1-\zeta^2)}$$

so that

$\omega_n = 4.4$ rad/s

Substituting for ω_n, I and K in equation (9.88) gives

$$19.33 = \frac{12}{(1.8 - 12k_a)}$$

from which

$\mathbf{k_a = 0.098\ s^2}$

Similarly, substituting for ζ, ω_n, I, K and k_a in equation (9.87) gives

$$5.35 = \frac{12k_v}{[1.8 - (12 \times 0.098)]}$$

from which

$\mathbf{k_v = 0.278\ s}$

Problem 8 The equation that describes the action of a three-term controller in which only derivative action is used is

$$\theta_{oc} = 10\left[\epsilon + \frac{T_d \mathrm{d}\epsilon}{\mathrm{d}t}\right]$$

where θ_{oc} is the output from the controller, ϵ is the error signal and T_d is the derivative action time. This controller is then used in order to control a process whose transfer operator is

$$\frac{20}{10D^2 + 60D + 800}$$

If negative unity feedback is used, determine the closed-loop transfer operator for the system. Calculate the derivative action time that is required in order to make the closed-loop damping ratio unity.

The controller transfer operator is

$$\frac{\theta_{oc}}{\epsilon} = 10(1 + T_d D) \qquad (9.89)$$

and the forward path transfer operator is

$$\frac{10(1 + T_d D)20}{10D^2 + 60D + 800} \qquad (9.90)$$

so that the closed-loop transfer operator is

$$\frac{10(1 + T_d D)20}{(10D^2 + 60D + 800)\left[1 + \frac{10(1 + T_d D)20}{10D^2 + 60D + 800}\right]} \qquad (9.91)$$

which reduces to

$$\frac{10(1 + T_d D)20}{10D^2 + 60D + 800 + 10(1 + T_d D)20} \quad (9.92)$$

Therefore, the closed-loop transfer operator is

$$\frac{\theta_o}{\theta_i} = \frac{20(1 + T_d D)}{D^2 + (6 + 20T_d)D + 100} \quad (9.93)$$

The **characteristic** equation of a control system is the equation of motion that determines the **free** response characteristics of the system, so that in this case the characteristic equation is

$$[D^2 + (6 + 20T_d)D + 100]\theta_o = 0 \quad (9.94)$$

It is evident from equation (9.94) that $\omega_n^2 = 100$ and $2\zeta\omega_n = (6 + 20T_d)$. Since the system is to be critically damped, then $\zeta = 1$, and $2 \times 1 \times 10 = (6 + 20T_d)$, so that T_d **= 0.7 s**

Problem 9 In a measurement system a pressure-sensitive transducer is connected to an amplifier which in turn is connected to a recorder. The transfer operators of the transducer and the recorder are respectively

$$\frac{2}{1 + 0.1D} \text{ and } \frac{1}{1 + 0.5D}$$

while the amplifier is set to a gain of 5. In order to test the system the pressure transducer is subjected to a step change in pressure of 5 units. If, at the instant that the step signal is applied, the recorder indicates a steady reading of 2 units, show that the output response of the recorder, θ_o is given by

$$10\left[5 + 6\exp(-2t)[\frac{1}{5}\exp(-8t) - 1]\right]$$

Sketch the expected transient response graph.

The overall open-loop transfer operator is

$$5 \times \frac{2}{1 + 0.1D} \times \frac{1}{1 + 0.5D}$$

so that

$$\frac{\theta_o}{\theta_i} = \frac{10}{(1 + 0.1D)(1 + 0.5D)} \quad (9.95)$$

and

$$(1 + 0.1D)(1 + 0.5D)\theta_o = 10\,\theta_i \quad (9.96)$$

is the equation of motion. The auxiliary equation is $(1 + 0.1m)(1 + 0.5m) = 0$, and $m = -10$ or $m = -2$, so that the transient solution is $\theta_{ot} = A\exp(-10t) + B\exp(-2t)$.

Since θ_i is a step input, set D = 0 in the left side of equation (9.96), so that the steady-state solution is $\theta_{oss} = 10\,\theta_i = 50$ and the complete solution is

$$\theta_o = 50 + A\exp(-10t) + B\exp(-2t) \quad (9.97)$$

In order to determine the values of the constants A and B, set $\theta_o = 2$ as $t = 0$, so that

$$2 = 50 + A + B \quad (9.98)$$

Also, $D\theta_o = 0$ as $t = 0$ (i.e. there is no **rate of change** in the recorder output at the instant that the step signal is applied to the transducer), and

$$D\theta_o = -10A\exp(-10t) - 2B\exp(-2t) \quad (9.99)$$

by differentiating equation (9.97).

Substituting the appropriate values in equation (9.99) gives

$$0 = -10A - 2B$$

from which

$B = -5A$. Substituting for B in equation (9.98) gives

$2 = 50 + A - 5A$

so that $A = 12$ and $B = -60$.

The complete solution is

$\theta_o = 50 + 12 \exp(-10t) - 60 \exp(-2t)$

which reduces to $\theta_o = 10\left[5 + 6 \exp(-2t)[\frac{1}{5} \exp(-8t) - 1]\right]$

The expected response is illustrated in *Fig 9.*

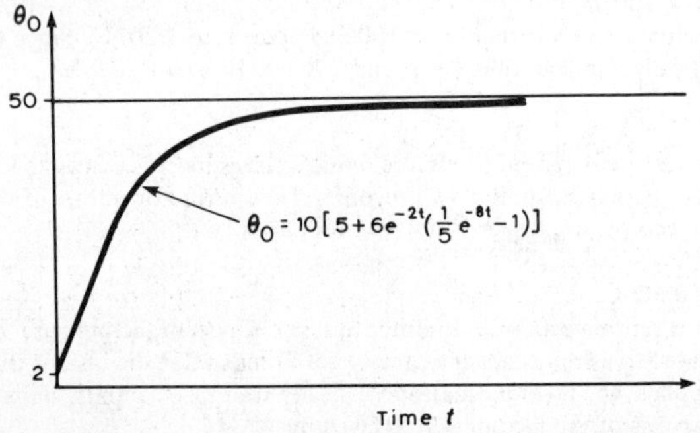

Fig 9

Problem 10 The temperature of a heat treatment furnace is regulated at a nominal 500°C by a two-step controller. Heat may be assumed to be lost from the furnace at a constant rate of 30 joule/s. The furnance temperature is controlled by switching electric heaters such that they are either fully on or fully off. In the fully on position, heat is supplied to the furnace at the constant rate of 50 joule/s. The thermal capacitance of the furnace is 100 joule/°C. The controller is set to give a differential of 10°C and the system dead-band time is 10 s.

Plot a graph illustrating the variation in the furnace temperature with time and deduce the maximum and the minimum furnace temperatures.

Consider the system with the heat switched on. The net flow of heat into the furnace is 50–30 = 20 joule/s, but the rate of flow of heat = $C\,d\theta/dt$, (see Chapter 8) where $d\theta/dt$ is the rate of change of the furnace temperature and C is the thermal capacitance of the furnace. In this case,

$$20 = 100 \frac{d\theta}{dt} \qquad (9.100)$$

so that the rate of change of temperature is 0.2°C/s.

The time taken for the furnace temperature to reach the upper differential limit from the set-point is 5/0.2 = 25 s (i.e. half the differential temperature of 10°). However, there is a time delay of 10 s between the temperature reaching the upper limit and the instant that the temperature begins to fall, so that the maximum temperature overshoots the maximum limit temperature. The overshoot due to the dead-band time is 10 × 0.2 = 2°C.

Consider the system with the heat switched off. The heat loss is 30 joule/s, and from equation (9.100) the reaction rate (rate of decrease of temperature) is 30/100 = 0.3°C/s. The time taken for the furnace temperature to reach the lower

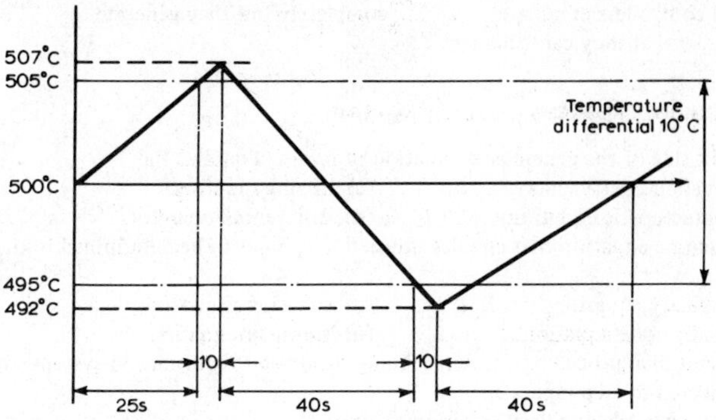

Fig 10

differential limit from the maximum temperature is $(10° + 2°)/0.3 = 40$ s. The overshoot due to the dead-band time = $10 \times 0.3 = 3°C$.

Finally, the time taken for the furnace temperature to reach the set-point temperature from the minimum temperature is $(3° + 5°)/0.2 = 40$ s. The characteristics of the two-step controlled furnace are as follows:

Maximum temperature = 500 + 5 + 2 = **507°C**
Minimum temperature = 500 − 5 − 3 = **492°C**
Cycling time = 25 + 10 + 40 + 10 + 40 = **2 min 5 s**

The response graph is illustrated in *Fig 10.*

C. FURTHER PROBLEMS ON THE DYNAMIC CHARACTERISTICS OF INSTRUMENT AND CONTROL SYSTEMS

(a) SHORT-ANSWER PROBLEMS

1 Linear differential equations that have . . . . coefficients can be solved by the method of . . . .

2 Temperature measuring instruments are . . . . instruments, since the highest differential power in their . . . . is . . . .

3 Accelerometers are usually . . . . instruments since their equations of motion contain . . . . terms.

4 The two solutions of a linear differential equation are known as the . . . . solution and the . . . . solution and the complete solution of the equation is the . . . . of the two solutions.

5 In order to evaluate the constants in a complete solution of a differential equation, the usual procedure is to insert . . . . conditions and to assume that the system is . . . . initially so that as $t = 0$, ... and . . . .

6 The three possible response characteristics of second-order systems are . . . . responses, ... responses and . . . . responses.

7 In the case of underdamped second-order systems, the roots of the auxiliary equations are . . . . pairs, so that the transient responses are . . . .

8 Proportional controllers generate . . . . that are . . . . to error signals but their main disadvantage is that they do not respond to . . . . on their outputs.

9 Derivative controllers respond to . . . . of error signals so that . . . . initial responses are generated but they must be combined with . . . . controllers.

10 Integral controllers eliminate . . . . completely but they generate . . . . motions so that they can become . . . .

(b) MULTI-CHOICE PROBLEMS (answers on page 184)

1 The right side of the generalised equation of motion contains the:
(a) constant coefficients; (c) driving function;
(b) characteristic equation; (d) differential operator.

2 The algebraic equation that enables transient responses to be determined is known as the:
(a) auxiliary equation, (c) equation of motion;
(b) steady-state equation; (d) transient equation.

3 The operational procedure for determining steady-state solutions to systems that are subjected to step inputs is:
(a) to equate the auxiliary equation to zero;
(b) dependent upon the driving function;
(c) dependent upon the transient response;
(d) to equate the differential operator to zero in the characteristic equation.

4 The speed of response of first-order systems is judged by the:
(a) transient response; (c) steady-state value;
(b) time-constant; (d) settling time.

5 The frequency at which an undamped second-order system freely oscillates is the:
(a) damping ratio; (c) resonance frequency;
(b) damped natural frequency; (d) undamped natural frequency.

6 In order for second-order systems to be critically damped the
(a) damping ratio must be less than 1;
(b) underdamped natural frequency must be greater than the damped natural frequency,
(c) damping ratio must equal 1,
(d) damping ratio must be greater than 1.

7 The time that is taken for an underdamped second-order system to reach a peak output in response to a step input is known as the
(a) rise-time; (b) overshoot; (c) response time; (d) settling time.

8 The range of controlled variable deviations that generate full outputs from proportional controllers is known as:
(a) derivative action time, (c) steady-state error;
(b) integral action time, (d) proportional-band.

9 The corrective actions of integral controllers occur at rates that are proportional to the:
(a) time derivatives of error signals; (c) error signals;
(b) time integrals of error signals; (d) two-step signals.

10 Two-step controllers regulate variables within upper and lower limits which are known as:
(a) two-step limits; (c) controller differentials;
(b) three-term limits; (d) controller states.

(c) CONVENTIONAL PROBLEMS

1 Define the following terms that are associated with the dynamical characteristics o measurement systems:
(a) Resonance (see Chapter 10);

(b) flat frequency response,
(c) time-constant.
Measurement systems are classified frequently as first-order or second-order systems. Explain the meaning of this terminology and sketch the responses of such systems as they are subjected to step input signals. Show clearly the effect of damping.

2 A thermocouple has a time-constant of 5 s. If it is suddenly plunged into a furnace that is heated to a temperature of 850°C, calculate the temperature that is indicated by the thermocouple after a time of 5 s. The initial thermocouple temperature can be considered to be zero. Comment upon this result.

[Indicated temperature = 537.3°C. As $t = \tau$, the output is 63.2% of the input]

3 The dynamical response of a temperature measuring instrument is characterised by the equation

$$\frac{d\theta_2}{dt} = K(\theta_1 - \theta_2)$$

where θ_1 is the actual temperature that is being measured, θ_2 is the indicated temperature and K is a constant. Determine the transfer operator for this instrument and derive an expression for its response to a step input. Calculate the time-constant for a particular instrument if it is plunged into a furnace that is heated to a temperature of 1200°C and the temperature that is indicated by the instrument after 7 s is 850°C. Assume that initially $\theta_2 = 0$ when $t = 0$.

$$\left[\text{Transfer operator} = \frac{1}{\tau D + 1}, \text{ where } \tau = 1/K. \text{ Time-constant} = 5.68 \text{ s}\right]$$

The dynamical responses of certain types of transducers are governed by the masses, the viscous damping forces and the stiffnesses of their internal members. State the characteristic equation of motion for such systems and define all the terms in the equation. Comment upon the effects of varying the damping factor and the stiffness of a particular transducer. A transducer of this type is subjected to a step input and is observed to generate an output that has a 20% initial overshoot in a rise-time of 0.01 s. Calculate the effective damping ratio and the undamped natural frequency of the transducer.

[$\zeta = 0.456$; $f_n = 56.18$ Hz]

A voltmeter has a scale that reads from 0 to 100 V. As 50 V is suddenly applied to its terminals, the pointer rises to a maximum reading of 65 V in 1 s before finally coming to rest. If this instrument is then used in order to indicate a voltage that is rising at a steady rate of 10 V/s, what would be the steady-state difference between the true voltage and the indicated voltage?

[Voltage error = 2.25 V]

The position of a machine-tool slide is controlled by the closed-loop control of the angular position of a lead screw. The effective inertia of the load masses referred to the drive shaft can be considered to be 2 kg m^2. The motion of the lead screw is resisted by a damping torque of 5 Nm per unit angular velocity of the drive shaft while the overall forward gain of the control system is 25 Nm/radian of error. Unity feedback of angular position is employed. If the system is subjected to a step input, calculate the percentage overshoot and the corresponding rise-time.

If the machine tool is required to machine a taper such that the slide is required to respond to an input velocity of 0.6 rad/s, calculate the steady-state velocity lag in degrees. (Velocity lag is an alternative term for the steady-state positional error). Describe a technique that is frequently used in order to synthesize the damping characteristics of such systems.

[Overshoot = 30.5%; rise-time = 0.95 s; velocity lag = 6.88°]

7 A closed-loop control system is used in order to regulate the angular position of a mass, the inertia of which is 80 kg m^2. The servomotor torque output is proportional to the misalignment. As the input member is rotated at a constant speed of 150 rev/min, the position of the mass is found to lag behind the input by 12 degrees. Determine the magnitude of the torque output from the servomotor per radian of misalignment and the damping torque per unit angular veloci that is present if the damping ratio is estimated to be 0.2.

In an attempt to improve the response of the system, derivative control action introduced. Show that the equation of motion in terms of the error for the new system is $ID^2\epsilon + (C + KT_d)D\epsilon + kK\epsilon = ID^2\theta_i + CD\theta_i$

Calculate the derivative action time T_d and the proportionality constant k that is required in order to reduce the steady-state velocity error to 2 degrees and to increase the damping ratio to 0.65.

[K = 72 kNm/rad of error; C = 960 Nm/rad/s, k = 6; T_d = 0.093

8 Discuss, with the aid of block diagrams, the advantages of derivative control actio velocity feedback control, and integral control action in servomechanisms. A serv mechanism which employs both positive acceleration and negative velocity feedback drives a load which has an inertia I = 4 kg m^2, forward gain K = 400 Nm/rad; damping force C = 10 Nm/rad/s. Determine the amount of gain that is necessary in each feedback loop in order to generate a response that has a dampir ratio of 0.3 and a natural damped frequency of 3 Hz.

[$k_a = 7.44 \times 10^{-3}\,s^2$; k_v = 0.02 s

9 Explain the purpose and the disadvantages of the following control actions: proportional; proportional-plus-derivative; proportional-plus-integral. Describe, with the aid of diagrams, the responses of each of these controllers to changes in controlled variables.

10 The liquid level in a reservoir is to be maintained at 3 m by a two-step controller. The outflow from the tank is constant at 0.02 m^3/s. Control is effected by varyir an inlet valve from its fully-open position to its fully-closed position. In the fully open position the inlet valve allows liquid to flow into the tank at a rate of 0.025 m^3/s. The tank has a cross-sectional area of 0.5 m^2. Limit switches are set so that there is a differential of 12 cm and the dead-band time is 5 s.

Plot a graph showing how the level varies with time and deduce the maximum and minimum levels and the cycling period that is to be expected.

[Maximum level = 3.11 m; minimum level = 2.74 m; cycling time = 46.25

10 System analysis

. METHODS OF FREQUENCY RESPONSE ANALYSIS

) RESPONSES OF SYSTEMS TO SINUSOIDAL INPUTS

ntroduction

The primary purpose of subjecting instruments and control systems to sinusoidal inputs is to examine the steady-state **stability** of such systems and to facilitate the manipulation of design parameters. It is explained in Chapter 7, section A.(c) (see page 108) that this procedure is known as **frequency response testing** and the responses of systems to sinusoidal inputs are known as **frequency responses**. Clearly, if systems are caused to oscillate sinuosidally, then their outputs are also sinusoidal but usually their outputs **lag behind** their inputs and can be magnified or diminished at particular frequencies depending upon the characteristics of individual systems. The amount by which an output lags behind an input is known as a **phase lag**. Usually, the output magnitude of a system is expressed as the ratio of the output amplitude of the system to the input amplitude. This ratio is known as an **amplitude ratio**.

Sinusoidal signals can be expressed mathematically as complex numbers that are similar in form to the second-order oscillatory transient response that is explained in Chapter 9, A.(b), case 3 (see page 000). In this case, equation (9.28) represents a damped sinusoidal oscillation where the real part of the equation represents the damping and the imaginary part of the equation represents an oscillation whose frequency is ω. However, in the case of a sinusoidal input signal there is no damping so that such signals can be represented by the imaginary term $j\omega_i$ where ω_i is an input frequency.

Only the operational methods of obtaining steady-state solutions are considered in the following cases.

rst-order systems

Consider a first-order system that can be represented by the transfer operator

$$\frac{\theta_o}{\theta_i} = \frac{1}{1 + \tau D} \qquad (10.1)$$

The operational method of calculating the responses of such systems to sinusoidal inputs is to set the operator $D = j\omega_i$, so that equation (10.1) becomes

$$\frac{\theta_o}{\theta_i} = \frac{1}{1 + j\tau\omega_i} \qquad (10.2)$$

Now, the denominator of equation (10.2) is a complex number which can be

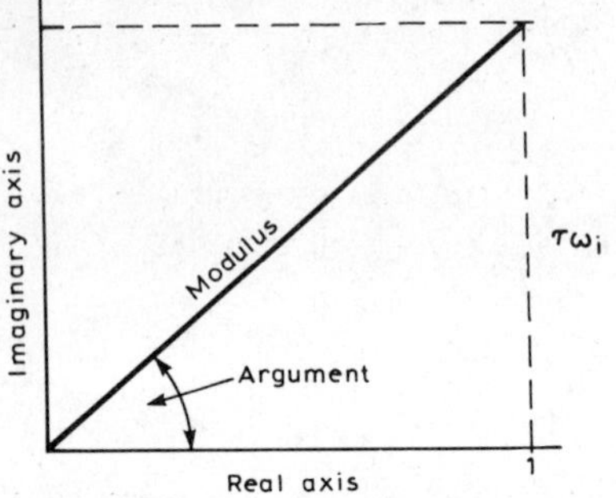

Fig 1

represented on an **Argand** diagram. *Fig 1* is the Argand diagram for the complex number $1 + j\tau\omega_i$. It is evident from *Fig 1*, that complex numbers can be represented by vectors and that the magnitude of a vector is known as the **modulus** and the angle that a vector makes with the zero axis is known as the **argument**.

In the case of the first-order system, the modulus is given by

modulus $= \sqrt{[1 + (\tau\omega_i)^2]}$ (using Pythagoras' theorem), (10.3

and the argument or **phase angle** is given by

$$\text{phase angle} = \arctan \frac{\tau\omega_i}{1} \quad (10.4$$

Clearly, if the system is subjected to a sinusoidal input whose frequency is ω_i, then the output will also be sinusoidal but the output amplitude will not necessarily be the same as the input amplitude. The ratio of the amplitudes is

$$\frac{\theta_o}{\theta_i} = \frac{1}{\sqrt{[1 + (\tau\omega_i)^2]}} \quad (10.5$$

Also, the output from the system will not necessarily be in phase with the input and the phase difference is given by

phase angle (rad) $\phi = \arctan \tau\omega_i$ (10.6

Fig 2 illustrates the relationship between an input frequency and the correspondin output frequency.

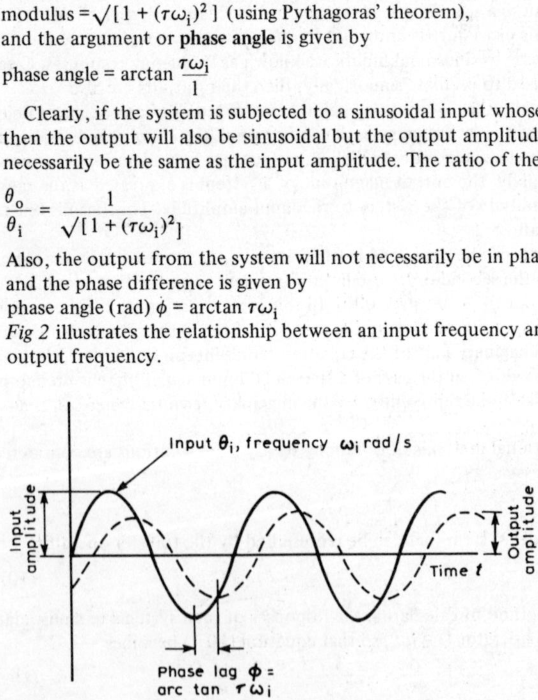

Fig 2

Second-order systems

3 The operational method of calculating the responses of second-order systems is similar to the first-order method. Consider the second-order equation of motion (9.22), then the corresponding transfer operator is

$$\frac{\theta_o}{\theta_i} = \frac{\omega_n^2}{(D^2 + 2\zeta\omega_n D + \omega_n^2)} \quad (10.7)$$

If this system is subjected to a sinusoidal signal that has a frequency ω_i, then set $D = j\omega_i$ in equation (10.7), so that

$$\frac{\theta_o}{\theta_i} = \frac{\omega_n^2}{(j\omega_i)^2 + 2\zeta\omega_n(j\omega_i) + \omega_n^2} \quad (10.8)$$

and

$$\frac{\theta_o}{\theta_i} = \frac{\omega_n^2}{(\omega_n^2 - \omega_i^2) + j(2\zeta\omega_n\omega_i)} \quad (10.9)$$

Clearly, the denominator of equation (10.9) is a complex number which has a

modulus of $\sqrt{[(\omega_n^2 - \omega_i^2)^2 + (2\zeta\omega_n\omega_i)^2]}$

and an argument $\arctan 2\zeta\omega_n\omega_i/(\omega_n^2 - \omega_i^2)$

Thus the system amplitude ratio is

$$\frac{\omega_n^2}{\sqrt{[(\omega_n^2 - \omega_i^2)^2 + (2\zeta\omega_n\omega_i)^2]}} \quad (10.10)$$

and the system phase lag is

$$\arctan\frac{2\zeta\omega_n\omega_i}{(\omega_n^2 - \omega_i^2)} \quad (10.11)$$

Occasionally, it is more convenient to express equations (10.10) and (10.11) in terms of the frequency ratio $r = \omega_i/\omega_n$, so that by dividing the numerators and

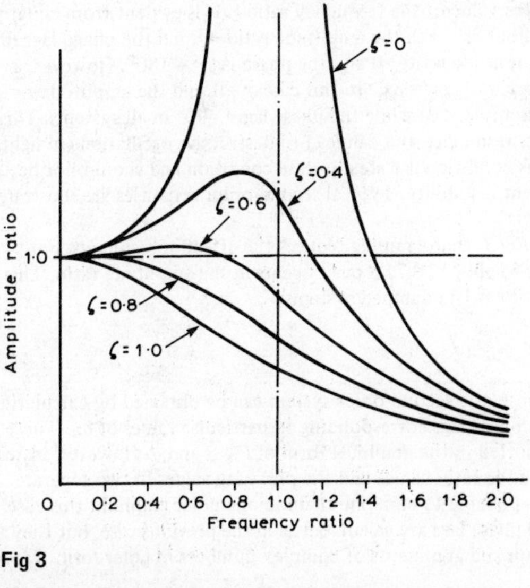

Fig 3

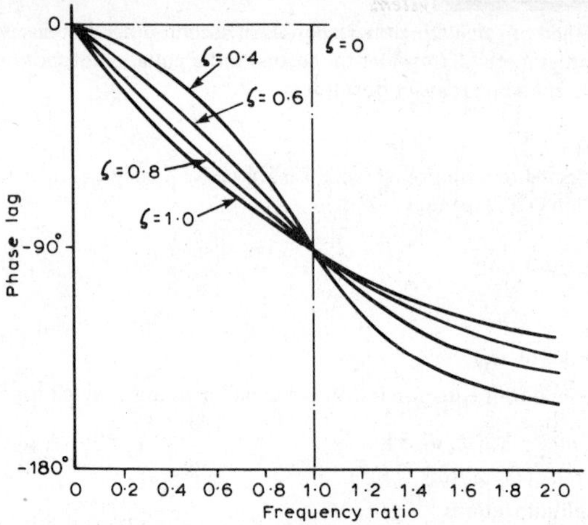

Fig 4

the denominators of equations (10.10) and (10.11) by ω_n^2 the amplitude ratio becomes

$$\frac{1}{\sqrt{[(1-r^2)^2+(2\zeta r)^2]}} \tag{10.12}$$

and the phase lag becomes

$$\arctan \frac{2\zeta r}{(1-r^2)} \tag{10.13}$$

Clearly, the values of the amplitude ratio and the phase lag depend upon the value of ζ and upon the value of the frequency ratio r. It is evident from equations (10.12) and (10.13), that as $r \to 0$, the amplitude ratio $\to 1$ and the phage lag $\to 0$. Also, as $r \to \infty$ the amplitude ratio $\to 0$ and the phase lag $\to -180°$. However, a particular situation occurs as $\omega_i = \omega_n$. In this case, $r = 1$ and the amplitude ratio $\to \infty$ in undamped systems ($\zeta = 0$) while the phase lag $\to -90°$ in all systems. This condition is known as **resonance** and can lead to destructive oscillations in lightly damped systems. This condition is a steady-state condition and should not be confused with transient instability. Typical second-order responses are illustrated in *Fig 3* and *4*.

It is evident from *Fig 3*, that damping reduces the effect of resonance but nevertheless, in cases where $\zeta < 0.71$ a peak occurs in the amplitude ratio. This peak does not occur at $r = 1$ in damped systems.

(b) NYQUIST DIAGRAMS

The frequency response of a second-order system can be obtained by calculating amplitude ratios and phase lags corresponding to particular values of ω_i. These values can then be plotted in the graphical form of *Fig 3* and *4*. However, instead of plotting the amplitude ratio values and the phase lag values in two separate cartesian graphs, it is possible to combine them in one polar graph. In this case, amplitude ratios and phase lags are calculated as in the previous case, but they are then plotted as moduli and arguments of complex numbers in polar form. *Fig 5*

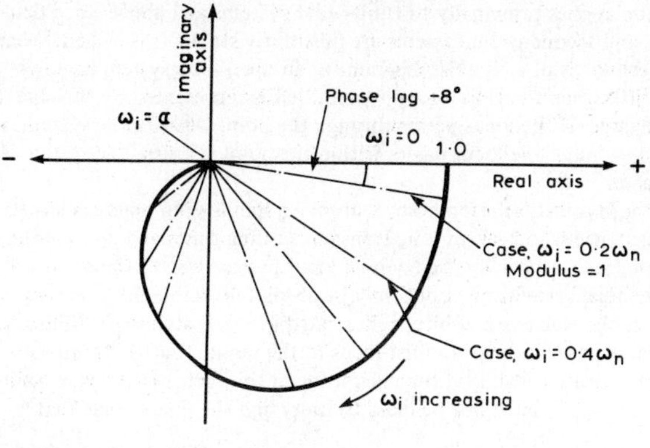

Fig 5 $\zeta = 0{\cdot}6$

illustrates a polar graph for the case $\zeta = 0.6$. This type of graph is known as a Nyquist diagram. This polar graph is typical of second-order systems but similar graphs can be plotted for any other type of system.

Frequently, it is not possible to analyse systems in this way and engineers are often confronted with physical hardware without knowing its dynamical characteristics. In such cases sinusoidal input signals can be applied physically and amplitude ratios and phase lags can be measured. Therefore, it is possible to plot Nyquist diagrams from measured data and to deduce the forms of transfer operators from the shapes of these diagrams.

Furthermore, it is possible to conduct such frequency response tests on **open-loop** systems that can become **unstable** in **closed-loop** conditions, since frequently instability is caused by closing loops. In these cases, it is possible to deduce from Nyquist diagrams whether **closed-loop** systems are stable or unstable and the adjustments to design parameters that need to be made in order to rectify unstable conditions. Nyquist formulated a certain condition that must be fulfilled in order to ensure **absolute** closed-loop stability and this is known as the **Nyquist Stability Criterion**. The Nyquist stability criterion is illustrated in *Fig 6*.

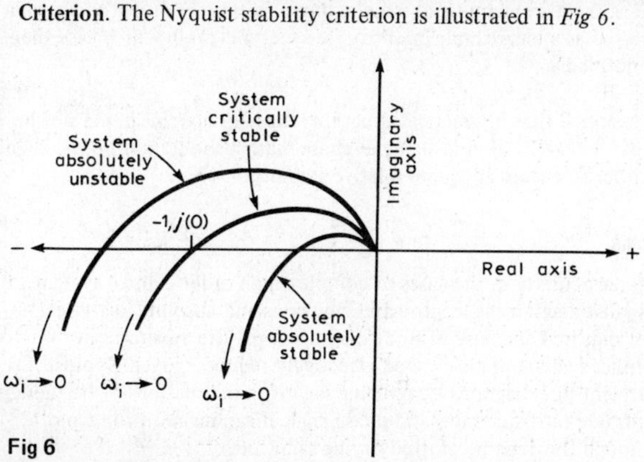

Fig 6

This criterion applies principally to third-order systems and above since first-order systems and second-order systems are inherently stable. It is evident from *Fig 6*, that if the locus of a Nyquist diagram for an open-loop system **encloses** the point $-1, j(0)$, then the closed-loop system that is represented by this diagram is **absolutely unstable**. If the locus passes **through** the point $-1, j(0)$, the system is **critically stable** while if the locus passes **within** the point $-1, j(0)$, the system is **absolutely stable**.

Although the Nyquist criterion ensures absolute stability, in practical situations this can be insufficient to prevent long transient settling times and continuous transient oscillations, especially if a Nyquist locus passes close to the point $-1, j(0)$. Therefore, practical systems must not only be absolutely stable but also they must be **relatively** stable. Relative stability is illustrated in *Fig 7*. Relative stability is a measure of the closeness of a Nyquist locus to the point $-1, j(0)$. In order to ensure adequate relative stability, the magnitude of the vector that corresponds to a phase angle of $-180°$ must not be close to unity and the phase angle that

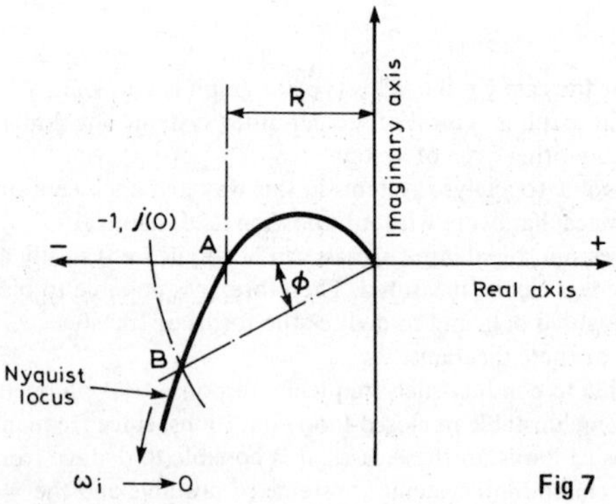

Fig 7

corresponds to the unit vector must not be close to $-180°$. These two criteria are known respectively as the **gain margin** and the **phase margin**. It is evident from *Fig 7* that $1-R$ is the gain margin and ϕ is the phase margin. Frequently, the gain margin is expressed as a logarithmic quantity (see section (c)) in which case the gain margin is defined as

$$20 \log_{10} (1/R) \text{ dB} \tag{10.14}$$

It is generally assumed that in practical situations the gain margin should not be less than approximately 10 dB and that the phase margin should not be less than about 50° in order to ensure adequate relative stability.

(c) BODE DIAGRAMS

In many cases, particularly in the cases of complex high-order control systems, the plotting of Nyquist diagrams is lengthy and laborious and absolute analytical accuracy is not required. The use of Bode diagrams provides an alternative way of analysing complex systems. This method effectively reduces curved Nyquist diagrams to straight-line diagrams by plotting logarithmic functions of frequency. However, amplitude ratio diagrams and phase angle diagrams need to be plotted separately although they can be plotted on the same axes.

In this case, amplitude ratios corresponding to a range of frequencies are expressed as decibels (dB) by calculating logarithms to the base 10 of the amplitude ratios and scaling them by multiplying by the scaler quantity 20. Phase lags are calculated and plotted in the normal way.

The algebraic factors that are encountered most frequently in transfer operators are (D), $(1 + \tau D)$ and $(\tau_1 D^2 + \tau_2 D + 1)$, and by setting $D = j\omega_i$, they become $(j\omega_i)$, $(1 + j\tau\omega_i)$ and $[\tau_1 (j\omega_i)^2 + \tau_2 (j\omega_i) + 1]$. These factors can occur in the numerators and in the denominators of transfer operators and transfer functions and can be raised to any power.

Case 1: Transfer function = $(j\omega_i)$ This is a complex number which has the form $0 + j\omega_i$, so that the modulus is ω_i and the argument is 90° for any value of ω_i. The modulus expressed in decibels is

$$20 \log_{10} \omega_i \qquad (10.15)$$

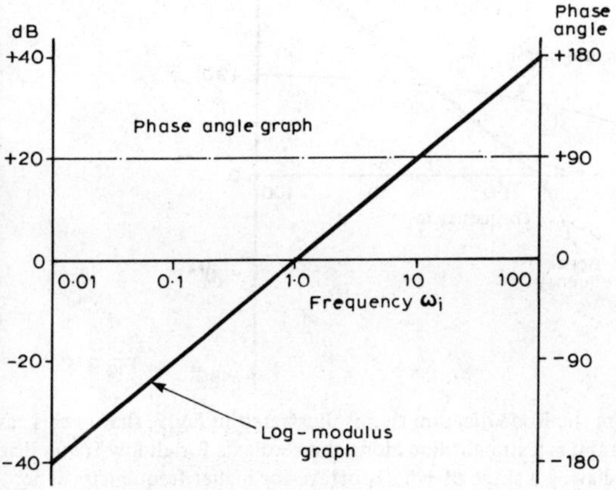

Fig 8

The table below shows the value of the log-modulus for a range of input frequencies and *Fig 8* illustrates the Bode diagram for this case. The frequency increments are usually considered to be in the ratio 2:1 or in the ratio 10:1. The former ratio is known as an **octave** and the latter ratio is known as a **decade**.

ω_i (rad/s)	*log-mod* (dB)
0.01	−40
0.10	−20
1.00	0
10.00	+20
100.00	+40

Clearly, in this case the slope of the log-modulus graph is uniform and is equal to +20 dB/decade. This is also equivalent to +6 dB/octave. The log-modulus graph for the inverse function $1/j\omega_i$ is also a straight-line graph but has a slope of −20 dB/decade or −6 dB/octave and a phase lag −90°. Any function which has the form $(j\omega_i)^n$ has a straight-line log-modulus graph and a slope $6n$ dB/octave.

Case 2: Transfer function = $(1 + j\tau\omega_i)$ This is a complex number that has a modul

$$\sqrt{(1 + \tau^2 \omega_i^2)} \quad (10.1$$

and an argument arctan $\tau\omega_i$. The modulus expressed in decibels is

$$20 \log_{10}\sqrt{(1 + \tau^2 \omega_i^2)} \quad (10.1$$

Clearly, values of the log-modulus depend upon the value of τ as well as values of ω_i.

Consider the case where $\tau\omega_i$ is much less than 1. Here, $\sqrt{(1 + \tau_i^2)} \rightarrow 1$ so that the log-modulus $\rightarrow$ 0 dB. Next, consider the case where $\tau\omega_i$ is equal to 1. Here, $\sqrt{(1 + \tau^2 \omega_i^2)} = \sqrt{2}$, so that the log-modulus = + 3 dB. Finally, consider the case where $\tau\omega_i$ is much greater than 1. Here, $\sqrt{(1 + \tau^2 \omega_i^2)} \rightarrow \tau\omega_i$ and the **slope** of the log-modulus graph $\rightarrow$ + 6 dB/octave in view of case 1 and the fact that τ is a constant.

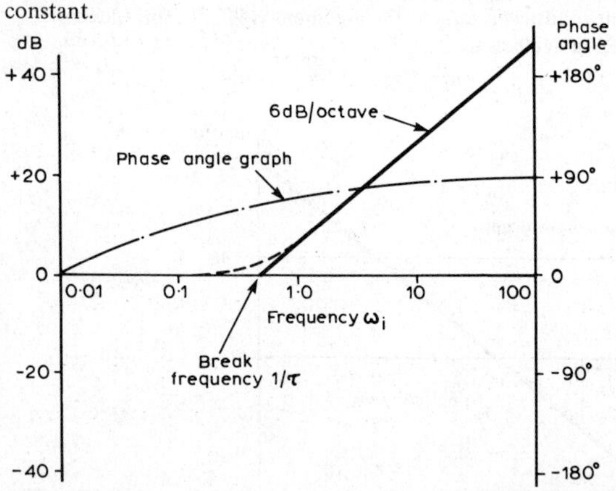

Fig 9

It is evident from the Bode diagram that is illustrated in *Fig 9*, that in this case the log-modulus graph is a straight line along the zero axis for all low frequencies and a straight line having a slope of + 6 dB/octave for higher frequencies. The frequency value at which the slope changes is known as the **break frequency** and i assumed to occur as $\tau\omega_i = 1$, so that the break frequency = $1/\tau$.

Although the actual log-modulus plot is a curve, these straight lines approxima to the curve. This method is known as the **asymptotic approximation method** and the maximum error occurs at $\omega_i = 1/\tau$ and never exceeds ± 3 dB. The phase angle varies from zero at zero frequency to + 90° at infinite frequency.

The log-modulus graph for the inverse function $1/(1 + j\tau\omega_i)$ is also a straight li along the zero axis for low frequencies and the slope breaks at $\omega_i = 1/\tau$. However in this case the slope of the log-modulus graph at higher frequencies is – 6 dB/ octave. The phase angle varies from zero at zero frequency to –90° at infinite frequency.

Case 3: Transfer function = $[\tau_1 (j\omega_i)^2 + \tau_2 (j\omega_i) + 1]$ This quadratic function car occur in the numerators and in the denominators of transfer functions but it is most frequently encountered in denominators. Quadratic functions can occasionally be factorised so that they form products of the case 2 functions. Th method of calculating the log-moduli and the phase angles of quadratic functions identical to the previous cases.

3. WORKED PROBLEMS ON THE FREQUENCY-RESPONSE ANALYSIS OF SYSTEMS

Problem 1 A thermocouple which has a time constant of 1.674 s is used in order to measure the temperature of a continuous process plant where the temperature varies sinusoidally between 725°C and 675°C over a time period of 15 s (i.e. half-cycle). Calculate the corresponding maximum and minimum temperatures that are indicated by the thermocouple, the time delay in seconds and the percentage dynamic error.

The time taken for the temperature to complete one cycle is 30 s, so that the cycling frequency is given by $f = 1/30$ Hz, and since $\omega = 2\pi f$, the frequency input to the thermocouple is

$$\omega_i = \frac{2\pi}{30} = 0.2094 \text{ rad/s}$$

Since thermocouples are first-order instruments, the amplitude ratio in this case is given by equation (10.5). Substituting values in equation (10.5) gives

$$\frac{\theta_o}{\theta_i} = \frac{1}{\sqrt{[1 + (1.674 \times 0.2094)^2]}} = 0.9437$$

The peak-to-peak temperature variation is 725°C – 675°C = 50°C, so that the temperature amplitude is 25°C. The corresponding thermocouple indicated amplitude is $\theta_o = 0.9437 \times 25 = 23.59$°C.

Thus the maximum indicated temperature is **723.59°C** and the minimum indicated temperature is **676.41°C**.

The phase angle is $\phi = \arctan\ \tau\omega_i = \arctan(1.674 \times 0.2094) = 0.3372$ rad so that the corresponding time delay is $\phi/\omega i$

i.e. $\dfrac{0.3372}{0.2094} = \mathbf{1.61\ s}$

Finally, the dynamic error is given by

$$\left(\frac{25 - 23.59}{25}\right)100 = \mathbf{5.64\%}$$

Problem 2 The transfer function for a second-order control system is

$$\frac{\theta_o}{\theta_i} = \frac{10}{s^2 + 5s + 25}$$

If the system is subjected to a unit-amplitude sinusoidal input signal which has a frequency of 0.5 Hz, establish an expression for the steady-state response of the system.

In this case, the input frequency, $\omega_i = 2\pi \times 0.5 = \pi$ rad/s. Also, the input amplitude is 1, so that the sinusoidal input signal can be expressed as

$$\theta_i = 1 \times \sin\pi t \qquad (10.18)$$

Now, sinusoidal quantities can be expressed as complex numbers, so that equation (10.18) can be written as

$$\theta_i = \exp(j\pi t) \qquad (10.19)$$

The transfer function for the control system can be expressed as

$$\theta_o = \frac{10\,\theta_i}{s^2 + 5s + 25} \qquad (10.20)$$

so that

$$\theta_o = \frac{10 \exp(j\pi t)}{s^2 + 5s + 25} \tag{10.21}$$

Set $s = j\omega_i$ in equation (10.21), so that

$$\theta_o = \frac{10 \exp(j\pi t)}{(j\omega_i)^2 + 5(j\omega_i) + 25} \tag{10.22}$$

$$\theta_o = \frac{10 \exp(j\pi t)}{-\pi^2 + 5j\pi + 25} \tag{10.23}$$

and

$$\theta_o = \frac{10 \exp(j\pi t)}{15.14 + j15.71} \tag{10.24}$$

The modulus of the complex number in the denominator of equation (10.24) is

$$\sqrt{(15.14^2 + 15.71^2)} \tag{10.25}$$

so that the modulus = 21.8 (10.26)

Also, the phase angle of the complex number in the denominator of equation (10.24) is

$$\phi = \arctan \frac{15.71}{15.14} = 46.06°$$

so that

$$\phi = 0.8039 \text{ rad} \tag{10.27}$$

Complex numbers such as that in the denominator of equation (10.24) can also be expressed in the form of equation (10.19) so that

$$15.14 + j15.71 = 21.8 \exp(j0.8039) \tag{10.28}$$

and equation (10.24) becomes $\theta_o = \dfrac{10 \exp(j\pi t)}{21.8 \exp(j0.8039)}$ (10.29)

Combining the complex numbers in the numerator and in the denominator of equation (10.29) gives

$$\theta_o = 0.459 \exp[j(\pi t - 0.8039)] \tag{10.30}$$

Rearranging equation (10.30) into sinusoidal form gives

$$\boldsymbol{\theta_o = 0.459 \sin(\pi t - 0.8039)} \tag{10.31}$$

It is evident from equation (10.31) that the control system output is a sinusoidal quantity whose amplitude is 0.459 (compared with unity input amplitude) and whose frequency is $\omega_i = \pi$. However, there is a phase lag of 0.8039 rad between the input and the output.

Problem 3 An accelerometer, an amplifier and a U/V recorder are used in order to measure vibration levels in a machine. The sensitivity of the accelerometer is 50 mV/g, the amplifier gain is set to 100 mA/mV and the recorder galvanometer has a transfer function

$$\frac{x_d}{x_i} = \frac{100}{s^2 + 380s + 10^5}$$

where x_d is the trace displacement (cm) and x_i is the input current (mA).

Establish an expression for the steady-state recorder movement as the measurement system monitors a sinusoidal vibration that has an acceleration amplitude of 1g at a frequency of 16 Hz. State the trace amplitude and the phase lag in degrees.

The overall transfer function for the measurement system is

$$\frac{x_d}{\theta_i} = \frac{5 \times 10^5}{s^2 + 380s + 10^5} \tag{10.32}$$

The input frequency, $\omega_i = 2\pi \times 16 = 32\pi$ rad/s and the input amplitude is 1g, so that

$$\theta_i = \sin 32\pi t = \exp(j32\pi t) \tag{10.33}$$

Set $s = j\omega_i$ in equation (10.32), so that

$$x_d = \frac{5 \times 10^5 \exp(j32\pi t)}{-(32\pi)^2 + 380j32\pi + 10^5} \tag{10.34}$$

$$x_d = \frac{5 \times 10^5 \exp(j32\pi t)}{(8.99 \times 10^4) + (j3.82 \times 10^4)} \tag{10.35}$$

and

$$x_d = \frac{50 \exp(j32\pi t)}{8.99 + j3.82} \tag{10.36}$$

The modulus of the complex number in the denominator of equation (10.36) is

$$\sqrt{(8.99^2 + 3.82^2)} \tag{10.37}$$

so that the modulus = 9.77 (10.38)

Also, the phase angle of the complex number in the denominator of equation (10.36) is

$$\phi = \arctan \frac{3.82}{8.99} = 23°$$

so that $\phi = 0.402$ rad (10.39)

Equation (10.36) becomes $x_d = \dfrac{50 \exp(j32\pi t)}{9.77 \exp(j0.402)}$ (10.40)

so that $x_d = 5.12 \exp[j(32\pi t - 0.402)]$ (10.41)

The steady-state recorder movement is therefore

$\mathbf{x_d = 5.12 \sin(32\pi t - 0.402)}$ (10.42)

In this case, the trace amplitude is 5.12 cm and the phase lag is 0.402 rad.

Problem 4 Plot a Nyquist diagram for a control system that has a performance characteristic that is governed by the open-loop transfer function

$$\frac{\theta_o}{\theta_i} = \frac{5}{1 + 0.1s}$$

Comment upon the closed-loop stability of this system.

Set $s = j\omega_i$ in the open-loop transfer function and calculate the amplitude ratio and the phase lag corresponding to a range of values of ω_i.

ω_i (rad/s)	$\sqrt{[1 + (0.1\omega_i)^2]}$	$\dfrac{5}{\sqrt{[1 + (0.1\omega_i)^2]}}$	$\phi = \arctan 0.1\omega_i$ (degrees)
1.0	1.0	5.0	− 6
2.0	1.02	4.9	−11
5.0	1.12	4.46	−27
10.0	1.41	3.55	−45
20.0	2.24	2.23	−63
50.0	5.10	0.98	−79
100.0	10.05	0.50	−84

The Nyquist diagram for this system is illustrated in *Fig 10*.

It is evident from *Fig 10* that the locus of the moduli does not extend beyond the first quadrant. Clearly, systems that are characterised by first-order transfer functions are inherently absolutely stable and relatively stable.

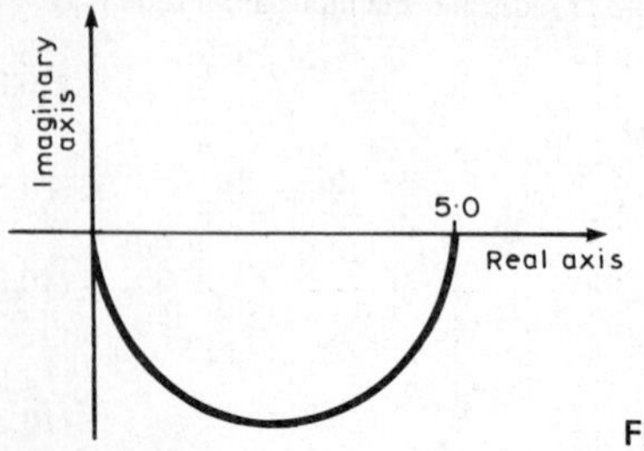

Fig 10

Problem 5 The performance of a third-order control system is characterised by the open-loop transfer function

$$\frac{\theta_o}{\theta_i} = \frac{2}{s(1+s)(1+0.5s)}$$

Plot a Nyquist diagram for this system and comment upon the absolute closed-loop stability of the system. Determine the gain and the phase margins and comment upon the relative closed-loop stability of the system.

Set $s = j\omega_i$ in the open-loop transfer function and calculate the amplitude ratio and the phase lag corresponding to a range of input frequencies. The modulus of the open-loop system is

$$\frac{2}{\omega_i \times \sqrt{(1+\omega_i^2)} \times \sqrt{[1+(0.5\omega_i)^2]}} = \frac{2}{\omega_i\, A.B}$$

where $A = \sqrt{(1+\omega_i^2)}$ and $B = \sqrt{[1+(0.5\omega_i)^2]}$

Similarly, the phase lag of the open-loop system is

$$-(\arctan \frac{\omega_i}{0} + \arctan\ \omega_i + \arctan\ 0.5\omega_i)$$

ω_i (rad/s)	$(j\omega_i)$		$(1+j\omega_i)$		$(1+0.5j\omega_i)$		*Amplitude*	*Phase*
	Mod	*Phase*	*A*	*Phase*	*B*	*Phase*	*ratio*	*lag*
0.8	0.8	90	1.28	39	1.08	22	1.81	−151
0.9	0.9	90	1.35	42	1.10	24	1.50	−156
1.0	1.0	90	1.41	45	1.12	27	1.27	−162
1.2	1.2	90	1.56	50	1.17	31	0.91	−171
1.5	1.5	90	1.80	56	1.25	37	0.59	−183
2.0	2.0	90	2.24	63	1.41	45	0.32	−198
5.0	5.0	90	5.10	79	2.69	68	0.03	−237

The Nyquist diagram for this system is illustrated in *Fig 11*. It is evident from *Fig 11* that the closed-loop system is absolutely stable since the locus of the moduli does not encompass the point −1, j(0). The phase margin for the closed-loop system is approximately 13° while the gain margin is approximately 20 $\log_{10}$ (1/0.66), so that the gain margin is approximately 3.61 dB. Clearly, although the system is absolutely stable, the relative stability is inadequate for most purposes.

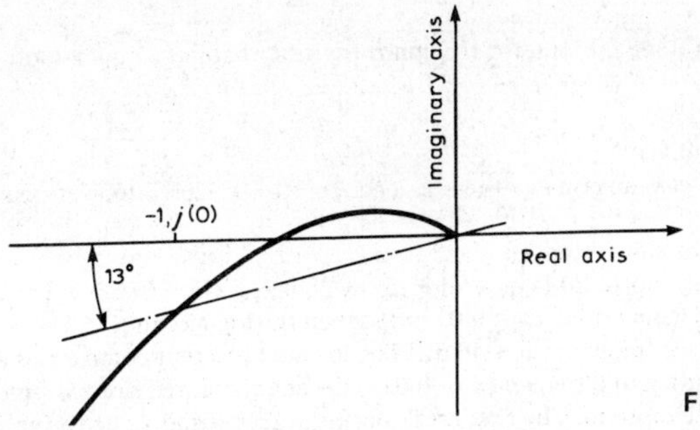

Fig 11

The relative stability of the system can be improved by reducing the overall gain from 2 to say 1.5 or 1.0.

Problem 6 Plot a Bode diagram for the control system whose open-loop transfer function is $10/(1 + 2s)$.

Set $s = j\omega_i$, so that the transfer function becomes

$$\frac{10}{1 + 2j\omega_i}$$

Let the input frequency be very low, say $\omega_i = 0.01$ rad/s. The log-modulus corresponding to this frequency is

$$20 \log_{10} 10 - 20 \log_{10} \sqrt{[1 + (2 \times 0.01)^2]} \simeq 20 \text{ dB}$$

Considering case 2 in section (c), it is evident that in this problem, the log-modulus is 20 dB at low frequencies and remains at that level until the frequency is high enough to influence the log-modulus. This occurs at the break frequency which is

$$\omega_i = \frac{1}{\tau} = \frac{1}{2} = 0.5 \text{ rad/s}$$

At frequencies higher than the break frequency, the slope of the log-modulus graph is –6 dB/octave. The phase angle varies from zero at zero frequency to –90° at infinite frequency.

The Bode diagram for this system is illustrated in *Fig 12*.

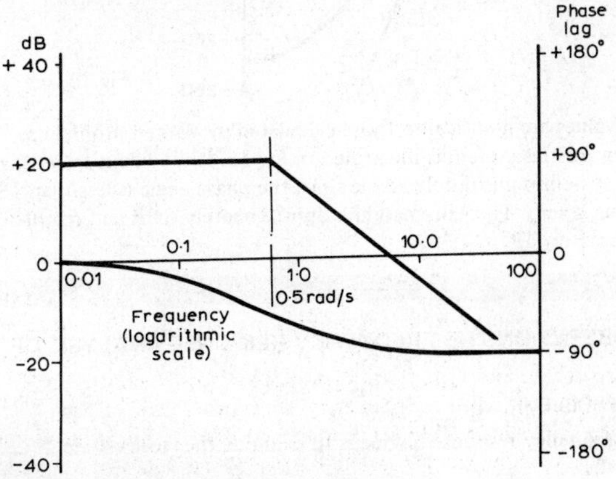

Fig 12

Problem 7 Draw a Bode diagram for the control system that has an open-loop transfer function

$$\frac{\theta_o}{\theta_i} = \frac{1}{s(1+s)(1+0.5s)}$$

and determine the gain margin and the phase margin for the closed-loop system.

The log-modulus for this system is:

$20 \log_{10} 1 - 20 \log_{10} \omega_i - 20 \log_{10} \sqrt{(1+\omega_i^2)} - 20 \log_{10} \sqrt{[1+(0.5\omega_i)^2]}$

Assume a low-frequency value, $\omega_i = 0.01$ rad/s, then the log-modulus corresponding to this frequency is + 40 dB. The log-modulus plot commences at + 40 dB corresponding to a frequency of 0.01 rad/s and the initial slope is −6 dB/octave due to the $1/\omega_i$ term. The first break occurs at $\omega_i = 1$ rad/s due to the largest time-constant, which is unity. The slope of the log-modulus graph after this break is −12 dB/octave due to the combined effects of the two most significant denominator terms. A second break occurs at $\omega_i = 2$ rad/s due to the second time-constant and the combined slope thereafter is −18 dB/octave.

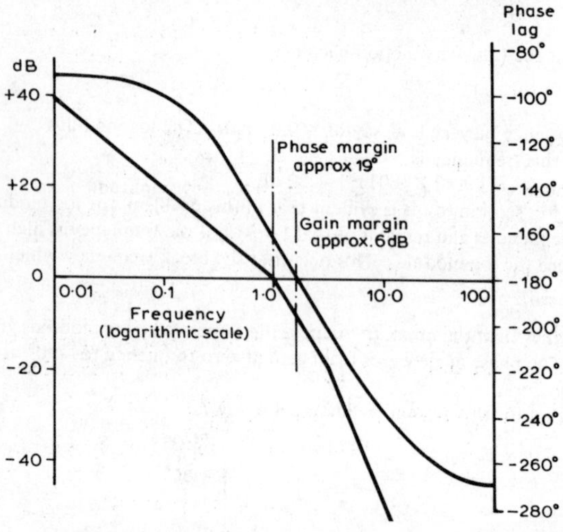

Fig 13

The phase-lag values are identical to those calculated in worked problem 5. The Bode diagram for this system is illustrated in *Fig 13*. It is evident from this diagram that the system is absolutely stable since the phase angle is less than 180° as the log-modulus is zero. The gain margin is approximately 6 dB and the phase margin is approximately 19°.

C. FURTHER PROBLEMS ON THE FREQUENCY RESPONSE ANALYSIS OF SYSTEMS

(a) SHORT ANSWER PROBLEMS

1 The purpose of frequency response testing is to examine the steady-state .... and to facilitate the ....

2 The amount by which an output lags behind an input is known as a . . . . lag and the ratio of the magnitude of an output to the magnitude of an input is known as the . . . . ratio.

3 A polar graph representing amplitude ratios and phase lags is known as a . . . . diagram.

4 Frequency response tests are conducted on . . . . systems since . . . . systems can become . . . .

5 A frequency response locus that encloses the point $-1, j(0)$ represents an . . . . system whereas a frequency response locus that passes through the point $-1, j(0)$ represents a . . . . system.

6 Practical control systems must be . . . . stable and also . . . . stable.

7 Bode diagrams are plotted by calculating . . . . functions of amplitude ratios which are expressed in . . . .

8 The frequency value at which the slope of a log-modulus plot changes abruptly is known as the . . . . and is assumed to occur as $\tau\omega_i =$ . . . .

(b) MULTI-CHOICE PROBLEMS (answers on page 184)

1 Subjecting instrumentation and control systems to sinusoidal inputs is known as:
(a) transient response testing, (b) ramp response testing, (c) frequency response testing; (d) step response testing.

2 Complex numbers can be represented by:
(a) frequency diagrams; (b) Argand diagrams; (c) Bode diagrams. (d) transient diagrams.

3 The condition that gives rise to a rapid increase in the output amplitude of an undamped second-order system as the driving frequency approaches the system natural frequency is known as:
(a) resonance; (b) instability; (c) an oscillation, (d) a vibration.

4 The condition that must be satisfied in order to ensure absolute closed-loop stability is known as:
(a) the Bode stability criterion; (b) the frequency response criterion; (c) the relative stability criterion; (d) the Nyquist stability criterion.

5 A frequency locus that passes within the point $-1, j(0)$ represents:
(a) a relatively stable system; (b) an absolutely stable system; (c) a critically stable system; (d) an absolutely unstable system.

6 Relative stability is measured by the:
(a) Nyquist criterion; (b) Bode criterion; (c) frequency response; (d) gain and phase margins.

7 A 2:1 frequency ratio is known as:
(a) an octave; (b) a decade; (c) a log-modulus; (d) a frequency increment.

8 The method of approximating log-modulus curves by straight lines is known as the:
(a) break frequency method; (b) asymptotic approximation method; (c) log-modulus method; (d) Nyquist method.

(c) CONVENTIONAL PROBLEMS

1 In a test on a temperature-measuring system, the response of a thermocouple was observed to be a simple lag having a time-constant 8 s. If the thermocouple were then used in order to measure the temperature of a furnace whose temperature fluctuates sinusoidally between 740°C and 700°C with a periodic time of 63 s,

determine the approximate maximum and minimum values that will be indicated by the thermocouple. Calculate the phase angle and the corresponding time lag between the temperature signals and the thermocouple output signals.

[Max. value = 735.6°; min. value = 704.4°; phase lag = 39°, time lag = 6.75 s]

2 A mercury-in-glass thermometer is calibrated by using it in order to measure the boiling temperature of water. It is observed that as the water temperature is 100°C, the thermometer reads 60°C, 4 s after being plunged into the water. Calculate the time-constant for the thermometer. The thermometer is then tested for frequency response by using it in order to monitor a fluctuating temperature. Calculate the maximum and the minimum readings on the thermometer as the temperature fluctuates sinusoidally between 80°C and 120°C in a cycle time of 50 s. Also calculate the time lag in seconds and the dynamic error.

[τ = 4.365 s; max. temp. = 117.54°C, min. temp. = 82.46°C; time lag = 4 s; dynamic error = 12.3%]

3 A piezo-electric pressure transducer exhibits a 10% overshoot in its output in a rise-time of 10^{-5} s, as it is subjected to a step input. Assuming that the transducer response is governed by the equation $(D^2 + 2\zeta\omega_n D + \omega_n^2)\theta_o = \omega_n^2\theta_i$, determine the transducer damping ratio and the undamped natural frequency. If the transducer is used in order to measure a pressure that varies sinusoidally at a frequency of 30 kHz and an amplitude of 800 kPa, calculate the output amplitude and the dynamic error.

[$\zeta = 0.59$; $\omega_n = 3.9 \times 10^5$ rad/s; amplitude = 837.43 kPa; dynamic error = 4.7%]

4 The motion of a second-order control system is governed by the transfer function

$$\frac{\theta_o}{\theta_i} = \frac{5}{s^2 + 6s + 36}$$

If the system is subjected to a sinusoidal input which has a frequency 0.5 Hz and an amplitude of 2 units, determine the corresponding output amplitude, output frequency and the phase lag.

[Output amplitude = 0.31; output frequency = π rad/s; phase lag = 0.625 rad]

5 Explain the purpose of frequency response testing and describe the type and the arrangement of equipment that is required in order to conduct such a test. Illustrate clearly the way in which control systems can be driven. Indicate the relevant parameters which are required to be measured and explain the techniques that are available for their determination.

6 Explain the Nyquist stability criterion and define absolute and relative stability. Define gain margin and phase margin.

7 Plot a Nyquist diagram for the control system that is represented by the open-loop transfer function

$$\frac{\theta_o}{\theta_i} = \frac{2}{s(1 + 0.3s)}$$

8 Plot a Nyquist diagram for the third-order control system that is represented by the open-loop transfer function

$$\frac{6}{(1 + 3s)(1 + s)(1 + 0.8s)}$$

and comment upon the stability of the closed-loop system. If the closed-loop system is absolutely stable, determine the gain margin and the phase margin.

[Gain margin = 3.74 dB (approx.); phase margin = 21° (approx.)]

9 Plot Bode diagrams for the two transfer functions:

(a) $\dfrac{\theta_o}{\theta_i} = \dfrac{1}{0.5s}$, (b) $\dfrac{\theta_o}{\theta_i} = \dfrac{5}{1 + 2s}$

0 Plot a Bode diagram for the system that is described in conventional problem 7.

1 Plot a Bode diagram for the system that is described in conventional problem 8 and compare the gain margins and the phase margins.

2 The harmonic responses of closed-loop control systems are often represented by plotting the gain and the phase characteristics in Bode diagrams. State the advantages of this method of representing response characteristics against polar plotting in the complex plane (Nyquist diagrams). The open-loop characteristics of a control system are represented by the transfer function

$$\frac{\theta_o}{\theta_i} = \frac{K}{0.5s(1 + 2s)^2}$$

Plot a Bode diagram for this system and determine a value for K which will ensure a phase margin of 30°.

[$K = 0.18$ (approx.)]

Answers to multi-choice problems

Chapter 1 (page 11)
1 (c); 2 (b); 3 (a); 4 (b); 5 (a); 6 (c), 7 (b); 8 (c); 9 (b); 10 (a).

Chapter 2 (page 33)
1 (b); 2 (c); 3 (d), 4 (a); 5 (a), 6 (b); 7 (c); 8 (b); 9 (a); 10 (d).

Chapter 3 (page 47)
1 (c); 2 (a); 3 (b); 4 (a); 5 (d); 6 (d); 7 (a), 8 (b); 9 (c); 10 (b).

Chapter 4 (page 75)
1 (d); 2 (b); 3 (a); 4 (a); 5 (c), 6 (b); 7 (d); 8 (c); 9 (a); 10 (d); 11 (b); 12 (c), 13 (a); 14 (c).

Chapter 5 (page 90)
1 (c); 2 (d); 3 (a); 4 (c); 5 (d); 6 (a), 7 (c); 8 (b); 9 (a), 10 (d).

Chapter 7 (page 124)
1 (b); 2 (d); 3 (d), 4 (a), 5 (c); 6 (a); 7 (a); 8 (b); 9 (c); 10 (b).

Chapter 9 (page 164)
1 (c); 2 (a); 3 (d); 4 (b), 5 (d), 6 (c); 7 (a); 8 (d); 9 (b); 10 (c).

Chapter 10 (page 181)
1 (c); 2 (b); 3 (a); 4 (d); 5 (b); 6 (d); 7 (a); 8 (b).

Appendix—Fundamental formulae

In the following formulae, E = modulus of elasticity (Pa), G = modulus of rigidity (Pa), and I = second moment of area (m^4), or moment of inertia (kgm^2).

1 STRESS AND STRAIN FORMULAE

Stress $= \dfrac{\text{force}}{\text{area}}$, expressed mathematically as $\sigma = \dfrac{F}{a}$ Pa

Strain $= \dfrac{\text{extension}}{\text{original length}}$, ... $\epsilon = \dfrac{\delta \ell}{\ell}$

$E = \dfrac{\text{stress}}{\text{strain}}$, ... $E = \dfrac{\sigma}{\epsilon}$ Pa

or $E = \dfrac{F\ell}{a\delta\ell}$

$\dfrac{\text{Transverse strain}}{\text{Longitudinal strain}}$ = Poisson's Ratio, denoted by τ.

Shear stress $= \dfrac{\text{shear force}}{\text{area}}$, expressed mathematically as $\tau = \dfrac{F}{a}$ Pa.

$G = \dfrac{\text{shear stress}}{\text{shear strain}}$, ... $G = \dfrac{\tau}{\phi}$

2 BEAM BENDING FORMULAE

(i) *Second moment of area* for a rectangular beam section with a breadth b and a depth d is

(a) about the neutral axis $I = \dfrac{bd^3}{12}$

(b) about the base $I = \dfrac{bd^3}{3}$

Second moment of area about the neutral axis for a circular beam section with a diameter d is $I = \dfrac{\pi d^4}{64}$

(ii) *Pure bending.* The relationship between bending moment m, second moment of area I, bending stress σ, half the beam thickness y, modulus of elasticity E, and radius of curvature R, is

$$\frac{M}{I} = \frac{\sigma}{y} = \frac{E}{R}$$

(iii) *Combined bending and direct stresses.*

Maximum stress $\sigma_1 = \dfrac{F}{a} + \dfrac{My_1}{I}$

Minimum stress $\sigma_2 = \dfrac{F}{a} - \dfrac{My_2}{I}$

(iv) *Beam deflection* formulae for *standard cases*;

(a) cantilever with concentrated end load W, $\delta = \dfrac{WL^3}{3EI}$

(b) cantilever with uniformly distributed load w/unit length,

$$\delta = \frac{wL^3}{8EI}$$

(c) simply supported beam with central point load W,

$$\delta = \frac{WL^3}{48EI}$$

(d) simply supported beam with uniformly distributed load w/unit length,

$$\delta = \frac{5wL^4}{384EI}$$

3 TORSION FORMULAE

(i) *The polar second moment* of area for a *circular shaft* about its axis is:

(a) for a solid shaft, $J = \dfrac{\pi d^4}{32}$

(b) for a hollow shaft, $J = \dfrac{\pi}{32}(D^4 - d^4)$

(ii) *Pure torsion.* The relationship between torque T, polar second moment of area J, shear stress τ, shaft radius, r, modulus of rigidity G, angle of twist θ, and shaft length L, is

$$\frac{T}{J} = \frac{\tau}{r} = \frac{G\theta}{L}$$

4 DYNAMICS FORMULAE

(i) *Linear motion* and *angular motion*:

Displacement $= x$ or θ

Velocity = rate of change of displacement $= \dfrac{dx}{dt}$ or $\dfrac{d\theta}{dt}$

Acceleration = rate of change of velocity $= \dfrac{d^2x}{dt^2}$ or $\dfrac{d^2\theta}{dt^2}$

(ii) *Newton's second law of motion* Force = mass × acceleration, expressed mathematically is

P (newtons) $= m$(kg) $\times f$(m/s²)

The equivalent angular case is: Torque = moment of inertia × angular acceleration, which expressed mathematically is

$T = I\alpha$, or $T = \dfrac{Id^2\theta}{dt^2}$

(iii) *Moment of inertia* is defined as the product of the mass of a particle and the square of its distance from an axis of rotation.

Hence $I = mk^2$, where k is known as the radius of gyration.

(iv) *Gyroscopic couple*:

torque = precesion velocity × spin velocity × moment of inertia, which expressed mathematically is

$T = \Omega\omega I$

VIBRATION AND CONTROL FORMULAE

Periodic time = $\dfrac{2\pi}{\text{angular velocity}}$, expressed mathematically as $t_p = \dfrac{2\pi}{\omega}$

Frequency = $\dfrac{1}{\text{periodic time}}$, ... $f = \dfrac{\omega}{2\pi}$

Maximum displacement is known as *amplitude*.

Transient solution of differential equations for standard cases:

(a) Real roots of auxiliary equation, $\theta_{ot} = A \exp(m_1 t) + B \exp(m_2 t) + \ldots$ etc.

(b) Conjugate complex roots of auxiliary equation,
$\theta_{ot} = \exp(mt)(A \cos \omega t + B \sin \omega t)$

(c) Repeated roots of auxiliary equation,
$\theta_{ot} = (A_1 + A_2 t + \ldots\ldots. A_p t^{p-1})\exp(mt)$

Soccer – Perfect Shooting Techniques

Photo Credits:
Cover Photos: dpa – Picture Alliance, © Thinkstock/Hemera, © Thinkstock/iStockphoto
Cover Design: Sabine Groten
Illustrations: www.easy2coach.net

For reasons of better readability we have decided to use the male (neutral) form of address throughout the book, which of course also includes the female form.

Soccer – Perfect Shooting Techniques

Thomas Dooley & Christian Titz

Meyer & Meyer Sport

Original title: Fußball – Perfekte Schusstechniken

Translated by Petra Haynes
AAA Translation, St. Louis, Missouri, USA
www.AAATranslation.com

British Library Cataloguing in Publication Data
A catalogue record for this book is available from the British Library

Thomas Dooley & Christian Titz
Soccer – Perfect Shooting Techniques
Maidenhead: Meyer & Meyer Sport (UK) Ltd., 2012
ISBN 978-1-84126-346-5

Auckland, Beirut, Budapest, Cairo, Cape Town, Dubai, Indianapolis,
Kindberg, Maidenhead, Sydney, Olten, Singapore, Tehran, Toronto
Member of the World
Sport Publishers' Association (WSPA)
www.w-s-p-a.org
Printed by: B.O.S.S Druck und Medien GmbH, Germany
ISBN 978-1-84126-346-5
E-Mail: info@m-m-sports.com
www.m-m-sports.com

Table of Contents

Preface

Goals decide games. It is therefore important to practice the successful finish. This book focuses extensively on the corresponding training. The many methodically designed training examples show what the training methods for learning the successful finish look like and how they can be successfully incorporated into the daily training routine.

What does methodical training to learn the correct finish and the required execution technique look like? What are the various options for a shot on goal? Which actions prior to a shot on goal must be adhered to or are often used in a game setting? What do the corresponding running lanes look like? From which distances are most goals scored?

This book will give you concise and comprehensive answers to all of these questions and many more, in the form of select training and playing methods.

All of the drills shown are the result of the authors' many years of practical experience in amateur and professional soccer.

In addition to the modern practice images, each drill is supplemented by extensive detailed information that will make the implementation of the drills easier and ensure a smooth training process.

We hope you enjoy reading and using this book!

Christian Titz

1. Fundamentals

Learning the techniques for ball and body movement with the critical timing of the shot and start requires a certain amount of time and therefore should be trained separately as well as in combination with passing and playing methods.

An accurate shooting technique is very important for a successful soccer game because after all, goals decide the game. It must therefore be practiced accordingly and rehearsed as typical preparatory action in connection with passing, feints, and receiving and moving with the ball. Mistakes in the execution must be corrected without fail.

Especially the training method for receiving and moving with the ball usingas few touches as possible at a high rate of speed before the shot on goal, or the direct shot after a fast pass from different positions are practiced much too infrequently, in spite of the fact that the correct execution often clinches a successful goal.

There are different ways to train shooting technique:

- With the inside of the foot (inside foot shot)
- With the instep (instep kick)
- With the outside of the foot
- With a inside foot kick
- Swerve (spin)
- With a drop kick
- Volley
- With a loft (lob)

The following should be considered during demonstrations:

1. The group should be positioned several yards in front of the trainer.
2. The motion sequence should be explained and shown slowly.
   The first step would be to demonstrate it slowly in front of the group so the players are able to see the sequence from the back (Note: Children in particular are better able to understand the exercise when they can view it from their own perspective.)
3. Start out slow and practice equally with both feet.

4. The motion sequence can be practiced as a dry run beforehand by asking the players to practice the motion sequence without the ball.

2. Aspects of a good trainer

- Always demand accuracy and speed (slow execution in the long-run does not lead to game-appropriate results).
- Explanations of exercises and subsequent corrections of mistakes must not lead to information overload (lack of concentration causes increased mistakes). They key is to find the right mix of correction and fluid execution of the exercise.
- Players should learn to observe (as during the game) and put their observations to use.
- Constantly correct mistakes to prevent the creeping in of incorrect automatisms.
- Address players in a manner that conveys matter-of-fact clarity as well as empathy.
- In good groups the trainer can simulate a stress situation during training that can prepare the player for pressure situations in a game (speaking loudly, critical tone/ language during execution of the exercise).
- Continuously demanding concentration.
- The trainer's demeanor (body language, tone of voice, corrections) fundamentally determines the quality of the training process.

Two basic aspects must always be consideredduring execution:
1. What is the arm doing?
2. What is the foot and body position?

3. Explanation of the different shooting techniques

3.1 General execution

- The supporting leg should be positioned about 10 inches to the side and level with the ball.
- The upper body is slightly bent over the ball.
- The foot swings from top to bottom.
- Arm-to-foot coordination during the shot is characterized by the following:
  a. Swing with the right leg – right arm moves back, left arm forward.
  b. Swing with the left leg – left arm moves back, right arm forward.
- For illustration purposes the player may kick into the air. "What is the arm doing?"
- At the moment of the kick the eyes are on the ball. The player anticipating the pass makes a small counter movement at the same time as the passing player swings his leg, or runs towards the passing player and receives the pass during the forward movement, and shoots directly on the goal.
- The starting motion of the receiving player/goalie coincides with the swinging motion of the passing player.
- Due to the high demand on the players' fine motor skills groups with a low playing standard (e.g. beginners and children) should have the ball passed in such a way that the children can run towards it, thereby utilizing the momentum of the approaching ball. This increases the sharpness or velocity of the ball because the player is able to exert more force on the ball.
- For the technical execution and the posture in the shooting techniques, the hardness of the pass/shot, the accuracy, the timing of shot and start are critical factors for a successful finish.

3.2 Instep kick

The toe points downward, the ankle is plantar-flexed and the upper body bent slightly over the ball. The contact area is the top of the foot.

3.3 Swerve

The ball is shot with the inside foot/toe and goes into a spin. The player goes into a more lateral position. A slightly supine backbend is not unusual.

3.4 Inside of the foot kick

The ball is played partly with the inside of the foot as well as the instep. The supporting leg is positioned to the side of the ball and the player's upper body is in a tilted position. The toes point downward; the position is similar to that of the instep kick.

3.5 Inside of the foot shot

The toe points upward, the ankle is firmly dorsi-flexed and opens 90°s to the outside. Lift the foot slightly and hit the ball in the center. Bring the body over the ball and do not bend back arching the back.

3.6 Outside of the foot shot

A slight backbend is possible when playing the ball with the outside of the foot. The ball is played with the outer toes and the outside of the foot and goes into a spin.

3.7 Drop kick

In a drop kick the ball is hit with the instep at the exact moment the ball touches the ground.

Learning aid:

- Take the ball into both hands, extend the arms and let the ball drop. The moment the ball touches the ground it must be struck with the instep. The leg follows through after contact. The ball should not rotate.
- Problems with the drop kick:
- The shot is taken too soon, before it touches the ground ==› demonstrate and explain.
- The shot is taken too late, when it bounces off the ground ==› demonstrate and explain.
- For some children this technique is very difficult to learn and requires some time until the motion sequence has become automated. It can be helpful to let the child kick next to the ball at the moment the ball touches the ground. This will allow him to develop the right feel/timing for the pointof impact without having to constantly retrieve the ball. Emphasizing the point of impact with a verbal "Go" can also be helpful. A good place to practice this is in front of a net fence.

3.8 Volley shot

During a volley shot the upper body is bent forward slightly. Contact with the ball is made at a low point (not too high). This gives the ball more force and makes the shot more accurate.

3.9 Lofting (Lobbing)

During a loft the foot is below the ball, lifting it with the instep.

4. Correction instructions for the trainer

- Strike the ball in front of the supporting leg.
- Let the leg follow trough after making contact.
- The toe points downward.

- The ankle is plantar-flexed.
- Pay attention to the arm position.
- Take small steps towards the ball.

5. Execution technique and posture – Receiving and moving with the ball

- Receiving and moving the ball should be done strictly with one touch.
- The ball can be received and moved with the inside/outside of the right or left foot.
- When receiving a high pass the player must settle the ball the instant it touches the ground. When properly executed the ball does not rebound from the ground and thus can be immediately moved by the player.
- To keep the ball from bouncing and to facilitate fluid and quick receipt and movement of the ball the player must have good timing and the proper ball handling technique.
- The example of receiving and moving the ball with the right inside foot should show the player moving the ball with the inside of his foot the instant it touches the ground. In doing so the leg swings right to left in direction of the ball (similar to the foot movement in a goal kick, but with a smaller swing) thereby keeping the ball from bouncing up and away. All the weight is on the supporting leg; the upper body rotates to the right in the hip joint (right shoulder rotates to the back). The eyes are on the ball which brings the upper body slightly over the ball.
- When receiving and moving the ball with the outside foot the ankle is turned to the inside. The lower leg is also rotated in at the knee so that the foot movement can occur from top to bottom and left to right in the direction of the ball. The ball's point of impact is the entire outside of the foot.

Variation:

Receiving and moving the ball behind the supporting leg to the left foot

This receiving technique combines receipt with an immediate lateral change of direction. This technique is executed with the inside of the foot. This is done with one touch and is a fluid motion. To do so the foot moves in the direction of the approaching ball. Just before contact the foot is pulled back (just a little slower than ball speed). Now the ball can be received slowly and at the same time be controlled with the inside of the foot.

6. Execution technique and posture – moving the ball with the bottom of the foot

In this variation the toes of the foot that will receive the ball are pulled up so that when the ball touches the ground the foot will partially cover the ball from above and keep it from bouncing up. At the same time the leg that receives the ball moves forward with the knee slightly bent. The upper body remains upright, the arms are at the sides and the elbows are bent. The palms face each other.

7. Execution technique and posture – Various directional changes / feints

Strictly applicable:

Feints are body fakes. This means attention must be paid to the upper body's motion sequence. Exercises should always be executed with both feet. Lots of touches on the ball, always controlling the ball and moving it close to the foot so the opponent can't get to the ball.

Tips:

The objective is to outplay and shake off the opponent; therefore it's important to:
Increase speed after executing a feint (short sprint for about 7 feet). Start out slow,

then gradually increase speed during practice. To memorize feints: Constantly correct, demonstrate and talk. A high rate of repetition with lots of touches is essential to acquiring new feints and ball handling techniques. Finally, the feint must be practiced with obstacles and against opponents.

Structure:

1. Position the group in front of the trainer.
2. Explain the exercise and break down and demonstrate the motion sequence at the beginning. First frontally in front of the group, then in a position that allows the players to see the exercise from the rear,making it easier to reconstruct.
3. Let the players repeat the exercise standing up, then correct mistakes and explain details about the respective exercises.
4. Let the players repeat the exercise slowly and then correct mistakes.
5. Continue to increase the speed until reaching maximum execution speed.
6. Use cones to represent opponents. A distance of about 7 feet to the cone serves as an orientation aid for proper start timing (start of the feint execution).
7. Essentially the success of a feint is not only determined by the technical quality of the feint's execution. Extremely relevant are accurate timing of the feint's initiation (not too early and not too late). When two players move towards each other at a high rate of speed, the feint is used at a distance of about 10 to 14 feet. If the player controlling the ball is running towards a waiting opponent, the distance is shortened to about 7 feet.
8. It is important that a noticeable upper body fake take place during the execution of the feint because the defender will usually react to that.

Exclusive offer:

As a purchaser of this book you are invited to view the described drills online in the form of free animated graphics and adapt them to your needs.

www.Easy2Coach.net

To do so, just follow these three easy steps:

1. Register for free at **www.easy2coach.net/motions**
2. Enter the coupon code in the coupon window. **Code: MM2012E2C01DS**
3. Watch the animations and adapt them as needed.

1 Simple shot on goal with rebounder

Purpose of training

- Ball handling techniques

Training emphasis

- Shooting techniques/shot on goal

Training aspects

Specific purpose:	**Speed of anticipation, outside of instep, moving the ball, speed of decision-making, insidefoot, insidefoot kick, combination, ball control technique with movement, instep**
Age group:	**Any**
Playing level:	**Anfänger, beliebig**
Form of training:	**Group**
Training structure:	**Main part/emphasis**
Intention:	**Improving individual quality**
Number of players:	**4 or more**
Number of participating players:	**Entire Team**
Training location	**Any**
Space requirements:	**Restricted playing field**
Length:	**10-15 min**
Physical aspects:	**Soccer-specific endurance, power**
Goalies:	**1 goalie**

Organization:
Set up a goal and a start cone for the players. One rebounder is positioned next to the goal. The balls are with the players at the start cone.

Execution:
The player at the start cone plays a pass to the rebounder next to the goal and runs towards the goal. The rebounder passes the ball back into the running lane so the player is able to take a direct shot on goal. Then the next player starts from the start cone, etc. The rebounder changes regularly.

Variations:

1. The starting player moves the ball and with the second touch takes a shot on goal.
2. The starting player makes a low pass or anair ball.
3. The rebounder returns the ball low or high.
4. Competition: count goals, the rebounder is allowed to count the rebound. In this variation the rebounder can leave his position after returning the pass and having actively used the rebound to his advantage.

Equipment : 1 regulation size goal(s), 2 cones

Tips:

- The objective is to learn the proper insidefoot shot, instep kick, and insidefoot kick swerve technique,

and thereby increase shot speed and precision.

- Also demand shots on goal with the weak foot (always alternate right and left, etc.)
- Pay attention to your posture when taking a shot (upper body over the ball; supporting leg is 12-16 inches to the side staggered with the ball, the foot points in shooting direction, the arms swing along; the arm closest to the shooting leg mimics the swinging motion of the leg (when shooting with the right leg, the right arm moves back to gather momentum, the left arm moves forward, at the moment of the shot the eyes are on the ball.)
- To avoid delays the next player starts immediately after one player takes a shot.
- If the starting player opens on the rebounder with an air ball it should be done with the inside of the instep. This gives the ball a linear and slightly upward trajectory and, compared to a curve ball played with the insidefoot, can be transferred from A to B much more quickly.
- As soon as the starting player initiates the swinging motion the rebounder makes a small counter movement and then briefly moves towards the ball.
- Receiving and moving the ball should be one fluid motion. Letting the ball rebound too far or deviating too far from the straight running lane when receiving and moving the ball, should be avoided.
- Receiving and moving the ball should occur strictly with one touch, hence the shot on goal is done with the second touch.

Field size: 25 yards x 20 yards

Distance between cones:
Goal cones vary according to age group, between 10 to 25 yards.

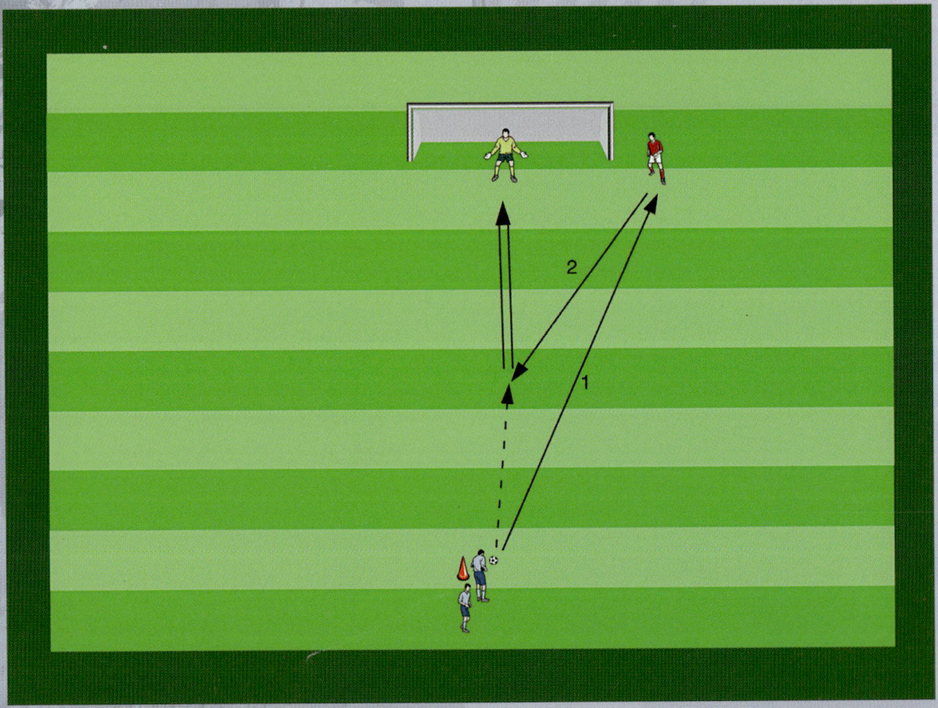

2 Obstacle course shooting drill with dribbling variations

Purpose of training

- Ball handling techniques

Training emphasis

- Shooting techniques/shot on goal

Training aspects

Specific purpose:	**Speed of anticipation, dribbling, speed of decision-making, inside foot, insidefoot kick, combination, ball control technique with movement, body fake, reaction speed, instep, swerve,**
Age group:	**Age 6 to seniors**
Playing level:	**Any**
Form of training:	**Stations**
Training structure:	**Main part/emphasis**
Intention:	**Improving individual quality**
Number of players:	**4 or more**
Number of participating players:	**Entire team**
Training location	**Any**
Space requirements:	**Restricted playing field**
Length:	**10-20 min**
Physical aspects:	**Soccer-specific endurance, power**
Goalies:	**1 goalie**

Organization:
Setting up an obstacle course for shots on goal as shown in the illustration. Players position themselves at each stationwith their ball.

Execution:
Group A: The player dribbles slalom through the cone course. He starts to dribble with the inside left foot next to the cone. The ball should be moved with both feet. This means, right foot on the right side of the cone, left foot on the left side of the cone. The shot on goal is a right foot swerve.

Group B 1: The player does a feint (Matthews) in front of the cone and shoots. Meaning the player moves the ball with the right inside foot to the left past the cone and then plays the ball (behind the cone) with the right outside foot to the right and makes an inside/instep kick on the big goal. The same motion sequence can also be done reversed left.

Group B 2: The player dribbles around the cones with the foot of his choice and takes a shot with the right foot.

Group C: The player dribbles slalom through the cone course. He begins dribbling to the right of the cone with the left outside foot. The ball should be controlled with both feet. That means left foot to the right of the cone, right foot to the left of the cone (outside foot). The shot on goal is a left foot swerve.

The groups can either stay at one station for a certain amount of time or change clockwise after each shot on goal.

If there is no goalie in a group, each player who misses a shot automatically becomes goalie.

Motivational aid:
Make a bet with the group: "You can't score 10 goals in 3 minutes; the loser has to do 15 pushups." Or make a bet, goalie against players; no 10 goals, the loser has to do 15 pushups.

Equipment:
1 regulation size goal(s), 18 cones, 2 mini goals(s)

Tips:
- Make sure that passes are made with one touch and the ball is played in running direction and not too far away from the teammate.
- The goalie should run towards the goal at a high rate of speed.
- Clean execution of the body feint. Receiving and moving the ball each are only one touch.
- Demand different shooting techniques (inside foot, instep, outside foot, swerve).
- Fast dribbling through the slalom course.
- Practice shots on goal with both feet.
- Demand correct posture.
- No stopping before taking a shot on goal, but shoot from a run.

Field size: 35 x 20 yards

Distance between cones:
Groups A and C: Distance between the individual cones is 1.5 yards. Shooting distance from the mini goal to the first cone is at maximum of 10 yards.
Group B 1: Distance between individual cones is 3 yards. Shooting distance from the big goal to the first cone is at maximum of 16 yards.
Group B 2: Distance between individual cones is 4 yards. Shooting distance from the big goal to the first cone is at maximum of 15 yards.

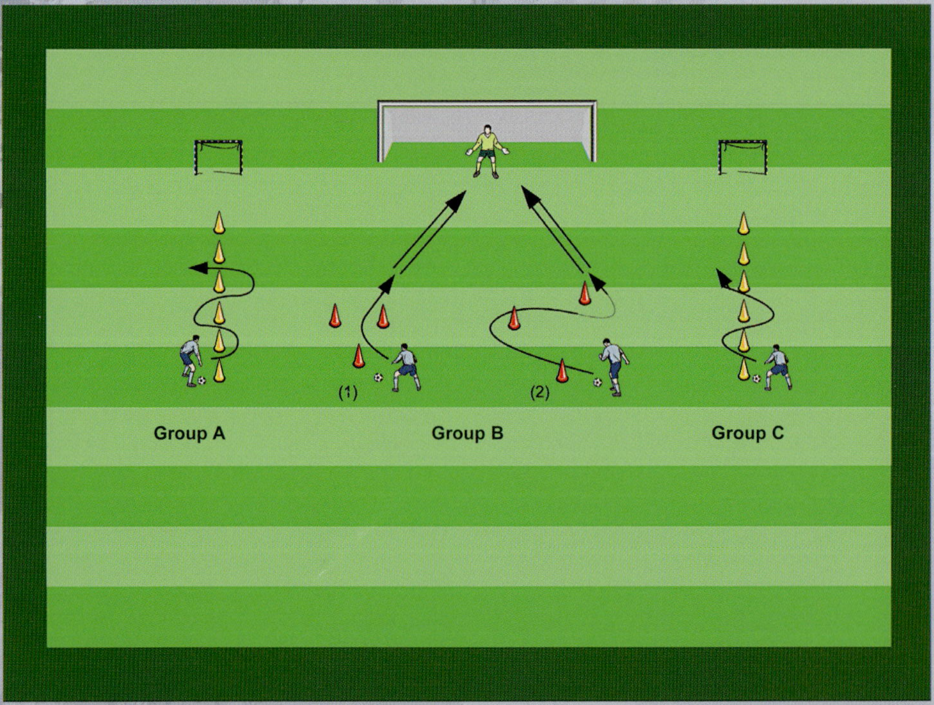

3 Obstacle course shooting drill with dribbling and passing

Purpose of training

- Ball handling techniques

Training emphasis

- Shooting techniques/shot on goals

Training aspects

Specific purpose:	Speed of action with the ball, attack performance, speed of anticipation, outside foot, moving with the ball, dribbling, speed of decision-making, inside foot, push pass (inside foot), combination ball handling technique with movement, passing in a triangle, passing over several stations, reaction speed, instep
Age group:	Any
Playing level:	Any
Form of training:	Group
Training structure:	Warm-up, main part/emphasis
Intention:	Offensive performance, improvement of individual quality
Number of players:	6 or more
Number of participating players:	Entire team
Training location	Any
Space requirements:	Restricted playing field
Length:	10-25 min
Physical aspects:	Soccer specific endurance, power
Goalies:	1 goalie

Organization:
Setting up an obstacle course for shots on goal,as shown in the illustration. The players position themselves at each station with their ball.

Execution:
Left outside station: The player dribbles slalom through the cone course. He begins dribbling on the left side of the cone with the left inside foot. The ball should be controlled with both feet. That means using the right foot to the right of the cone, and the left foot to the left of the cone. The shot on goal is taken with a right foot swerve.

Center station: A passes the ball to C and overlaps C, C plays to B, B plays a diagonal pass in running direction of A, who takes a shot on goal. Positions change after each round.
Afterwards the passing combination is practiced in reverse. A passes to B and overlaps B, B plays to C, C plays a diagonal pass in running direction of A, who takes the shot on goal. Positions change after each round.

Right outside station: The player dribbles slalom through the cone course. He begins to dribble on the right side of the cone with the left outside foot. The ball should be controlled with both feet.

This means left foot on the right side of the cone, right foot (outside foot) on the left side of the cone. The shot on goal is taken with a left foot swerve.
The groups can either practice at one station for a certain period of time or change stations clockwise after every shot on goal. If there is no goalie in a group, each player who misses a shot automatically becomes goalie.

Motivational aid:
Make a bet with the group: "You can't score 10 goals in 3 minutes; the loser has to do 15 pushups." Or make a bet, goalie against players; no 10 goals, the loser has to do 15 pushups.

Equipment:
1 regulation size goal(s), 15 cones, 2 mini goals

Tips:
- Make sure that passes are made with one touch and the ball is played in running direction and not too far away from the teammate.
- The shooter should run towards the goal at a high rate of speed.
- The players anticipating the ball, B and C, make a counter motion before the pass.
- Demand different shooting techniques (inside foot, instep, outside foot, inside instep, swerve).
- Fast dribbling through the slalom course.
- Practice shots on goal with both feet.
- Demand correct posture.
- No stopping before taking a shot on goal, but shoot from a run.

Field size: 35 x 20 yards

Distance between cones:
Outside stations: Distance between individual cones is at maximum 1.5 yards. Shooting distance from the mini goal to the first cone is at maximum 10 yards.
Center station: Distances between individual cones is at maximum 6 yards. Shooting distance form the big goal to the first cone is at maximum 16 yards.

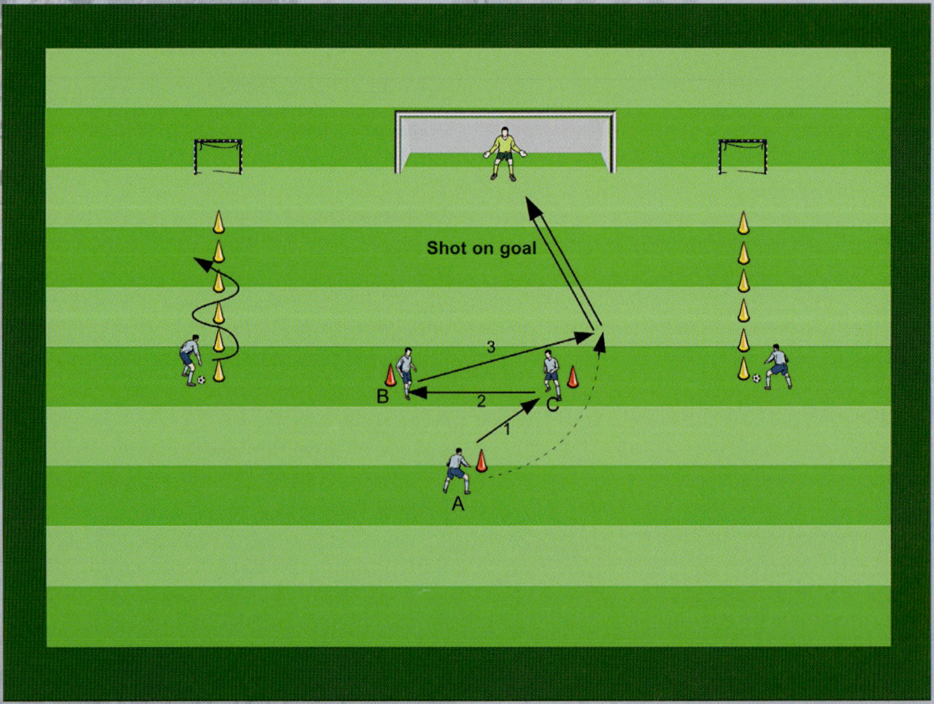

4 Shot on goal with a fixed rebounder, variation I

Purpose of training

- Ball handling techniques

Training emphasis

- Shooting techniques/shot on goal

Training aspects

Specific purpose:	**Speed of action with the ball, speed of anticipation, speed of decision-making, push pass (inside foot), inside foot kick, instep**
Age group:	**Any**
Playing level:	**Any**
Form of training:	**Group**
Training structure:	**Main part/emphasis**
Intention:	**Improving individual quality**
Number of players:	**4 or more**
Number of participating players:	**Entire team**
Training location	**Any**
Space requirements:	**Restricted playing field**
Length:	**10-15 min**
Physical aspects:	**Soccer-specific endurance, power**
Goalies:	**1 goalie**

Organization:
Setting up one goal, two start cones, and one cone where the rebounder positions himself, as shown in the illustration. The players are divided evenly between the two start cones. The balls are also distributed to the two start cones. The starting players always have a ball.

Execution:
The respective starting players from the two groups take turns playing a low, short, and quick pass to the rebounder. He lets the ball bounce back into the running lane of the starting player and positions himself towards the starting player from the second group. The starting player shoots the ball directly on goal. Afterwards he gets in line at the other start cone. Once the rebounder has passed the ball back the start player at the other cone starts his pass. The rebounder changes regularly. This creates a passing and shooting drill with both feet.

Equipment: 1 regulation size goal(s), 3 cones

Tips:
- Make sure the shot on goal is practiced with left and right. To do so you can only shoot and pass with the left from one cone, and with the right from the other cone.
- Pay attention to your posture when taking a shot (upper body over the ball; supporting leg is 12-16 inches to the side staggered with the ball, the foot points in shooting direction, the arms swing along; the arm closest to the shooting leg mimics the swinging motion of the leg (when shooting with

the right leg, the right arm moves back to gather momentum, the left arm moves forward), at the moment of the shot the eyes are on the ball.)

- As soon as the starting player initiates the swinging motion the rebounder makes a small counter movement and then briefly moves towards the ball.
- Different shooting techniques (inside foot kick, instep kick, swerve) can be practiced where appropriate (at the trainer's command).
- Make sure that the waiting starting player begins with the drill as soon as the rebounder has passed the ball back to the active player.
- After making his pass the starting player only begins to run when the rebounder initiates his swing.

Field size: 10 x 25 yards

Distance between cones:
Goal to rebounder cone: 16 yards
Rebounder cone to start cones: 5-9 yards

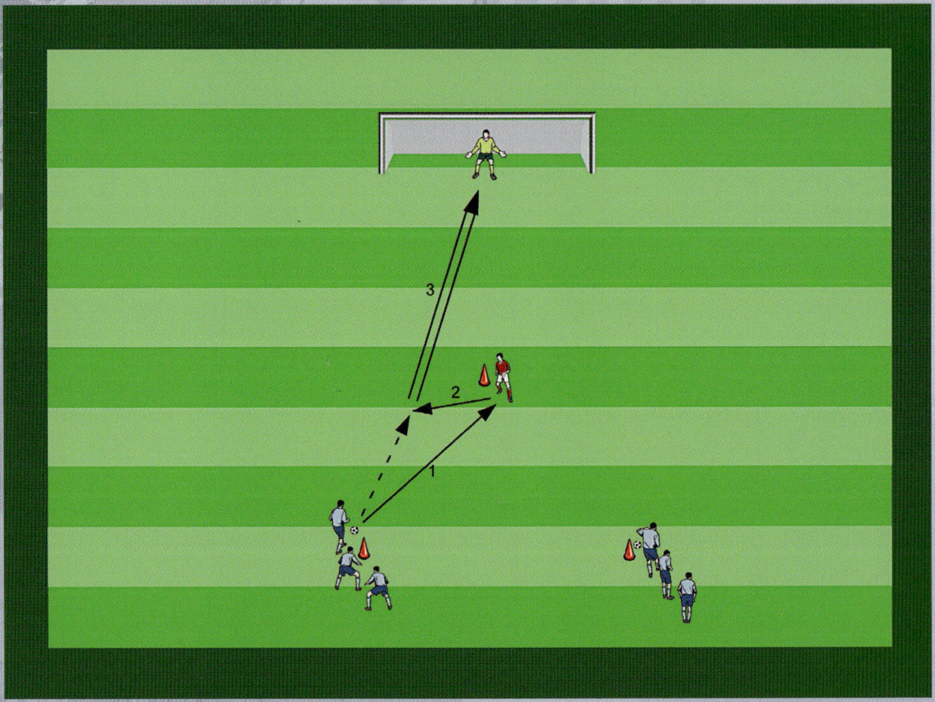

5 Shot on goal with a fixed rebounder, variation II

Purpose of training
- Ball handling techniques

Training emphasis
- Shooting techniques/shot on goal

Training aspects

Specific purpose:	**Push-off power, speed of action with the ball, speed of anticipation, outside instep, receiving and moving the ball, double pass, speed of decision-making, inside foot, push pass (inside foot), Inside foot kick, combination ball handling technique with movement, reaction speed, instep**
Age group:	**Any**
Playing level:	**Any**
Form of training:	**Group**
Training structure:	**Mainpart/emphasis**
Intention:	**Improving individual performance**
Number of players:	**4 or more**
Number of participating players:	**Entire team**
Training location	**Any**
Space requirements:	**Restricted playing field**
Length:	**10-15 min**
Physical aspects:	**Soccer-specific endurance, power**
Goalies:	**1 goalie**

Organization:
Setting up one goal, two start cones and one cone where the rebounder positions himself, as shown in the illustration. The players are divided evenly between the two start cones. The balls are also distributed to the two start cones. The starting players always have a ball.

Execution:
The respective starting players from the two groups take turns passing to the rebounder. He lets the ball bounce back into the running lane. Now the ball is received and played with one touch, or with weaker groups with 2-3 touches. The shot on goal is taken after a brief fast dribble. The rebounder changes regularly.

Equipment: 1 regulation size goal(s), 3 cones

Tips:
- Make sure the shot on goal is practiced with left and right. To do so you can only shoot and pass with the left from one cone, and with the right from the other cone.
- Pay attention to your posture when taking a shot (upper body over the ball; supporting leg is 12-16 inches to the side staggered with the ball, the foot points in shooting direction, the arms swing along; the arm closest to the shooting leg mimics the swinging motion of the leg (when shooting withthe right leg, the right arm moves back to gather momentum, the left arm moves forward), at the moment of the shot the eyes are on the ball.)
- As soon as the starting player initiates the swinging motion the rebounder

makes a small counter movement and then briefly moves towards the ball.

- After making his pass the starting player only begins to run when the rebounder initiates his swing.
- Receiving and moving the ball should be one fluid motion. Letting the ball rebound too far or deviating too far from the straight running lane when receiving and moving the ball, should be avoided.
- Different shooting techniques (inside foot kick, instep kick, swerve) can be practiced where appropriate (at the trainer's command).

Field size: 10 x 25 yards

Distance between cones:
Goal to rebounder cone: 16 yards
Rebounder cone to start cones: 6-9 yards

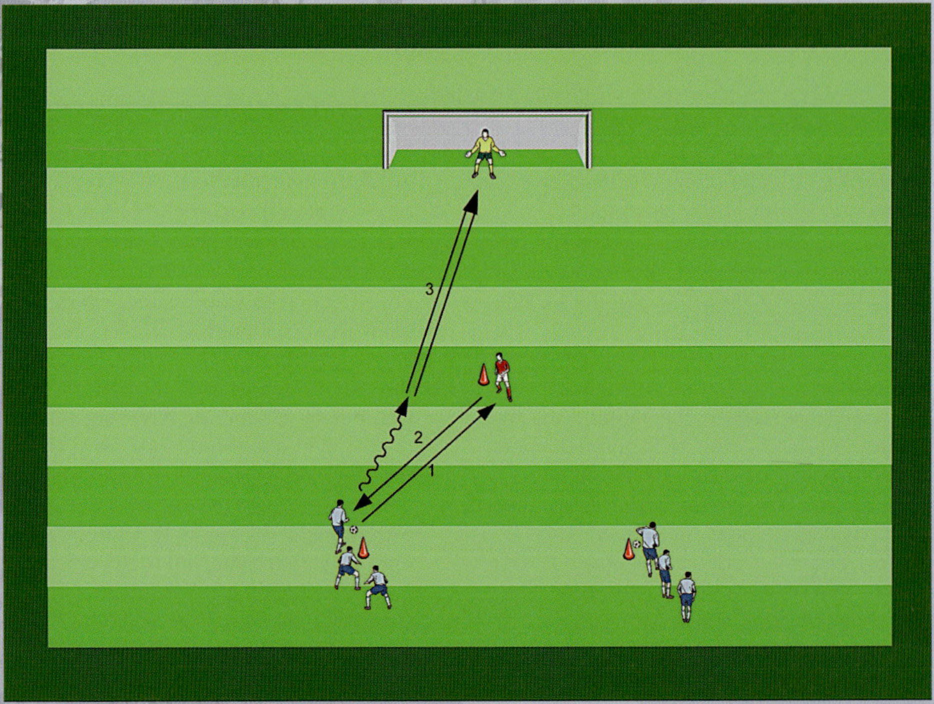

6 Shot on goal with a fixed rebounder, variation III

Purpose of training
- Ball handling techniques

Training emphasis
- Shooting techniques/shot on goal

Training aspects

Specific purpose:	**Speed of action with the ball, speed of anticipation, outside instep, moving with the ball, speed of decision-making, combination ball handling technique with movement, header while moving, short passes, volley, instep, swerve**
Age group:	**Age 9 to seniors**
Playing level:	**Advanced**
Form of training:	**Group**
Training structure:	**Main part/emphasis**
Intention:	**Improving individual quality**
Number of players:	**6 or more**
Number of participating players:	**Entire Team**
Training location	**Any**
Space requirements:	**Restricted playing field**
Length:	**10-15 min**
Physical aspects:	**Soccer-specific endurance**
Goalies:	**1 goalie**

Organization:
Setting up one goal, two start cones and one cone where the rebounder positions himself, as shown in the illustration. The players are divided evenly between the two start cones. The balls are also distributed to the two start cones. The starting players always have a ball.

Execution:
The two groups' respective starting players take turns lobbing the ball to the rebounder. Depending on his performance level, he has two options:
a) He catches the ball and throws it to the starting player for a header, or b) he stops the ball with his chest and plays it back high. The receiving player must receive the ball with this head and put it in the net. In the beginning he should receive the ball with the head and then control it with the foot; later he should shoot a volley immediately after receiving the ball with the head. The next player starts as soon as the ball has been received. The rebounder changes regularly.

Equipment: 1 regulation size goal(s), 3 cones

Tips:
- To do a lob the foot is positioned underneath the ball and lifts the ball with the instep towards the rebounder.
- Pay attention to your posture when taking a shot (upper body over the ball; supporting leg is 12-16 inches to the side staggered with the ball, the foot points in shooting direction, the arms swing along; the arm closest to the shooting leg mimics the swinging

motion of the leg (when shooting withthe right leg, the right arm moves back to gather momentum, the left arm moves forward), at the moment of the shot the eyes are on the ball.)

- During the volley the upper body is bent slightly forward. The point of contact on the ball is low (not too high). This gives the ball more force and accuracy.
- Make sure that the waiting starting player begins with the drill as soon as the rebounder has thrown/passed the ball back to the active player.
- When receiving or moving the ball with the head it is important to keep the ball as low as possible in running direction (forehead contact area points slightly downward) and not let it bounce up or to the side. (Head is tilted back)

Field size: 10 x 25 yards

Distance between cones:
Goal to rebounder cone: 16 yards
Rebounder cone to start cones: 3-9 yards

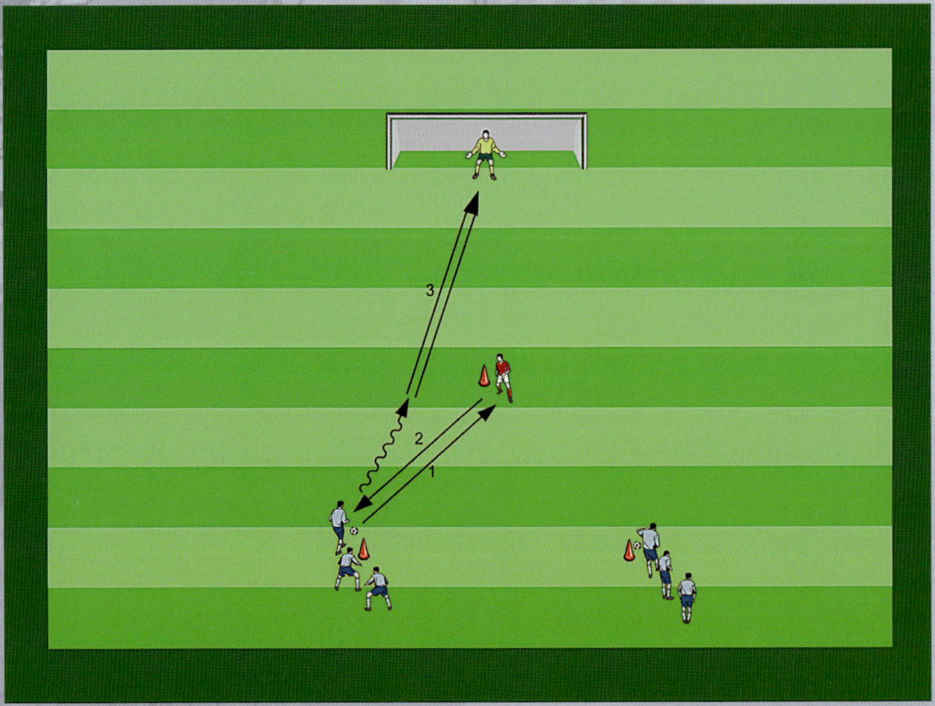

7 Shot on goal with a fixed rebounder, variation IV

Purpose of training
- Ball handling techniques

Training emphasis
- Shooting techniques/shot on goal

Training aspects

Specific purpose:	**Speed of action with the ball, speed of anticipation, moving with the ball, double pass, speed of decision-making, combination ball handling techniques with movement, reaction speed, volley, instep**
Age group:	**Age 11 to seniors**
Playing level:	**Advanced**
Form of training:	**Group**
Training structure:	**Main part/ emphasis**
Intention:	**Improving individual quality**
Number of players:	**4 or more**
Number of participating players:	**Entire Team**
Training location	**Any**
Space requirements:	**Restricted playing field**
Length:	**10-15 min**
Physical aspects:	**Soccer-specific endurance**
Goalies:	**1 goalie**

Organization:
Setting up one goal, two start cones and one cone where the rebounder positions himself, as shown in the illustration. The players are divided evenly between the two start cones. The balls are also distributed to the two start cones. The starting players always have a ball.

Execution:
The two groups' respective starting players take turns playing a high ball (lob) to the rebounder. He lets the ball rebound high into the starting player'srunning lane and orientates himself to the starting player from the second group. The starting player now receives/moves the ball a) at a run with one touch and with the second touch takes a volley on goal, or b) shoots directly on goal without first receiving the ball. Afterwards he gets in line at the other start cone. Once the rebounder has passed the ball back, the starting player from the other cone begins his pass. The rebounder changes regularly.

Equipment: 1 regulation size goal(s), 3 cones

Tips:
- To do a lob the foot is positioned underneath the ball and lifts the ball with the instep towards the rebounder.
- Pay attention to your posture when taking a shot (upper body over the ball; supporting leg is 12-16 inches to the side staggered with the ball, the foot points in shooting direction, the arms swing along; the arm closest to the shooting leg mimics the swinging motion of the leg (when shooting with

the right leg, the right arm moves back to gather momentum, the left arm moves forward), at the moment of the shot the eyes are on the ball.)

- During the volley the upper body is bent slightly forward. The point of contact on the ball is low (not too high). This gives the ball more force and accuracy.
- Make sure that the waiting starting player begins with the drill as soon as the rebounder has passed the ball back to the active player.
- As soon as the starting player initiates the swinging motion the rebounder makes a small counter movement and then briefly moves towards the ball.
- Receiving and moving the ball should be one fluid motion. Letting the ball rebound too far or deviating too far from the straight running lane when receiving and moving the ball, should be avoided.
- As soon as the ball has left the rebounder's foot the starting player runs in direction of the ball/goal.

Field size: 20 x 35 yards

Distance between cones:
Goal to rebounder cone: 12-16 yards
Rebounder cone to start cones: 3-9 yards

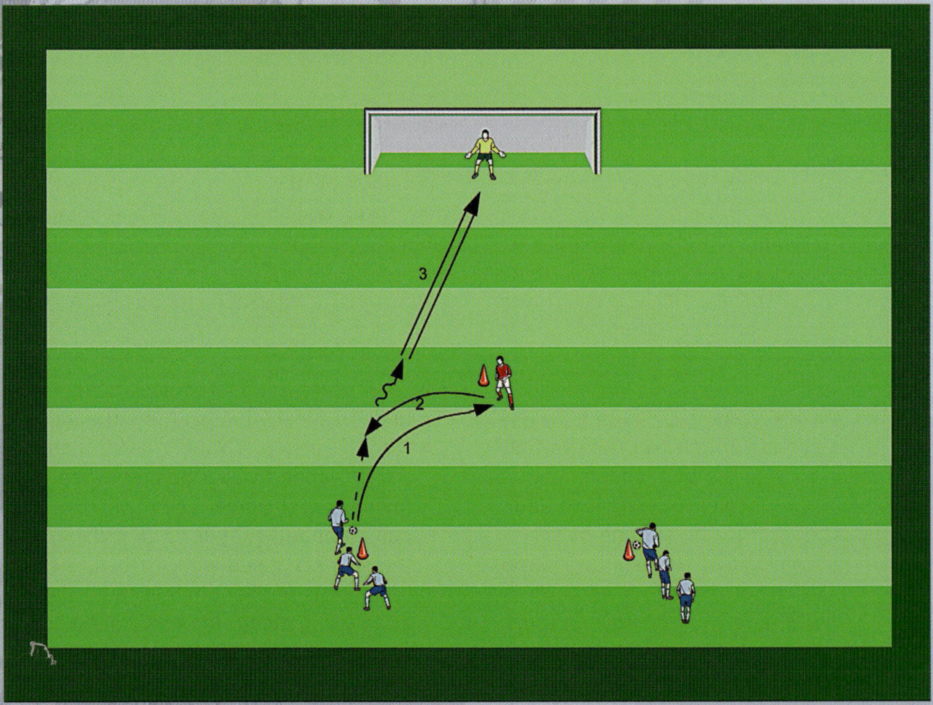

8 Shot on goal with a fixed rebounder, variation V

Purpose of training

- Ball handling techniques

Training emphasis

- Explosiveness
- Feints/tricks
- Shooting techniques, shot on goal

Training aspects

Specific purpose:	**Push-off power, speed of action with the ball, speed of anticipation, receiving and moving the ball, double pass, dribbling, speed of decision-making, inside foot, push pass (inside foot), combination ball handling technique with movement, body feints, reaction speed, instep, swerve**
Age group:	**Any**
Playing level:	**Any**
Form of training:	**Group**
Training structure:	**Main part/emphasis**
Intention:	**Improving individual quality**
Number of players:	**4 or more**
Number of participating players:	**Entire team**
Training location	**Any**
Space requirements:	**Restricted playing field**
Length:	**10-15 min**
Physical aspects:	**Soccer-specific endurance, power**
Goalies:	**1 goalie**

Organization:
Setting up one goal, one start cone where the players line up, and one where the rebounder positions himself. The players at the start cone have the balls.

Execution:
The starting player passes the ball to the rebounder, who lets it bounce back. Now the player attempts to play a feint off the rebound and put the ball in the net. Once the player has passed the rebounder the next player immediately starts his pass. Rebounders change regularly.

Equipment: 1 regulation size goal(s), 2 cones

Tips:

- The feint against a standing opponent must be initiated about 2 yards away.
- Demand different feints (scissors, pirouettes, feint shot on goal, etc.)
- The player doing the feint runs to the ball as soon as it has left the rebounder's foot.
- Demand that shots on goal also be done with the weak foot (always alternate right and left).
- Pay attention to your posture when taking a shot (upper body over the ball; supporting leg is 12-16 inches to the side staggered with the ball, the foot points in shooting direction, the

arms swing along; the arm closest to the shooting leg mimics the swinging motion of the leg (when shooting with the right leg, the right arm moves back to gather momentum, the left arm moves forward), at the moment of the shot the eyes are on the ball.)

- To avoid delays the next player starts immediately after the previous player has passed the rebounder.
- As soon as the starting player initiates the swinging motion the rebounder makes a small counter movement and then briefly moves towards the ball.
- Receiving and moving the ball should be one fluid motion. Letting the ball rebound too far or deviating too far from the straight running lane when receiving and moving the ball, should be avoided.
- Receiving and moving the ball should be done strictly with only one touch.
- The trainer can also act as rebounder.
- The rebounder's play can be passive, partially active or active, meaning physical play.

Field size: 10 x 25 yards

Distance between cones:
Goal to rebounder cone: 12-18 yards
Rebounder cone to start cone: 6-12 yards

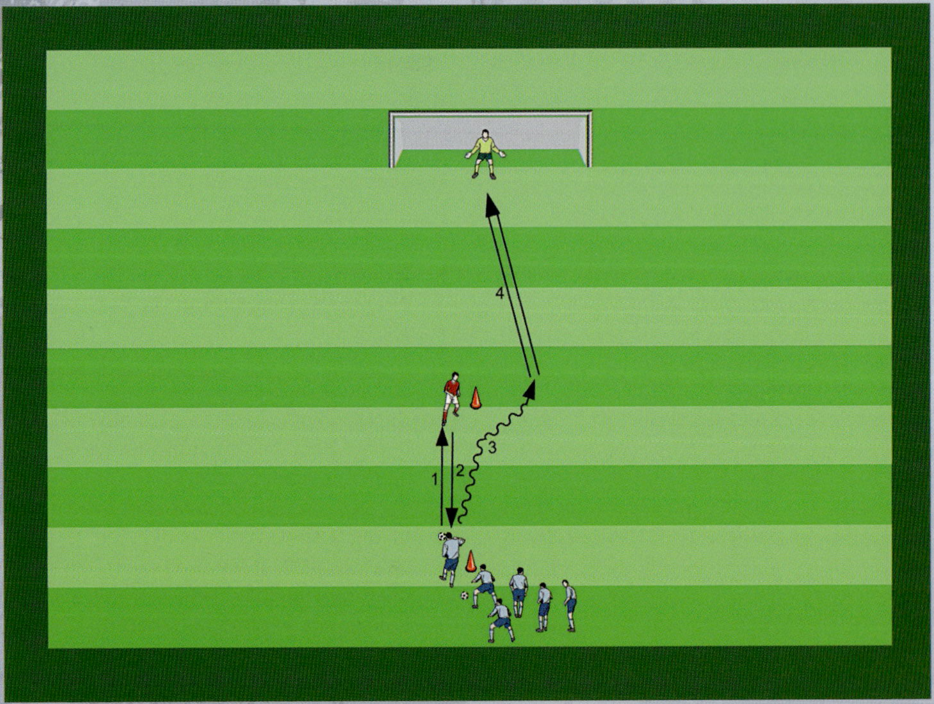

9 Shot on goal setting up your own shot

Purpose of training
- Ball handling techniques

Training emphasis
- Shooting techniques/ shot on goal

Training aspects

Specific purpose:	**Push-off power, speed of action with the ball, speed of anticipation, drop kick, speed of decision-making, push pass (inside foot), combination ball handling technique with movement, short passes, body feints, reaction speed, volley, instep**
Age group:	**Any**
Playing level:	**Any**
Form of training:	**Group**
Training structure:	**Main part/emphasis**
Intention:	**Improving individual quality**
Number of players:	**2 or more**
Number of participating players:	**Entire team**
Training location	**Any**
Space requirements:	**Restricted playing field**
Length:	**10-15 min**
Physical aspects:	**Soccer-specific endurance, power**
Goalies:	**1 goalie**

Organization:
Setting up one goal, one orientation cone and one start cone,as shown in the illustration. Players and balls are positioned at the start cone.

Execution:
The player passes the ball to himself about 2-3 yards into the run-up and shoots on goal while moving.

Variation 1:
The player lobs the ball forward and after the ball bounces a few times, shoots a volley on goal.

Variation 2:
Like variation 1, but this time the player shoots the volley from the air without the ball having touched the ground.

Variation 3:
The player lobs the ball forward and when the ball bounces up, makes a drop kick on goal.

Equipment: 1 regulation size goal(s), 2 cones

Tips:
- Demand that shots on goal also be done with the weak foot (always alternate right and left).
- Pay attention to your posture when taking a shot (upper body over the ball; supporting leg is 12-16 inches to the side staggered with the ball, the foot points in shooting direction, the arms swing along; the arm closest to the shooting leg mimics the swinging motion of the leg (when shooting with the right leg, the right arm moves back

to gather momentum, the left arm moves forward), at the moment of the shot the eyes are on the ball.)

- During the volley the upper body is bent slightly forward. The point of contact on the ball is low (not too high). This gives the ball more force and accuracy.
- When executing a drop kick contact is made with the instep the instant the ball touches the ground.
- To avoid delays the next player starts immediately after the previous player has taken a shot.
- The orientation cone serves as a visual aid. The shot should be taken when the ball is level with the cone.
- The pass should not be played too hard, but also not too slow.

Field size: 10 x 25 yards

Distance between cones:

Goal to orientation cone: 8-16 yards

Orientation cone to start cone: 3-9 yards

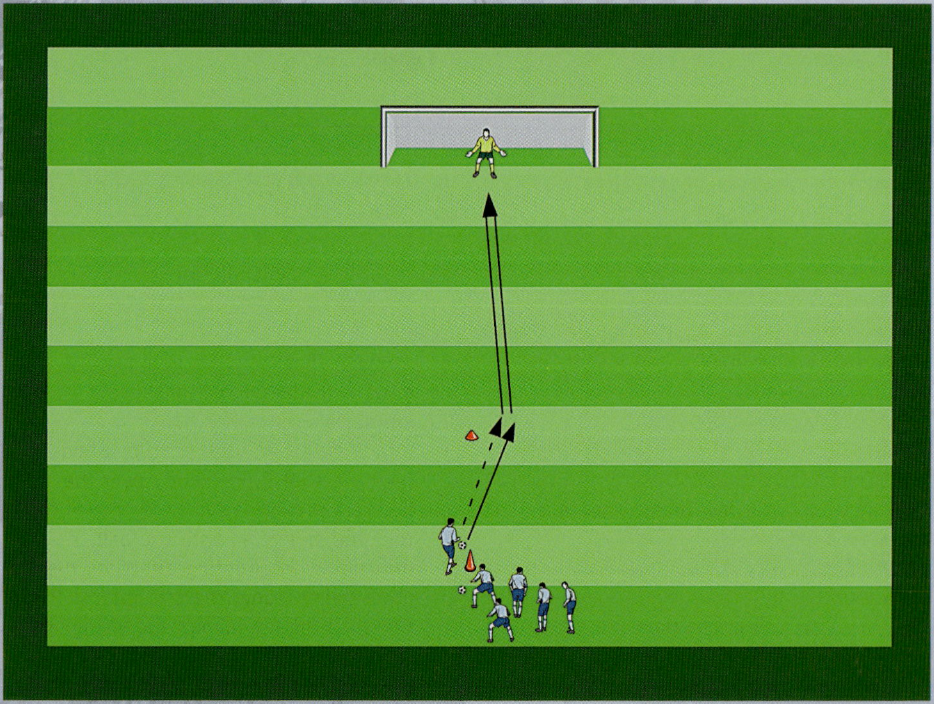

10 Shot on goal after dribbling with a feint

Purpose of training

- Ball handling techniques

Training emphasis

- Feints
- Shot on goal

Training aspects

Specific purpose:	**Speed of action with the ball, speed of anticipation, outside instep, moving with the ball, dribbling, speed of decision-making, inside foot, push pass (inside), combination ball handling technique with movement, body feint, reaction speed, instep, swerve**
Age group:	**Any**
Playing level:	**Advanced**
Form of training:	**Group**
Training structure:	**Main part/emphasis**
Intention:	**Improving individual quality**
Number of players:	**2 or more**
Number of participating players:	**Entire team**
Training location	**Any**
Space requirements:	**Restricted playing field**
Length:	**10-15 min**
Physical aspects:	**Soccer-specific endurance, power**
Goalies:	**1 goalie**

Organization:
Setting up one goal, one orientation cone and one start cone as shown in the illustration. Players and balls are positioned at the start cone.

Execution:
The starting player starts to dribble as fast as he can. He does a feint in front of the orientation cone and immediately takes a shot on goal. As soon as he has completed the feint, the next player starts.

Equipment: 1 regulation size goal(s), 2 cones

Tips:

- While dribbling make sure the ball stays close to the outside instep (ball no more than 20 inches from foot).
- Execute the feint about 2 yards from the orientation cone. Try to take the shot when level with the cone or just past it.
- Demand different types of feints (scissors, pirouettes, feint shot on goal, Matthews, etc.)
- Shots on goal should be trained with the right and left foot.
- Pay attention to your posture when taking a shot (upper body over the ball; supporting leg is 12-16 inches to the side staggered with the ball, the foot points in shooting direction, the arms swing along; the arm closest to the shooting leg mimics the swinging motion of the leg (when shooting with the right leg, the right arm moves back to gather momentum, the left arm

moves forward), at the moment of the shot the eyes are on the ball.)

- Different shooting techniques (inside foot kick, instep kick, swerve) can be practiced where appropriate (at the trainer's command).
- As soon as the active player has taken a shot on goal the next player begins to dribble.

Field size: 10 x 25 yards.

Distance between cones:
Goal to orientation cone: 8-16 yards
Orientation cone to start cone: 8-9 yards

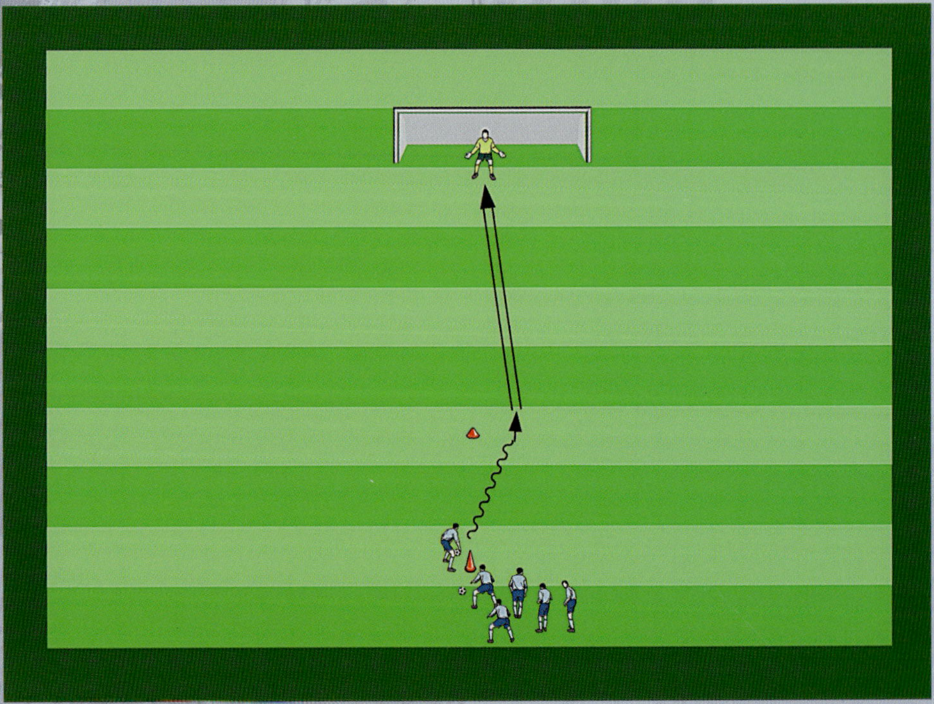

11 Controlling the ball with your back to the goal

Purpose of training

- Ball handling techniques
- Wing play/centering (cross)

Training emphasis

- Receiving and moving with the ball
- Shot on goal

Training aspects

Specific purpose:	**Push-off power, speed of action with the ball, speed of anticipation, outside instep, moving with the ball, speed of decision-making, inside foot, push-pass (inside), combination ball handling technique with movement, short passes, body feints, reaction speed, instep**
Age group:	**Any**
Playing level:	**Any**
Form of training:	**Group**
Training structure:	**Main part/emphasis**
Intention:	**Improving individual quality**
Number of players:	**4 or more**
Number of participating players:	**Entire team**
Training location	**Any**
Space requirements:	**Restricted playing field**
Length:	**10-15 min**
Physical aspects:	**Soccer-specific endurance, power**
Goalies:	**1 goalie**

Organization:
Setting up one goal, cones in a square, and one start cone, as shown in the illustration. One player is positioned inside the square. The others are positioned at the start cone with the ball.

Execution:
The starting player plays a low pass to the player inside the cone square who has his back to the goal. The player turns with the ball and takes a shot on goal. The shot on goal should be taken from inside the square. The shooter retrieves the ball and the passing player now goes inside the square, etc.

Variation:
An air ball can be substituted for a low pass.

Equipment: 1 regulation size goal(s), 5 cones

Tips:

- Shots on goal should be taken with both the right and the left foot.
- Pay attention to your posture when taking a shot (upper body over the ball; supporting leg is 12-16 inches to the side staggered with the ball, the foot points in shooting direction, the arms swing along; the arm closest to the shooting leg mimics the swinging motion of the leg (when shooting with the right leg, the right arm moves back to gather momentum, the left arm moves forward), at the moment of the shot the eyes are on the ball.)
- Turning and receiving the ball should be one fluid motion. Letting the ball

rebound too far or deviating too far from the straight running lane when receiving and moving the ball, should be avoided.

- Initiate a starting motion (to the side or rear and move towards the passing player) before moving with the ball.
- Different shooting techniques (inside foot kick, instep kick, swerve) can be practiced where appropriate (at the trainer's command).
- When receiving the ball with the chest the upper body must be turned towards the goal when contact is made with the ball, thus directing the ball in the desired direction.
- As soon as the ball has left the foot of the passing player, he runs inside the square in anticipation of the next pass.

Field size: 10 x 35 yards.

Distance between cones:
Goal to cone square: 16-20 yards
Cone square to start cone: 8-15 yards (low pass/air ball)
Cones in square: 3-5 yards

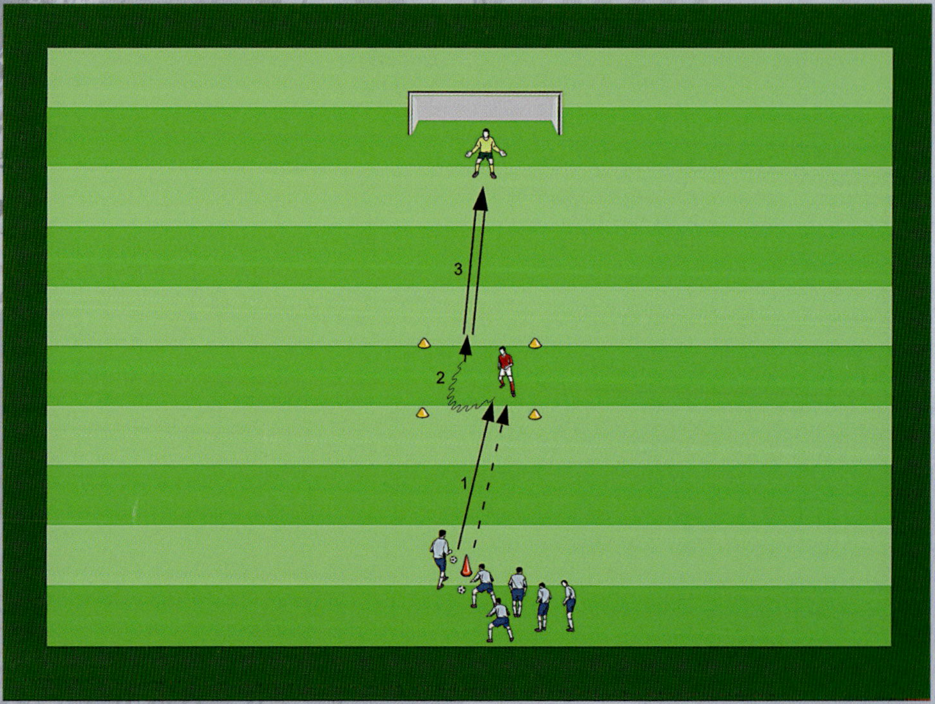

12 Shot on goal after a pass combination

Purpose of training
- Ball handling techniques
- Wing play/centering (cross)

Training emphasis
- Receiving and moving with the ball
- Shot on goal

Training aspects

Specific purpose:	**Speed of action with the ball, speed of anticipation, outside instep, moving with the ball, direct pass play, speed of decision-making, inside pass, push-pass (inside), combination ball handling technique with movement, passing to multiple stations, volley, instep, swerve**
	Age 9 to seniors
Age group:	**Advanced**
Playing level:	**Group**
Form of training:	**Main part/emphasis**
Training structure:	**Group**
Intention:	**Bonding, improving individual quality**
Number of players:	**6 or more**
Number of participating players:	**Entire Group**
Training location	**Any**
Space requirements:	**Restricted playing field**
Length:	**10-15 min**
Physical aspects:	**Soccer-specific endurance, power**
Goalies:	**1 goalie**

Organization:
Setting up one goal, two start cones (A+B) where players line up, and one where the rebounder is positioned. Balls are with group A players.

Execution:
Starting player A juggles the ball. Then he passes it with a volley to the rebounder, who plays it directly to player B. Player B traps the ball with one touch and takes a shot on goal.

Variation:
Player B has to immediately utilize the ball from the rebounder. The subsequent position changes take place as follows: starting player A becomes the rebounder, the rebounder lines up with Group B, and starting player B lines up with Group A after he retrieves the ball.

Equipment: 1 regulation size goal(s), 3 cones

Tips:
- Demand shots on goal with the weak foot (always alternate right and left).
- Pay attention to your posture when taking a shot (upper body over the ball; supporting leg is 12-16 inches to the side staggered with the ball, the foot points in shooting direction, the arms swing along; the arm closest to the shooting leg mimics the swinging motion of the leg (when shooting with the right leg, the right arm moves back

to gather momentum, the left arm moves forward), at the moment of the shot the eyes are on the ball.)

- As soon as starting player A has passed the ball to the rebounder he runs to the rebounder's position who, immediately after his pass, lines up with Group B.
- As soon as starting player A initiates the swinging motion the rebounder makes a small counter movement and then briefly moves towards the ball.
- Receiving and moving the ball should be one fluid motion. Letting the ball rebound too far or deviating too far from the straight running lane when receiving and moving the ball, should be avoided.
- Receiving and moving the ball should be done strictly with only one touch.
- During a volley shot the upper body is bent forward slightly. Contact with the ball is made at a low point (not too high). This applies more force to the ball and makes the shot more accurate

Distance between cones:

Goal to rebounder cone: 8-16 yards

Rebounder cone to start cones: 5-8 yards

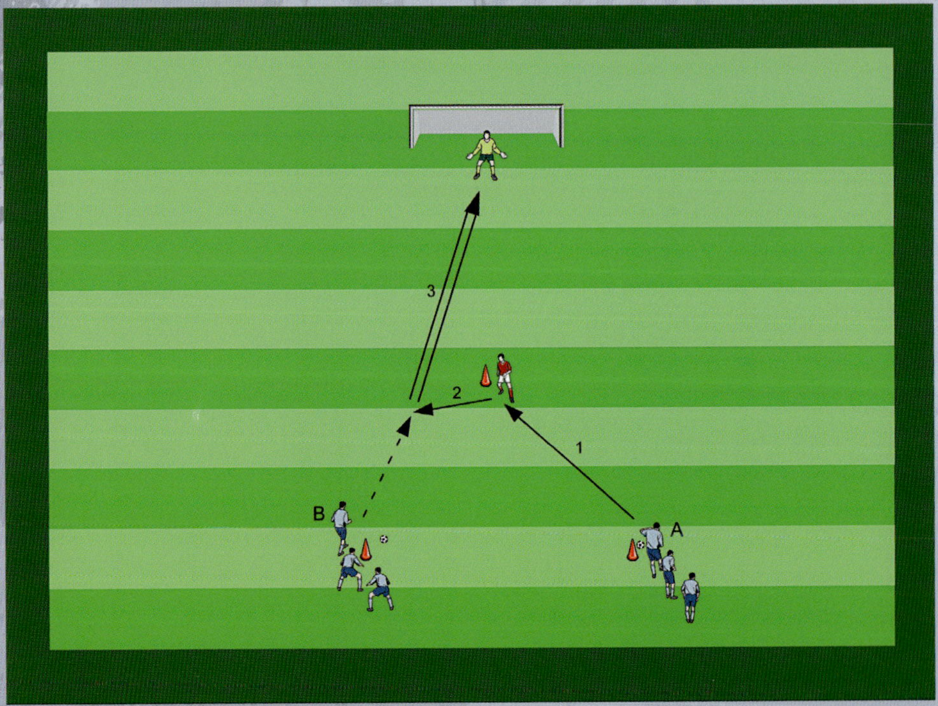

13 Shot on goal after a lateral double pass

Purpose of training
- Ball handling techniques

Training emphasis
- Shot on goal

Training aspects

Specific purpose:	**Push-off power, speed of action with the ball, speed of anticipation, outside instep, direct passing, speed of decision-making, inside foot, push-pass (inside), combination ball handling technique with movement, reaction speed, swerve**
Age group:	**Any**
Playing level:	**Any**
Form of training:	**Group**
Training structure:	**Main part/emphasis**
Intention:	**Improving individual quality**
Number of players:	**4 or more**
Number of participating players:	**Entire team**
Training location	**Any**
Space requirements:	**Restricted playing field**
Length:	**10-15 min**
Physical aspects:	**Soccer-specific endurance, power**
Goalies:	**1 goalie**

Organization:
Setting up one goal, one start cone where players line up, and one cone where the rebounder is positioned. Balls are with the players at the start cone.

Execution:
The starting player passes the ball with the right foot to the rebounder's left foot. He lets the ball bounce off to the side in such a way that the starting player, after a short sprint, is able to shoot it on goal (swerve) out of a turn from directly behind the cone with the right foot.

The exercise is set up twice so it can be executed with the left foot from the other side the second time.

Equipment: 1 regulation size goal(s), 2 cones

Tips:
- Swerve: Shoot the ball with the inside/ toe to put an arched spin on the ball (swerve). To do this, the player's upper body moves into a slightly more lateral position. A slight backbend is also not uncommon.
- The next player starts immediately after the shot.
- The players' run up is nearly parallel to the rebounder.
- The objective is to learn how to successfully finish with a moving ball.

Field size: 10 x 20 yards

Distance between cones:
Goal to rebounder cone: 8-18 yards
Start cone to rebounder cone: length – 2 yards/width 3-4 yards

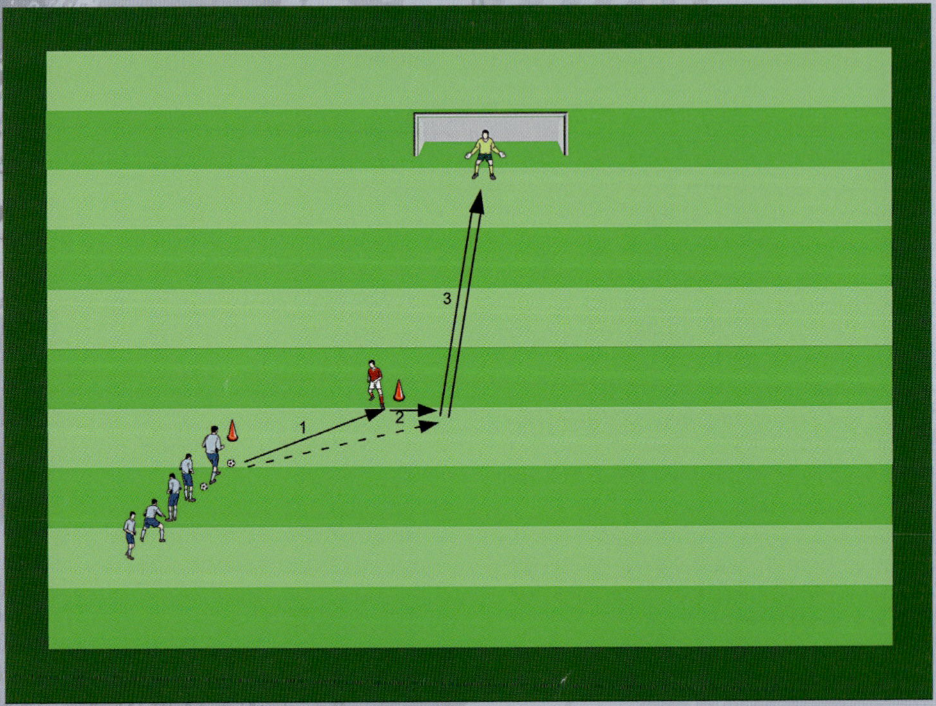

14 Shot on goal by a third player after a double pass

Purpose of training

- Ball handling techniques
- Wing play/centering (cross)

Training emphasis

- Receiving and moving with the ball
- Shooting techniques/shot on goal

Training aspects

Specific purpose:	**Push-off power, speed of action with the ball, speed of anticipation, outside instep, receiving and moving with the ball, double pass, dribbling, speed of decision-making, inside foot, push-pass (inside), combination ball handling technique with movement, instep, swerve**
Age group:	**Age 9 to seniors**
Playing level:	**Advanced**
Form of training:	**Group**
Training structure:	**Main part/emphasis**
Intention:	**Improving individual quality**
Number of players:	**6 or more**
Number of participating players:	**Entire team**
Training location	**Any**
Space requirements:	**Restricted playing field**
Length:	**10-15 min**
Physical aspects:	**Soccer-specific endurance, power**
Goalies:	**1 goalie**

Organization:
Setting up one goal, two start cones where players line up, and one cone where the rebounder is positioned. Balls are with the players at the group A start cone.

Execution:
Player A passes the ball to the rebounder. He passes the ball low (later on medium-high or high) back into the running lane of player A. Now player A passes the ball directly into the running lane of player B, who controls the ball and finishes the action with a shot on goal.

Next A becomes the rebounder. The rebounder lines up with Group B and the Group B player lines up with Group A.

Equipment: 1 regulation size goal(s), 2 cones

Tips:

- As soon as the starting player initiates the swinging motion the rebounder makes a small counter movement and then briefly moves towards the ball.
- Player B starts parallel with player A's swinging motion, before A plays the pass into B's running lane.
- Receiving and moving the ball should be one fluid motion. Letting the ball rebound too far or deviating too far from the straight running lane when receiving and moving the ball, should be avoided.
- Different shooting techniques (inside foot kick, instep kick, swerve) can be practiced where appropriate (at the trainer's command).
- Pay attention to your posture when taking a shot (upper body over the

ball; supporting leg is 12-16 inches to the side staggered with the ball, the foot points in shooting direction, the arms swing along; the arm closest to the shooting leg mimics the swinging motion of the leg (when shooting with the right leg, the right arm moves back to gather momentum, the left arm moves forward), at the moment of the shot the eyes are on the ball.)

Field size: 10 x 25 yards

Distance between cones:
Goal to rebounder cone: 8-18 yards
Rebounder cone to start cones: 5-8 yards
Start cone A to start cone B: 2-3 yards

15 Direct volley on goal with your back to the passing player

Purpose of training

- Ball handling techniques

Training emphasis

- Receiving and moving with the ball
- Shot on goal

Training aspects

Specific purpose:	**Push-off power, speed of action with the ball, speed of anticipation, outside instep, moving with the ball, direct passing, dribbling, speed of decision-making, speed of action, inside foot, reaction speed, volley, instep, speed of perception**
Age group:	**Any**
Playing level:	**Any**
Form of training:	**Group**
Training structure:	**Main part/emphasis**
Intention:	**Improving individual quality**
Number of players:	**4 or more**
Number of participating players:	**Entire team**
Training location	**Any**
Space requirements:	**Restricted playing field**
Length:	**10-15 min**
Physical aspects:	**Soccer-specific endurance, power**
Goalies:	**1 goalie**

Organization:
Setting up one goal as well as two start cones, as shown in the illustration. All but one of the players line up with balls at cone A, one player goes to cone B.

Execution:
Player A lobs the ball over player B from a standing position or from a short run up. Player B starts for the ball and shoots a direct volley or drop kick on goal. Player A then immediately runs to cone B, player B runs to cone A after retrieving the ball.

Equipment: 1 regulation size goal(s), 2 cones

Tips:

- To do a lob the foot is positioned underneath the ball and lifts the ball with the instep towards the rebounder.
- Demand shots on goal with the weak foot (always alternate right and left).
- To avoid delays the next player starts immediately after one player takes a shot.
- During a volley shot the upper body is bent forward slightly. Contact with the ball is made at a low point (not too high). This applies more force to the ball and makes the shot more accurate.
- In a drop kick the ball is hit with the instep at the exact moment the ball touches the ground.

Field size: 10-x 25 yards

Distance between cones:
Goal to cone B: 11-20 yards
Goal to cone A: 16-25 yards
Cone B to cone A: 5 yards

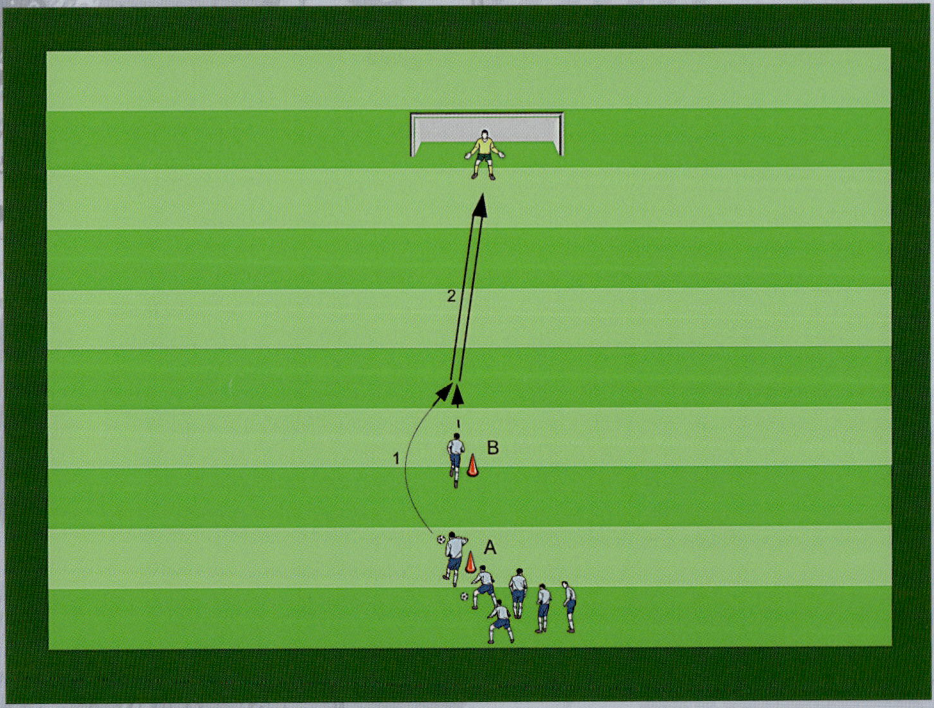

16 Shot on goal after a double pass

Purpose of training
- Ball handling techniques

Training emphasis
- Shooting techniques/shot on goal

Training aspects

Specific purpose:	**Push-off power, speed of action with the ball, speed of anticipation, outside instep, double pass, speed of decision-making, push-pass (inside), inside foot kick, combination ball handling technique with movement, reaction speed, instep, swerve**
Age group:	**Any**
Playing level:	**Any**
Form of training:	**Group**
Training structure:	**Main part/emphasis**
Intention:	**Improving individual quality**
Number of players:	**4 or more**
Number of participating players:	**Entire team**
Training location	**Any**
Space requirements:	**Restricted playing field**
Length:	**10-15 min**
Physical aspects:	**Soccer-specific endurance, power**
Goalies:	**1 goalie**

Organization:
Setting up one goal, as well as one start cone and one rebounder cone, as shown in the illustration. One of the players is positioned at the rebounder cone, the rest are at the start cone with the balls.

Execution:
The starting player plays a double pass with the rebounder and utilizes the ball as a volley.

Option:
Shooting competition. Goals are counted; the rebounder can utilize the rebound.

Equipment: 1 regulation size goal(s), 2 cones

Tips:
- The pass to the rebounder is played to his strong foot.
- As soon as the starting player initiates the swinging motion the rebounder makes a small counter movement and then briefly moves towards the ball.
- Pay attention to your posture when taking a shot (upper body over the ball; supporting leg is 12-16 inches to the side staggered with the ball, the foot points in shooting direction, the arms swing along; the arm closest to the shooting leg mimics the swinging motion of the leg (when shooting with the right leg, the right arm moves back to gather momentum, the left arm

moves forward), at the moment of the shot the eyes are on the ball.)

- Different shooting techniques (inside foot kick, instep kick, swerve) can be practiced where appropriate (at the trainer's command).

Field size: 10 x 25 yards

Distance between cones:
Goal to cone B: 9-16 yards
Goal to cone A: 16-25 yards
Cone B to cone A: 7 yards

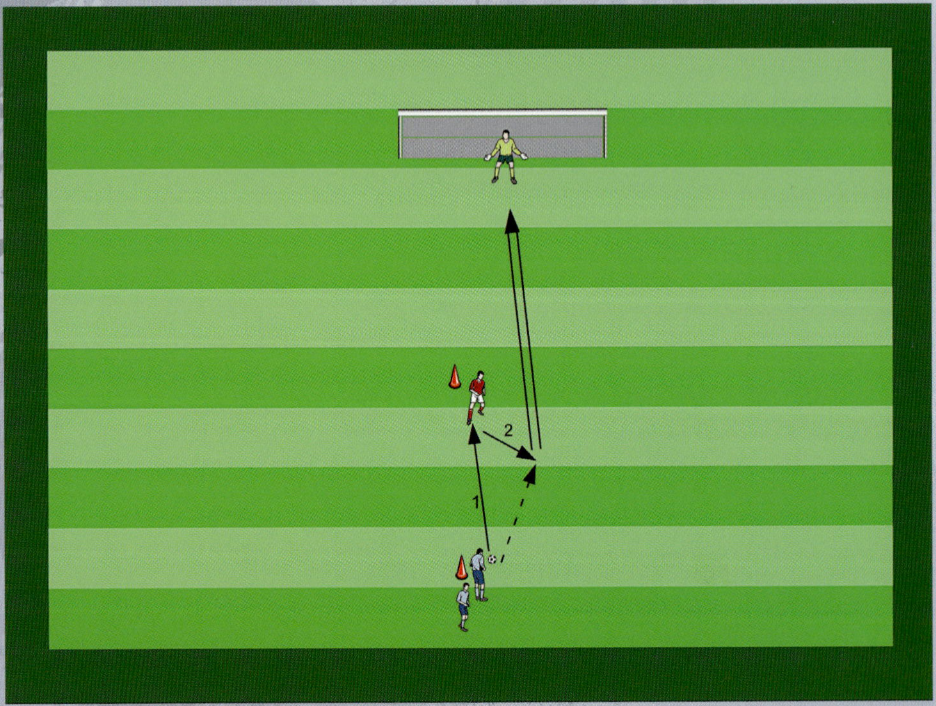

17 Scoring after a pass between the legs with your back to the goal

Purpose of training

- Ball handling techniques

Training emphasis

- Shooting techniques/shot on goal

Training aspects

Specific purpose:	**Push-off power, speed of action with the ball, speed of anticipation, outside instep, direct passing, speed of decision-making, action speed, inside foot, push-pass (inside), inside foot kick, combination ball handling technique with movement, reaction speed, instep, speed of perception**
Age group:	**Any**
Playing level:	**Any**
Form of training:	**Group**
Training structure:	**Main part/emphasis**
Intention:	**Improving individual quality**
Number of players:	**4 or more**
Number of participating players:	**Entire team**
Training location	**Any**
Space requirements:	**Restricted playing field**
Length:	**10-15 min**
Physical aspects:	**Soccer-specific endurance, power**
Goalies:	**1 goalie**

Organization:
Setting up one goal, one cone A and one cone B, as shown in the illustration. One player stands at cone B, the other players at cone A with balls.

Execution:
Player A passes the ball to player B through the legs, who stands with his back to the goal. Player B abruptly pivots and sprints to the ball as fast as he can, and shoots on goal.

Player A now takes player B's position and player B lines up at cone A.

Equipment: 1 regulation size goal(s), 2 cones

Tips:

- Pay attention to your posture when taking a shot (upper body over the ball; supporting leg is 12-16 inches to the side staggered with the ball, the foot points in shooting direction, the arms swing along; the arm closest to the shooting leg mimics the swinging motion of the leg (when shooting with the right leg, the right arm moves back to gather momentum, the left arm moves forward), at the moment of the shot the eyes are on the ball.)
- Player B starts as soon as the ball has rolled through his legs.
- Different shooting techniques (inside foot kick, instep kick, swerve) can be

practiced where appropriate (at the trainer's command).

- The passing player has to time his pass very well so the shooting player
- -if players are older than 16- is able to reach the ball preferably before the 18 yard line and can take a shot on goal.

Field size: 10 x 25

Distance between cones:

Goal to cone B: 15-20 yards

Cone B to cone A: 4-17 yards

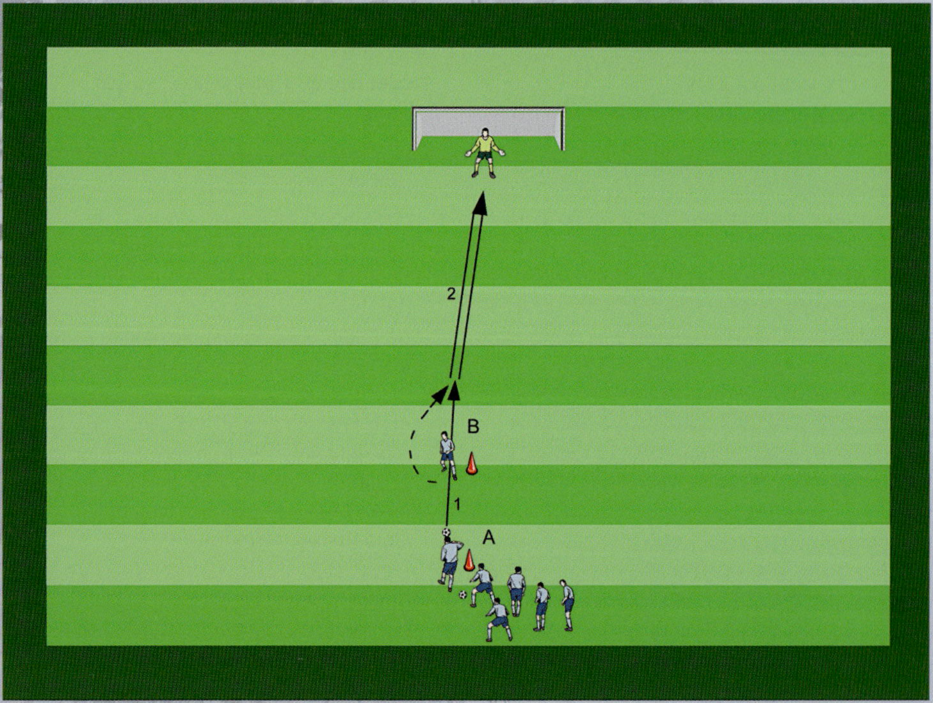

18 Shot on goal after a short dribble

Purpose of training
- Ball handling techniques

Training emphasis
- Shot on goal

Training aspects

Specific purpose:	Push-off power, speed of action with the ball, speed of anticipation, outside instep, moving with the ball, dribbling, speed of decision-making, action speed, inside foot, push-pass (inside), combination ball handling technique with movement, reaction speed, instep, speed of perception
Age group:	Any
Playing level:	Any
Form of training:	Group
Training structure:	Main part/emphasis
Intention:	Improving individual quality
Number of players:	4 or more
Number of participating players:	Entire team
Training location	Any
Space requirements:	Restricted playing field
Length:	10-15 min
Physical aspects:	Soccer-specific endurance, power
Goalies:	1 goalie

Organization:
Setting up one goal, one orientation cone, and one start cone. The players line up at the start cone. Balls are with the players.

Execution:
The player dribbles the ball in direction of the goal. When he is level with the orientation cone, he takes a running shot on goal. As soon as he reaches he cone the next player starts his dribble, etc.

Equipment: 1 regulation size goal(s), 2 cones

Tips:
- Make sure shots on goal are practiced with both right and left foot. Only shoot with the left foot from one cone, and only the right foot from the other cone.
- Pay attention to your posture when taking a shot (upper body over the ball; supporting leg is 12-16 inches to the side staggered with the ball, the foot points in shooting direction, the arms swing along; the arm closest to the shooting leg mimics the swinging motion of the leg (when shooting with the right leg, the right arm moves back to gather momentum, the left arm moves forward), at the moment of the shot the eyes are on the ball.)
- Different shooting techniques (inside foot kick, instep kick, swerve) can be practiced where appropriate (at the trainer's command).

- The following criteria must be adhered to when dribbling:
    - Take your eyes off the ball at regular intervals (alternate looking at the ball and looking ahead).
    - Keep your speed up.
    - As many touches as possible.
    - Keep the ball close (ball should not be more than 20 inches away).

Field size: 10 x 25 yards

Distance between cones:
Goal to orientation cone: 8-18 yards
Orientation cone to start cone: 5-7 yards

1 Dribbling
2 Shot on goal

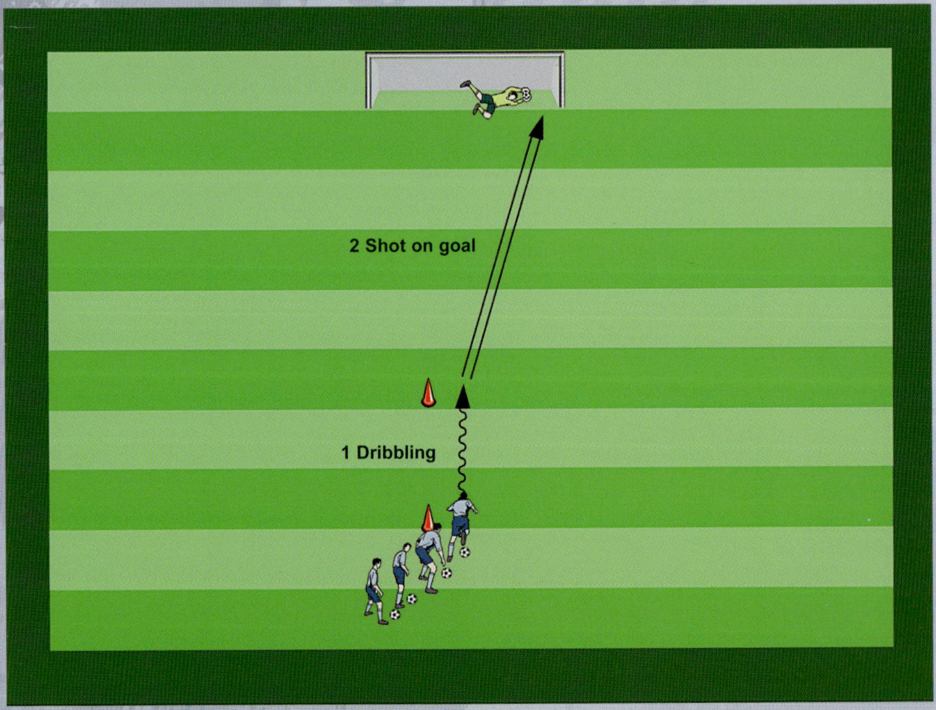

19 Shot on goal setting up your own shot

Purpose of training
- Ball handling techniques

Training emphasis
- Shooting techniques/shot on goal

Training aspects

Specific purpose:	Push-off power, speed of action with the ball, speed of anticipation, outside instep, speed of decision-making, action speed, push-pass (inside), inside foot kick, combination ball handling technique with movement, short passes, reaction speed, instep, speed of perception, swerve
Age group:	Any
Playing level:	Any
Form of training:	Group
Training structure:	Main part/emphasis
Intention:	Improving individual quality
Number of players:	4 or more
Number of participating players:	Entire team
Training location	Any
Space requirements:	Restricted playing field
Length:	10-15 min
Physical aspects:	Soccer-specific endurance, power
Goalies:	1 goalie

Organization:
Setting up one goal, one start cone, and one orientation cone, as shown in the illustration. The players line up at the start cone. Each player should have a ball if possible.

Execution:
The players set up their own shot on goal. In doing so, they must take the shot before the orientation cone, but no later than when they are level with it.

Equipment: 1 regulation size goal(s), 2 cones

Tips:
- The correct speed is critical when setting up the shot. It must be timed so the player is able to sprint to the ball in time.
- Pay attention to your posture when taking a shot (upper body over the ball; supporting leg is 12-16 inches to the side staggered with the ball, the foot points in shooting direction, the arms swing along; the arm closest to the shooting leg mimics the swinging motion of the leg (when shooting with the right leg, the right arm moves back

to gather momentum, the left arm moves forward), at the moment of the shot the eyes are on the ball.)

- Different shooting techniques (inside foot kick, instep kick, swerve) can be practiced where appropriate (at the trainer's command).

Field size: 10 x 25 yards

Distance between cones:
Goal to cone B: 15-20 yards
Cone B to cone A: 4-7 yards

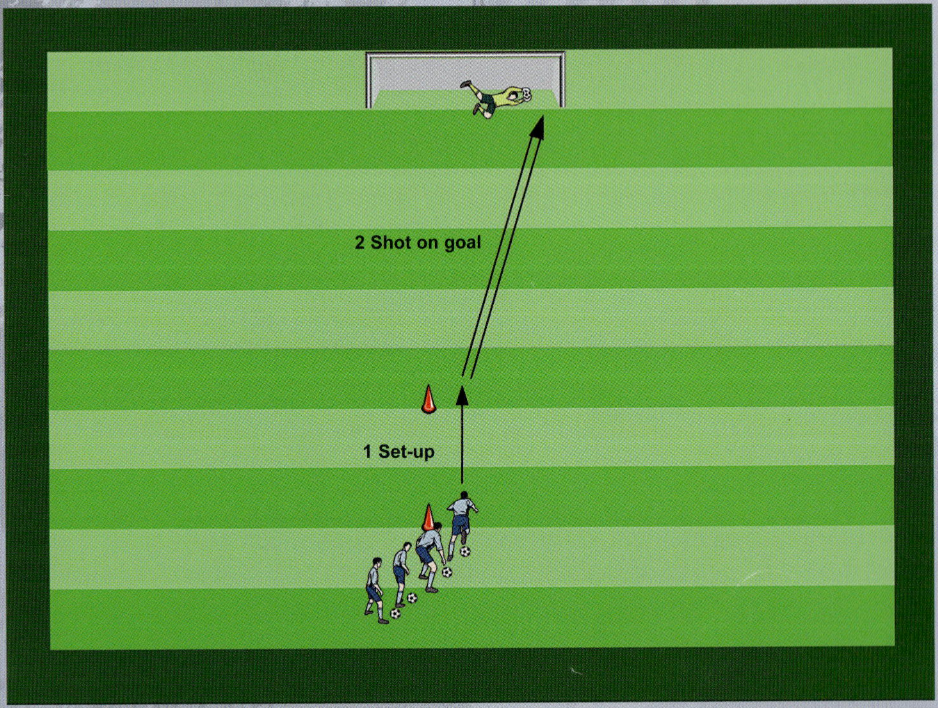

20 Volley shot

Purpose of training
- Ball handling techniques
- Wing play/centering (cross)

Training emphasis
- Lifting the ball
- Shot on goal

Training aspects

Specific purpose:	Push-off power, speed of action with the ball, speed of anticipation, speed of decision-making,action speed, combination ball handling technique with movement, short passes, reaction speed, volley, instep, speed of perception
Age group:	Any
Playing level:	Beginner, advanced
Form of training:	Group
Training structure:	Main part/emphasis
Intention:	Improving individual quality
Number of players:	4 or more
Number of participating players:	Entire team
Training location	Any
Space requirements:	Restricted playing field
Length:	10-15 min
Physical aspects:	Soccer-specific endurance, powe
Goalies:	1 goalie

Organization:
Setting up one goal, as well as one start cone where the players can line up with balls.

Execution:
The player lobs the ball for himself and then shoots a volley on goal.

Equipment: 1 regulation size goal(s), 1 cone

Tips:
- To do a lob the foot is positioned underneath the ball and lifts the ball with the instep.
- During the volley the upper body is bent slightly forward (over the ball). The point of contact on the ball is low (not too high). This gives the ball more force and accuracy.

Field size: 10 x 20 yards

Distance between cones:
Goal to start cone: 12-20 yards

21 Receiving and controlling the ball with your back to the goal

Purpose of training
- Ball handling techniques
- Wing play/centering (cross)

Training emphasis
- Lifting the ball
- Shot on goal

Training aspects

Specific purpose:	**Push-off power, speed of action with the ball, speed of anticipation, outside instep, moving with the ball, drop kick, action speed, combination ball handling technique with movement, short passes, reaction speed, volley, instep, speed of perception**
Age group:	**Any**
Playing level:	**Any**
Form of training:	**Group**
Training structure:	**Main part/emphasis**
Intention:	**Improving individual quality**
Number of players:	**4 or more**
Number of participating players:	**Entire team**
Training location	**Any**
Space requirements:	**Restricted playing field**
Length:	**10-15 min**
Physical aspects:	**Soccer-specific endurance, power**
Goalies:	**1 goalie**

Organization:
Setting up one goal as well as two start cones (I + II), as shown in the illustration. One player stands at cone II with his back to the goal, the rest of the players are at cone I with the ball.

Execution:
Player A plays a high ball to player B. Player B receives the ball out of the air while turning towards the goal, and finishes with the second touch. Right after the pass player A takes player B's position, etc.

Equipment: 1 regulation size goal(s), 2 cones

Tips:
- Shots on goal should be trained with the right and left foot.
- Receiving and moving the ball should be one fluid motion. Letting the ball rebound too far or deviating too far from the straight running lane when receiving and moving the ball, should be avoided.
- When receiving the ball with the chest the upper body is turned towards the goal, so a targeted shot on goal can be taken with the next touch.
- During a volley shot the upper body is bent forward slightly. Contact with the

ball is made at a low point (not too high). This applies more force to the ball and makes the shot more accurate.

- When executing a drop kick contact is made with the instep the instant the ball touches the ground.

Field size: 10 x 25 yards

Distance between cones:
Goal to cone I: 8-18 yards
Cone I to cone II: 4-7 yards

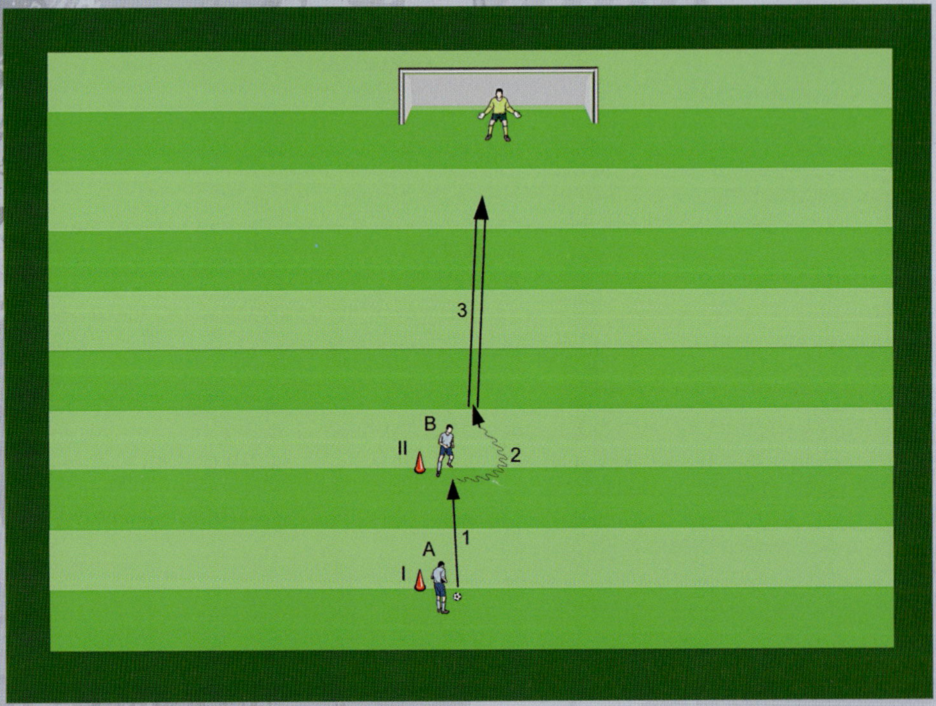

22 Pass and finish after a sprint

Purpose of training
- Ball handling techniques

Training emphasis
- Shooting techniques/shot on goal

Training aspects

Specific purpose:	**Push-off power, speed of anticipation, outside instep, direct pass play, speed of decision-making, action speed, inside foot, push-pass (inside), inside foot kick, combination ball handling technique with movement, reaction speed, instep, speed of perception, swerve**
	Any
Age group:	**Any**
Playing level:	**Group**
Form of training:	**Main part/emphasis**
Training structure:	**Improving individual quality**
Intention:	**4 or more**
Number of players:	**Entire team**
Number of participating players:	**Any**
Training location	**Restricted playing field**
Space requirements:	**10-15 min**
Length:	**Soccer-specific endurance, power, Speed**
Physical aspects:	**endurance**
Goalies:	**1 goalie**

Organization:
Setting up one goal, as well as two start cones (A+B) and two orientation cones (I+II), as shown in the illustration. The players and balls are evenly divided between the two start cones to the left and right of the goal.

Execution:
Player A starts with a pass in the direction of orientation cone II. At the moment he initiates his swing, player B starts to sprint to cone II in order to reach the ball before it passes the cone. In doing so player B runs around the cone and takes a running shot on goal.

After that the next player from group B passes the ball in the direction of cone I, where the next player from group A tries to shoot the ball on goal before it passes cone I. The group that opens with the pass alternates after each shot.

Equipment: 1 regulation size goal(s), 4 cones

Tips:
- Make sure shots on goal are practiced with both right and left foot.
- Pay attention to your posture when taking a shot (upper body over the ball; supporting leg is 12-16 inches to the side staggered with the ball, the footpoints in shooting direction, the arms swing along; the arm closest to the shooting leg mimics the swinging motion of the leg (when shooting with

the right leg, the right arm moves back to gather momentum, the left arm moves forward), at the moment of the shot the eyes are on the ball.)

- Different shooting techniques (inside foot kick, instep kick, swerve) can be practiced where appropriate (at the trainer's command).
- To avoid delays and prevent long waiting periods, the next opening pass is played immediately after the shot on goal.
- The passing players must develop a good sense of timing for the passing speed since the receiving player has to get to the ball before it reaches the respective orientation cone. The same applies to the receiving player. To be able to reach the ball before it passes the cone he must adapt the timing of his start and his running speed to the speed of the ball.

Field size: 28 x 16 yards

Distance between cones:
Left goal post to start cone B: 10 yards
Right goal post to start cone A: 10 yards
Start cone A to orientation cone I: 16 yards
Start cone B to orientation cone II: 16 yards

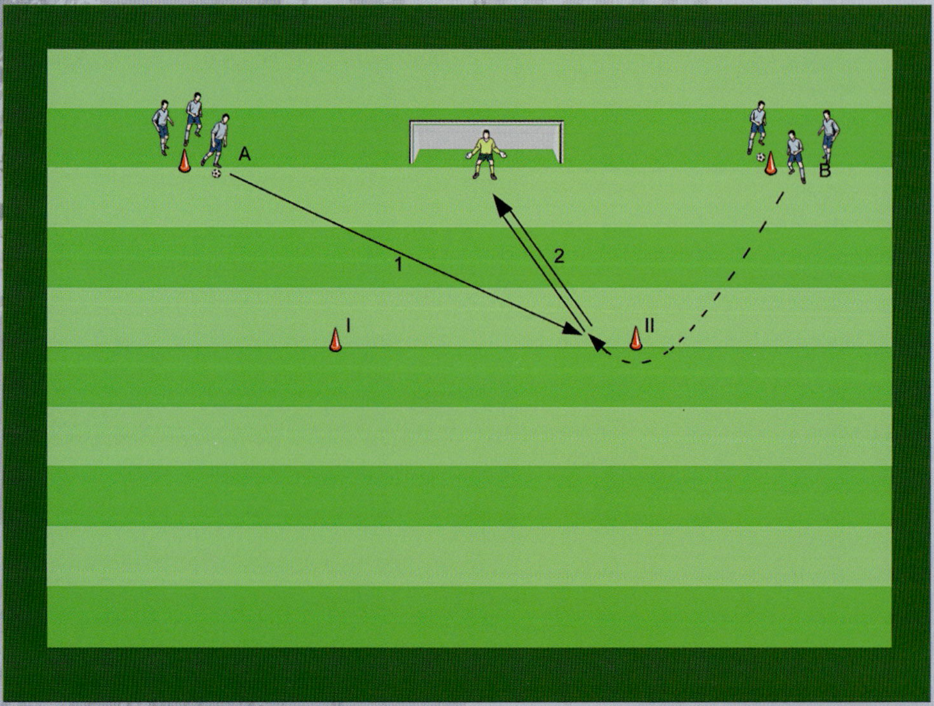

23 Shot on goal after a lateral pass

Purpose of training
- Ball handling techniques

Training emphasis
- Shooting techniques/shot on goal

Training aspects

Specific purpose:	Push-off power, speed of action with the ball, offensive playspeed of anticipation, moving with the ball, direct pass play, speed of decision-making, action speed, inside foot, push-pass (inside), inside foot kick, combination ball handling technique with movement, reaction speed, instep, speed of perception
Age group:	Age 9 to seniors
Playing level:	Advanced
Form of training:	Group
Training structure:	Main part/emphasis
Intention:	Offensive play, improving individual quality
Number of players:	6 or more
Number of participating players:	Entire team
Training location	Any
Space requirements:	Restricted playing field
Length:	10-15 min
Physical aspects:	Soccer-specific endurance, power
Goalies:	1 goalie

Organization:
Setting up one goal, one orientation cone, as well as two start cones (A+B), as shown in the illustration. The players are evenly divided between the two start cones, balls are with the players at cone A.

Execution:
The red player at cone A opens with a low pass in the direction of the orientation cone. At the moment he initiates his swing the blue player at cone B begins to sprint towards the orientation cone and approaches the ball to reach it before it passes the cone. In doing so player B runs around the cone and picks up the ball as he turns, and takes a shot on goal.

Afterwards the players switch their start cones so they are alternately making the pass and receiving the pass.

Equipment: 1 regulation size goal(s), 3 cones

Tips:
- Make sure shots on goal are practiced with both right and left foot.
- Pay attention to your posture when taking a shot (upper body over the ball; supporting leg is 12-16 inches to the side staggered with the ball, the foot points in shooting direction, the arms swing along; the arm closest to the shooting leg mimics the swinging motion of the leg (when shooting with

the right leg, the right arm moves back to gather momentum, the left arm moves forward), at the moment of the shot the eyes are on the ball.)

- Different shooting techniques (inside foot kick, instep kick, swerve) can be practiced where appropriate (at the trainer's command).
- To avoid delays and prevent long waiting periods, the next opening pass is played immediately after the shot on goal.
- The passing players must develop a good sense of timing for the passing speed since the receiving player has to get to the ball before it reaches the respective orientation cone. The same applies to the receiving player. To be able to reach the ball before it passes the cone he must adapt the timing of his start and his running speed to the speed of the ball.
- The pass should be played in such a way that the receiving player can only reach it close to the cone.
- Receiving and moving the ball should be one fluid motion. Letting the ball rebound too far or deviating too far from the straight running lane when receiving and moving the ball, should be avoided.
- Receiving and moving the ball should be done strictly with only one touch, hence the shot on goal is done with the second touch.

Field size: 15 x 20 yards

Distance between cones:
Goal to orientation cone: 10-20 yards
Orientation cone to start cone A/B: 10 yards

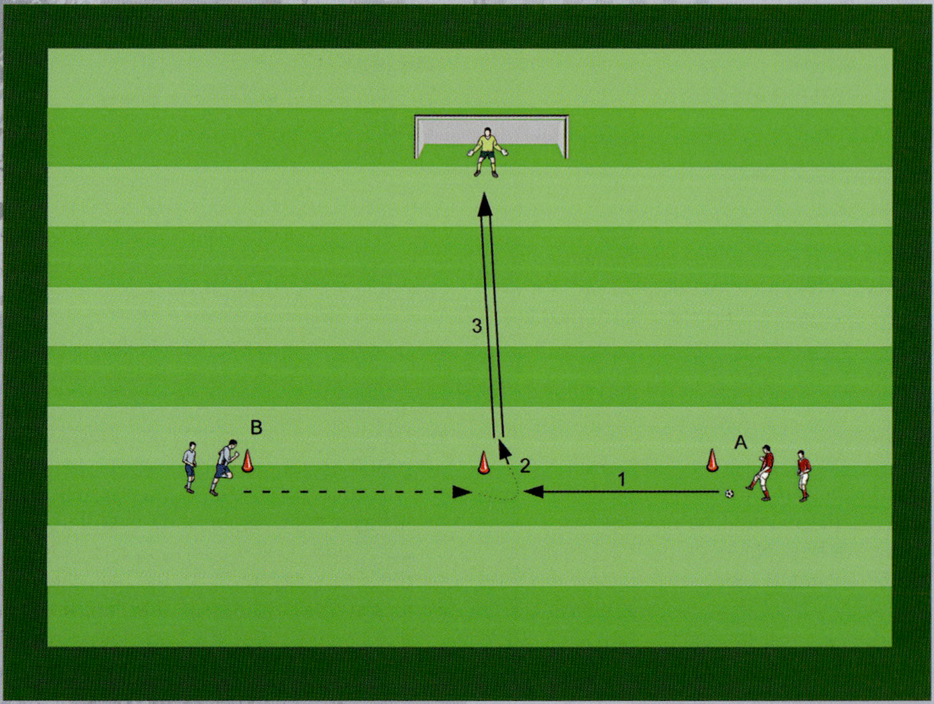

24 Controlling the ball with your back to the goal and double pass

Purpose of training

- Ball handling techniques

Training emphasis

- Receiving and moving with the ball
- Shooting techniques/shot on goal

Training aspects

Specific purpose:	**Push-off power, speed of action with the ball, speed of anticipation, outside instep, moving with the ball, double pass, speed of decision-making, action speed, inside foot, push-pass (inside), inside foot kick, combination ball handling technique with movement, long passes, reaction speed, instep, speed of perception, swerve**
Age group:	**Age 13 to seniors**
Playing level:	**Advanced, professional**
Form of training:	**Group**
Training structure:	**Main part/emphasis**
Intention:	**Improving individual quality**
Number of players:	**6 or more**
Number of participating players:	**Entire team**
Training location	**Any**
Space requirements:	**Restricted playing field**
Length:	**10-15 min**
Physical aspects:	**Soccer-specific endurance, power**
Goalies:	**1 goalie**

Organization:
Setting up one goal, a cone square, as well as a start cone, as shown in the illustration. One player stands inside the cone square, one player (rebounder) stands diagonally behind it, and the other players stand at the start cone with the ball.

Execution:
The blue starting player plays a fly ball to the player inside the cone square who has his back to the goal. He turns with the ball and plays a double pass with the rebounder and then shoots on goal.

The blue starting player now goes inside the cone square, the player from the cone square becomes the rebounder, and the rebounder lines up at the start cone after retrieving the ball.

Equipment: 1 regulation size goal(s), 5 cones

Tips:

- Make sure shots on goal are practiced with both right and left foot.
- Pay attention to your posture when taking a shot (upper body over the ball; supporting leg is 12-16 inches to the side staggered with the ball, the foot points in shooting direction, the arms swing along; the arm closest to the shooting leg mimics the swinging motion of the leg (when shooting with the right leg, the right arm moves back to gather momentum, the left arm

moves forward), at the moment of the shot the eyes are on the ball.)

- Turning and receiving and moving with the ball should be one fluid motion. Letting the ball rebound too far or deviating too far from the straight running lane when receiving and moving the ball, should be avoided.
- Initiate a starting motion (to the side or rear and move towards the passing player) before moving with the ball.
- Different shooting techniques (inside foot kick, instep kick, swerve) can be practiced where appropriate (at the trainer's command).
- When receiving the ball with the chest the upper body is turned towards the goal at the moment of contact, thus guiding the ball in the desired direction.
- As soon as the ball has left the passing player's foot he immediately runs inside the square in anticipation of the next pass.

Field size: 20 x 45 yards

Distance between cones:
Goal to cone square: 20-25 yards
Cone square to start cone: 15-20 yards
Cones in the square: 5 yards

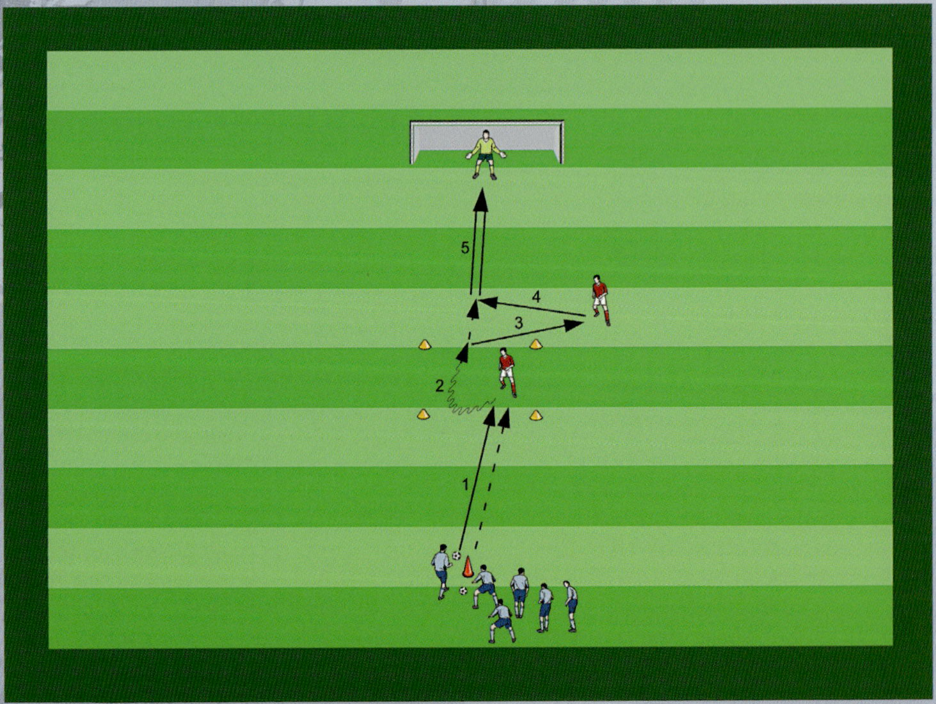

25 Target shooting

Purpose of training
- Ball handling techniques

Training emphasis
- Shooting techniques/shot on goal

Training aspects

Specific purpose:	**Outside instep, inside foot, inside foot kick, combination ball handling technique with movement, instep, swerve**
Age group:	**Age 13 to 14, age 15 to seniors**
Playing level:	**Advanced**
Form of training:	**Group**
Training structure:	**Warm-up, main part/emphasis, finish**
Intention:	**Improving individual quality**
Number of players:	**2 or more**
Number of participating players:	**Entire team**
Training location	**Any**
Space requirements:	**Restricted playing field**
Length:	**10-15 min**

Organization:
A smaller goal is set up inside a regulation size goal, as shown in the illustration. Two cones are set up level with each other, and the players are positioned next to each other in a line between the two cones. Each player has a ball.

Execution:
The placement of the smaller goal inside the regulation size goal creates different target zones, which in the illustrationare identified by different colors. The players now have to take turns shooting into the zones as specified by the trainer.

Option:
Each successful shot is worth one point. The player with the most points wins.

Equipment:
1 regulation size goal(s), 2 cones, 1 mini goal(s)

Tips:
- Pay attention to your posture when taking a shot (upper body over the ball; supporting leg is 12-16 inches to the side staggered with the ball, the foot points in shooting direction, the arms swing along; the arm closest to

the shooting leg mimics the swinging motion of the leg (when shooting with the right leg, the right arm moves back to gather momentum, the left arm moves forward), at the moment of the shot the eyes are on the ball.)

- Shooting drills should always be done with booth feet.
- Different shooting techniques (inside foot kick, instep kick, swerve) can be practiced where appropriate (at the trainer's command).

Field size: 10 x 20 yards

Distance between cones:
Goal to cone line: 11-20 yards

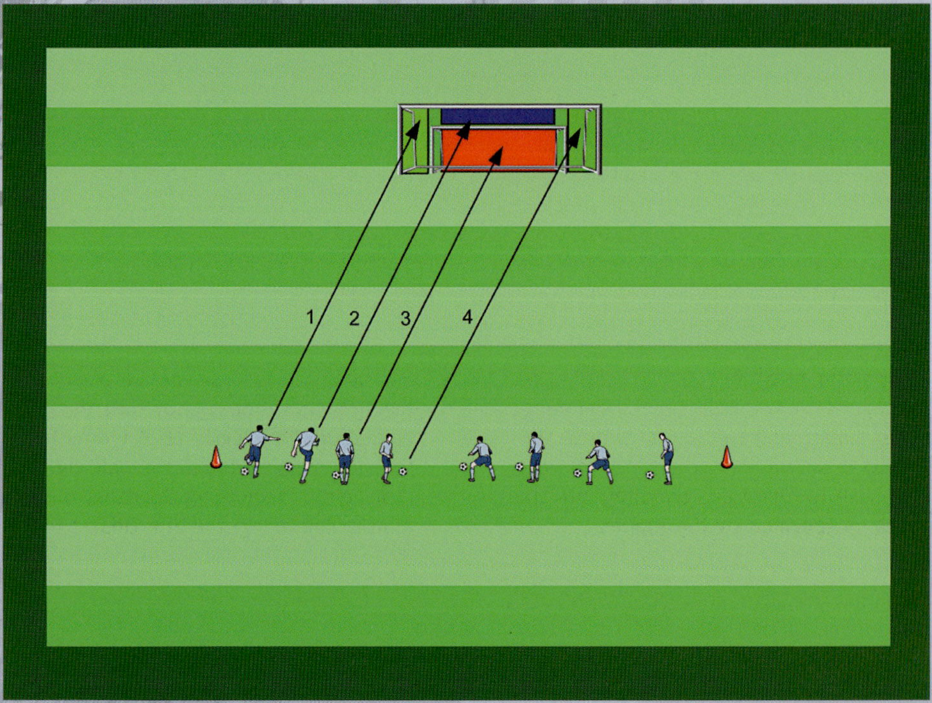

26 Shooting competition with multiple goals

Purpose of training
- Ball handling techniques

Training emphasis
- Shooting techniques/shot on goal

Training aspects

Specific purpose:	**Push-off power, speed of action with the ball, speed of anticipation, outside instep, double pass, speed of decision-making, action speed, inside foot, inside foot kick, combination ball handling technique with movement, reaction speed, instep**
Age group:	**Age 9 to 12, age 13 to 14, age 15 to seniors**
Playing level:	**Any**
Form of training:	**Group**
Training structure:	**Conclusion, warm-up, main part/ emphasis**
Intention:	**Fun training, improving individual quality**
Number of players:	**10 or more**
Number of participating players:	**Entire team**
Training location	**Any**
Space requirements:	**Restricted playing field**
Length:	**10-30 min**
Physical aspects:	**Soccer-specific endurance, power**
Goalies:	**3 goalies**

Organization:
Setting up three goals side by side as well as two start cones (A+B) and a rebounder cone. One player (or the trainer) stands at the rebounder cone, the others are divided equally between the two start cones. Each player has a ball.

Execution:
Shooting competition on three goals
The starting player from one of the two groups starts the drill by playing a double pass with the rebounder, and then takes a shot on one of the three goals. As soon as the player has taken the shot, the starting player from the next group starts.

Shots on goal from cone A are taken with the left foot, from cone B with the right foot. Players switch start cones after each shot. The rebounder changes regularly if the trainer does not play that position.

Option:
If the players score three consecutive goals, the goalies have to do five push-ups. If they have three consecutive saves, the field players have to do five push-ups.

Equipment: 3 regulation size goal(s), 3 cones

Tips:

- Pay attention to your posture when taking a shot (upper body over the ball; supporting leg is 12-16 inches to the side staggered with the ball, the foot points in shooting direction, the arms swing along; the arm closest to the shooting leg mimics the swinging motion of the leg (when shooting with the right leg, the right arm moves back to gather momentum, the left arm moves forward), at the moment of the shot the eyes are on the ball.)
- Shooting drills should always be done with booth feet.
- Different shooting techniques (inside foot kick, instep kick, swerve) can be practiced where appropriate (at the trainer's command).
- The next player starts immediately after a player takes a shot on goal.

Field size: 30 x 25 yards

Distance between cones:

Goal line to rebounder cone: 9-14 yards
Goal line to start cone: 15-25 yards
Rebounder cone to start cone: 5-8 yards

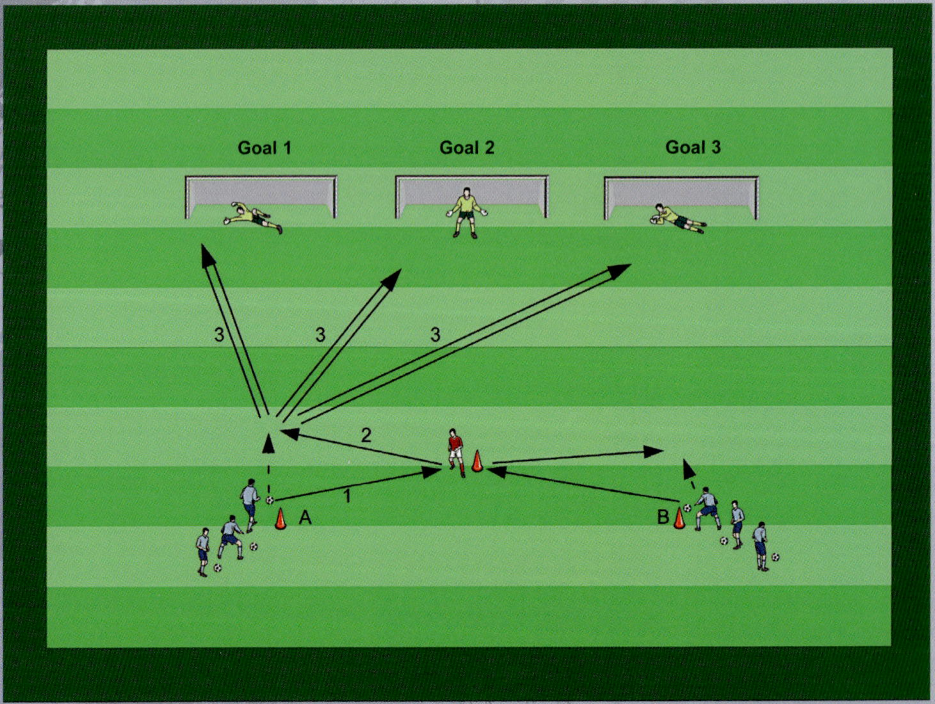

27 Shooting competition goalie against field players

Purpose of training

- Ball handling techniques

Training emphasis

- Shooting techniques/shot on goal

Training aspects

Specific purpose:	**Outside instep, inside foot, inside foot kick, combination ball handling technique with movement, instep, swerve**
Age group:	**Any**
Playing level:	**Beginner, any**
Form of training:	**Group**
Training structure:	**Conclusion, warm-up, main part/ emphasis**
Intention:	**Fun training, improving individual quality**
Number of players:	**6 or more**
Number of participating players:	**Entire Team**
Training location	**Any**
Space requirements:	**Restricted playing field**
Length:	**10-20 min**
Goalies:	**1 goalie**

Organization:
Setting up one goal, and also two cones that are level with teach other. Players line up next to each other between the two cones. Each player has a ball.

Execution:
Each player has one shot; the player all the way to the left starts. The players then take turns shooting on goal.

Option:
If more than half the shots taken on goal are successful the shooters won and the goalie has to do 10 push-ups. If they score less than 50%, the players have to do 10 push-ups.

Equipment: 1 regulation size goal(s), 2 cones

Tips:

- Pay attention to your posture when taking a shot (upper body over the ball; supporting leg is 12-16 inches to the side staggered with the ball, the foot points in shooting direction, the arms swing along; the arm closest to the shooting leg mimics the swinging motion of the leg (when shooting with the right leg, the right arm moves back to gather momentum, the left arm moves forward), at the moment of the shot the eyes are on the ball.)
- Shooting drills should always be done with booth feet.
- Different shooting techniques (inside foot kick, instep kick, swerve) can be practiced where appropriate (at the trainer's command).

Field size: 20 x 20 yards

Distance between cones:
Goal to cones: 9-20 yards
Cone to cone: 20 yards

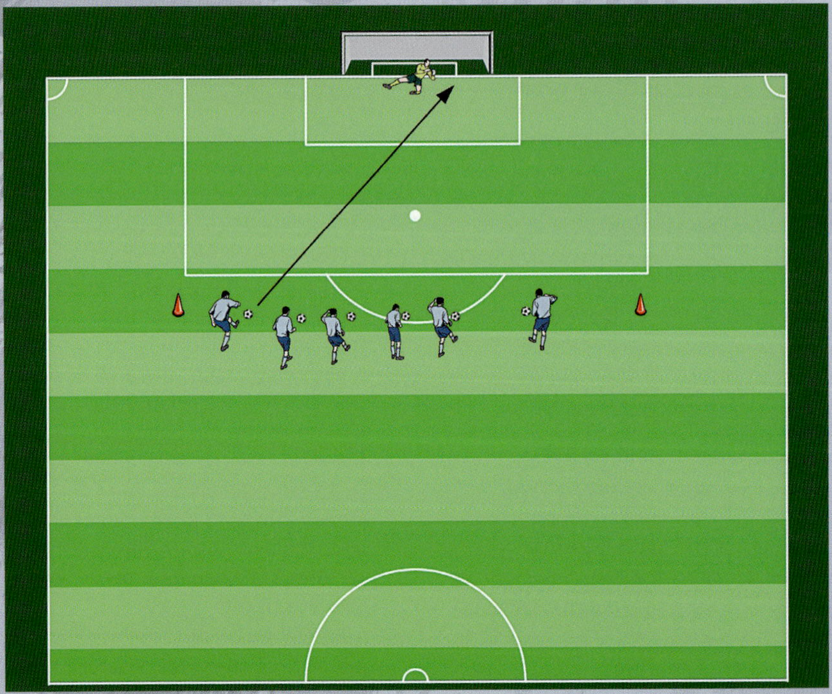

28 Speed training alternating shots on goal

Purpose of training

- Ball handling techniques

Training emphasis

- Shooting techniques/shot on goal

Training aspects

Specific purpose:	**Push-off power, speed of action with the ball, outside instep, speed of decision-making, inside foot, inside foot kick, interval method, combination ball handling technique with movement, instep, swerve**
Age group:	**Age 9 to seniors**
Playing level:	**Any**
Form of training:	**Partner**
Training structure:	**Main part/emphasis**
Intention:	**Fun training, stress training, improving individual quality**
Number of players:	**2**
Number of participating players:	**Entire team**
Training location	**Any**
Space requirements:	**Restricted playing field**
Length:	**5 min**
Physical aspects:	**Soccer-specific endurance, power, speed endurance**
Goalies:	**2 goalies**

Organization:
Setting up two goals facing each other (I+I), as well as two cones, as shown in the illustration. An equal number of balls are set up next to each other in two rows on a level with the cones. One player stands at each of the two rows of balls.

Execution:
At the trainer's signal both players simultaneously start shooting on goal. The blue player starts on goal I, the red player starts on goal II. After each shot they switch to the nearest ball in the other row of balls, thus alternating goals. The player who scores the most goals wins.

Equipment: 2 regulation size goal(s), 2 cones

Tips:

- Pay attention to your posture when taking a shot (upper body over the ball; supporting leg is 12-16 inches to the side staggered with the ball, the foot points in shooting direction, the arms swing along; the arm closest to the shooting leg mimics the swinging motion of the leg (when shooting with the right leg, the right arm moves back to gather momentum, the left arm moves forward), at the moment of the shot the eyes are on the ball.)
- Shooting drills should always be done with booth feet.
- Different shooting techniques (inside foot kick, instep kick, swerve) can be practiced where appropriate (at the trainer's command).

- Both players must try to finish at approximately the same time.
- If necessary the trainer may have to ensure the tempo of the exercise through encouragement or time limits.
- After each round the waiting players set up the drill again and the next two players start.

Field size: 15 x 37 yards

Distance between cones:
Goal to cones: 10-16 yards
Cone to cone: 5 yards
Goal to goal: 25-37 yards

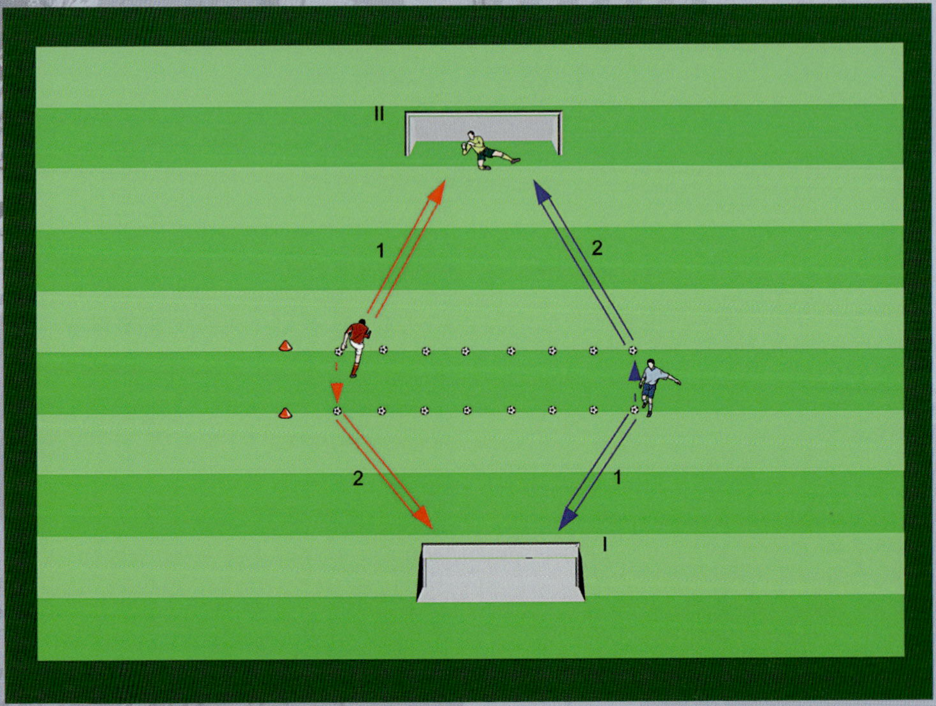

29 Shooting competition between two field players or goalies

Purpose of training

- Ball handling techniques

Training emphasis

- Shooting techniques/shot on goal

Training aspects

Specific purpose:	**Push-off power, speed of action with the ball, speed of anticipation, outside instep, speed of movement without the ball, drop kick, speed of decision-making, action speed, inside foot, inside foot kick, interval method, combination ball handling technique with movement, reaction speed, volley, instep, speed of perception, swerve**
Age group:	**Any**
Playing level:	**Any**
Form of training:	**Partner**
Training structure:	**Conclusion, Warm-up, main part/ emphasis**
Intention:	**Fun training, goalie performance, improving individual quality**
Number of players:	**2**
Number of participating players:	**Entire Group**
Training location	**Any**
Space requirements:	**Restricted playing field**
Length:	**5-20 min**
Physical aspects:	**Soccer-specific endurance, strength endurance, speed endurance**
Goalies:	**2 goalies**

Organization:
Setting up a small field with two goals facing each other, as shown in the illustration. One player (field player or goalie) stands in each goal. The balls are divided between the two goals.

Execution:
The players take turns acting as goalie and shooter. In doing so they try to score goals and also attempt to save the other player's shots. Both players take turns shooting. Both players can utilize the space between their goal lines and the two closest smaller cones. They can have three touches per action: one for receiving/defense, one to set up, and one to shoot on goal. If the ball bounces outside the marked square when receiving or defending, or a player sets up a shot outside the marked square, the opposing player can immediately get a new ball from inside the goal and attempt to score a goal.

Drill will be played for time or point limit.

Option:
Depending on group size, the drill can also be played with more or fewer touches, or the marked play area can be made smaller or larger.

Equipment: 2 regulation size goal(s)
8 cones

Tips:

- Pay attention to your posture when taking a shot (upper body over the ball; supporting leg is 12-16 inches to the side staggered with the ball, the foot points in shooting direction, the arms swing along; the arm closest to the shooting leg mimics the swinging motion of the leg (when shooting with the right leg, the right arm moves back to gather momentum, the left arm moves forward), at the moment of the shot the eyes are on the ball.)
- Shooting drills should always be done with booth feet.
- Depending on how a player receives the ball, shots on goal can be taken from the ground, as volleys or drop kicks.
- During the volley the upper body is bent slightly forward. The point of contact on the ball is low (not too high). This gives the ball more force and accuracy.
- When executing a drop kick contact is made with the instep the instant the ball touches the ground.
- Correct the goalie's performance: push off from the ball of the foot, shorten the angle, quick reaction, incorporate different types of shots/throws, switch quickly from defense to starting/shooting.

Field size: 20 x 30 yards

Distance between cones:
Outside goal post to goal line cone: 6.5 yards
Goal line cone to small cone: 5-10 yards
Goal to goal: 15-30 yards

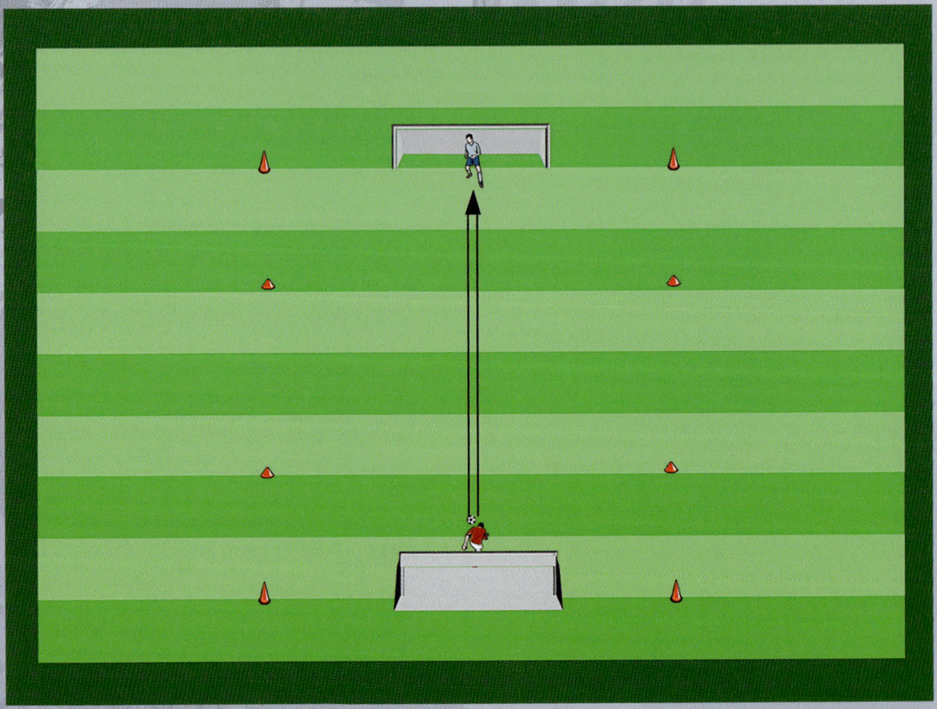

30 Dribble shooting competition

Purpose of training

- Ball handling techniques

Training emphasis

- Dribbling
- Feints/tricks
- Shooting techniques/shot on goal

Training aspects

Specific purpose:	**1 on 1, push-off power, defensive/offensive performance, speed of action with the ball, speed of anticipation, outside instep, moving with the ball, dribbling, speed of decision-making, inside foot, push-pass (inside), combination ball handling technique with movement, body feint, reaction speed, instep, swerve**
Age group:	**Any**
Playing level:	**Any**
Form of training:	**Group**
Training structure:	**Conclusion, warm-up, main part/ emphasis**
Intention:	**Fun training, improving individual quality**
Number of players:	**6 or more**
Number of participating players:	**Entire team**
Training location	**Any**
Space requirements:	**Restricted playing field**
Length:	**10-15 min**
Physical aspects:	**Soccer-specific endurance, power**

Organization:
Setting up one goal and one start cone. The players stand at the start cone with balls.

Execution:
Dribble knock out is a rule-based dribbling/ shooting competition.
The starting player dribbles the ball and tries to outplay the goalie. Any player who doesn't score becomes the goalie. A penalty point is issued for each goal scored. Any player with three penalty points is knocked out of the game. If a goal is scored on a player who already has two penalty points, causing him to accumulate a third one, the shooter still has to serve as goalie since the other player is knocked out of the competition. Whoever is left at the end wins the competition.

Equipment: 1 regulation size goal(s), 1 cone

Tips:
- Pay attention to your posture when taking a shot (upper body over the ball; supporting leg is 12-16 inches to the side staggered with the ball, the foot points in shooting direction, the arms swing along; the arm closest to the shooting leg mimics the swinging motion of the leg (when shooting with the right leg, the right arm moves back to gather momentum, the left arm

moves forward), at the moment of the shot the eyes are on the ball.)

- When dribbling the upper body is initially bent forward slightly. It straightens up when the player stops or pulls back the ball.
- When executing a body feint the center of gravity shifts because the upper body bends to the right or left side respectively, as is typical in body feints.
- Do not lean back!
- The arms are bent and move at the sides in normal running/walking rhythm.
- The knee should be bent when receiving the ball.
- Contact with the ball is light ("gentle"). A feel for the ball must be developed.
- The eyes should be taken off the ball at regular intervals (alternate looking at the ball and straight ahead).
- Keep up speed.
- As many touches as possible.
- During execution the knees are slightly bent.
- Keep the ball close (ball should not be more than 20 inches away).

Field size: 12 x 25 yards

Distance between cones:
Goal to start cone: 12-25 yards

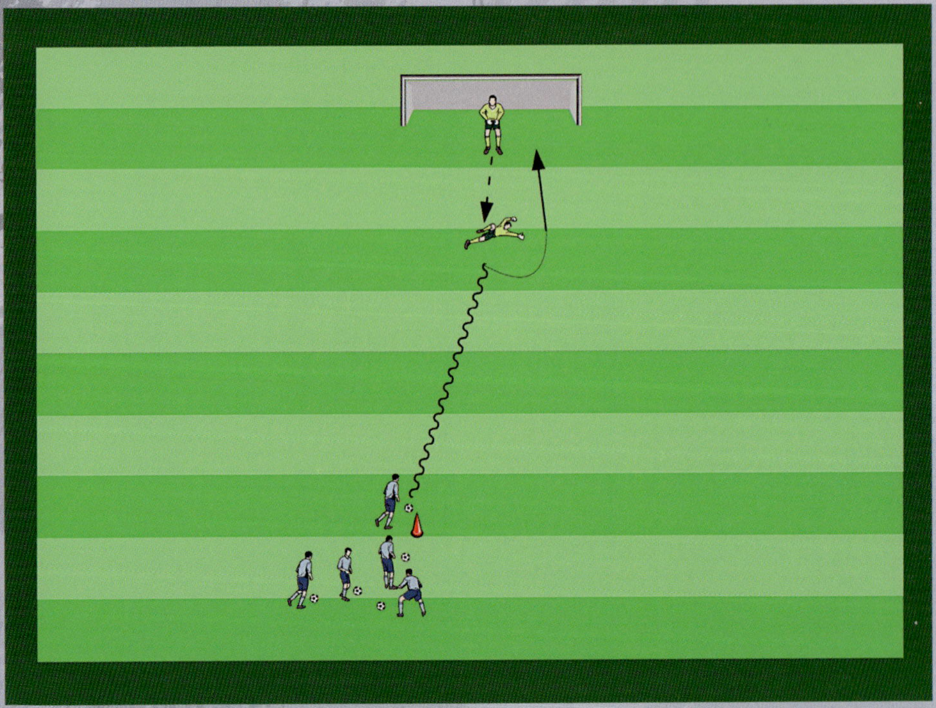

31 Shooting on two goals after receiving and controlling the ball/ various actions

Purpose of training

- Ball handling techniques

Training emphasis

- Receiving and moving with the ball
- Feints/tricks
- Shooting techniques/shot on goal

Training aspects

Specific purpose:	**Push-off power, speed of action with the ball, speed of anticipation, outside instep, moving with the ball, agility, dribbling, speed of decision-making, action speed, inside foot, push-pass (inside), combination ball handling technique with movement, short passes, body feint, reaction speed, instep, speed of perception, swerve**
Age group:	**Age 6 to seniors**
Playing level:	**Any**
Form of training:	**Group**
Training structure:	**Main part/emphasis**
Intention:	**Improving individual quality**
Number of players:	**8 or more**
Number of participating players:	**Entire team**
Training location	**Any**
Space requirements:	**Restricted playing field**
Length:	**20-40 min**
Physical aspects:	**Soccer-specific endurance**
Goalies:	**2 goalies**

Organization:
Setting up two goals facing each other and six cones (see illustration). The players are evenly divided between the four outside start cones. Balls are with the players from groups A and B.

Execution:
Drill sequence I:
A plays a low pass to A1. A1 dribbles to the center cone, passes it on the inside and takes a shot on goal. At the same time B passes the ball to B1, who also dribbles to the center cone, passes it on the inside and takes a shot on goal. Start out with swerve balls into the corners of the goal, then with the instep or inside foot kick on goal.

Drill sequence II:
Like I, but now execute a feint in front of the center cone.

Players switch sides after 5 minutes in all exercise variations to practice the sequences with both feet (A becomes B/A1 becomes B1).

Variation I:
Each player has a ball. A and B start simultaneously and meet up in the exact

center. Both players link their left arm and make one complete turn (fling). Then shoot in running direction. Next the same sequence with B1 and A1.

Variation II:
Each player has a ball. Players A and B start dribbling simultaneously from their cones and after 2-3 yards pass their ball into each other's running lane so each player is able to take a shot on goal when he is at a level with the center cone. Next A1 and B1 start with the same exercise.

Variation III:
Player A plays a double pass with player A1, who is waiting at the center cone. Next player A crosses the ball from the goal line to player A1 who has started for the goal box looking for the finish. Parallel sequence with B and B1.

Variation IV:
A plays the ball to player A1, who is waiting at the center cone, and runs diagonally in direction of the goal. Player A1 lets the ball bounce into A's running lane, briefly runs after his own pass and receives a deep pass from A (in direction of the goal line). Player A1 crosses that ball into the penalty box, where player A finishes. Parallel sequence with B and B1. After each round players A and A1 as well as B and B1 switch positions.

Equipment: 2 regulation size goal(s), 6 cones

Tips:

Shot on goal:
- Pay attention to your posture when taking a shot (upper body over the ball; supporting leg is 12-16 inches to the side staggered with the ball, the foot points in shooting direction, the arms swing along; the arm closest to the shooting leg mimics the swinging motion of the leg (when shooting with the right leg, the right arm moves back to gather momentum, the left arm moves forward), at the moment of the shot the eyes are on the ball.)
- During a volley shot the upper body is bent forward slightly. Contact with the ball is made at a low point (not too high). This applies more force to the ball and makes the shot more accurate.
- When executing a header the contact area is the forehead. The force is generated by the tension of the arched upper body (player arches his back). Just before the player makes contact with the ball he releases that tension by suddenly jerking his head forward and hitting the ball in front of the body. The arms are bent and move back.

Passing:
- When passing to the rebounder make sure to play to his strong foot.
- Receiving and moving the ball should be one fluid motion. Letting the ball rebound too far or deviating too far from the straight running lane when receiving and moving the ball, should be avoided.
- When passing into the running lane the ball should be passed so the receiver can start the consecutive action (e.g. the cross) as directly (from a run) as possible.

Feints:
- Execute feints approximately 1-2 yards from the center cone. Afterwards briefly increase speed, finish.

Dribbling:
- When dribbling the upper body is initially bent forward slightly. It straightens up when the player stops or pulls back the ball.
- When executing a body feint the center of gravity shifts because the upper body bends to the right or left side respectively, as is typical in body feints.

- Do not lean back!
- The arms are bent and move at the sides in normal running/walking rhythm.
- When movingwith the ball the knee is bent.
- Contact with the ball is light ("gentle"). A feel for the ball must be developed.
- Take your eyes off the ball at regular intervals (alternate looking at the
- ball and looking ahead).
- Keep up speed.
- As many touches as possible.
- During execution the knees are slightly bent.
- Keep the ball close (ball should not be more than 20 inches away).

Rebounder:

- As soon as the starting player initiates the swinging motion the rebounder makes a small counter movement and then briefly moves towards the ball.

Field size: 28 x 40 yards

Distance between cones:
Outside goal post to nearest outside cone: 10 yards
Outside cone to nearest center cone: 12.5-20 yards deep + 5 yards off-center
Goal to goal: 25-40 yards

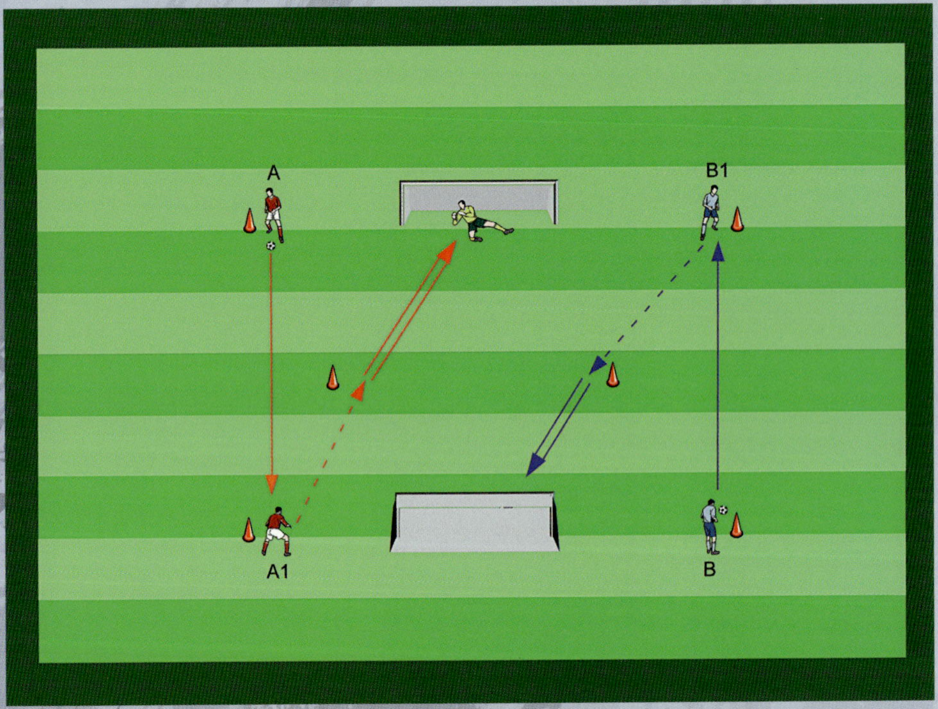
A
B1
A1
B

32 Shooting on two goals after a pass

Purpose of training

- Ball handling techniques

Training emphasis

- Shooting techniques/shot on goal

Training aspects

Specific purpose:	**Speed of action with the ball, speed of anticipation, outside instep, receiving and moving with the ball, dribbling, speed of decision-making, inside foot, instep**
Age group:	**Any**
Playing level:	**Any**
Form of training:	**Group**
Training structure:	**Main part/emphasis**
Intention:	**Improving individual quality**
Number of players:	**4**
Number of participating players:	**Entire team**
Training location	**Any**
Space requirements:	**Double penalty area**
Length:	**10-15 min**
Physical aspects:	**Soccer-specific endurance**
Goalies:	**2 goalies**

Organization:
Setting up two goals facing each other. One cone each on the baseline to the left and right of the goal, and another on the field as shown in the illustration. Sufficient number of balls.

Execution:
The players are divided evenly between the cones. Player A dribbles to the center cone and passes the ball off to player A1. After receiving the ball, he takes a direct shot on goal. The same sequence is played by B and B1. Afterwards the positions are switched so that player A1 dribbles to the center cone and passes the ball off to A, who takes a shot on goal.

Equipment: 2 regulation size goal(s), 6 cones

Tips:

- Receiving and moving the ball should occur with one touch, and the ball should not bounce too far from the foot
- Demand different shooting techniques (inside foot, instep, outside foot, inside instep...).
- Fast dribble to the center cone. The player waiting for the ball must be able to accurately anticipate the dribbling speed to be able to reach the cone at the same time as the dribbler.
- Practice shots on goal with both feet.

Field size: 27 x 32 yards

Distance between cones:
Goal to side goal line cones: 10 yards
Goal line cones to center cone: 16 yards

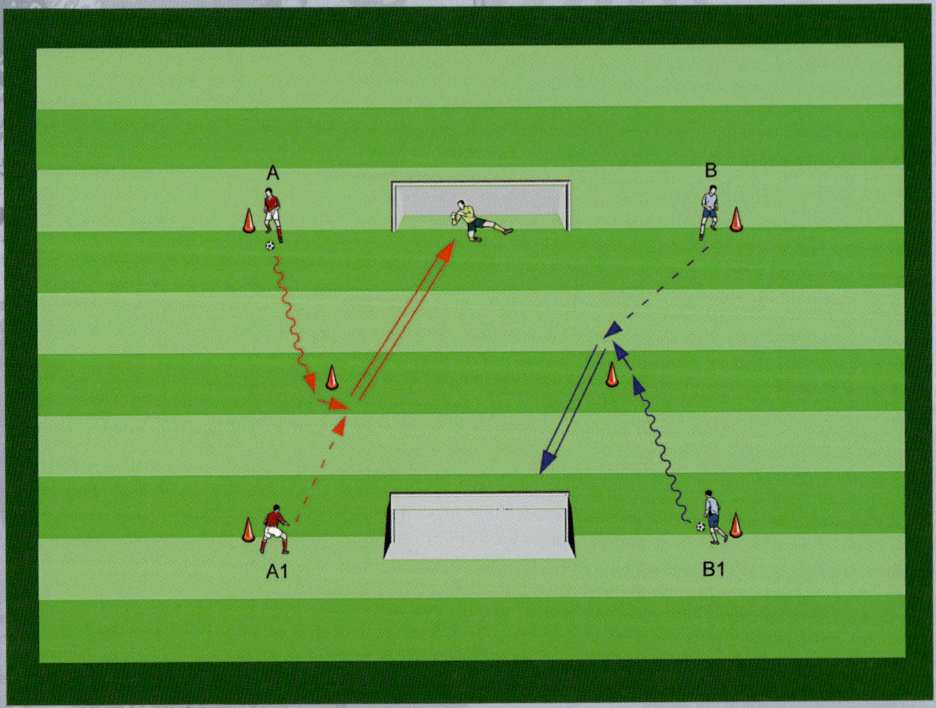

33 Shooting on two goals after a diagonal pass

Purpose of training

- Ball handling techniques

Training emphasis

- Shooting techniques/shot on goal

Training aspects

Specific purpose:	**Push-off power, speed of action with the ball, speed of anticipation, speed of decision-making, action speed, push-pass, inside foot kick, combination ball handling technique with movement, reaction speed, instep, speed of perception, swerve**
Age group:	**Age 9 to seniors**
Playing level:	**Advanced**
Form of training:	**Group**
Training structure:	**Main part/emphasis**
Intention:	**Improving individual quality**
Number of players:	**8 or more**
Number of participating players:	**Entire team**
Training location	**Any**
Space requirements:	**Restricted playing field**
Length:	**10-15 min**
Physical aspects:	**Soccer-specific endurance, power**
Goalies:	**2 goalies**

Organization:
Setting up two goals facing each other, as well as two rebounder cones (see illustration). One player stands at each of the rebounder cones (A1 and B1), the remaining players are divided evenly between the two positions next to the goals (A+B) with balls.

Execution:
Player A passes the ball to player A1. At the same time player B passes the ball to player B1. Now player A1 as well as player B1 briefly let the ball bounce off to the side. Player B shoots the ball that was passed by A1 on goal, and player A shoots the ball passed by B1.

Next the positions change clockwise: player A takes the rebounder position of B1, player B1 retrieves the ball shot by player A and lines up with group B. Player B takes the rebounder position of A1, who in turn retrieves the ball shot by B and lines up with group A.

Equipment: 2 regulation size goal(s), 2 cones

Tips:

- Pay attention to your posture when taking a shot (upper body over the ball; supporting leg is 12-16 inches to the side staggered with the ball, the foot points in shooting direction, the arms swing along; the arm closest to the shooting leg mimics the swinging motion of the leg (when shooting with the right leg, the right arm moves back to gather momentum, the left arm moves forward), at the moment of the shot the eyes are on the ball.)

- As soon as the starting player initiates the swinging motion the rebounder makes a small counter movement and then briefly moves towards the ball.
- When passing to the rebounder make sure to play to his strong foot.
- As soon as the ball has left his foot the passing player takes off in order to be able to directly utilize the ball coming form the rebounder.
- To ensure smooth progression of the drill, the players from groups A and B must make sure they always start at the same time.
- Different shooting techniques (inside foot kick, instep kick, swerve) can be practiced where appropriate (at the trainer's command).

Field size: 20 x 35 yards

Distance between cones:
Goal to group A/B: 5-7 yards
Goal to goal: 20-35 yards
Goal to nearest rebounder cone: 10-20 yards

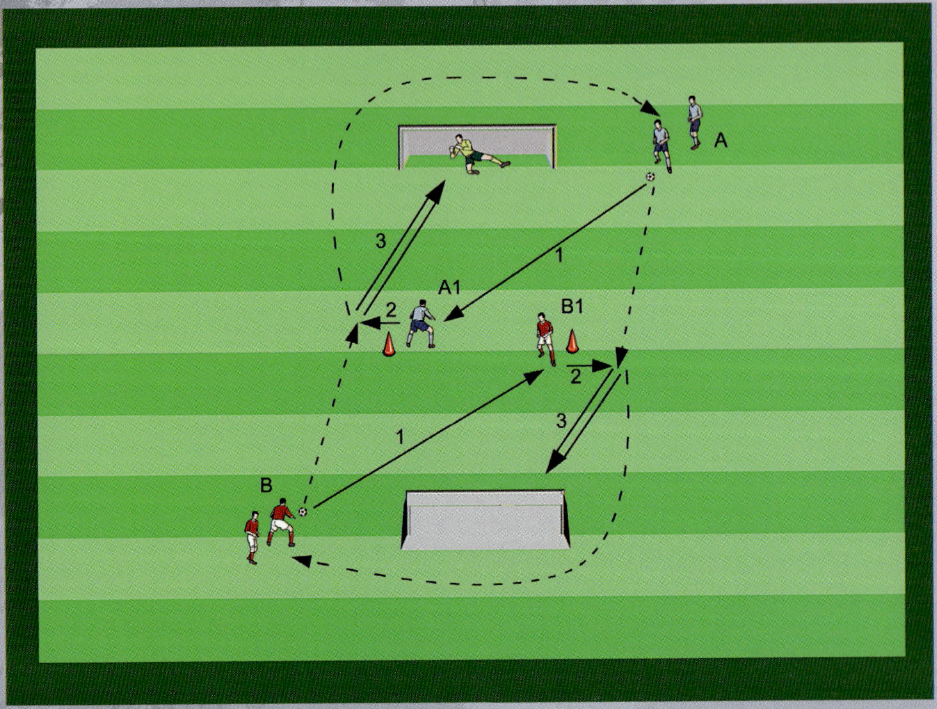

34 Alternating shots on two goals

Purpose of training
- Ball handling techniques

Training emphasis
- Shooting techniques/shot on goal

Training aspects

Specific purpose:	**Push-off power, speed of action with the ball, speed of anticipation, outside instep, receiving and moving with the ball, double pass, speed of decision-making, inside foot, push-pass (inside), inside foot kick, combination ball handling technique with movement, short passes, reaction speed, instep, swerve**
Age group:	**Age 9 to seniors**
Playing level:	**Any**
Form of training:	**Group**
Training structure:	**Main part/emphasis**
Intention:	**Improving individual quality**
Number of players:	**8 or more**
Number of participating players:	**Entire team**
Training location	**Any**
Space requirements:	**Restricted playing field**
Length:	**10-15 min**
Physical aspects:	**Soccer-specific endurance, power**
Goalies:	**2 goalies**

Organization:
Setting up two goals facing each other, as well as two start cones and one rebounder cone (see illustration). One player stands at the rebounder cone, the remaining players are divided evenly between the two start cones with balls.

Execution:
The player from the red group B plays a double pass with the rebounder and subsequently shoots directly on goal. Now the rebounder turns to the other side and receives a pass from the player of the blue group A. He also lets this pass bounce off to the side for a shot on goal. The players who have taken a shot retrieve their ball and line up behind the other group.

Option:
The rebounder can also let the ball bounce into the passing player's running lane who then has to briefly receive/control the ball at a run, before shooting on goal.

The rebounder changes regularly.

Equipment: 2 regulation size goal(s), 3 cones

Tips:
- Pay attention to your posture when taking a shot (upper body over the ball; supporting leg is 12-16 inches to the side staggered with the ball, the foot points in shooting direction, the arms swing along; the arm closest to the shooting leg mimics the swinging

motion of the leg (when shooting with the right leg, the right arm moves back to gather momentum, the left arm moves forward), at the moment of the shot the eyes are on the ball.)

- As soon as the starting player initiates the swinging motion the rebounder makes a small counter movement and then briefly moves towards the ball.
- After the double pass the rebounder immediately has to turn to the other side to play the next double pass with the other group.
- The pass to the rebounder should be played to his strong foot.
- The passing player starts as soon as the rebounder initiates his swing.
- Different shooting techniques (inside foot kick, instep kick, swerve) can be practiced where appropriate (at the trainer's command).
- Receiving and moving the ball should be done with one touch.

Field size: 20 x 32 yards

Distance between cones:
Goal to rebounder cone: 8-16 yards, depending on the age group
Start cone to rebounder cone: 3-4 yards

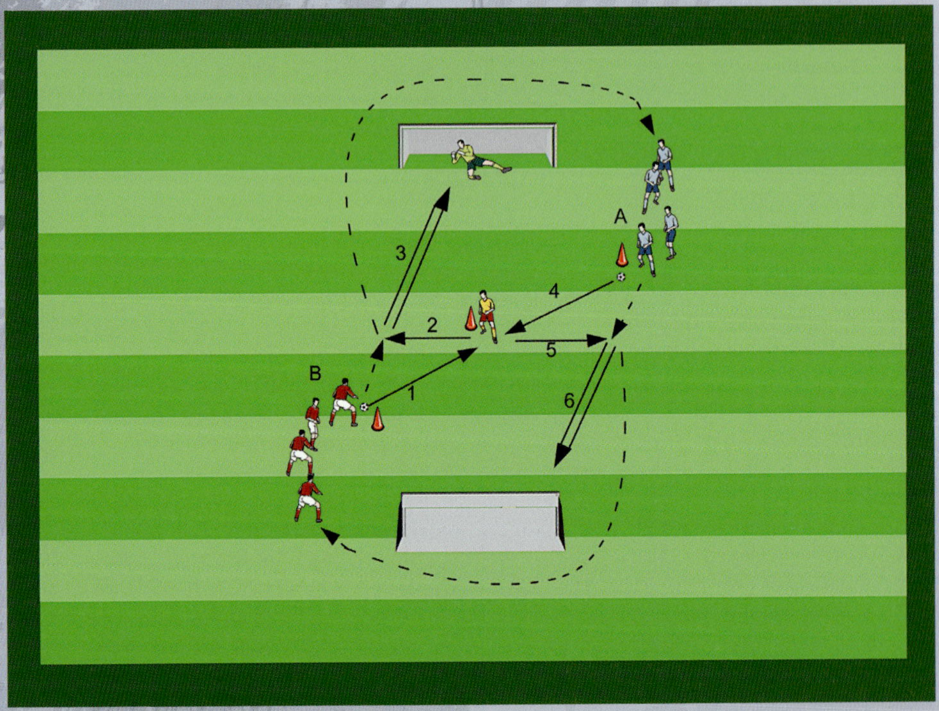

35 Shooting on two goals after a pass combination

Purpose of training

- Ball handling techniques

Training emphasis

- Shooting techniques/shot on goal

Training aspects

Specific purpose:	Push-off power, speed of action with the ball, speed of anticipation, outside instep, direct pass play, basic move, speed of decision-making, inside foot, push-pass (inside), inside foot kick, combination ball handling technique with movement, triangle passing, reaction speed, quick play to the forward, instep, swerve
Age group:	Age 9 to seniors
Playing level:	Advanced
Form of training:	Group
Training structure:	Main part/emphasis
Intention:	Offensive play, improving individual quality
Number of players:	10 or more
Number of participating players:	Entire team
Training location	Any
Space requirements:	Restricted playing field
Length:	10-15 min
Physical aspects:	Soccer-specific endurance, power
Goalies:	2 goalies

Organization:
Setting up two goals facing each other, as well as four start cones and one rebounder cone (see illustration). One player stands at the rebounder cone, the remaining players are evenly divided between the four start cones. The players in groups A and B have the balls.

Execution:
Player A opens with a pass to the rebounder. He makes a side pass to A1, who takes a direct shot on goal. Next both players switch to the opposite groups (A to B1 and A1 to B), the rebounder turns and receives a pass from B, which he turns into a side pass to B1, who takes a shot on goal. Afterwards these two also switch to the opposite groups.

Option:
A second rebounder positions himself next to the first rebounder. Now the drill runs parallel, meaning both groups (A + A1 and B+ B1) start simultaneously.

Equipment: 2 regulation size goal(s), 4 cones

Tips:
The drill progresses as follows:

- Player A/B initiates the swinging motion for a pass => rebounder's counter

movement (brief backwards movement followed by brief 1-2 yard movement towards passing player).

- The rebounder initiates swinging motion for a pass => player A/B starts.
- Pay attention to your posture when taking a shot (upper body over the ball; supporting leg is 12-16 inches to the side staggered with the ball, the foot points in shooting direction, the arms swing along; the arm closest to the shooting leg mimics the swinging motion of the leg (when shooting with the right leg, the right arm moves back to gather momentum, the left arm moves forward), at the moment of the shot the eyes are on the ball.)
- As soon as the starting player initiates the swinging motion the rebounder makes a small counter movement and then briefly moves towards the ball.
- Immediately after the pass the rebounder must turn to the other side to play the next pass with the other group.
- The pass to the rebounder should be played to his strong foot.
- Different shooting techniques (inside foot kick, instep kick, swerve) can be practiced where appropriate (at the trainer's command).

Field size: 20 x 32 yards

Distance between cones:
Goal/start cones to rebounder: 8-16 yards, depending on the age group

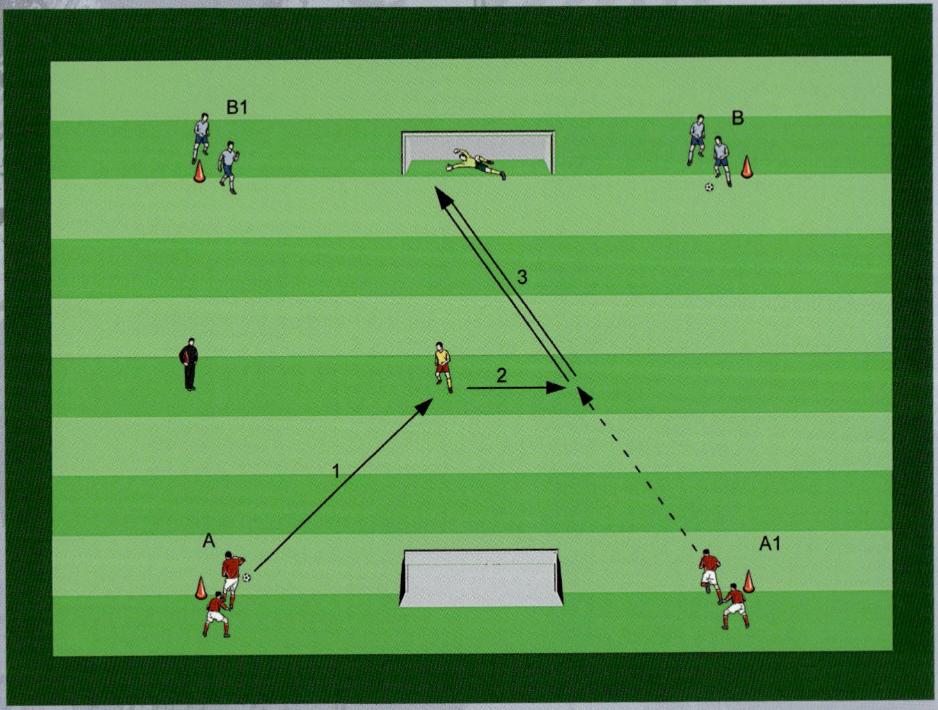

36 Shooting on two goals after a pass assist

Purpose of training
- Ball handling techniques

Training emphasis
- Shooting techniques/shot on goal

Training aspects

Specific purpose:	**Push-off power, speed of action with the ball, offensive play, speed of anticipation, outside instep, basic move, speed of decision-making, inside foot, push-pass (inside), inside foot kick, combination ball handling technique with movement, reaction speed, quick play to the forward, instep, speed of perception, swerve**
Age group:	**Age 9-12, 13-14, 15 to seniors**
Playing level:	**Advanced**
Form of training:	**Group**
Training structure:	**Main part/emphasis**
Intention:	**Offensive play, improving individual quality**
Number of players:	**10 or more**
Number of participating players:	**Entire team**
Training location	**Any**
Space requirements:	**Restricted playing field**
Length:	**10-15 min**
Physical aspects:	**Soccer-specific endurance, power**
Goalies:	**2 goalies**

Organization:
Setting up two goals facing each other, as well as four start cones (see illustration). Players are evenly divided between the four start cones. The players of groups A and B have the balls.

Execution:
Players set up shots on goal for each other. Player A opens with a diagonal ball to player B1. Next player B sets up a shot on goal for player A1. After each action the players switch positions with their neighboring cone (A with A1/B with B1, and vice versa).

Equipment: 2 regulation size goal(s), 4 cones

Tips:
- The receiving player startsas soon as the passing player initiates his swing.
- Pay attention to your posture when taking a shot (upper body over the ball; supporting leg is 12-16 inches to the side staggered with the ball, the foot points in shooting direction, the arms swing along; the arm closest to the shooting leg mimics the swinging motion of the leg (when shooting with the right leg, the right arm moves back to gather momentum, the left arm moves forward), at the moment of the shot the eyes are on the ball.)
- Shots on goal should be trained with the right and left foot. On one side

shots can only be taken with the left foot and on the other side only withthe right foot.

- Different shooting techniques (inside foot kick, instep kick, swerve) can be practiced where appropriate (at the trainer's command).

Field size: 20 x 30 yards

Distance between cones:
Goal to side cone: 7 yards
Goal to goal: 20-30 yards
Distances between cones vary according to age.

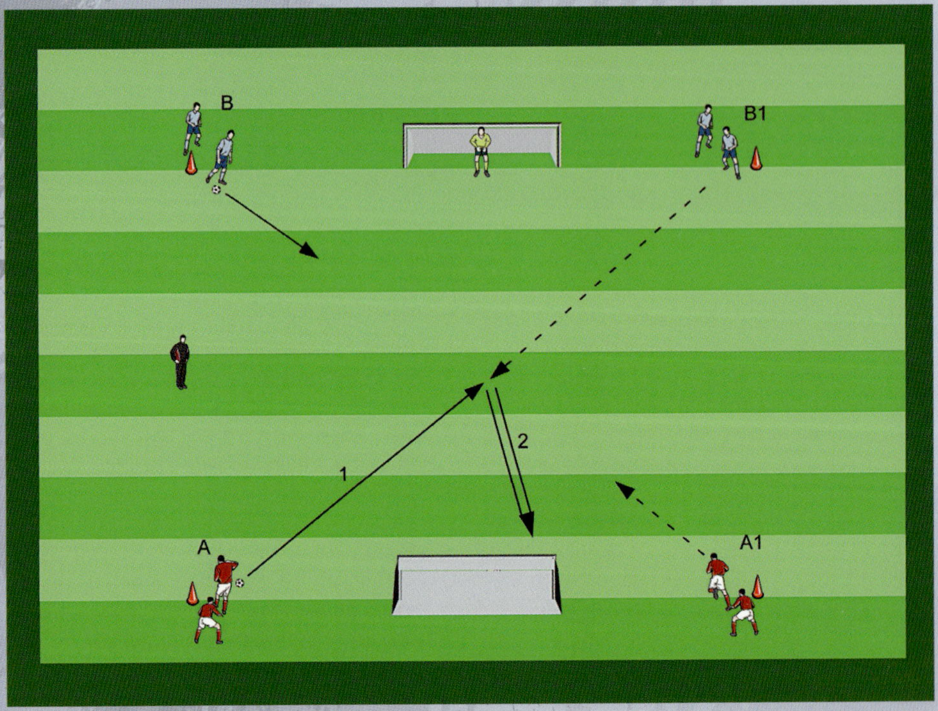

37 Shooting on two goals after a pass down the line

Purpose of training
- Ball handling techniques

Training emphasis
- Shooting techniques/shot on goal

Training aspects

Specific purpose:	**Push-off power, speed of action with the ball, speed of anticipation, outside instep, moving with the ball, speed of decision-making, inside foot, push-pass (inside), inside foot kick, combination ball handling technique with movement, short passes, reaction speed, instep, swerve**
Age group:	**Any**
Playing level:	**Any**
Form of training:	**Group**
Training structure:	**Main part/emphasis**
Intention:	**Improving individual qualit**
Number of players:	**10 or more**
Number of participating players:	**Entire team**
Training location	**Any**
Space requirements:	**Restricted playing field**
Length:	**10-15 min**
Physical aspects:	**Soccer-specific endurance, power**
Goalies:	**2 goalies**

Organization:
Setting up two goals facing each other, as well as four start cones (see illustration). Players are evenly divided between the four start cones. The players of groups A and B1 have the balls.

Execution:
The players pass to each other down the line for a shot on goal. Player A starts with a pass into the running lane of player B, and player B1 with a pass into the running lane of player A1. Players B and A1 turn these passes into direct shots on goal. Next the players switch positions clockwise.
To change the shooting foot, players B and A1 pass the ball and B and A1 take the shot on goal.

Option:
Shot on goal is taken after previously receiving and moving the ball (low/high).

Equipment: 2 regulation size goal(s), 4 cones

Tips:
- The receiving player starts as soon as the passing player initiates his swing.
- Pay attention to your posture when taking a shot (upper body over the ball; supporting leg is 12-16 inches to the side staggered with the ball, the foot points in shooting direction, the arms swing along; the arm closest to the shooting leg mimics the swinging motion of the leg (when shooting with the right leg, the right arm moves back to gather momentum, the left arm moves forward), at the moment of the shot the eyes are on the ball.)
- Make sure the shot on goal is practiced with left and right foot. To do so you can only allow shots with the left foot from one side and with the right from the other side, or switch passing players.

- Different shooting techniques (inside foot kick, instep kick, swerve) can be practiced where appropriate (at the trainer's command).
- Receiving and moving the ball should be one fluid motion. Letting the ball rebound too far or deviating too far from the straight running lane when receiving and moving the ball, should be avoided.
- Receiving and moving the ball should occur strictly with one touch, hence the shot on goal is done with the second touch.
- If the starting player opens with a high ball it should be executed with the inside instep. This gives the ball a linear, slightly upward trajectory and can be transferred much more quickly from A to B than a curve ball played with the instep.
- When receiving the ball with the chest the upper body must be turned towards the goal when contact is made with the ball, thus directing the ball in the desired direction.
- During a volley shot the upper body is bent forward slightly. Contact with the ball is made at a low point (not too high). This applies more force to the ball and makes the shot more accurate.

Field size: 20 x 32 yards

Distance between cones:
Goal to side cone: 6.5 yards
Goal to goal: 15-30 yards
Distances between cones vary according to age.

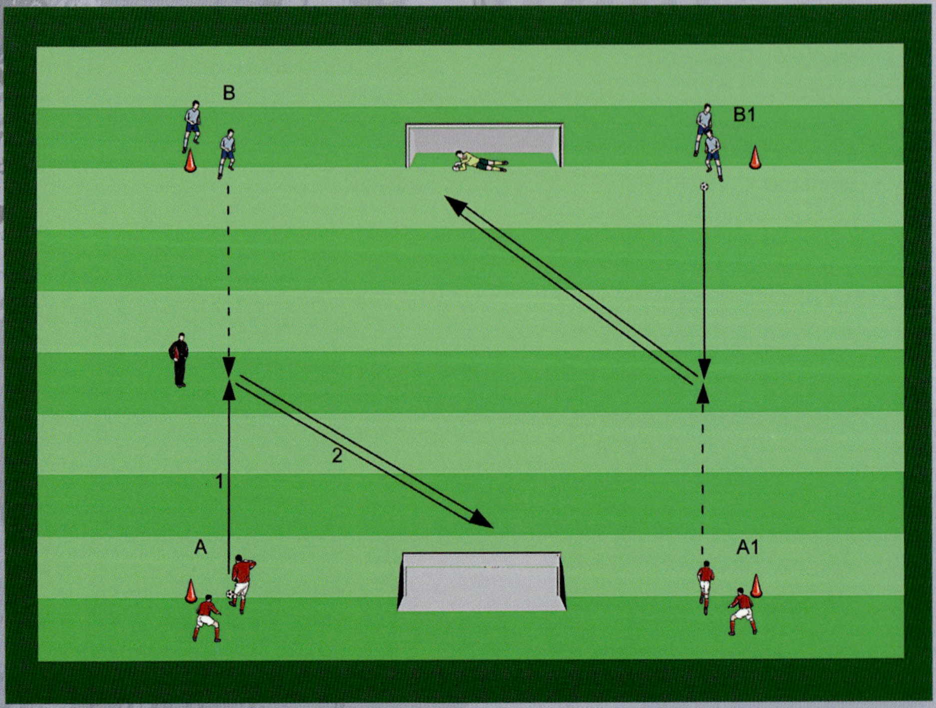

38 Shooting on two goals with follow-up action

Purpose of training
- Ball handling techniques

Training emphasis
- Feints/tricks
- Shooting techniques/shot on goal

Training aspects

Specific purpose:	**Push-off power, speed of action with the ball, offensive play, speed of anticipation, outside instep, moving with the ball, double pass, dribbling, speed of decision-making, inside foot, push-pass (inside), inside foot kick, combination ball handling technique with movement, body feint, reaction speed, instep, speed of perception, swerve**
Age group:	**Age 13-14, age 15 to seniors, U12, U13**
Playing level:	**Advanced**
Form of training:	**Group**
Training structure:	**Main part/emphasis**
Intention:	**Offensive play, improving individual quality**
Number of players:	**8 or more**
Number of participating players:	**Entire team**
Training location	**Any**
Space requirements:	**Restricted playing field**
Length:	**10-15 min**
Physical aspects:	**Soccer-specific endurance, speed endurance, power**
Goalies:	**2 goalies**

Organization:
Setting up two goals facing each other, as well as four outside cones. Players and balls are evenly divided between the two diagonally opposite outside start cones (see illustration). An additional inside cone square is set up.

Execution:
Player A dribbles the ball to the inside of the cone square and takes a shot on goal from within the square. Next he sprints around the cone situated to his front left, and briefly back towards the start cone. At the halfway point player B plays a double pass with him. After the double pass player B also dribbles into the cone square and from there takes a shot on goal. The same sequence then repeats itself. The blue players (C) execute the same drill on the opposite goal. Afterwards the players line up again at the start cone.

Option:
After the ball has been received a feint can be executed in front of the first cone on the left of the inside cone square.

Equipment: 2 regulation size goal(s), 8 cones

Tips:

- Keep the ball close while dribbling (ball should not be more than 20 inches away from foot).
- It is important to execute the feint at the right moment (1-2 yards from the cone) and to use the correct technique.
- Receiving and moving the ball should be one fluid motion. Letting the ball rebound too far or deviating too far from the straight running lane when receiving and moving the ball, should be avoided.
- Receiving and moving the ball should occur strictly with one touch.
- Pay attention to your posture when taking a shot (upper body over the ball; supporting leg is 12-16 inches to the side staggered with the ball, the foot points in shooting direction, the arms swing along; the arm closest to the shooting leg mimics the swinging motion of the leg (when shooting with the right leg, the right arm moves back to gather momentum, the left arm moves forward), at the moment of the shot the eyes are on the ball.)
- Demand that shots on goal also be executed with the weak foot (always alternate right and left, etc.)
- Demand correct timing, accuracy and force of passes.

Field size: 30 x 32 yards

Distance between cones:
Goal to side cone: 11.5 yards
Goal to goal: 32 yards
Cones of inside cone square: 5-8 yards respectively
Distances between cones vary according to age.

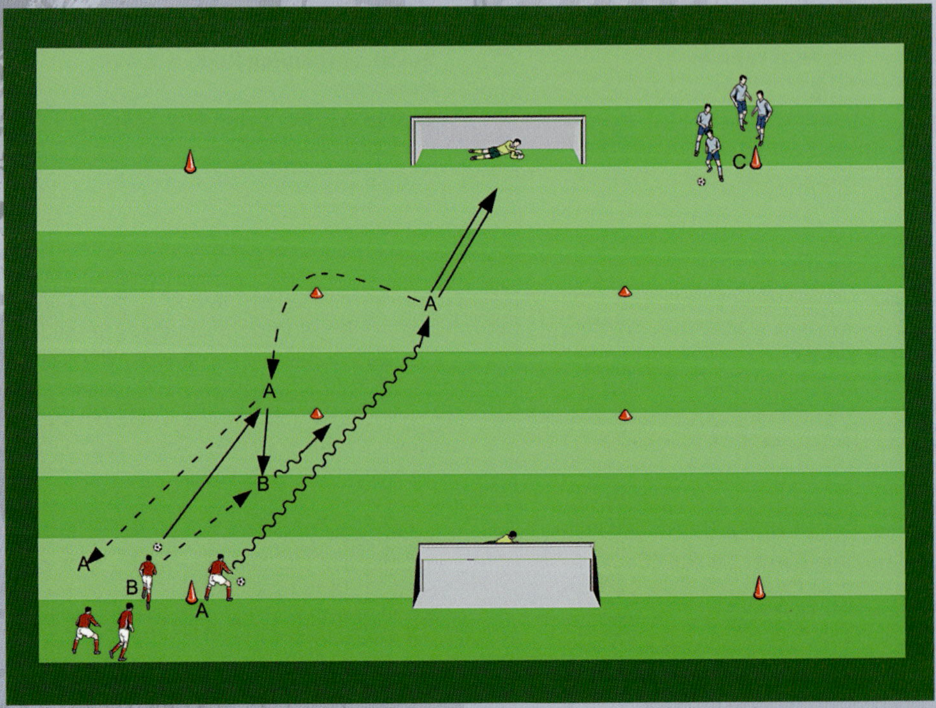

39 Shot on goal with two double passes

Purpose of training
- Ball handling techniques

Training emphasis
- Shooting techniques/shot on goal

Training aspects

Specific purpose:	Push-off power, speed of action with the ball, offensive play, speed of anticipation, speed of movement without the ball, direct pass play, double pass, speed of decision-making, action speed, push-pass (inside), inside foot kick, combination ball handling technique with movement, short passes, dribbling, swerve
Age group:	9-12, 13-14, 15 to seniors
Playing level:	Advanced, pro
Form of training:	Group
Training structure:	Main part/emphasis
Intention:	Improving individual quality
Number of players:	10 or more
Number of participating players:	Entire team
Training location	Any
Space requirements:	Restricted playing field
Length:	10-15 min
Physical aspects:	Soccer-specific endurance, speed endurance
Goalies:	1 goalie

Organization:
Setting up one goal and three cones, as shown in the illustration. One player stands at each of the two cones closest to the goal (B and C), the remaining players (A) are positioned at the third cone with ball.

Execution:
Player A plays a double pass with B and then a double pass with C. After that comes a brief dribble followed by a shot on goal. The shooter retrieves the ball and again lines up behind group A. The two rebounders change regularly.

Equipment: 1 regulation size goal(s), 3 cones

Tips:
- As soon as the starting player initiates his swing the rebounder makes a small counter movement and then briefly moves towards the ball.
- The pass to the rebounder should be played to his strong foot.
- Receiving and moving the ball should be one fluid motion. Letting the ball rebound too far or deviating too far from the straight running lane when receiving and moving the ball, should be avoided.
- Keep the ball close while dribbling.
- Pay attention to your posture when taking a shot (upper body over the

ball; supporting leg is 12-16 inches to the side staggered with the ball, the foot points in shooting direction, the arms swing along; the arm closest to the shooting leg mimics the swinging motion of the leg (when shooting with the right leg, the right arm moves back to gather momentum, the left arm moves forward), at the moment of the shot the eyes are on the ball.)

- Make sure the shot on goal is practiced with the left and right foot.
- Different shooting techniques (inside foot kick, instep kick, swerve) can be practiced where appropriate (at the trainer's command).

Field size: 10 x 35 yards

Distance between cones:
Goal to cone C: 16-25 yards
Cone C to cone B to cone A: 5 yards

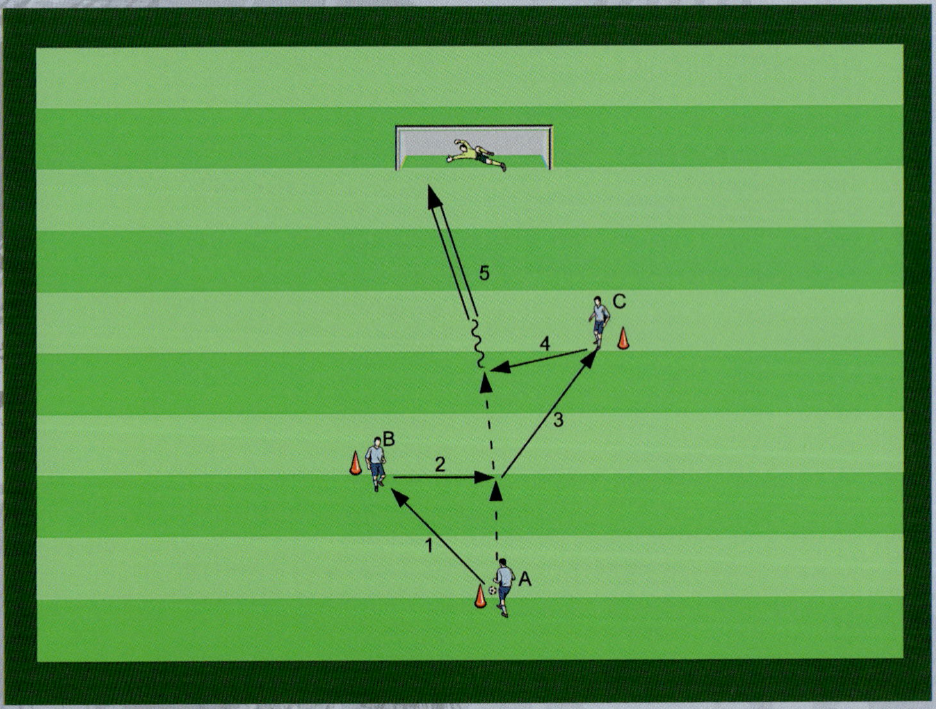

40 Shot on goal after multiple double passes

Purpose of training
- Ball handling techniques

Training emphasis
- Shooting techniques/shot on goal

Training aspects

Specific purpose:	**Push-off power, speed of action with the ball, speed of anticipation, outside instep, speed of movement without the ball, direct pass play, double pass, speed of decision-making, action speed, inside foot, push-pass (inside), inside foot kick, combination ball handling technique with movement, short passes, reaction speed, instep, speed of perception, swerve**
Age group:	**Age 13 to seniors**
Playing level:	**Advanced, pro**
Form of training:	**Group**
Training structure:	**Main part/emphasis**
Intention:	**Improving individual quality**
Number of players:	**10 or more**
Number of participating players:	**Entire team**
Training location	**Any**
Space requirements:	**Restricted playing field**
Length:	**10-15 min**
Physical aspects:	**Soccer-specific endurance, speed endurance**
Goalies:	**1 goalie**

Organization:
Setting up one goal as well as two rows of three cones each opposite each other (see illustration), and a start cone. One player stands at each cone. The remaining players are positioned at starting position A.

Execution:
The player at starting position A plays a double pass with each player on the plains of all three cones, starting with a double pass to player B. After the pass relay he takes a shot on goal. The next player startsafter pass 5 (see illustration). The rebounders change regularly.

Equipment: 1 regulation size goal(s), 7 cones

Tips:
- As soon as the passing player initiates his swing, the respective double pass partner (rebounder) makes a small counter movement and then briefly moves towards the ball.
- The pass to the rebounder is played to his strong foot.
- All passes should be direct if possible.
- Pay attention to your posture when taking a shot (upper body over the ball; supporting leg is 12-16 inches to the side staggered with the ball, the foot points in shooting direction, the arms swing along; the arm closest to the shooting leg mimics the swinging motion of the leg (when shooting with

the right leg, the right arm moves back to gather momentum, the left arm moves forward), at the moment of the shot the eyes are on the ball.)

- Make sure the shot on goal is practiced with the left and right foot.
- Different shooting techniques (inside foot kick, instep kick, swerve) can be practiced where appropriate (at the trainer's command).

Field size: 20 x 40 yards

Distance between cones:
Goal to pair of cones closest to goal: 10-15 yards
Cone to cone/ width: 15 yards
Cone to cone/depth: 10 yards
Start cone/first rebounder cone: 5 yards
Distances between cones vary according to age.

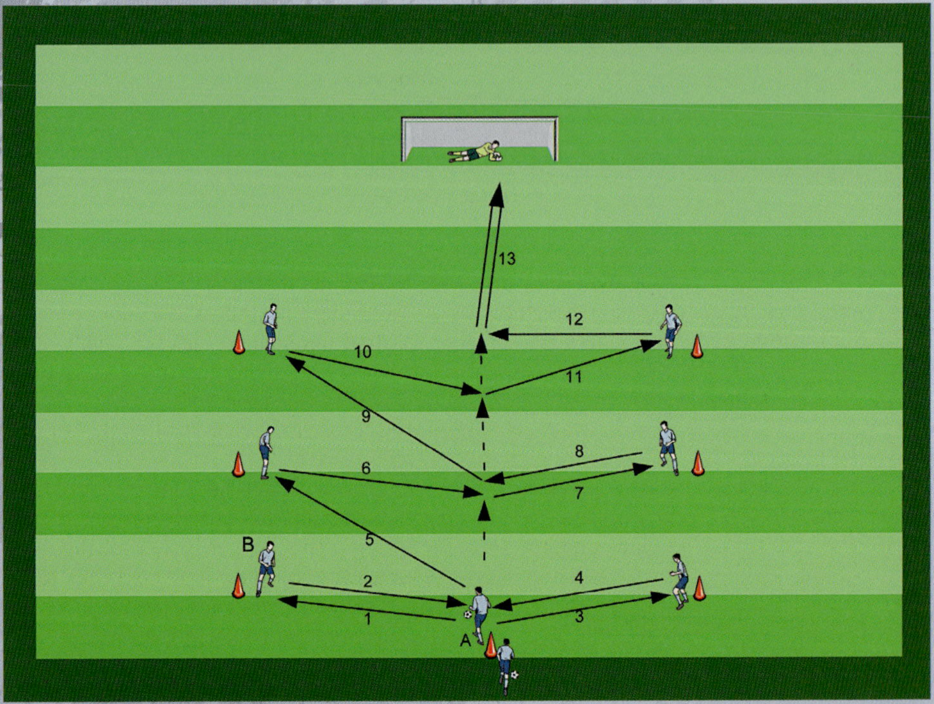

41 Shot on goal with double pass and overlap

Purpose of training

- Ball handling techniques

Training emphasis

- Shooting techniques/shot on goal

Training aspects

Specific purpose:	**Push-off power, speed of action with the ball, offensive play, speed of anticipation, outside instep, speed of movement without the ball, direct pass play, double pass, speed of decision-making, overlapping, inside foot, push-pass (inside), inside foot kick, combination ball handling technique with movement, passing to multiple stations, reaction speed, instep, swerve**
Age group:	**Age 9-12, 13-14,15 to seniors**
Playing level:	**Advanced**
Form of training:	**Group**
Training structure:	**Main part/emphasis**
Intention:	**ffensive play, improving individual quality**
Number of players:	**6 or more**
Number of participating players:	**Entire team**
Training location	**Any**
Space requirements:	**Restricted playing field**
Length:	**10-15 min**
Physical aspects:	**Soccer-specific endurance, power**
Goalies:	**1 goalie**

Organization:
Setting up one goal, two rebounder cones (B+C), and a start cone (A), as shown in the illustration. One player stands at each of the rebounder cones, the remaining players line up at the start cone with a ball.

Execution:
Player A plays a double pass with player B and then passes the ball directly to player C. After A has played his second pass he takes the position of B. Player B directly overlaps A after playing the pass back to him, and turns the pass from C (4) into a shot on goal. Player B takes the position of C and player C runs to the position of player A.

Equipment: 1 regulation size goal(s), 3 cones

Tips:

- As soon as the starting player initiates the swinging motion the rebounder makes a small counter movement and then briefly moves towards the ball.
- The pass to the rebounder should be played to his strong foot.
- Pay attention to your posture when taking a shot (upper body over the ball; supporting leg is 12-16 inches to the side staggered with the ball, the foot points in shooting direction, the arms swing along; the arm closest to the shooting leg mimics the swinging

motion of the leg (when shooting with the right leg, the right arm moves back to gather momentum, the left arm moves forward), at the moment of the shot the eyes are on the ball.)

- Make sure the shot on goal is practiced with the left and right foot.
- Different shooting techniques (inside foot kick, instep kick, swerve) can be practiced where appropriate (at the trainer's command).
- Player B starts as soon as he has passed the ball back to player A.
- The subsequent position changes must take place quickly to avoid delays.

Field size: 10 x 40 yards

Distance between cones:
Goal to cone C: 10-16 yards
Cone C to cone B: 6-10 yards
Cone B to cone A: 6-10 yards
Distances between cones vary according to age.

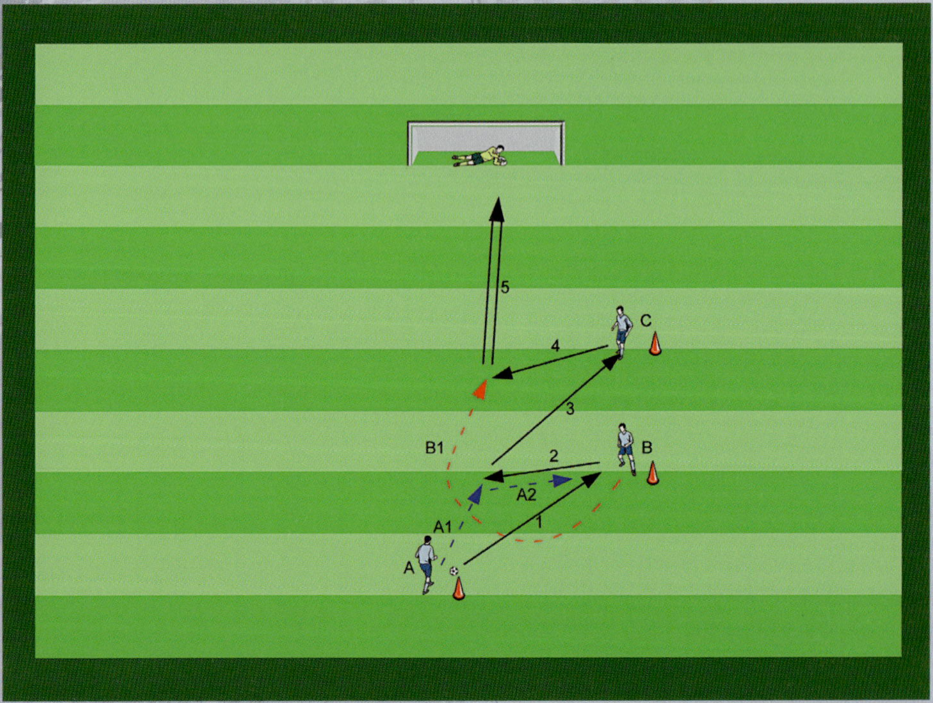

42 Shot on goal after a back pass

Purpose of training
- Ball handling techniques

Training emphasis
- Shooting techniques/shot on goal

Training aspects

Specific purpose:	Push-off power, speed of action with the ball, offensive play, speed of anticipation, outside instep, basic play, speed of decision-making, action speed, inside foot, push-pass (inside), inside foot kick, combination ball handling technique with movement, reaction speed, instep, swerve
Age group:	Age 9 to seniors
Playing level:	Any
Form of training:	Group
Training structure:	Main part/emphasis
Intention:	Offensive play, improving individual quality
Number of players:	4 or more
Number of participating players:	Entire team
Training location	Any
Space requirements:	Restricted playing field
Length:	10-20 min
Physical aspects:	Soccer-specific endurance, power
Goalies:	1 goalie

Organization:
Setting up one goal and two start cones, as shown in the illustration. The players are evenly divided between the cones. The players in group A have the balls.

Execution:
The red player A plays a long diagonal ball into the running lane of the blue player B. Player B starts the moment Player A initiates his swing, and passes/crosses the ball back into the running lane of the red player. The red player then shoots a volley on goal. After that the players switch groups.

Equipment: 1 regulation size goal(s), 2 cones

Tips:
- The diagonal opening ball should be played fast and low from a run. This means the ball must be played with an inside foot kick (half inside foot half instep; the ankle is turned up).
- The subsequent cross should ideally be played direct from a run, but can also be executed after first receiving and moving with the ball.
- After he has played the opening ball Player A immediately moves to a central and slightly offset position relative to the second goal post at a level with the penalty box.
- Pay attention to your posture when taking a shot (upper body over the

ball; supporting leg is 12-16 inches to the side staggered with the ball, the foot points in shooting direction, the arms swing along; the arm closest to the shooting leg mimics the swinging motion of the leg (when shooting with the right leg, the right arm moves back to gather momentum, the left arm moves forward), at the moment of the shot the eyes are on the ball.)

- During a volley shot the upper body is bent forward slightly. Contact with the ball is made at a low point (not too high). This applies more force to the ball and makes the shot more accurate.

Field size: 30 x 35 yards

Distance between cones:
Start cone A to start cone B: 25-30 yards
Goal to start cone A: 20-25 yards

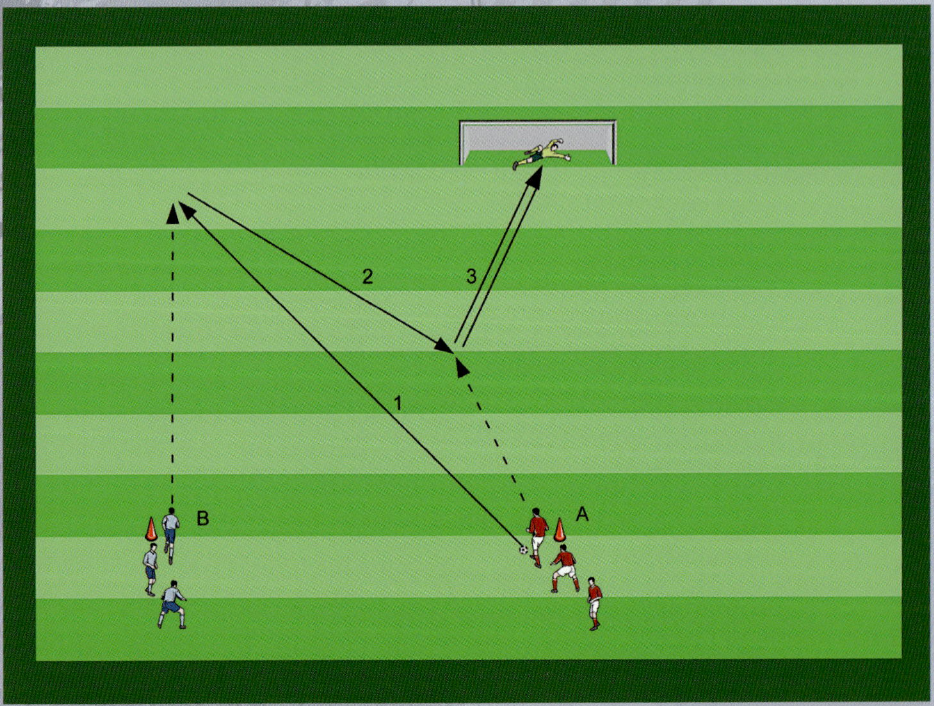

43 Shot on goal with a double pass and through pass

Purpose of training

- Ball handling techniques

Training emphasis

- Shooting techniques/shot on goal

Training aspects

Specific purpose:	**Push-off power, speed of action with the ball, attack through the middle, speed of anticipation, outside instep, direct pass play, speed of decision-making, action speed, inside foot, push-pass (inside), inside foot kick, combination ball handling technique with movement, passing to multiple stations, reaction speed, instep, swerve**
Age group:	**Age 13 to seniors**
Playing level:	**Advanced**
Form of training:	**Group**
Training structure:	**Main part/emphasis**
Intention:	**Offensive play, improving individual quality**
Number of players:	**6 or more**
Number of participating players:	**Entire team**
Training location	**Any**
Space requirements:	**Restricted playing field**
Length:	**10-15 min**
Physical aspects:	**Soccer-specific endurance, power**
Goalies:	**1 goalie**

Organization:
Setting up one goal and four cones (A-D), as shown in the illustration. One player each at cones B-D, the remaining players stand at start cone A with the balls.

Execution:
Player A plays a pass to player B. B plays a direct pass to player C, who lets the ball rebound into the running lane of player D, who takes a shot on goal. The players start their action with a counter movement the moment the front player initiates his swing,before playing a pass. Players change positions clockwise.

Equipment: 1 regulation size goal(s), 4 cones

Tips:

- As soon as the starting player initiates the swinging motion the rebounder makes a small counter movement and then briefly moves towards the ball.
- The pass to the rebounder should be played to his strong foot.
- Pay attention to your posture when taking a shot (upper body over the ball; supporting leg is 12-16 inches to the side staggered with the ball, the foot points in shooting direction, the arms swing along; the arm closest to the shooting leg mimics the swinging motion of the leg (when shooting with the right leg, the right arm moves back to gather momentum, the left arm

moves forward), at the moment of the shot the eyes are on the ball.)

- Shots on goal should be trained with the right and left foot.
- Different shooting techniques (inside foot kick, instep kick, swerve) can be practiced where appropriate (at the trainer's command).

Field size: 20 x 30 m

Distance between cones:
Goal to cone B: 15 yards
Cone A to cones B/C/D: 12 yards respectively

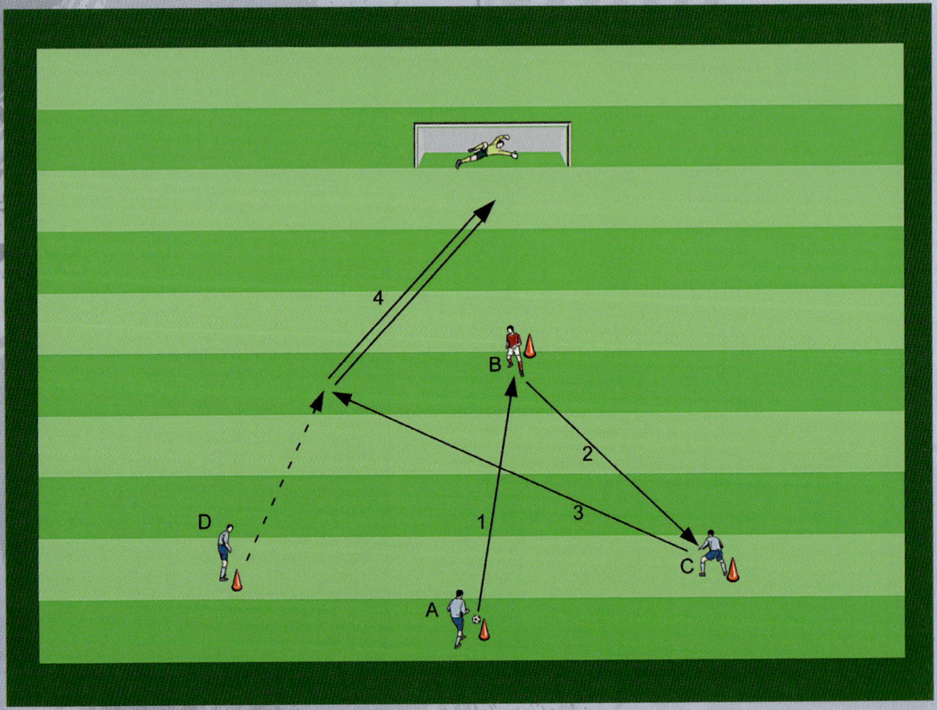

44 Successful finish after a pass

Purpose of training
- Ball handling techniques

Training emphasis
- Shooting techniques/shot on goal

Training aspects

Specific purpose:	**Push-off power, speed of action with the ball, speed of anticipation, direct pass play, speed of decision-making, inside foot, push-pass (inside), inside foot kick, combination ball handling technique with movement, reaction speed, instep, swerve**
Age group:	**Any**
Playing level:	**Any**
Form of training:	**Small groups of 2-6 players**
Training structure:	**Main part/emphasis**
Intention:	**Improving individual quality**
Number of players:	**4 or more**
Number of participating players:	**Entire team**
Training location	**Any**
Space requirements:	**Restricted playing field**
Length:	**10-15 min**
Physical aspects:	**Soccer-specific endurance, power**
Goalies:	**1 goalie**

Organization:
Setting up one goal and three cones (A-C), as shown in the illustration. One player stands at each cone. The remaining players stand at cone A. The players at cone A have the balls.

Execution:
Player A passes to player C. C lets the ball rebound into the running lane of player B. B takes a shot on goal. C lines up at the back of Group A. Player A takes the position of Player B, and B runs to Player C's position.

Equipment: 1 regulation size goal(s), 3 cones

Tips:
- Player C makes a counter movement the moment A initiates his swing, and briefly moves towards the ball for the rebound.
- Player B starts down his running lane as soon as C initiates his pass.
- The pass to the rebounder should be played to his strong foot.
- The passing game should be forceful and tight.
- Pay attention to your posture when taking a shot (upper body over the ball; supporting leg is 12-16 inches to the side staggered with the ball, the foot points in shooting direction, the

arms swing along; the arm closest to the shooting leg mimics the swinging motion of the leg (when shooting with the right leg, the right arm moves back to gather momentum, the left arm moves forward), at the moment of the shot the eyes are on the ball.)

- Shots on goal should be trained with the right and left foot.
- Different shooting techniques (inside foot kick, instep kick, swerve) can be practiced where appropriate (at the trainer's command).

Field size: 15 x 30 yards

Distance between cones:
Goal to cone C: 10-18 yards
Cone A to cone B to cone C: 8 yards

45 Shot on goal after a pass relay

Purpose of training

- Ball handling techniques

Training emphasis

- Shooting techniques/shot on goal

Training aspects

Specific purpose:	**Push-off power, speed of action with the ball, speed of anticipation, direct pass play, speed of decision-making, push-pass (inside), inside foot kick, combination ball handling technique with movement, reaction speed, instep, swerve**
Age group:	**Any**
Playing level:	**Any**
Form of training:	**Small groups of 2-6 players**
Training structure:	**Main part/emphasis**
Intention:	**Improving individual quality**
Number of players:	**4 or more**
Number of participating players:	**Entire team**
Training location	**Any**
Space requirements:	**Restricted playing field**
Length:	**10-15 min**
Physical aspects:	**Soccer-specific endurance, power**
Goalies:	**1 goalie**

Organization:
Setting up one goal and three cones (A-C), as shown in the illustration. One player stands at each cone. The remaining players stand at cone A. The players at cone A have the balls.

Execution:
Player A passes to player B. B plays the ball directly to C, who takes a shot on goal on the turn. Afterwards positions change clockwise (A->B/B->C/C->A).

Equipment: 1 regulation size goal(s), 3 cones

Tips:

- The opening pass to the rebounder should be played to his strong foot.
- The receiving player makes a counter movement before each pass.
- The passing game should be forceful and tight.
- Pay attention to your posture when taking a shot (upper body over the ball; supporting leg is 12-16 inches to the side staggered with the ball, the foot points in shooting direction, the arms swing along; the arm closest to the shooting leg mimics the swinging

motion of the leg (when shooting with the right leg, the right arm moves back to gather momentum, the left arm moves forward), at the moment of the shot the eyes are on the ball.)

- Shots on goal should be trained with the right and left foot.
- Different shooting techniques (inside foot kick, instep kick, swerve) can be practiced where appropriate (at the trainer's command).
- The shooter should take a direct shot on goal out of his countermovement and before the cone.

Field size: 15 x 30 yards

Distance between cones:
Goal to cone C: 10-18 yards
Cone A to cone C/B: 8 yards

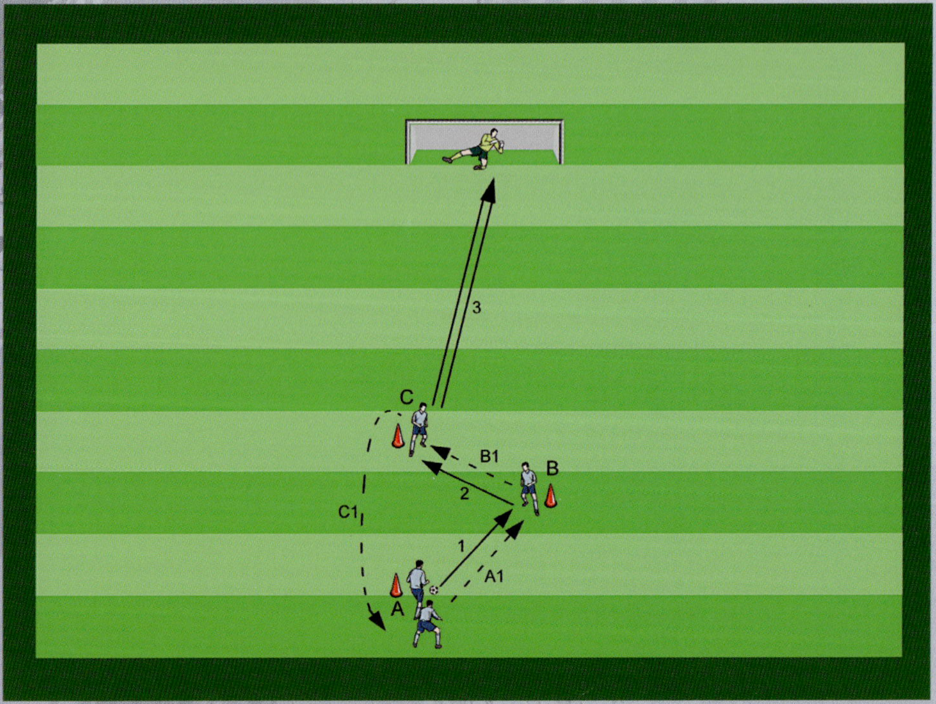

46 Shot on goal after a double pass and deep pass

Purpose of training
- Ball handling techniques

Training emphasis
- Shooting techniques/shot on goal

Training aspects

Specific purpose:	**Push-off power, speed of action with the ball, speed of anticipation, direct pass play, double pass, speed of decision-making, inside foot, push-pass (inside), inside foot kick, combination ball handling technique with movement, short passes, quick play to the forward, instep, speed of perception, swerve**
Age group:	**Age 13-14, 15 to seniors, U12, U13**
Playing level:	**Advanced**
Form of training:	**Small groups of 2-6 players**
Training structure:	**Main part/emphasis**
Intention:	**Offensive play, improving individual quality**
Number of players:	**4 or more**
Number of participating players:	**Entire team**
Training location	**Any**
Space requirements:	**Restricted playing field**
Length:	**10-15 min**
Physical aspects:	**Soccer-specific endurance, power**
Goalies:	**1 goalie**

Organization:
Setting up one goal, one rebounder cone, and one start cone, as shown in the illustration. One player stands at the rebounder cone, the others line up with the balls at the start cone.

Execution:
A plays a double pass with B, whereby B plays the ball into the running lane of A (see illustration). Next A plays the ball so deep that B has to chase it to take a shot on goal. After completion of the action player A takes the place of player B, and B switches to the start cone.

Equipment: 1 regulation size goal(s), 2 cones

Tips:
- The opening pass to the rebounder should be played to his strong foot.
- Player B makes a counter movement at the moment A initiates his swing, and briefly moves towards the ball for the rebound.
- The passing game should be forceful and tight.
- The deep pass must be timed so the receiver can utilize it at a run before he reaches the penalty box.
- Pay attention to your posture when taking a shot (upper body over the ball; supporting leg is 12-16 inches to the side staggered with the ball, the foot points in shooting direction, the

arms swing along; the arm closest to the shooting leg mimics the swinging motion of the leg (when shooting with the right leg, the right arm moves back to gather momentum, the left arm moves forward), at the moment of the shot the eyes are on the ball.)

- Shots on goal should be trained with the right and left foot.
- Different shooting techniques (inside foot kick, instep kick, swerve) can be practiced where appropriate (at the trainer's command).

Field size: 15 x 35 yards

Distance between cones:
Goa to cone B: 16-25 yards
Cone B to start cone A: 10 yards
Distances between cones vary according to age.

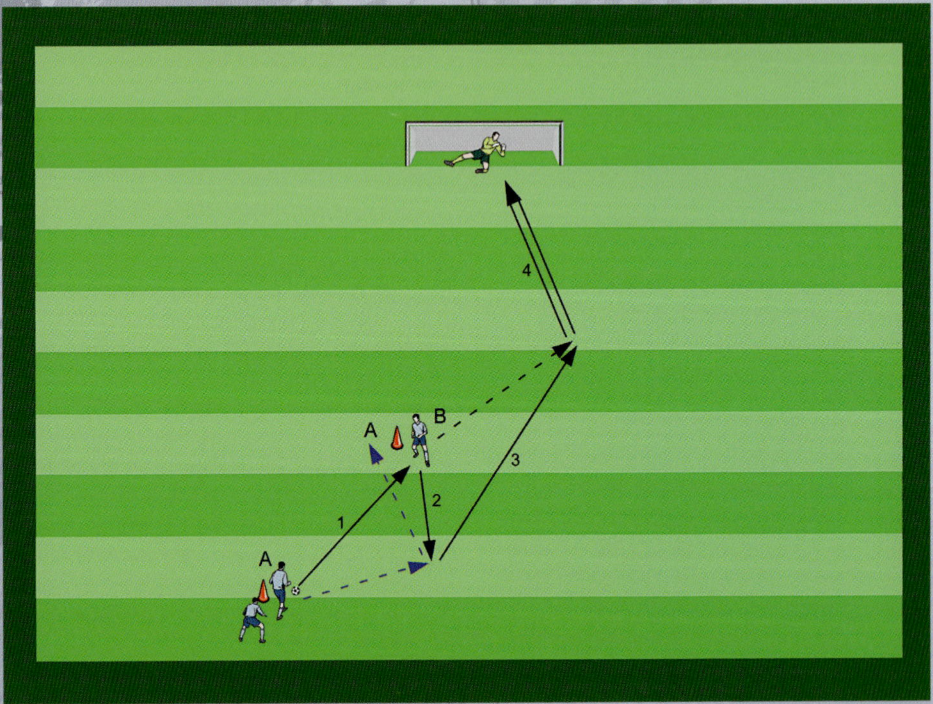

47 Shot on goal after pass relay

Purpose of training

- Ball handling techniques

Training emphasis

- Shooting techniques/shot on goal

Training aspects

Specific purpose:	Push-off power, speed of action with the ball, speed of anticipation, outside instep, moving with the ball, direct pass play, speed of decision-making, inside foot, push-pass (inside), inside foot kick, combination ball handling technique with movement, short passes, long passes, passing to multiple stations, reaction speed, instep, swerve
Age group:	Age 13-14, 15 to seniors
Playing level:	Advanced
Form of training:	Group
Training structure:	Main part/emphasis
Intention:	Improving individual quality
Number of players:	6 or more
Number of participating players:	Entire team
Training location	Any
Space requirements:	Half field
Length:	10-20 min
Physical aspects:	Soccer-specific endurance, speed endurance, power
Goalies:	1 goalie

Organization:
Setting up one goal and three cones (A-C), as shown in the illustration. One player stands at cone C, the others are divided between cones A and B. The players at cone A have the ball.

Execution:
Player A plays a linear high ball to player B. He plays a double pass with C and then shoots the ball passed by C on goal. Next player A takes B's position and player B takes C's position.

Option:
The fly ball played by A can also be received and utilized by B during the first step, before the pass to player C.

Equipment: 1 regulation size goal(s), 3 cones

Tips:

- Player B makes a counter movement at the moment A initiates his swing, and then briefly moves towards the ball for the rebound. The same goes for player C, who starts his counter movement the moment B initiates his swing.
- The passing game should be forceful and tight.
- The fly ball (A) should be played as an inside foot kick, partly with the

inside foot and partly with the instep (linear trajectory). This type of pass can generate a high rate of passing speed.
- When receiving the ball with the chest it is important to lightly bunt the ball in passing direction to player C.
- Pay attention to your posture when taking a shot (upper body over the ball; supporting leg is 12-16 inches to the side staggered with the ball, the foot points in shooting direction, the arms swing along; the arm closest to the shooting leg mimics the swinging motion of the leg (when shooting with the right leg, the right arm moves back to gather momentum, the left arm moves forward), at the moment of the shot the eyes are on the ball.)
- Shots on goal should be trained with the right and left foot.
- Different shooting techniques (inside foot kick, instep kick, swerve) can be practiced where appropriate (at the trainer's command).

Field size: Half of playing field

Distance between cones:
Right goal post to cone A: 10-30 yards
Cone A to cone B: 30-50 yards
Cone B to cone C: 15-35 yards
Distances between cones vary according to age.

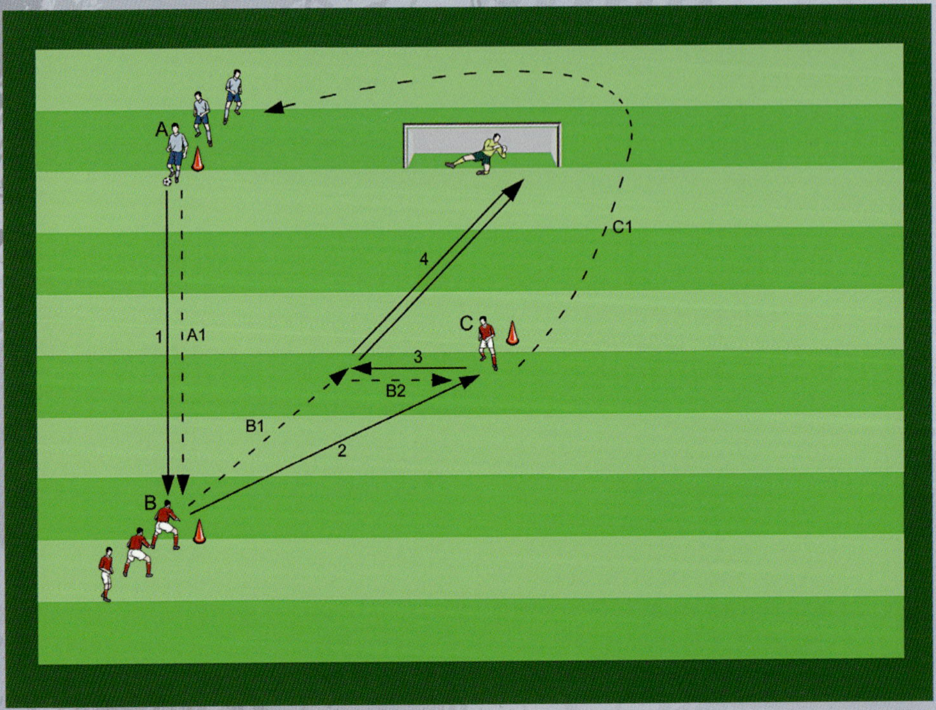

48 Passing combination with overlap and successful finish

Purpose of training

- Ball handling techniques

Training emphasis

- Shooting techniques/shot on goal

Training aspects

Specific purpose:	**Push-off power, speed of action with the ball, offensive play, speed of anticipation, outside instep, ball control, speed of movement without the ball, direct pass play, speed of decision-making, overlap, inside foot, push-pass (inside), inside foot kick, combination ball handling technique with movement, header while moving, short passes, long passes, passing to multiple stations, volley, instep, speed of perception, swerve**
Age group:	**Age 13 to seniors**
Playing level:	**Advanced**
Form of training:	**Group**
Training structure:	**Main part/emphasis**
Intention:	**Offensive play, improving individual quality**
Number of players:	**8 or more**
Number of participating players:	**Entire team**
Training location	**Any**
Space requirements:	**Restricted playing field**
Length:	**10-15 min**
Physical aspects:	**Soccer-specific endurance, speed endurance, power**
Goalies:	**1 goalie**

Organization:
Setting up one goal as well as five cones. Cones I and II are orientation cones. The players are divided evenly between the remaining three cones. Players A have the balls.

Execution:
Player A opens the drill with a pass to player C. At the moment of the pass player B starts from his cone towards cone II. Player A starts in direction of cone I, and in doing so overlaps player B. Now player C passes the ball played by A into the running lane of B, who plays the ball diagonally in direction of cone I when he is approximately on a level with cone II. Players B and C now move towards the goal and crisscross as soon as player A crosses the ball passed to him by B into the penalty box, to make use of it there. After the finish the players switch cones clockwise (A->B; B->C; C->A).

Equipment: 1 regulation size goal(s), 5 cones

Tips:

- The opening pass to player C should be played to his strong foot.

- Player C makes a counter movement the moment A initiates his swing, and briefly moves towards the ball.
- The passing game should be forceful and tight.
- The deep pass to cone II must be timed so player A can pass it from a run just before the cone. The same goes for the pass A plays in direction of cone I.
- The finish is determined by how the ball is played into the box (low pass, medium high/high cross). A volley should be executed regardless.
- If the finish is a shot, the following posture is important: upper body over the ball; supporting leg is 12-16 inches to the side staggered with the ball, the foot points in shooting direction, the arms swing along; the arm closest to the shooting leg mimics the swinging motion of the leg, the other arm moves forward; at the moment of the shot the eyes are on the ball.
- The header is executed with the forehead.
- During a header the neck does not move sideways but forward.
- During a flick header the head is turned to the side up to 45° from a straight position.
- Momentum is gathered with a hollow back (bow tension).
- Eyes are on the ball; eyes are closed during a header (this is a natural reflex and cannot be changed).
- Elbows are bent, hands (usually fists) point upward and are used to gather momentum.

Field size: 30 x 35 yards

Distance between cones:
Right goal post to cone I: 20 yards width and 5 yards from the end line
Goal to cone II: 16-20 yards
Cone II to cone C: 6-8 yards
Cone C to cone A: 5 yards
Cone C to cone B: 5 yards

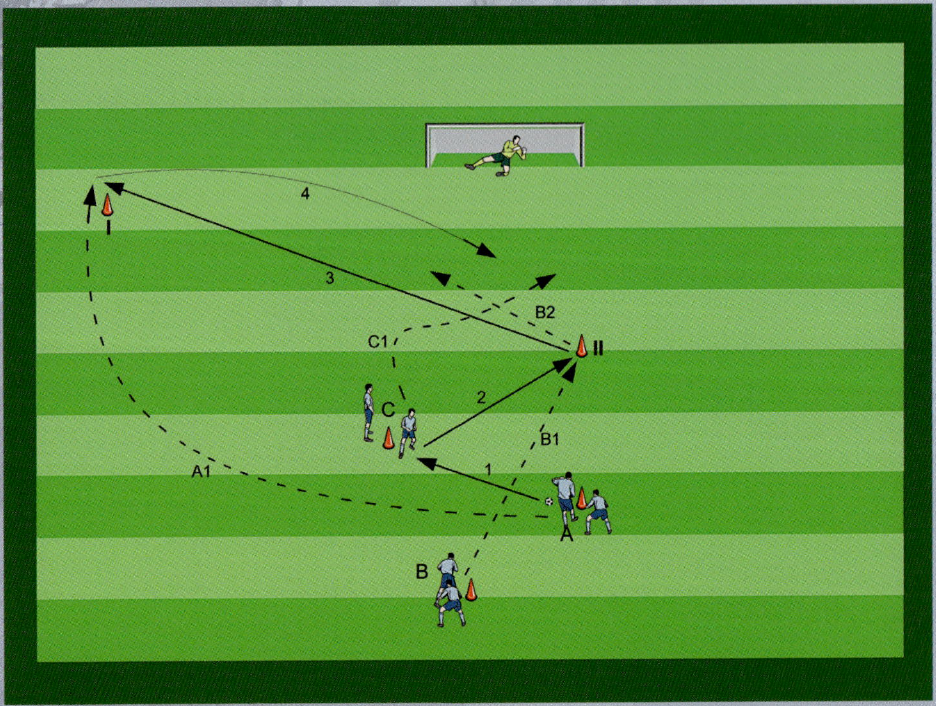

49 Shooting on two goals with overlaps, crossing, crisscross, and successful finish

Purpose of training
- Ball handling techniques

Training emphasis
- Shooting techniques/shot on goal

Training aspects

Specific purpose:	**Push-off power, speed of action with the ball, speed of anticipation, outside instep, moving with the ball, speed of movement without the ball, double pass, speed of decision-making, wing play without an opponent, action speed, overlap, inside foot, push-pass (inside), inside foot kick, combination ball handling technique with movement, header while moving, body feint, reaction speed, volley, instep, swerve**
Age group:	**Age 13 to seniors**
Playing level:	**Advanced**
Form of training:	**Group**
Training structure:	**Main part/emphasis**
Intention:	**Offensive play, improving individual quality**
Number of players:	**8 or more**
Number of participating players:	**Entire team**
Training location	**Any**
Space requirements:	**Half field**
Length:	**15-30 min**
Physical aspects:	**Soccer-specific endurance, GAT II, speed, speed endurance**
Goalies:	**2 goalies**

Organization:
Mark off a field with four cones. Set up one goal at each end, and one start cone to the side of each goal. Form two groups (blue/red). Both groups position themselves at the start cones (with ball) and in pairs at the respective positions on the field, as shown in the illustration.

Execution:
Example red group:
Player A starts the drill with a low pass to player B, who receives the ball as he makes an inside turn and then does a brief fastdribble. After his pass, player A immediately sprints in direction of the baseline. Now player B passes the ball into the running lane of A and together with player C runs into the penalty box. Player A crosses the ball from a run in front of the goal. B and C crisscross and try to make use of the cross. The drill is done simultaneously on the other side (blue group) with the same running and passing lanes.

Both of the two positions in the field are manned by two players. After each round the players move to the next position (A->B; B->C; C->A).

Equipment: 1 regulation size goal(s), 2 cones

Tips:

- The opening pass to player B should be played to his strong foot.
- Player B makes a counter movement the moment A initiates his swing, and briefly moves towards the ball.
- The passing game should be forceful and tight.
- Receiving the ball while turning should be a fluid movement and can be executed with the inside as well as the outside of the foot.
- The ball should be kept close while dribbling and the start should be explosive.
- The deep pass to player A must be timed so the player can execute a cross from a run just before the baseline.
- The finish is determined by how the ball is played into the box (low pass, medium high/high cross). A volley should be executed regardless.
- If the finish is a shot, the following posture is important: upper body over the ball; supporting leg is 12-16 inches to the side staggered with the ball, the foot points in shooting direction, the arms swing along; the arm closest to the shooting leg mimics the swinging motion of the leg, the other arm moves forward; at the moment of the shot the eyes are on the ball.

Field size: 40 x 50 yards

Distance between cones:
Field marked by cones: Width 30 yards, length varies according to age 30-50 yards
Right goal post to start cone: 16 yards
Goal to player C: 16 yards

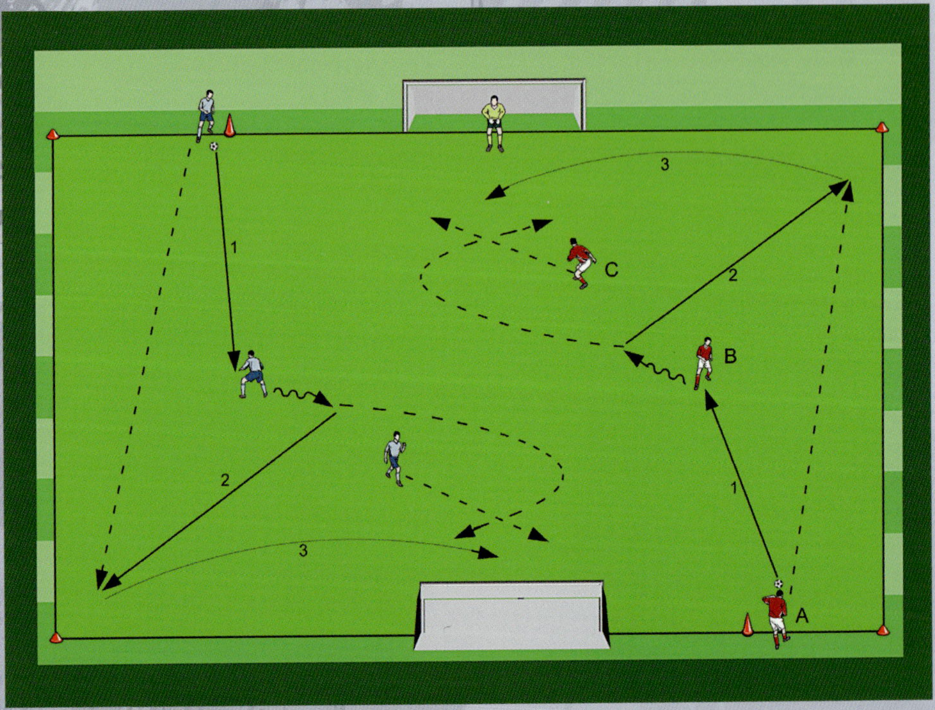

50 Shooting on two goals after a cross

Purpose of training
- Ball handling techniques

Training emphasis
- Shooting techniques/shot on goal

Training aspects

Specific purpose:	Push-off power, speed of action with the ball, speed of anticipation, outside instep, moving with the ball, direct pass play, speed of decision-making, inside foot, push-pass (inside), inside foot kick, combination ball handling technique with movement, header while moving, short passes, long passes, reaction speed, wing play, volley, instep, swerve
Age group:	Age 13 to seniors
Playing level:	FAdvanced, pro
Form of training:	Group
Training structure:	Main part/emphasis
Intention:	Offensive play, improving individual quality
Number of players:	8 or more
Number of participating players:	Entire team
Training location	Any
Space requirements:	Restricted playing field
Length:	15-25 min
Physical aspects:	Soccer-specific endurance, GAT II, speed endurance, power
Goalies:	2 goalies

Organization:
Mark off a field with four cones. Set up one goal at each end. Players are evenly divided between the four positions (A-D) shown in the illustration on either side of the goals. One player is positioned in the middle of the field.

Execution:
Player Aopens with a low pass to the rebounder in the middle and then sprints diagonally to the midfield position I. The rebounder passes the ball on to player B. B then passes the ball directly into the running lane of A and sprints in direction of the penalty box. There he tries to utilize the cross that A plays to him while running. The drill is now executed on the other side with the same running and passing lanes.
After each action the players line up at the position oppositetheir own. The rebounder changes regularly.

Equipment: 2 regulation size goals(s), 4 cones

Tips:
- The pass to the rebounder should be played to his strong foot.
- The rebounder makes a counter movement the moment A initiates his swing, and briefly moves towards the ball.

- The passing game should be forceful and tight.
- The diagonal ball played by player B into the running lane of A is a low, diagonal inside foot kick (half inside foot, half instep).
- Player A receives the ball at a full run and crosses it directly to B, who has moved up.
- After the action the rebounder immediately turns to the other group.
- B waits near the 18-yard area and starts when the crossing player initiates his swing.

Field size: 30 x 35 yards

Distance between cones:
Cones marking the field: Width 30 yards/ length 35 yards
Player positions A-D-goal: 15 yards

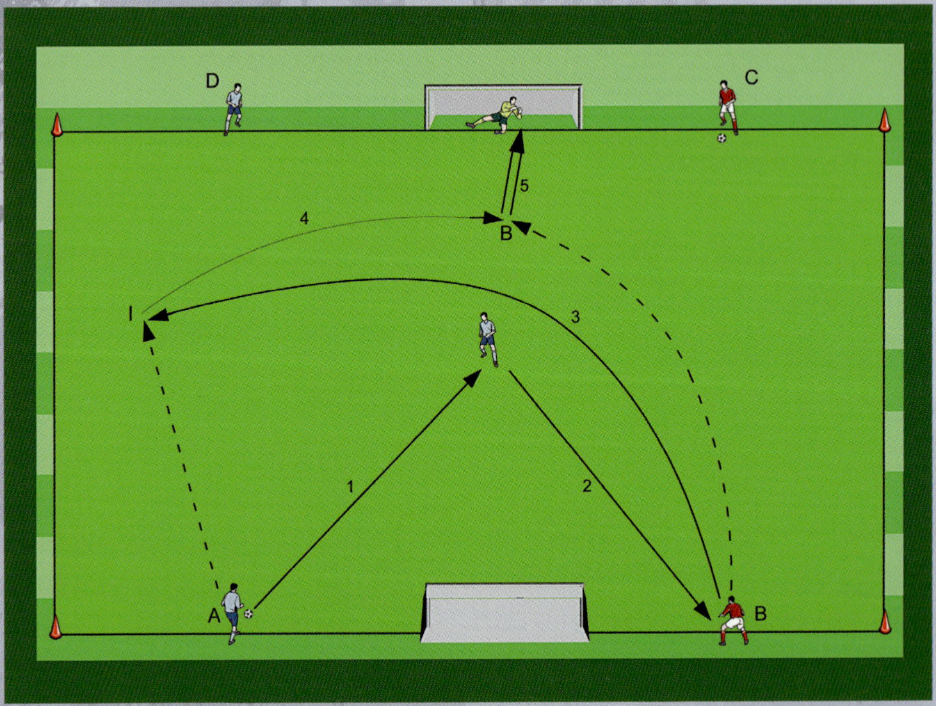

51 Shooting on two goals with overlap, dribbling, crossing, and successful finish

Purpose of training
- Ball handling techniques

Training emphasis
- Shooting techniques/shot on goal

Training aspects

Specific purpose:	**Push-off power, speed of action with the ball, offensive play, speed of anticipation, outside instep, receiving and moving with the ball, speed of movement without the ball, dribbling, speed of decision-making, wing play without an opponent, action speed, overlap, inside foot, push-pass (inside), inside foot kick, combination ball handling technique with movement, header while moving, short passes, long passes, reaction speed, volley, instep, swerve**
Age group:	**Age 13-14, age 15 to seniors**
Playing level:	**Advanced**
Form of training:	**Team**
Training structure:	**Main part/emphasis**
Intention:	**Offensive play, improving individual quality**
Number of players:	**8 or more**
Number of participating players:	**Entire team**
Training location	**Any**
Space requirements:	**Restricted playing field**
Length:	**15-25 min**
Physical aspects:	**Physical aspects: Soccer-specific endurance, GAT II, speed endurance, power**
Goalies:	**2 goalies**

Organization:
Mark off a field with four cones. Set up one goal at each end. Form two groups (blue/red) who position themselves on either side of the two goals, as shown in the illustration. The blue players A and the players of the opposite red group have the balls. An additional cone is set up in the middle of the field.

Execution:
Player A opens the drill with a flat, diagonal pass, which player B reaches. Player A overlaps B in direction of the baseline. Player B traps the ball and dribbles in direction of the middle cone and then plays the ball into A's running lane. B then runs into the penalty box and tries to utilize A's cross.

After the sequence is complete both players run behind the goal they played on and line up with the group whose original starting position was diagonally across from their own. Now the red group starts with the same running and passing lanes.

Equipment: 2 regulation size goals(s), 5 cones

Tips:

- The opening ball played by A should be timed so player B is able to reach it after a short sprint.
- The ball should be kept close while dribbling and the running speed should remain high.
- The diagonal deep pass to player A must be timed so the player is able to do a cross just before the baseline while running.
- Player B waits at a level with the penalty box until player A initiates his swing for the cross. Only then does he run into the penalty box for the finish.
- The finish is determined by how the ball is played into the box (low pass, medium high/high cross). A volley should be executed regardless.
- If the finish is a shot, the following posture is important: upper body over the ball; supporting leg is 12-16 inches to the side staggered with the ball, the foot points in shooting direction, the arms swing along; the arm closest to the shooting leg mimics the swinging motion of the leg, the other arm moves forward; at the moment of the shot the eyes are on the ball.

Field size: 30 x 40 yards

Distance between cones:
Cones marking the field: Width 30 yards, length 40 yards
Goal to middle orientation cone: 20 yards
Goal post to starting position players: 15 yards

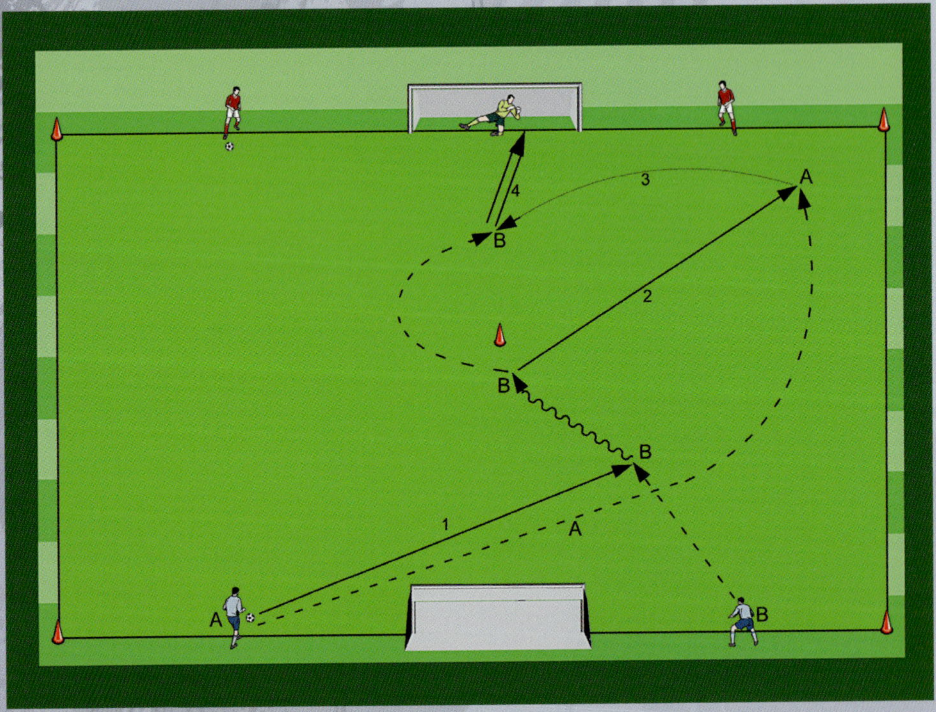

52 Shot on goal after a deep pass

Purpose of training

- Ball handling techniques

Training emphasis

- Shooting techniques/shot on goal

Training aspects

Specific purpose:	**Push-off power, speed of action with the ball, attack through the middle, speed of anticipation, outside instep, moving with the ball, speed of decision making, inside foot, push-pass (inside), inside foot kick, combination ball handling technique with movement, short passes, quick play to the forward, instep, swerve**
Age group:	**Any**
Playing level:	**Any**
Form of training:	**Group**
Training structure:	**Main part/emphasis**
Intention:	**improving individual quality**
Number of players:	**4 or more**
Number of participating players:	**Entire team**
Training location	**Any**
Space requirements:	**Restricted playing field**
Length:	**10-15 min**
Physical aspects:	**Soccer-specific endurance, speed endurance, power**
Goalies:	**1 goalie**

Organization:
Setting up one goal and two poles, as shown in the illustration. The players are evenly divided between the two poles. The balls are with group A.

Execution:
Player A makes a slightly diagonal pass into the 18-yard area. Player B sprints after the ball and takes a shot on goal. Positions change after each round.

Equipment: 1 regulation size goal(s), 2 pole(s)

Tips:

- The opening pass into the 18-yard area must be timed so the player is able to reach the ball with a linear sprint.
- Pay attention to your posture when taking a shot (upper body over the ball; supporting leg is 12-16 inches to the side staggered with the ball, the foot points in shooting direction, the arms swing along; the arm closest tothe shooting leg mimics the swinging motion of the leg (when shooting with the right leg, the right arm moves back to gather momentum, the left arm moves forward), at the moment of the shot the eyes are on the ball.)

- Shots on goal should be trained with the right and left foot.
- Different shooting techniques (inside foot kick, instep kick, swerve) can be practiced where appropriate (at the trainer's command).
- The receiving player startswhen the passing player initiates his swing.

Field size: 15 x 25 yards

Distance between cones:
Goal to pole: 25 yards
Pole to pole: 15 yards

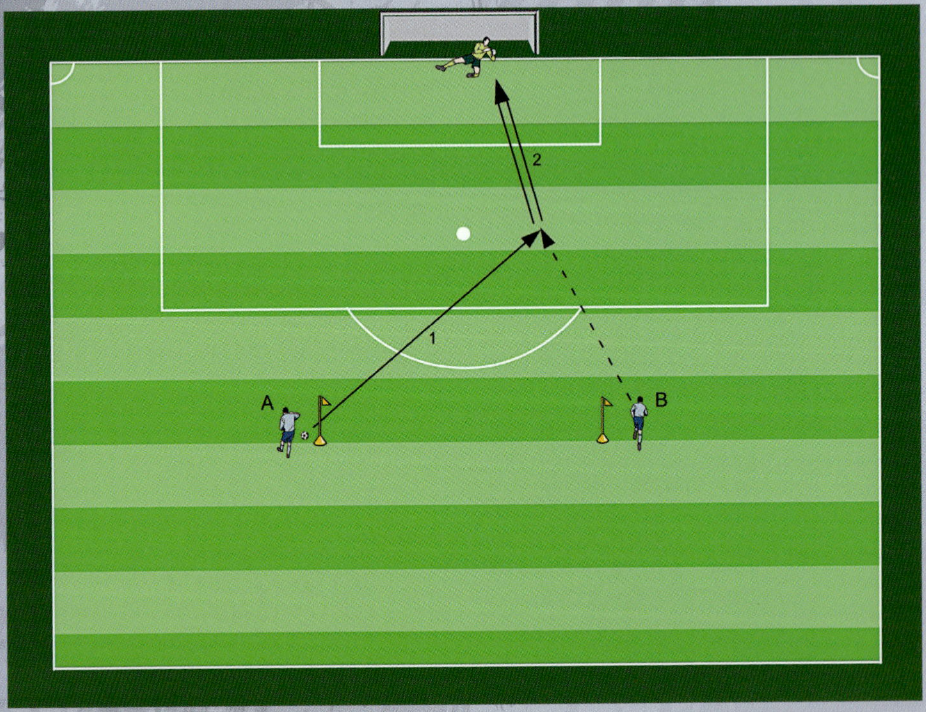

53 Shot on goal with passing game and simulated opponents

Purpose of training

- Ball handling techniques

Training emphasis

- Shooting techniques/shot on goal

Training aspects

Specific purpose:	**Push-off power, speed of action with the ball, attack through the middle, speed of anticipation, outside instep, moving with the ball, dribbling, speed of decision making, action speed, inside foot, push-pass (inside), inside foot kick, combination ball handling technique with movement, body feint, quick play to the forward, instep, swerve**
Age group:	**Age 9 to seniors**
Playing level:	**Advanced**
Form of training:	**Group**
Training structure:	**Main part/emphasis**
Intention:	**Offensive play, improving individual quality**
Number of players:	**6 or more**
Number of participating players:	**Entire team**
Training location	**Any**
Space requirements:	**Restricted playing field**
Length:	**10-15 min**
Physical aspects:	**Soccer-specific endurance, speed endurance, power**
Goalies:	**1 goalie**

Organization:
Setting up one goal, three poles, and two start cones, as shown in the illustration. The players are evenly divided between the two start cones. The balls are with group A.

Execution:
Player A dribbles from the start cone in direction of the two closest poles. At the same time player B starts down his running lane alongside the pole. When A arrives there he plays a deep pass, which player B reaches and turns into a direct volley or, after briefly trapping and moving with the ball, a shot on goal. Positions change after each round.

Equipment: 1 regulation size goal(s), 3 pole(s)

Tips:
- Dribbling should be explosive and the ball should stay close to the foot.
- The opening pass into the 18-yard area must be timed so the player is able to reach the ball with a linear sprint.
- As soon as A initiates his pass, B starts in direction of the goal.
- The ball-oriented running lane of player B is the shortest way to the ball (do not run in an arc).
- Pay attention to your posture when taking a shot (upper body over the ball; supporting leg is 12-16 inches to

the side staggered with the ball, the foot points in shooting direction, the arms swing along; the arm closest to the shooting leg mimics the swinging motion of the leg (when shooting with the right leg, the right arm moves back to gather momentum, the left arm moves forward), at the moment of the shot the eyes are on the ball.)

- Shots on goal should be trained with the right and left foot.
- Different shooting techniques (inside foot kick, instep kick, swerve) can be practiced where appropriate (at the trainer's command).

Field size: 35 x 25 yards

Distance between cones:
Goal to poles: 25 yards
Start cone A to pole I: 6-8 yards
Pole I to pole II: 12 yards
Pole II to pole III: 10 yards
Start cone B to pole III: 5 yards

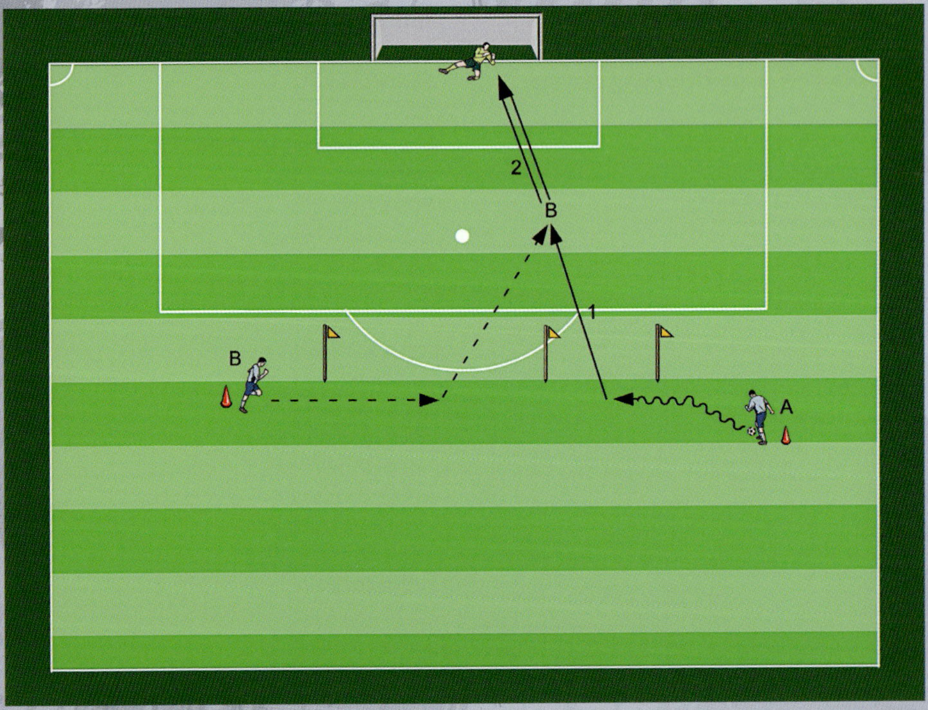

54 Shot on goal after passing game and follow-up action

Purpose of training

- Ball handling techniques

Training emphasis

- Shooting techniques/shot on goal

Training aspects

Specific purpose:	**Push-off power, speed of action with the ball, offensive play, speed of anticipation, outside instep, moving with the ball, direct pass play, double pass, speed of decision making, wing play without an opponent, action speed, inside foot, push-pass (inside), inside foot kick, combination ball handling technique with movement, header while moving, reaction speed, volley, instep, speed of perception, swerve**
Age group:	**Age 13 to seniors**
Playing level:	**Advanced**
Form of training:	**Group**
Training structure:	**Main part/emphasis**
Intention:	**Offensive play, improving individual quality**
Number of players:	**8 or more**
Number of participating players:	**Entire team**
Training location	**Any**
Space requirements:	**Restricted playing field**
Length:	**15-25 min**
Physical aspects:	**Soccer-specific endurance, GAT II, speed endurance, power**
Goalies:	**1 goalie**

Organization:
Setting up one goal, three poles, and an equal number ofstart cones, as shown in the illustration. The players are evenly divided betweenthe start cones. The balls are with group A, as well as with the trainer and the second goalie, who stands next to the goal.

Execution:
Player A plays a pass to player B, who passes the ball back to A in direction of the baseline. Immediately after the pass players B and C start in direction of the goal and crisscross the moment player A reaches the ball played by B and crosses it into the 18-yard box. Band C finish the action with a shot on goal. Player C then has to utilize a second ball from the trainer or from the second goalie. Positions change after each round.

Equipment: 1 regulation size goal(s), 3 cones

Tips:
- The opening pass from A should be played to B's strong foot.

- B must time his pass so A is able to reach it just before the baseline and can then cross it directly into the 18-yard box.
- B and C start immediately after B has passed the ball to A.
- Crisscross at the moment A initiates his swing for the cross.
- The finish is determined by how the ball is played into the box (low pass, medium high/high cross). A volley should be executed regardless.
- The following posture is importantwhen taking a shot on goal: upper body over the ball; supporting leg is 12-16 inches to the side staggered with the ball, the foot points in shooting direction, the arms swing along; the arm closest to the shooting leg mimics the swinging motion of the leg, the other arm moves forward; at the moment of the shot the eyes are on the ball.

Field size: 30 x 30 yards

Distance between cones:
Goal to poles: 25 yards
Cone A to B: 15 yards
Cone B to C: 15 yards
Cone A to pole I: 5 yards
Pole I to pole II: 10 yards
Pole II to pole III: 15 yards

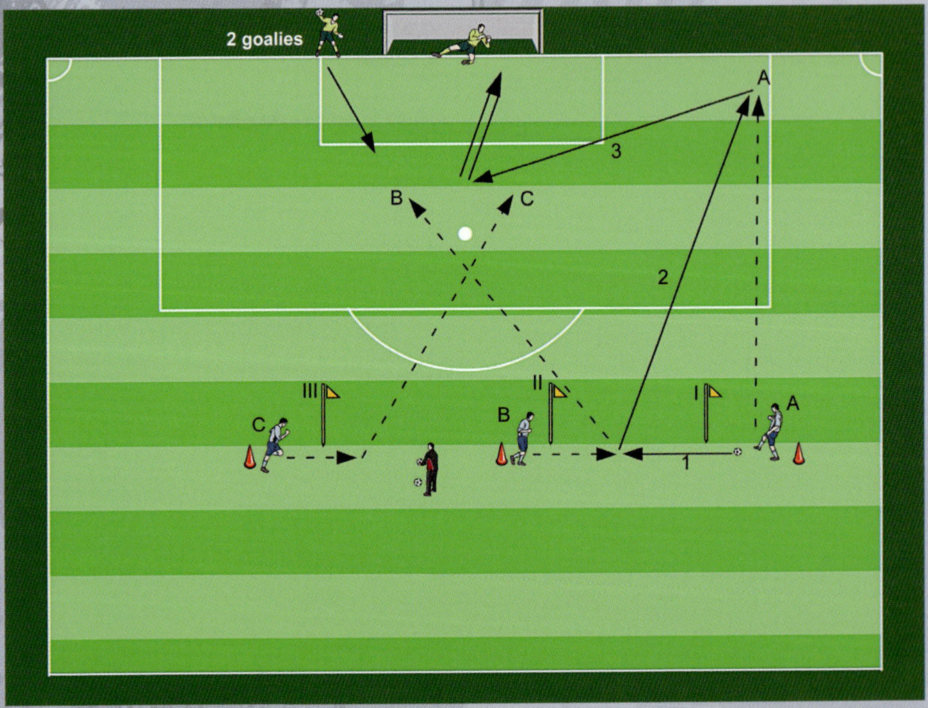

55 Shooting on two goals after combination passes

Purpose of training

- Ball handling techniques

Training emphasis

- Shooting techniques/shot on goal

Training aspects

Specific purpose:	Push-off power, speed of action with the ball, speed of anticipation, outside instep, double pass, speed of decision making, inside foot, push-pass (inside), inside foot kick, combination ball handling technique with movement, reaction speed, instep, swerve
Age group:	Age 13 to seniors
Playing level:	Any
Form of training:	Group
Training structure:	Main part/emphasis
Intention:	Improving individual quality
Number of players:	10 or more
Number of participating players:	Entire team
Training location	Any
Space requirements:	Restricted playing field
Length:	10-20 min
Physical aspects:	Soccer-specific endurance, power
Goalies:	2 goalies

Organization:
Mark off a field with four cones and two goals facing each other. The players are evenly divided between the four cones. One ball for each pair of players.

Execution:
Player A plays a long ball to player B and runs in direction of the goal. Player B lets the ball rebound to A so that A can then take a shot on goal. After the shot on goal A runs to B and takes his position, and B takes the position of A. The drill is done alternately from both sides.

Equipment: 2 regulations size goal(s), 4 cones

Tips:

- The long opening pass can be played as a linear fly ball or a low pass. In both cases it is important that the ball is played with an inside foot kick (contact area is half inside foot, half instep). Contrary to the low pass, in a fly ball the foot is farther underneath the ball and the player leans back slightly.
- The pass as well as the subsequent lay-off should be played to the strong foot.
- Pay attention to your posture when taking a shot (upper body over the ball; supporting leg is 12-16 inches to the side staggered with the ball, the foot points in shooting direction, the

arms swing along; the arm closest to the shooting leg mimics the swinging motion of the leg (when shooting with the right leg, the right arm moves back to gather momentum, the left arm moves forward), at the moment of the shot the eyes are on the ball.)

Field size: 25 x 32 yards

Distance between cones:
Width: 25 yards
Length: 25-32 yards, depending on the age

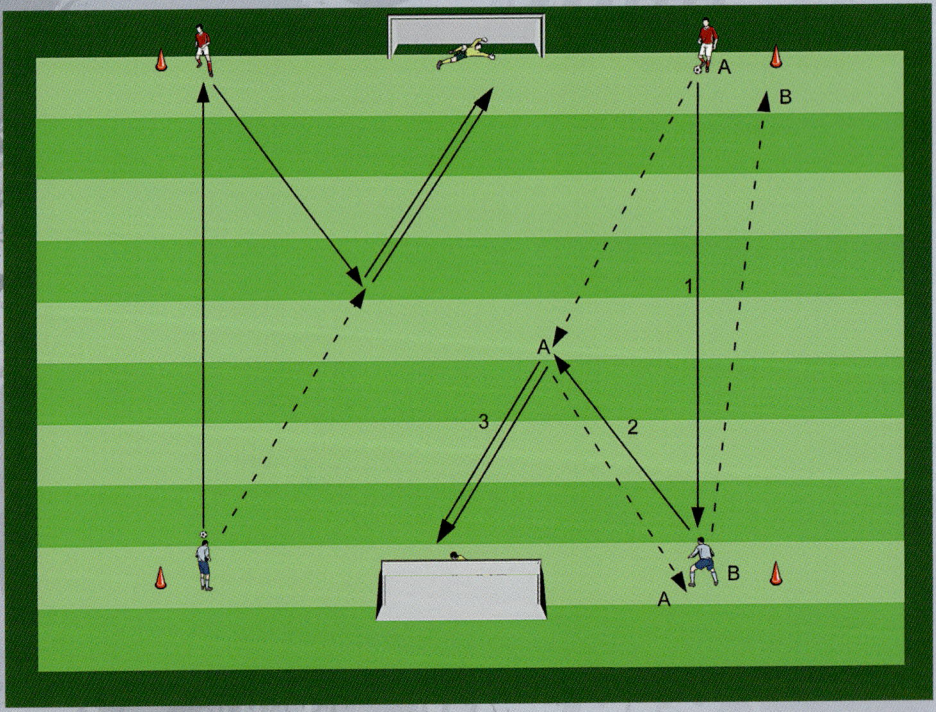

56 Shooting on two goals after a diagonal pass

Purpose of training

- Ball handling techniques

Training emphasis

- Shooting techniques/shot on goal

Training aspects

Specific purpose:	**Push-off power, speed of action with the ball, speed of anticipation, outside instep, moving with the ball, direct pass play, speed of decision making, action speed, inside foot, push-pass (inside), inside foot kick, combination ball handling technique with movement, reaction speed, instep, swerve**
Age group:	**Age 13 to seniors**
Playing level:	**Advanced, pro**
Form of training:	**Team training**
Training structure:	**Main part/emphasis**
Intention:	**Improving individual quality**
Number of players:	**10 or more**
Number of participating players:	**Entire team**
Training location	**Any**
Space requirements:	**Restricted playing field**
Length:	**10-15 min**
Physical aspects:	**Soccer-specific endurance, power**
Goalies:	**2 goalies**

Organization:
Mark off a field with four cones and two goals facing each other. The players are evenly divided between the four cones. The balls are divided between cone stations A and C.

Execution:
Player A opens with a long ball to player B, who lets the ball rebound diagonally into the middle of the field. Player C sprints to the ball, dribbles, and then takes a shot on goal. After that the players change positions clockwise. The diagonal opening balls are played alternately from positions A and C.

Equipment: 2 regulation size goal(s), 4 cones

Tips:

- The long opening ball can be played as a fly ball or a low pass. In both cases it is important that the ball is played as an inside foot kick (contact area is half inside foot, half instep). Contrary to the low pass, in a fly ball the foot is farther underneath the ball and the player leans back slightly.
- The pass as well as the subsequent lay-off should be played to the strong foot.
- As soon as the passing player initiates his swing, the player receiving the ball makes a small counter movement and briefly moves towards the ball.
- Short, explosive dribble with tight ball control.

- Pay attention to your posture when taking a shot (upper body over the ball; supporting leg is 12-16 inches to the side staggered with the ball, the foot points in shooting direction, the arms swing along; the arm closest to the shooting leg mimics the swinging motion of the leg (when shooting with the right leg, the right arm moves back to gather momentum, the left arm moves forward), at the moment of the shot the eyes are on the ball.)
- Different shooting techniques (inside foot kick, instep kick, swerve) can be practiced where appropriate (at the trainer's command).

Field size: 30 x 30 yards

Distance between cones:
Width/length: 30 yards

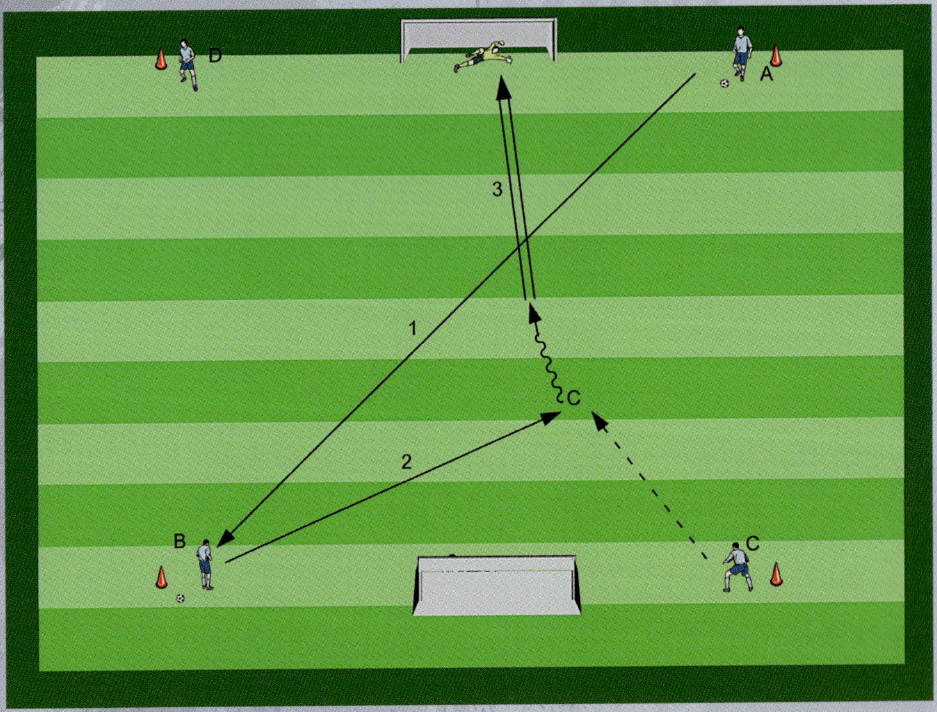

57 Shooting competition after a pass relay

Purpose of training
- Ball handling techniques

Training emphasis
- Shooting techniques/shot on goal

Training aspects

Specific purpose:	Push-off power, speed of action with the ball, speed of anticipation, outside instep, moving with the ball, direct pass play, dribbling, speed of decision making, action speed, inside foot, push-pass, (inside) inside foot kick, combination ball handling technique with movement, passing to multiple stations, instep, swerve
Age group:	Age 9 to seniors
Playing level:	Advanced
Form of training:	Team training
Training structure:	Warm-up, main part/emphasis
Intention:	Fun training, improving individual quality
Number of players:	10 or more
Number of participating players:	Entire team
Training location	Any
Space requirements:	Restricted playing field
Length:	10-15 min
Physical aspects:	Soccer-specific endurance, power

Organization:
Set up two cone courses with one mini or team handball goal per course, as shown in the illustration. Form two groups and divide them between the two stations. The balls are at starting position A and the corresponding station of group B.

Execution:
Example group A:
Player A plays a double pass with B. He then plays the return ball diagonally into the running lane of C, who started with A's swinging motion in direction of the cone goalfrom his cone. C receives the ball, briefly dribbles, and then takes a shot on the mini goal through the cone goal. After each action the stations within the two groups change sequentially (A->B, B->C, etc.). Count each group's successful shots: shooting competition.

Equipment: 12 cones, 2 mini goal(s)

Tips:
- As soon as the passing player initiates his swing, the player receiving the ball makes a small counter movement and briefly moves towards the ball.
- The pass as well as the subsequent lay-off should be played to the strong foot.
- The pass to C must be played centrally in front of the cone goal.
- When receiving and moving the ball at full speed it must be kept close.
- Short, explosive dribble with tight ball control.

- Pay attention to your posture when taking a shot (upper body over the ball; supporting leg is 12-16 inches to the side staggered with the ball, the foot points in shooting direction, the arms swing along; the arm closest to the shooting leg mimics the swinging motion of the leg (when shooting with the right leg, the right arm moves back to gather momentum, the left arm moves forward), at the moment of the shot the eyes are on the ball.)
- Quick position changes to ensure a swift flow.

Field size: 30 x 30 yards

Distance between cones:
Cone A to cone B: 10-15 yards
Cone B to cone C: 8-10 yards
Mini goal to cone goal: 10-16 yards
End line to cone A: 5 yards

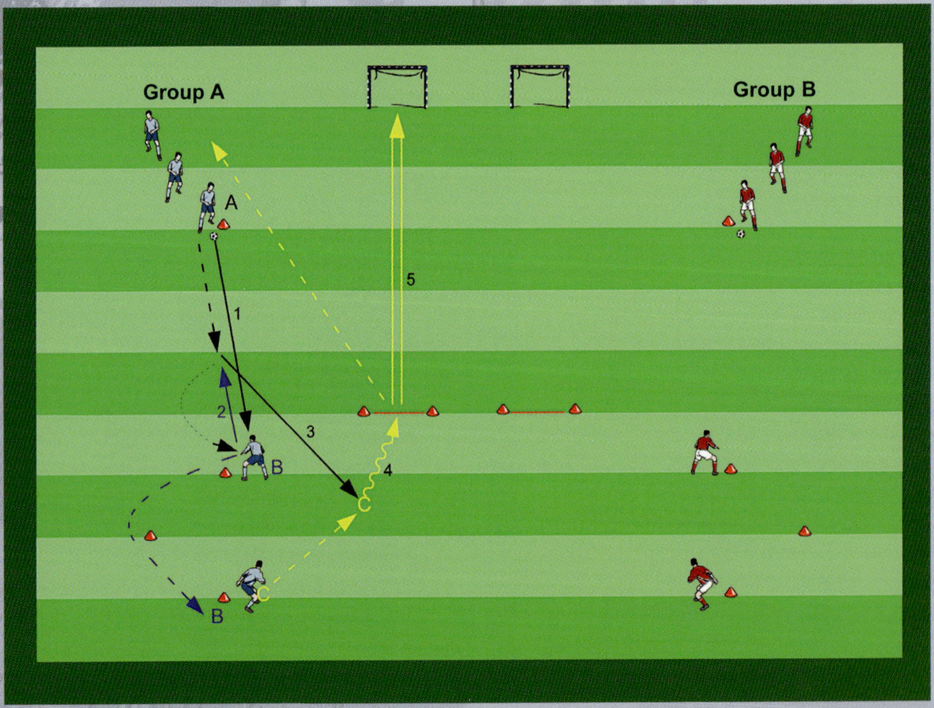

58 Passing game in double diamond with successful finish

Purpose of training

- Ball handling techniques

Training emphasis

- Shooting techniques/shot on goal

Training aspects

Specific purpose:	**Push-off power, speed of action with the ball, attack through the middle, speed of anticipation, direct pass play, speed of decision making, action speed, inside foot, push-pass (inside), inside foot kick, combination ball handling technique with movement, short passes, passing to multiple stations, instep, swerve**
Age group:	**Age 9 to seniors**
Playing level:	**Advanced**
Form of training:	**Medium groups, 5-8 players**
Training structure:	**Main part/emphasis**
Intention:	**Team bonding, improving individual quality**
Number of players:	**8**
Number of participating players:	**Entire team**
Training location	**Any**
Space requirements:	**Restricted playing field**
Length:	**10-15 min**
Physical aspects:	**Soccer-specific endurance, power**
Goalies:	**1 goalie**

Organization:
Set up one goal and six cones, as shown in the illustration. There are two players positioned at starting position A. The balls are also at cone A. There is one player positioned at each of the remaining cones.

Execution:
Player A begins the drill with a diagonal pass to player B, who lets the ball rebound to player C. C plays a diagonal pass to player D, who in turn lets the ball rebound to player E. Finally E passes the ball with the inside foot around player D, into the running lane of A, who receives the ball at a run and takes a shot on goal. Positions change clockwise. The exercise is repeated as soon as all of the players have taken a shot and have reached their starting position, but this time counter-clockwise.

Equipment: 12 cones, 2 mini goal(s)

Tips:
- As soon as the passing player initiates his swing, the respective receiving player makes a small counter movement and then briefly moves towards the ball.
- Passes should always be played to the strong foot.
- Receiving and moving the ball should be one fluid motion. Letting the ball rebound too far or deviating too far from the straight running lane when receiving and moving the ball, should be avoided.

- Player A starts to sprint as soon as E initiates his swing.
- Pay attention to your posture when taking a shot (upper body over the ball; supporting leg is 12-16 inches to the side staggered with the ball, the foot points in shooting direction, the arms swing along; the arm closest to the shooting leg mimics the swinging motion of the leg (when shooting with the right leg, the right arm moves back to gather momentum, the left arm moves forward), at the moment of the shot the eyes are on the ball.)
- Different shooting techniques (inside foot kick, instep kick, swerve) can be practiced where appropriate (at the trainer's command).

Field size: 20 x 45 yards

Distance between cones:
10 yards respectively

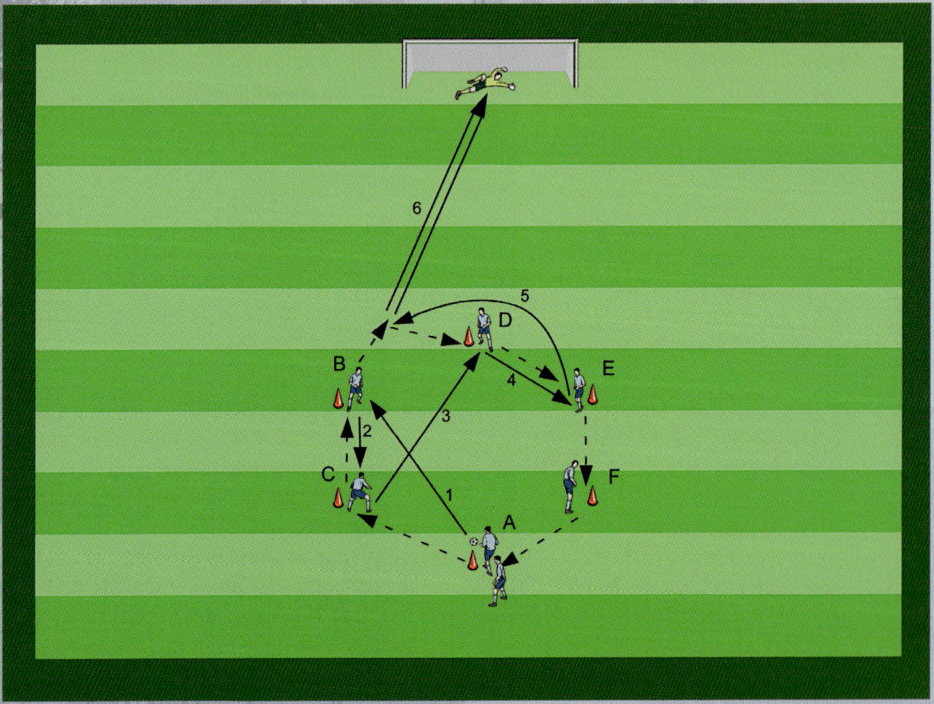

59 Double pass with sprint competition and successful finish

Purpose of training

- Ball handling techniques

Training emphasis

- Shooting techniques/shot on goal

Training aspects

Specific purpose:	**Push-off power, speed of action with the ball, speed of anticipation, outside foot, double pass, speed of decision making, inside foot, push-pass (inside), inside foot kick, combination ball handling technique with movement, liveliness, instep, speed of perception, swerve**
Age group:	**Age 9 to seniors**
Playing level:	**Advanced**
Form of training:	**Team training**
Training structure:	**Main part/emphasis**
Intention:	**Fun training, improving individual quality**
Number of players:	**6 or more**
Number of participating players:	**Entire team**
Training location	**Any**
Space requirements:	**Restricted playing field**
Length:	**15-20 min**
Physical aspects:	**Physical aspects: Soccer-specific endurance, speed, power**
Goalies:	**1 goalie**

Organization:
Setting up one goal, two pass cones, two start cones, as well as two flags, as shown in the illustration. The players form two groups (A+B). One player from each group is positioned at start cones III and IV respectively, the others line up at start cones I + II. The balls are at the two pass cones and with the trainer.

Execution:
At the trainer's command the red players at the pass cones pass the ball to the blue players at the start cones, who then turn to the passing players at the trainer's command and let the ball rebound. After that they immediately sprint around the pole and try to utilize the trainer's pass before the player from the other group does.

Equipment: 1 regulation size goal(s), 4 cones, 2 pole(s)

Tips:
- At the trainer's command the red player immediately passes while the blue player turns.
- Accurate pass to the blue player's strong foot.
- Dynamic turn and explosive sprint around the pole and to the ball.
- The player must stay close to the pole when running around it.
- In case of a tackle the body must be actively used (shoulder contact, screen

the ball with the foot closest to the ball, position your body between the ball and the opponent).

- Next break away from the opponent by reaccelerating and taking the shortest way to the goal.
- The ball can be shot on goal with the first touch, or after receiving and briefly moving with it.
- Pay attention to your posture when taking a shot (upper body over the ball; supporting leg is 12-16 inches to the side staggered with the ball, the foot points in shooting direction, the arms swing along; the arm closest to the shooting leg mimics the swinging motion of the leg (when shooting with the right leg, the right arm moves back to gather momentum, the left arm moves forward), at the moment of the shot the eyes are on the ball.)

Field size: 20 x 25 yards

Distance between cones:
Base line to cones I and II: 10 yards
Base line to cones III and IV: 18 yards
Base line to pole: 22 yards

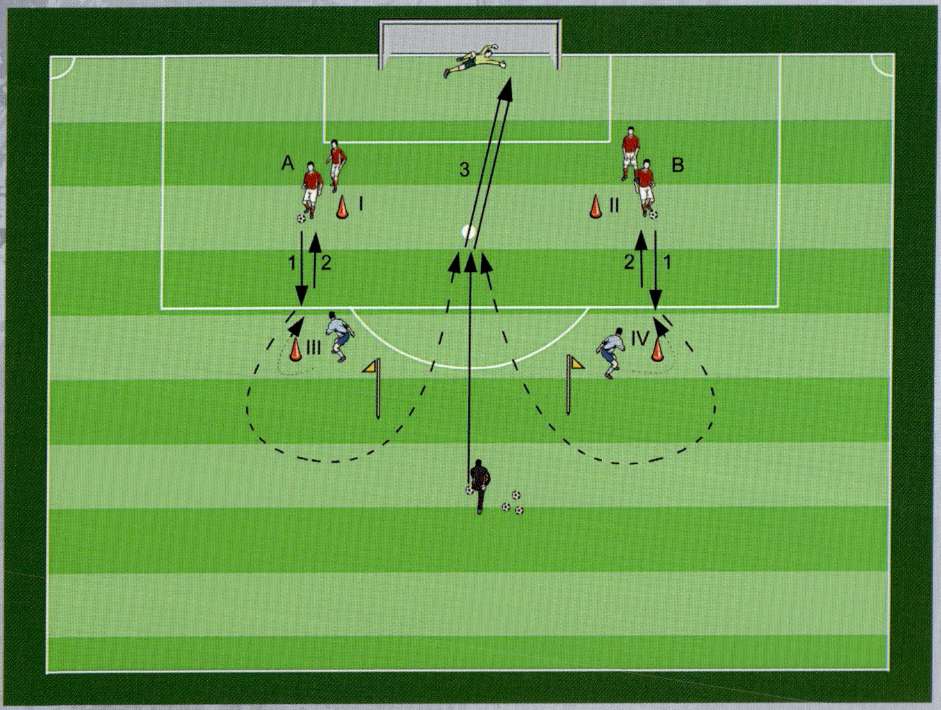

Thank you

Many years ago, I developed the desire to publish the experiences and ideas I accumulated as player and trainer, as well as the impressions I acquired through lectures, trainer seminars, and from countless conversations with soccer-enthusiasts. This work and many others have now turned that dream into reality.

I would like to thank the following individuals and entities:

Easy2Coach, whose graphics software Easy2Coach Draw provided me with innovative ways to present the many training drills.

Through collaboration with Meyer & Meyer Publishing my idea for worldwide publication of a training tool in various media formats (book form, e-book, diverse training packages, as well as drills in an on-line data bank with integrated graphic and animation software) was realized.

Günter Limbach for his trust and legal advice.

My father, Johannes Titz, whom I could always rely upon, who first exposed me to soccer, and who never showed fatigue or irritation while creating illustrations of the drills.

Meyer & Meyer Publishing, and especially Jürgen Meyer, for his confidence, his conviction, and the many helpful suggestions.

Sebastian Stache, who was always at my side as a reliable partner, critic, and friend, and who is one of the most capable editors any author could wish for.

My friend, Dr. Steve Dooley, whose constructive criticism inspired me.

Thomas Dooley for his professional co-authorship and his faith in this training theory. Timo Nagel, my long-time friend and fellow-trainer, who was on hand with help and advice.

Furthermore I would like to thank all the individuals and friends who accompanied me on this journey and inspired my creativity. I am especially thankful to my family, who backed me up and offered me limitless support during this time.

Christian Titz

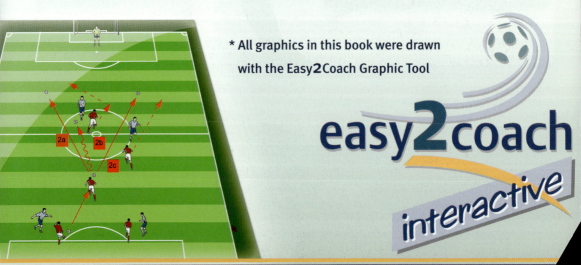

DSU

www.dooleysoccer.us

DOO[...]R UNIVERSITY

More than soccer!

[...]SU stands for a
[...]g, based on a self
[...]ch more.

[...]cer camps

[...] Sports